African Immigrant Religions in America

African Immigrant Religions in America

Edited by

Jacob K. Olupona and Regina Gemignani

New York University Press

New York and London

NEW YORK UNIVERSITY PRESS
New York and London
www.nyupress.org

LIBRARY OF CONGRESS CATALOGING-IN-PUBLICATION DATA
African immigrant religions in America / edited by Jacob K. Olupona and Regina Gemignani.
p. cm.
Includes bibliographical references and index.
ISBN-13: 978-0-8147-6211-0 (cloth : alk. paper)
ISBN-10: 0-8147-6211-5 (cloth: alk. paper)
ISBN-13: 978-0-8147-6212-7 (pbk. : alk. paper)
ISBN-10: 0-8147-6212-3 (pbk. : alk. paper)
1. African Americans—Religion. 2. Africa, Sub-Saharan—Emigration and immigration—Religious aspects. I. Olupona, Jacob Obafemi Kehinde.
II. Gemignani, Regina.
BR563.N4A368 2007
200.89'96073—dc22 2006102212

New York University Press books are printed on acid-free paper, and their binding materials are chosen for strength and durability.

Manufactured in the United States of America
10 9 8 7 6 5 4 3 2 1

Contents

Acknowledgments

The editors would like to thank our colleagues in the Working Group on African Immigrant Religion in the United States, many of whom wrote chapters for this volume, for their important contributions to the developing conversation on this topic. Their work has helped to shape our own ideas and insights, to chart directions for future research, and to advance the study of African immigrant religion in America.

We greatly appreciate the assistance provided by the many individuals who have helped in organizing this project and in the production of this publication. We thank John Ortiz and Aklil Bekele, in the African American and African Studies Program, and Connie Zeiller, Andre Des Boine, and Sam Peterson, at Hart Interdisciplinary Programs, University of California, Davis, for their skilled administrative and technical assistance. This volume would not have been possible without the help of the following students and researchers: Marilu Carter, Morrie Amodu, and Ana Rodas. We wish to acknowledge the contribution of the faculty of African American and African Studies for their ongoing support, especially Moradewun Adejunmobi, the director, and Bettina Ngweno, who chaired conference sessions and generously offered their feedback and encouragement. Professor Ogbu Kalu also provided his invaluable insight and guidance to this work. We wish to thank the Ford Foundation and the Davis Humanities Institute, especially George Van Den Abbeele and Ronald Saufley, for the financial support that brought this project to fruition.

Finally, we give a special thanks to all of those who provided the information that is contained in this volume. We appreciate the enthusiastic involvement of the leaders and members of the many religious communities that participated in these studies and whose interest, cooperation, and support have been vital to the success of this project.

Introduction

Jacob K. Olupona and Regina Gemignani

The chapters in this volume document a rising phenomenon on the North American religious scene—the churches, mosques, and shrines established and led by African immigrants.[1] African-born immigrants are a small but growing segment of immigrants to the United States and Canada. Despite their modest numbers, they are making a significant social and cultural impact, especially through the proliferation of religious communities. Representing an array of denominations, organizational styles, and sociopolitical concerns, these communities are increasingly visible contributors to religious diversity in North America. Several years ago, Jacob Olupona established the African Immigrant Religious Communities Project in order to examine the scope and significance of these religious communities within the context of the American religious landscape and cultural pluralism. As part of this project, and with the aim of advancing the study of African immigrant religion, this volume brings together groundbreaking research on this topic. Here, fourteen scholars contribute insights and perspectives from the fields of theology, religious studies, history, sociology, and anthropology. Their work focuses on a wide range of topics and a variety of faith traditions within African Christianity and Islam. Taken as a whole, the chapters demonstrate the profound significance of religion in the lives of many African immigrants and the richness and diversity of their community life.

African Immigrant Religion in the United States

From the late 1980s to the present, there has been a substantial increase in the number of Africans immigrants in the United States. The U.S. census estimates that, in 2003, more than one million African-born immigrants were residing in the country, compared to only 230,000 in 1990.[2] As discussed in the following chapters, causes for increased migration from Africa are well known and can be located within economic and political crises, including economic transformation, political tension, and war that engulfed the continent during this period. Kalu points to additional factors that shaped emigration patterns, including the lack of work incentives, disabling political cultures, and personal quests for meaning and self-development. Africans have been able to enter the United States in larger numbers through the Diversity Visa Program (often referred to as "The Visa Lottery") that was introduced as part of the 1990 Immigration Act. This opening up of immigration opportunities in the United States contrasts with increased restrictions on immigration in the former colonial powers such as Great Britain and France, and, as a result, the United States has replaced those countries as the favored destination of African immigrants.

While in the United States, African immigrants have been struggling to redefine themselves, create a distinct identity, maintain contact with kin in Africa, and express their cultural values. One of the ways they are doing this is through their religious affiliations. Many of the immigrants have found sanctuary in different religious groups established by persons of their own ethnic, national, or regional (e.g., West African) origin, where they can profoundly assert themselves. The rapid spread of African immigrant religious communities is found in gateway cities such as New York, Washington, D.C., Chicago, Atlanta, Houston, Miami, and Los Angeles, as well as in a number of smaller cities and towns such as Lewiston and Portland, both in Maine, and New Brunswick, New Jersey. These communities represent various faith traditions including Islam, mainline Christianity (e.g., Catholics, Episcopalians, Lutherans), pentecostal/charismatic churches, African Initiated Churches (AICs, such as Church of the Lord (Aladura), Christ Apostolic Church, Celestial Church of Christ), and African Indigenous Religion. To give an idea of the numbers of communities, Biney (this volume) estimates that there are approximately 40 Ghanaian Christian communities in New York City alone, and the total number of African Christian churches in New York is more than 120.[3] There are also at least ten African-led mosques in the city. Even in regions less populated by African immigrants, such as Northern California, there is a proliferation of religious communities led by Africans and attended largely by African immigrants.[4]

As evidenced by the abundance of articles in the national press, African immigrants are drawing increased public attention.[5] However, there has been little research on these groups. Although there are two major studies of immigrant religion in the United States, including projects led by Warner and by Ebaugh,[6] these volumes scarcely mention African immigrants.[7] Several monographs on African immigrants exist, including studies by Arthur, Stoller, Abusharaf, Copeland-Carson, D'Alisera, and Tettey in North America, as well as work by ter Haar and by Adogame and Weisskoeppel in Europe.[8] However, African immigration and especially the subtopic of African immigrant religion have not received the scholarly attention that they deserve. One important reason for this is the prior invisibility of the African immigrant population. Despite the popularity of notions of immigrant identity, agency, and cultural pluralism, African immigrants are still understood according to a "melting pot" model of immigration and are expected to identify with a segment of the host society, African Americans. Many Africans are conscious of the need to develop a voice and a presence that represent their unique, and heterogeneous, perspectives and contributions. This idea was the motivating force behind the African Immigrant Religious Communities Project[9] and the current volume.

The contributors to this volume on African religion and immigration were asked to explore the subject broadly, and their work accordingly traverses rich and diverse terrain. Despite the variation in topics and approaches, a number of common themes emerge that stimulate discussion and raise questions for future investigations. The following represents several of the key themes found in this work.

Emerging Themes

This project is interested in questions about the nature of the African immigrant religious communities, what they aim to accomplish, and their wider social impact. A thematic analysis helps to understand some of the ways in which scholars are approaching these questions. The five overarching themes found in this work include social identities, transnationalism, migration as process, civic engagement and political incorporation, and gender relations.

Identities

As often pointed out in recent studies of immigration, ideals of cultural and religious pluralism have created a context in which immigrants are no longer expected to assimilate to an external norm. Religious communities become less the isolated ethnic enclave of the past, instead emerging as sites for a vital expression and agency that aims to establish one's place in a multicultural America. Most of the chapters in this volume address this issue of identity formation. Several of the chapters attend specifically to the ways in which aspects of gender, ethnicity, race, and religion define (or do not define) these imagined communities.

For many, the imagining of community involves the connection to, and remembrance of, an African homeland. Community members emphasize the importance of speaking their language and hearing it spoken, the chance to enjoy special food delicacies, and the opportunity to sing familiar songs of praise. Services and events often include ethnic markers such as flags and clothing styles, and one often finds reference to cultural beliefs and values (such as respect for elders) that members suggest are defining attributes of their community. Such findings have led some of the contributors to foreground the role of ethnicity and nationalism in the construction of identity. For example, Nida describes how ideals of Ethiopian cultural identity are sustained in the Orthodox church; being connected to one's "Ethiopian roots" provides community "in a strange and racialized American cultural and social environment." Gemignani's chapter also suggests that tribal, national, and "African" identities are relevant to identity formation in the pentecostal/charismatic churches she has studied. She examines the implications of ethnoreligious identities for the negotiation of gender relations in these communities. Beck's research illustrates the significant connections between Islam and ethnicity in the U.S. context, where national, regional, and ethnic identities are associated with affiliation in New York City mosques. Sodiq similarly stresses the emphasis on Yoruba language and culture in mosques affiliated with the Nigerian Muslim Association. These examples provide support for what D'Alisera has described as "an emerging national-ethnic identity that has become interwoven with Islam in the American context."[10]

Other contributors, such as Bongmba and Biney, emphasize that collective identities in these groups are not always organized around ethnic or national structures of belonging. Biney critiques Ebaugh and Chafetz's view that a primary sociological function of immigrant congregations is the reproduction of ethnicity. On the basis of his research with the Presbyterian Church of Ghana in New York, he suggests that, while members of this church are concerned with "reinforcing and redefining their sense of who they are," this is essentially about community and spirituality, constructed against impersonal and "adulterated" Western religious life. Bongmba's chapter on the Brotherhood of the Cross and Star also deemphasizes ethnicity. He finds that, in order to champion the cause of a global mission and to challenge popular beliefs that "African" churches are local, specialized, and thereby historically inconsequential in the West, members of this group tend to eschew ethnic identification and promote instead a universal Christian identity. Criticizing, with ter Haar,[11] the way in which the public "insists on highlighting the Africanness" of the congregations, Bongmba's findings suggest that some religious groups may consciously downplay ethnicity in order to counter an objectifying racial discourse.

As suggested by Zinn, the discursive construction of African immigrants' subjectivity must be viewed in the context of complex relations of power with attention to the way in which immigrants "endow their migration experience with self-empowering meanings."[12] Our contributors' varied views on identity formation attest to the diversity of experiences within the religious communities and the fact that identities within these groups are multiple and fluid and involve a dynamic intersection of religion, race, ethnicity, class, and gender. All the authors foreground the agency of the immigrant religious community members as they negotiate their identities in engagement with their social world, including new challenges, divisions, and inequities.

Racial stratification in the United States is central to the migration experiences of African immigrants and plays a central role in processes of identity construction.[13] For many African immigrants, racial identities are conflicting and ambiguous. To a certain degree, one finds a conscious effort to confront racism in its various forms. For example, as in Jeung's research on pan-Asian religious community formation in America, pan-African identities are common in the religious communities. These identities "infuse old symbols with new meanings and interpretations," eliciting strong sentiment among community members in ways that often challenge racial hierarchies.[14] In some communities, special events are planned to honor community role models who have experienced and challenged racial discrimination. In one African-led church, a special celebration was held to honor community elders—both African and African American—who over the years have helped African immigrants overcome social and economic challenges. During another church's anniversary celebration, guest ministers from a Native American "sister" church described their shared experiences of cultural and racial marginalization in the United States and the different ways they have supported one another in their community-building efforts.

Despite points of connection concerning race relations and a strong desire for improved relationships with the African American community, there are also differences that have been an ongoing obstacle in strengthening this relationship. Much of the difficulty stems from the relatively low priority that African immigrants typically give to race as an issue as they struggle to obtain the American dream and disengage themselves, and especially their children, from discrimination and the prospect of segmented assimilation into racially defined categories. As suggested by Casanova, the positive affirmation of religious identity itself can be viewed as part of the "common defensive reaction by most immigrants groups against ascribed racialization, particularly against the stigma of racial darkness."[15] This point is discussed further in chapter 1.

Perceptions of self and other in the African immigrant community are bound up with these negotiations. It is not uncommon to hear stereotypes, discussed in this volume by Beck and elsewhere by Waters, that suggest that African Americans are "crippled by their experience with American race relations," and there is a significant degree to which Africans construct their identities against these perceptions and biases.[16] For example, in discussions of identities, African community members often describe their own ethnic or national group as proud and not lacking in self-esteem, forward-looking and not mired in the past, and so forth. Conversely, African American stereotypes of African immigrants often imply opportunism and implicit sanctioning of racial bias. In this volume, Beck explores racial relations and identities among the African Muslim community and the role of religion both in fueling tensions and as a potential unifying and mobilizing force.

Religious affiliation shapes African immigrant identities in multiple and profound ways, through commonly held beliefs and values, through forms of social interaction, and through religious performance. The uniqueness of religious style and performance is one of the most common reasons immigrants give for attending African-led religious communities. As stated by one church member in Sacramento, "In a Nigerian church, the style and the zeal and the commitment make the difference. . . . I doubt if I could get that in any culture anywhere." In most if not all African immigrant congregations, music and dance are integral to this religious experience and to the understanding and experience of community. Stokes states that in the context of immigration, music defines "a moral and political community in relation to the world in which they find themselves." Music is a significant contributor to identity formation as it "evokes and organizes collective memories and present experience of place with an intensity, power and simplicity unmatched by any other social activity."[17] Although none of the chapters focus on this topic at length, the significance of music in shaping a sense of belonging is described by several of the researchers working across the religious spectrum from Islam to pentecostal/charismatic Christianity to the Ethiopian Orthodox Church (see chapters by Biney, Nida, Tettey, and Sodiq).

Transnationalism

As is increasingly true for immigrant populations in general, Africans in America lead transnational lives. Their social ties, economic ventures, political activities, and cultural beliefs and practices span the Atlantic, linking them not only with their home countries but also with African immigrants in European nations such as France, Great Britain, and Germany. These essays suggest that immigrant religious communities provide a key site in which Africans actively articulate their complex sense of self and identity in their new surroundings. In his work, Tettey aptly illustrates some of the linkages between religion and transnational immigrant experiences and subjectivities. Drawing on Anthias's concept of "translocational positionality," he analyzes the various ways in which Ghanaian church members in Canada deploy identity markers that make sense of, and give purpose to, transnational experiences. Examples include the use of the concept of the "home church," a fluid construct of religious familiarity and belonging, as well as the movement between North America and Africa of ministers, ideas, and liturgical genres in which new religious approaches and practices are continuously exchanged. He suggests that such processes play a key role in carving out a space for Ghanaians and helping them to overcome the dissonance of their transnational lives.

Other chapters similarly demonstrate the ability of global religious movements to provide symbols and practices that transcend fixed notions of place and identity. As described later, many immigrants interpret their presence in America as "part of a divine plan which allows them to move with their faith and plant new churches in the West" (Bongmba, this volume). As pointed out by Bongmba, this ideal of spiritual agency provides not only purpose but a sense of home, which is interpreted as wherever one is sent to go to preach. Such findings can be viewed as evidence for the "new awareness and vitality manifested in immigrant identities"[18] as they creatively address and adapt to a world characterized by movement and dislocation.

Migration as Process

Another common theme found in these chapters is the sense in which religious experience is shaped by, and influences, the process of migration from the homeland. Several of the authors criticize what Benmayor and Skotnes suggest is a general tendency in the literature and popular thought to view migration as "a single movement in space and a single moment in time."[19] Instead, they put forth the concept of migration as a dynamic process that many African immigrants infuse with religious significance and that, in turn, shapes religious practice and community building.

For many African Christians, the notion of "reverse mission" is central to the way religion provides meaning and direction at different stages in the migration process. A large percentage of African religious community leaders and members view their migration to the United States in the context of an evangelical mission to the West. Here the process of migration becomes invested with agency beyond social and economic objectives.[20] The critique of Western cultural values, especially what is viewed as a lack of spirituality and adherence to God's word (for example, the image in Biney's chapter of a Western Christian who inserts his own writings into his Bible) is a factor in the decision to emigrate and in the interpretation of, and responses to, challenges and hardships along the way. African immigrants often describe periods in which they strayed from their faith, later to return with renewed religious fervor. The notion of reverse mission also has a significant impact on the evolving civic participation of African Christian communities. As suggested by Kalu in his previous work on African pentecostalism, the aim to transform "the dark sides of the modern socioeconomic and political culture" creates a politically empowering "theology of engagement."[21] In this volume, the essays by Bongmba and Akinade deal explicitly with the missionary impulse that is shaping African Christian movements in the United States and across the globe.

Our authors suggest that studying migration as a dynamic and ongoing process can help to illuminate many aspects of immigrant religious life. Tettey points out that descriptions of immigrant social and cultural practices and institutions too often fail to incorporate an historical analysis of the individual and collective events and experiences that have influenced their development. Arguing for a more longitudinal framework and drawing on work by Hagan and Ebaugh, he investigates six stages in the migration process and discusses how each of these stages shapes Ghanaian religious participation in Canada. Kalu's contribution is also important here in that he examines the linkages between past and present experience and between migration as imagined and lived. His text weaves together the physical hardships and struggles of migration, "the impact of broken dreams" in the Diaspora, and the solace and strength found in religious fellowship.

Civic Participation and Political Expression

A related set of issues explored in these chapters is concerned with the social and political incorporation of African religious communities. Warner has suggested that immigrant religious communities have gradually assumed a "congregational" form, one of the effects of which is to promote community building and broad-based participation.[22] For most immigrant religious institutions, social involvement begins at home. As they respond to the many needs of fellow immigrants, they develop as instruments of mutual aid and support in civil society. Like the authors of a number of recent studies of immigrant religion in Asian and Latino communities,[23] the authors in this volume describe the various formal and informal approaches used by the communities to improve the lives of immigrants, often aimed at both members and nonmembers (e.g., legal advice, financial assistance, counseling services, support and employment networks). The deep sense of trust that pervades relationships within the religious groups emerges as an important part of their efficacy in addressing immigrant concerns about what are often considered private matters, such as finances or family relationships.

Many African immigrants believe strongly in the power of God to perform miracles in their lives and, as a result, to bring about prosperous changes in their social conditions. Especially in the pentecostal/charismatic and AIC communities, ritual practices, including prayer, prophesy, healing and testimony, are directed toward members' aspirations in a multitude of areas, including education, entrepreneurship, professional success, health, and relationships. These communities provide encouragement for an often uphill struggle toward financial security and personal betterment, as well as the hope to sustain their members' efforts. Akinade discusses the concept of Spirit that infuses all aspects of human life and provides "enabling power" to overcome life's challenges. Biney similarly describes deliverance services enacted in order to cast out the hindering spirits that impede human progress. These practices are a principle aspect of weekly services and also are enacted during many informal and formal events and gatherings. Biney also describes the diversity in class and status that characterizes the typical Sunday service, where teachers, nurses, accountants, doctors, janitors, hotel and bar attendants, and aides to the elderly sit side by side. Akinade points out that the opportunity for immigrants to witness and learn from others who have "made it" in America is highly relevant to their ability to provide encouragement in the face of chaos and uncertainty.[24]

A significant level of political involvement is found among many first- and second-generation African immigrants; while Barack Obama's rise to political fame is exceptional, it is one instance of a much wider trend. One finds numerous examples of political advocacy by Africans at state and local levels encompassing broad issues of culture, identity, and citizenship. The religious communities have played a central role in shaping political expression, especially through the explicit or implied messages conveyed by leaders and through informal community gatherings (such as in conversation after a service), which often serve as forums for political discussion and debate.

Several of the contributors to this volume analyze this engagement with broader social and political concerns. Okome's findings uncover heterogeneous political views among the leadership of African pentecostal communities. She investigates the way in which immigrant values translate to the American political context, and suggests continuities with, and departures from, the political agendas of the Christian Right. Okome describes the reluctance of many church members to become politically involved and suggests a need for greater unity in order to achieve more effective community mobilization. At the same time, she suggests that the churches have a strong commitment to social change and are emerging as advocates on a number of issues, including immigration and refugee policy, social welfare, and race relations.[25] Hinted at in this work, and deserving of further study, are the linkages between African spiritualism and political agency. Beck's study also provides insight relevant to the political engagement of African immigrant communities. Like Okome, she emphasizes the diverse opinions and ambiguous political classification of African Muslim immigrants. She also describes how alliances with African American politicians are providing an opportunity for greater representation and influence.

Transnationalism is an important factor shaping political expression in these communities. Bongmba, Nida, and Tettey each describe the continuing engagement of the members of religious communities with social and political concerns in the homeland. Issues at the forefront of immigrant concerns include democratization, economic development, the AIDS epidemic, and debt relief. For many communities, the wave of democratic transitions in the homeland has been a central area of concern and advocacy. It also has served to inspire and mobilize civic participation more generally.

Women and Gender

As reflected in contributions to this volume and in other recent literature, gender relations are a final but not least important theme in the evolving research on immigrant religion. Recent studies on gender, religion, and immigration highlight the opportunities for women to develop their autonomy through their leadership experiences in the religious communities.[26] In the African religious congregations, one finds wide variation in the degree of women's involvement and leadership. In contrast to Ebaugh and Chafetz, we do not suggest that such variation is largely an outcome of men's interest in filling leadership roles themselves.[27] Instead, we argue that it is common to find women in religious communities actively pressing for, and gaining, a more influential voice. Two notable examples include the Ethiopian communities (both pentecostal/charismatic and Orthodox), and the Islamic communities. In this volume, Nida reports that transformations in Ethiopian Orthodox religious practice in the American context have meant that women may now chant the mass or *kidase* and are beginning to assume leadership roles in the *kidase* classes. Similarly, the chapter by Sodiq describes the increased participation of women on leadership committees in the Nigerian mosques. In some African pentecostal churches in the United States, women have begun to serve as head pastors, something that is quite rare at home. Women also are highly involved in transnational religious networks. Women leaders travel worldwide to plant churches, present sermons, and hold seminars. They are also leaders of missionary and development efforts on the African continent. In contrast to ethnic associations, which are in certain cases dominated by men, religion may serve as an important arena in which women can participate equally with men in social and economic projects in the homeland, thereby gaining status and political influence.[28]

Despite the substantial evidence for women's leadership opportunities in the religious communities, few of the churches ordain women as pastors, and there are no women Imams. In addition, as reported by Crumbley and Cline-Smythe (this volume), the voices of women may not be heard despite their formal leadership roles. In the Church of the Lord (Aladura), women are ordained as ministers and hold a great deal of political power. This is evident in the gender parity that characterizes all levels of the church leadership structure. Yet, because of cultural beliefs, women leaders are expected to show deference to men, for example in their interactions with other church leaders. Also, their findings suggest that women leaders' ceremonial power in some AICs may be constrained through menstrual rites that segregate them from holy spaces and objects.

As religious communities aim to assist and guide immigrants in their social integration, marriage and the family emerges as a critical arena in the study of religion and gender. In the African immigrant communities, an important factor influencing the family is the increasing work opportunities and incomes of wives in relation to their husbands. As women, many of whom hold skilled positions in the nursing field, become major wage earners in African immigrant households, a certain level of conflict between husbands and wives has arisen. Although the relationship between employment and women's social and economic autonomy is complex,[29] there is evidence that the increased labor force opportunities available to African women has elevated their status and strengthened their position in decision making. At the same time, men are faced with the reality that their participation in childcare and homemaking is necessary for the household to function.

As a result of transformations in the division of labor, religious communities are emerging as a key context for the negotiation of gender relations. In some ways, African immigrant religious communities reproduce gender divisions, promoting men's role as the household head and redirecting women toward the sphere of homemaking and childcare. However, the religious community also serves as a site for the reinterpretation of gender ideologies and relations. Religious leaders have taken a lead role here, offering counseling services, marriage seminars, and study groups that aim to help ease the transition for men and women. Women have also created their own associations for mutual support related to employment, marriage, and child rearing, and they are actively engaged in the construction of gender relations in their communities. In this volume, Gemignani discusses gender and religion in African immigrant communities, basing her observations on pentecostal/charismatic African churches in Sacramento and in the San Francisco Bay Area. Demonstrating the ways in which women use religious teachings to reinterpret patriarchal authority, she provides evidence for Shibley's thesis that evangelicalism serves as a "flexible ideological resource" for reconstituting relations of gender and the family.[30]

The Scope and Content of This Book

The chapters in this volume illuminate African immigrant religion from the varied perspectives of a diverse group of scholars. Contributors were asked to address the topic according to their area of interest and expertise, and the volume reflects a wide range of approaches. All the chapters, with the exception of Daniels's theoretical work, involve ethnographic research in the religious communities. Many of the authors have spent extensive periods observing activities and speaking with community members, with varying degrees of identification and immersion. For example, in addition to their positions as researchers and scholars, Moses Biney is an ordained minister and Yushau Sodiq is a leader in the Muslim community. As Christianity is the dominant faith among the educated class in much of sub-Saharan Africa, several of the authors, especially scholars of religion, have worshipped at African churches for a number of years. This accounts for the large presence among the authors of those who profess to be Christians. As discussed further in chapter 1, Christian hegemony in Africa since the colonial era explains the relative silence of other voices. We suggest that the positionality of many of the authors as both scholars and believers in their faith shapes their perspectives while also facilitating important personal insights into their subject matter—the role of religion in immigrant lives.

African religious communities are diverse, and several groups are covered in these works. The book contains three chapters on African Initiated Churches (Akinade, Bongmba, Crumbley), one on the Ethiopian Orthodox Church (Nida), four on pentecostal/charismatic churches (Biney, Gemignani, Okome, Tettey), and two on Islam (Beck, Sodiq). No essays on African Indigenous Religion in the United States were submitted for the volume. This is largely a result of the fact that only a small portion of the membership of these communities in the United States are immigrants from Africa, and so scholars studying immigration have tended to focus on other religious groups. However, the growth of African-led shrines and temples that are rapidly gaining a multiethnic following across America is a particularly intriguing phenomenon that deserves further investigation.

This volume includes chapters that address historical and theoretical aspects of the phenomenon of African immigrant religion, as well as more specific ethnographic studies that focus on a particular religious community or communities. A number of chapters provide helpful background information about the origins of the groups and their establishment in North America. Although there is a certain degree of overlap in thematic content, the chapters of the volume can be divided into four sections: (1) Historical and Theoretical Perspectives (Olupona, Daniels, Kalu), (2) Reverse Mission: Faith, Practice and the Immigrant Journey (Akinade, Bongmba), (3) Gender, Ethnicity, and Identity (Gemignani, Crumbley, Beck, Nida) and (4) Civic Engagement and Political Incorporation (Tettey, Okome, Biney, Sodiq). The paragraphs that follow describe some of the highlights of the chapters.

In chapter 1, "Communities of Believers: Exploring African Immigrant Religion in the United States," Jacob Olupona describes his ongoing research project on African immigrant religious communities in the United States. Since 2000, his project has been involved in the mapping and in-depth ethnographic study of African-led religious communities across seven major U.S. metropolitan centers. This chapter outlines the historical background and scope of the project, as well as its relevance to U.S. public concerns and policy agendas. Olupona discusses the role of religious community in promoting the integration of African immigrants, as well as the broader relationships between religion, immigration, and civic participation. The chapter provides examples of some of the ways the African immigrant groups are actively addressing crucial social, cultural, economic, and political issues and problems facing their nascent community. Project findings relating to African immigrant religious identities, spatial patterns of growth, transglobalism, patronage, and Americanization are also summarized.

In chapter 2, "African Immigrant Churches in the United States and the Study of Black Church History," David Daniels points out that "contemporary African church life" (in contrast to church life in precolonial and colonial Africa) has thus far remained "outside the purview of Black Church history." He argues for the need to include African immigrant denominations within Black Church studies, suggesting that the advent of African immigrant churches in the United States since 1965 has created a new moment in the study of the Black Church. The chapter explores the conceptual frameworks used to study the Black Church, placing in dialogue the historiography of African Christianity and the historiography of African American Christianity. The initial challenge, he suggests, is how we as scholars place African immigrant denominations on the religious map of the United States. Where are they located? How are they best categorized? How are they best defined? In this chapter, Daniels contends that a serious engagement of the African immigrant churches by Black Church historians would require a reconceptualization of the Black Church as a rubric.

Chapter 3, "The Andrew Syndrome: Models in Understanding Nigerian Diaspora," provides background and insightful analysis of the problem of African emigration, using Nigeria as an example. In this chapter, Ogbu Kalu views migration as a process and identifies four interrelated phases of the problem: the unfavorable conditions at home that compel emigration, the perilous routes of migration, a fragmented Diaspora, and the unlikely prospects of reentry. Woven through his analysis are two competing metaphors, Exile and Crossing Jordan, which shape the individual psyche and the social body. Participation in religious organizations and other forms of association meet the needs of both of these to connect to the homeland. However, as reported by Kalu, social life is fraught with contradictions, especially in regard to the structural changes in marriage and the family and in regard to the second generation. Many families are changed under the trauma of migration and struggle for day-to-day survival, especially when they try to instill African family values in the younger generation. Often, the dilemma facing an immigrant is whether to feel like an exile or to celebrate a successful crossing.

In his conclusion, Kalu argues for what he terms "stewardship in exile," a concept that would replace the current focus on migration problems such as "brain drain" and the unheeded call for exiles to return and would search for ways that migration patterns could benefit the homeland. In order to rebuild local capacity in Africa, leaders and policymakers at home and abroad must devise ways to contribute to national development, attracting resources by developing centers of excellence, training programs, grant-writing workshops, and support for specialized study abroad. In this way, the dysfunctional pattern of migration can be redirected as a strategy of stewardship for developing the homeland.

Akintunde Akinade contributes chapter 4, "Non-Western Christianity in the Western World: African Immigrant Churches in the Diaspora." Akinade declares Christianity an "authentic world religion," citing a radical demographic shift in which most of the world's Christians now live outside the West. African Christian leaders are gaining prominence, as evidenced by the influence of Archbishop Peter Akinola in the Episcopal Church (and more recently during the debates preceding the election of Pope Benedict XVI). In this current context, "salient issues within world Christianity are being determined from multiple centers." Akinade calls for greater understanding of these changes, of the unique perspectives and contributions of African Christianity. He advocates for dialogical engagement between Christian traditions and for a pluralistic approach that champions "theological mutuality and reciprocity."

Akinade describes African Initiated Churches in the United States as vibrant communities that respond to the immigrant condition by providing a spiritual environment for "experiencing God here and now in the midst of urban chaos, poverty, racism, confusion, anomie and alienation." He suggests that AICs are positioned to address the challenges of immigrant life immigrants, as they have historically composed a grassroots tradition that encompasses the needs and interests of marginalized groups. Akinade also foregrounds the role of African cultural identity in the AICs and suggests that a history of colonial, racial, and religious subordination plays a role in their formation, as "many Africans believe that their religious affiliation and identity are the antidote against acute deracination."[31]

Elias Bongmba, in his chapter, "Portable Faith: The Global Mission of African Initiated Churches," provides a thoughtful analysis of global Christianity—this time based on research with one specific African Initiated Church in Houston. This church was established by Nigerian and Cameroonian immigrants as part of the religious movement The Brotherhood of the Cross and Star and is referred to by the biblical name Bethel. Bongmba emphasizes that Bethel represents a longstanding and respected Christian tradition charged with expanding the "divine mission" to preach the gospel to other parts of the world. This sense of mission profoundly shapes the engagement of the church members with their new societies. Bongmba also illustrates the crucial role of the social support networks established through the church. The Brotherhood of the Cross and Star is a dynamic movement whose members believe that they walk with the Supreme Being, who gives them energy. His respondents describe this not as ideational but as part of their "concrete experience": "You can always feel the energy that is there with you, at home, work, school and everywhere you go." According to the founder's millennial vision and proscriptions, the group's mission, the promotion of brotherly love, unity, and peace will usher in the reign of God on earth. A spiritual commission infuses the transnational experience of the church members and provides a sense of purpose and meaning, as well as a deep sense of community.

In chapter 6, "Gender, Identity, and Power in African Immigrant Evangelical Churches," Regina Gemignani explores gender relations in African immigrant Christian communities. Contrary to studies that view immigrant women's concern for family unity and their feminist interests as opposed to one another, her research suggests a more complex view of women's agency in which both religious proscription and women's opportunities and advancement are paramount. Gemignani describes the journey of African immigrant women who are training to enter the nursing profession in the United States; they take courses, sit in board exams, seek out sponsors, and await work authorization, all with the untiring assistance of fellow church members. She suggests that, beyond this, the religious communities provide the symbolic resources to negotiate shifts in the gender division of labor. Key to her argument is the idea of "power in vulnerability"[32] that is made possible by the multiple and shifting interpretations of religious ideals such as "submission" and "wisdom."

Chapter 7, "Gender and Change in an African Immigrant Church: An Anthropologist and a (Former) Prophetess Reflect," is the outcome of a collaborative study on gender relations in the Church of the Lord Aladura (CLA), undertaken by Dr. Deidre Helen Crumbley and former CLA Prophetess Gloria Cline-Smythe. Although the research at its inception was not designed as a collaboration, issues of power and representation came to the fore during the project's course, and Crumbley consequently adapted her methodology to address these issues. She points out the nuanced analysis and critique offered by Cline-Smythe, especially concerning menstrual rites, as well as Cline-Smythe's concern that her faith not be represented as "the faith of backwards people from a backwards continent."

In this work, the authors advocate for greater inclusion of women's voices in scholarly and public discourse on African immigrant religion. Gender relations in the CLA are described in some detail, and the authors highlight the significant degree of political power held by women in this church. Of particular interest is the ordination of women and the gender parity within the church hierarchy. Nevertheless, gender inequities perpetuated in ideologies about the "respectful woman" pose challenges for women leaders. Another important contribution of this research is the exploration of methodological issues. The authors suggest that electronic media and the telephone are playing an important role in studies of African immigrant religious communities, the members of which are often geographically dispersed. They report that Web sites, e-mail, and telephone calls were all instrumental in sharing both research findings and interactions in the field. Furthermore, prayer and worship take place over the telephone, suggesting the prominence of this mode of communication within the religious community itself.[33] The authors recommend further study of the implications of these unconventional methods for fieldwork and the ethnographic process.

As suggested by its title, "West African Muslims in America: When Are Muslims Not Muslims?," chapter 8, by Linda Beck, investigates issues of identity among African Muslim communities. Through research on relationships with other Muslim and African American communities in New York City, the author analyzes the contexts in which West African Muslims identify and are identified as Muslims and the implications for their socioeconomic and political incorporation. Beck's work provides insight on a number of salient topics, including the contradictory effects of September 11, 2001, and its aftermath on intra-Muslim relations, the evolving relationships between Africans and African Americans in New York, and the trend toward increasing political participation.

In chapter 9, "African Religious Beliefs and Practices in Diaspora: An Ethnographic Observation of Activities at an Ethiopian Orthodox Christian Church in Los Angeles," Worku Nida presents his findings on liturgical chanting of the *kidase* or mass, as taught and learned by Ethiopian immigrants at the Virgin Mary's Ethiopian Orthodox Tewahedo Church, located in Compton, a city in South-Central Los Angeles. Nida reports on the changes in Diaspora in cultural and religious traditions. He examines how Ethiopian immigrants transform religious practices as they re-create their self and collective identities in their new home. Nida's chapter presents the historical background of the Ethiopian Orthodox Church in Ethiopia and in Los Angeles and provides a sociolinguistic analysis of the *kidase* performance. He states that the establishment of an Orthodox church in Los Angeles represented an important opportunity for Ethiopian communities to preserve and cultivate their personal and social identity, cultural traditions, religious ritual, and numerous languages (Amharic as well as several Ethiopian ethnic languages, including Guragegna, Oromogna, Tigrigna, Walyatigna, and Hadiyigna). The particular culture and history taught through *kidase* emphasizes an orthodoxy that often omits significant aspects of Ethiopian cultures and histories, especially those associated with Islam and traditional religions, as well as certain political stances. At the same time, social identities in the church are far from static, and religious practice provides an opportunity to accommodate change in some areas while reconfirming core values and practices in others. Nida's study shows that such exploration and negotiation may take place within the seemingly inflexible context of liturgical chanting.

In Chapter 10, "Transnationalism, Religion, and the African Diaspora in Canada: An Examination of Ghanaians and Ghanaian Churches," Wisdom Tettey illustrates the ways in which the immigrant churches serve as conduits in the construction of a dynamic and fluid transnational identity. The synchronization that defines religious settings across the Atlantic "helps bridge the gap between those who occupy in-between spaces between the two worlds." A major focus of his work is the interaction between religion and civic life. Drawing on his ethnographic research among Ghanaian pentecostal communities in Canada, Tettey illustrates the support provided by these churches for immigrants who may encounter unforeseen social marginalization, underemployment, bigotry, condescension, patronizing, violence, and intolerance in their new societies. Tettey suggests that religious immigrant organizations provide fellowship, support, and care that can mitigate psychological duress. Social networks, as well as the status associated with church leadership positions, are instrumental in contributing to individuals' positive self-image. The churches also provide direct assistance or link members with resources in order to address areas of concern such as immigration and naturalization, employment, housing, financial stability, healthcare, and family harmony. Religious youth conferences and ministries are held across Canada to engage and encourage the youth.

Chapter 11, "Singing the Lord's Song in a Foreign Land: Spirituality, Communality, and Identity in a Ghanaian Immigrant Congregation," investigates the motives that prompt immigrants to join African-led Christian churches. Moses Biney bases his analysis on ethnographic work that he conducted at the Presbyterian Church of Ghana, a charismatic church in New York City, composed mainly of Ghanaian immigrants. He outlines the intriguing history of the New York church, which, he explains, was established during a time of instability and anxiety over the future survival of the Ghanaian immigrant community. He describes how the two most important goals of the church—spirituality and community—

are linked to the nature of the African immigrant experience in the United States, including the perceived lack of spirituality of the American populace and the feeble welcome received in some predominantly White churches. As argued by Biney, the African Christian communities take on the opposite traits, providing "religious emotion, vibrant singing and dancing, strong belief in God as creator of all and Jesus as redeemer, belief in individual and corporate sin, a holistic understanding of human life and a strong emphasis on community and fellowship."

In chapter 12, "African Immigrant Churches and the New Christian Right," Mojubaolu Okome examines the political engagement of African Christian communities in the United States and offers a glimpse into the beliefs and motivations that spark civic and political participation. She outlines the debate over the level of political agency among African pentecostals, contrasting Gifford's view that these are largely an apolitical economic movement with Kalu's emphasis on the spiritual power of the new pentecostalist churches as they "struggle to proclaim the gospel and serve society." Okome adopts the middle ground, acknowledging the current lack of mobilization and unity among African pentecostals/AICs in the United States but also describing their proclivity for political thought and action and their well-articulated vision for social change.

Much of this chapter is devoted to a presentation of ethnographic material gathered during interviews with three prominent African pastors. Okome's data highlight the emphasis placed by these leaders on building viable communities, especially through community self-help initiatives and personal motivation. The pastors demonstrate an acute awareness of the challenges faced by African immigrants and the steps that must be taken to address issues of alienation, discouragement, and division. Okome also points out that these individuals are politically minded in ways that fail to conform to current configurations of religion-based politics in the United States. She describes the role of transnational religion both as a motivating factor for social agency (e.g., African pentecostals' mission to effect change in the world) and as a set of relationships, practices, and understandings with which African religious leaders are particularly adept and upon which they might productively draw in their interactions with the American social and religious landscape.

The establishment of Muslim communities by Nigerian immigrants is the subject of chapter 13, "African Immigrant Muslims in the United States: The Nigerian Case," by Yushau Sodiq. Sodiq draws upon interviews with

Muslim leaders, as well as his personal observations and experiences, to examine the phenomenon of Nigerian-led mosques in the United States. Such mosques have recently proliferated under the umbrella organization, the Nigerian Muslim Association (NMA). The role of the mosque in the construction of immigrant community and identity is especially crucial for Muslim immigrants, who often experience a profound sense of alienation from their religious life. These communities promote youth development, support women's leadership opportunities, and cultivate positive relationships with other Muslim and Christian communities.

Cultivating Islamic values and spiritual commitment and transmitting these to the youth are foremost among the NMA's goals. Sodiq suggests that Yoruba cultural identity is integral to the mosques, and he points out the wide use of the Yoruba language. He suggests that the prevalence of certain contested cultural values and practices raises questions in these mosques about "whether and how to separate religion from the culture" and observes that issues such as gender separation and modes of worship have become important topics of discussion and debate in the American context. There are also concerns that putting too strong an emphasis on Islamic education represents a "selling-out of 'Yoruba culture' to 'Arab culture.'" A major focus of this chapter is the organization of these emergent communities. Sodiq discusses a number of challenges faced by the NMAs, including the lack of leadership experience among some Imams, the need for greater incentives and accountability, and the divided priorities of Imams and the administrative leadership. Among other things, Sodiq recommends an integration of Islamic knowledge and education that will serve to unite the leadership and build stronger communities.

Notes

1. By "African immigrant religious community" we refer to religious communities formed by immigrants who self-identify as African. Most of these immigrants are from sub-Saharan Africa. In many cases, the communities are ethnically diverse and are composed of members from several African countries, although they may include non-Africans, as well.

2. According to U.S. census estimates, the African-born U.S. population totaled 1,147,378 persons in 2004. As is often pointed out, these census numbers exclude a large population of undocumented immigrants. Data source: U.S. Census Bureau American Factfinder Web site, Table B05006, Place of Birth for the Foreign-Born

Population, 2004 American Community Survey, available online at www.factfinder.census.gov (accessed August 2005).

3. Mark Gornik, "How African Christianity Explains the World," paper presented at the Conference on African Immigrants, Religion and Cultural Pluralism in the United States, U.C. Davis, December 3, 2004.

4. In Sacramento and in the San Francisco Bay Area, there are currently more than forty African churches.

5. These were a few of the articles published in 2005: "More Africans Enter the U.S. Than in the Days of Slavery," *New York Times,* 21 February 2005; "Papal Choice Fuels Immigrant Interest," *Chicago Tribune,* 18 April 2005; "A Texas Town Nervously Awaits a New Neighbor," *New York Times,* 21 August 2005.

6. See R. Stephen Warner and Judith G. Wittner, eds., *Gatherings in Diaspora: Religious Communities and the New Immigration* (Philadelphia: Temple University Press, 1998), and Helen R. Ebaugh and Janet S. Chafetz, eds., *Religion and the New Immigrants, Continuities and Adaptations in Immigrant Congregations* (Walnut Creek, Calif.: Alta Mira Press, 2000).

7. Warner defines what he terms the "new immigrants" as those "with origins in East and South Asia, the Middle East, the Caribbean and Latin America." See "Immigration and Religious Communities in the United States," in Warner and Wittner, *Gatherings in Diaspora,* 5. Other than a chapter by Abusharaf on a mosque that was once, but is no longer, attended mainly by Sudanese immigrants, there is no mention of African immigrants in the volume. In Ebaugh and Chafetz's volume, there is only a brief discussion of a small group of Nigerian families who attend a multiethnic Catholic church.

8. See John Arthur, *Invisible Sojourners: African Immigrant Diaspora in the United States* (New York: Praeger, 2000); Paul Stoller, *Money Has No Smell: The Africanization of New York City* (Chicago: University of Chicago Press, 2002); Rogaia Mustafa Abusharaf, *Wanderings: Sudanese Migrants and Exiles in North America* (Ithaca, N.Y.: Cornell University Press, 2003); Jacqueline Copeland-Carson, *Creating Africa in America: Translocal Identity in an Emerging World City* (Philadelphia: University of Pennsylvania Press, 2004); JoAnn D'Alisera, *An Imagined Geography: Sierra Leonean Muslims in America* (Philadelphia: University of Pennsylvania Press, 2004); W. Tettey and K. Puplampu, *Negotiating Identity and Belonging: The African Diaspora in Canada* (Calgary: University of Calgary Press, 2005); Gerrie ter Haar, *Halfway to Paradise: African Christians in Europe* (Cardiff, U.K.: Cardiff Academic Press, 1998); and Afe Adogame and Cordula Weisskoeppel, eds., *Religion in the Context of African Migration* (Bayreuth: Bayreuth African Studies Series no. 5, 2005). Other notable works on African immigration include the analysis of Ethiopian refugees in the book on postrevolution migration by Peter H. Koehn, *Refugees from Revolution: U.S. Policy and Third World Migration* (Boulder: Westview Press, 1991), and a small but growing number of articles on African Muslims in New York City (see references at the end of chapter 13).

9. The project combines scholarly research with support for the religious communities (e.g., providing access to information, networking, establishing an interfaith dialogue.). A national conference, African Immigrant Religious Community Leaders in the United States, was held at U.C. Davis in April 2005 and was attended by thirty-five prominent African Imams, pastors, and traditional priests from across the country.

10. D'Alisera, *An Imagined Geography,* 84.

11. Ter Haar, *Halfway to Paradise,* 84.

12. Dorothy L. Zinn, "The Senegalese Immigrants in Bari," in R. Benmayor and A. Skotnes, eds., *Migration and Identity* (New York: Oxford University Press, 1994), 58.

13. A growing body of work attests to the centrality of race and racial identity in the process of immigrant incorporation. Several theorists have described the ways in which racial structures are shaping the opportunities and responses of black immigrants to the United States. Some of the most important recent studies include Alex Stepick, *Pride Against Prejudice: Haitians in the United States* (Boston: Allyn and Bacon, 1998); Mary C. Waters, *Black Identities: West Indian Immigrant Dreams and American Realities* (New York: Russell Sage Foundation, 1999); Nancy Foner and G. Fredrickson, eds., *Not Just Black and White: Historical and Contemporary Perspectives on Immigration, Race and Ethnicity in the United States* (New York: Russell Sage Foundation, 2004).

14. Russell Jeung, "New Asian Churches and Symbolic Racial Identity," in Jane N. Iwamura and Paul Spickard, *Revealing the Sacred in Asian and Pacific America* (New York: Routledge, 2003), 225–240.

15. Jose Casanova, "Immigration and the New Religious Pluralism: A E.U./U.S. Comparison," paper presented at the Conference on the New Religious Pluralism and Democracy, Georgetown University, April 21–22, 2005, 25.

16. Mary Waters, *Black Identities,* 71.

17. Martin Stokes, ed., *Ethnicity, Identity and Music: The Musical Construction of Place* (New York: Berg, 1994), 3.

18. Nigel Rapport, "Coming Home to a Dream: A Study of the Immigrant Discourse of 'Anglo-Saxons' in Israel," in N. Rapport and A. Dawson, eds., *Migrants of Identity: Perceptions of Home in a World of Movement* (New York: Berg, 1998), 79.

19. Benmayor and Skotnes, *Migration and Identity,* 8.

20. This notion has spurred an important discussion among scholars on the necessity of viewing globalization as a multidirectional exchange in which Christian communities from the South, and African religious communities in particular, are assuming an active and influential role. Also relevant is Newham Freston's description of Pentecostalism as "globalization from below." See N. Freston, "Evangelicalism and Globalization: General Observations and Some Latin American Dimensions," in M. Hutchinson and O. Kalu, eds., *A Global Faith? Essays on Evangelicalism and Globalization* (Sydney: Center for the Study of Australian Christianity, 1998).

21. Ogbu Kalu, "'Globelecalization' and Religion: The Pentecostal Model in Contemporary Africa," in J. Cox and G. ter Haar, eds., *Uniquely African? African Christian Identity from Cultural and Historical Perspectives* (Trenton, N.J.: Africa World Press, 2003), 239.

22. Warner, "Immigration and Religious Communities in the United States," in Warner and Wittner, *Gatherings in Diaspora*, 21.

23. For example, see Pyong Gap Min and Jung Ha Kim, *Religions in Asian America: Building Faith Communities* (New York: Alta Mira Press, 2002).

24. Similar points are made by Luis Leon with respect to a pentecostal church attended by Latino immigrants in Los Angeles in which the pastor and other successful members represent "living embodiment(s) of the power of God." See "Born Again in East LA: The Congregation as Border Space," in Warner and Wittner, eds., *Gatherings in Diaspora.*

25. Okome's views were corroborated at the recent meeting convened by the project for African religious leaders across the United States. The leaders expressed a strong desire to have their congregations act as a vehicle for social change and a collaborative engagement that will unite their efforts.

26. Ebaugh and Chafetz, *Religion and the New Immigrants.*

27. Ebaugh and Chafetz state that "the pace at which women enter such [formal leadership] roles is substantially a function of men's desire to fill them." See H. R. Ebaugh and J. S. Chafetz, "Agents for Cultural Reproduction and Structural Change: The Ironic Role of Women in Immigrant Religious Institutions," *Social Forces* 78, no. 2 (1999): 585–613.

28. For example, Goldring describes Mexican women's marginalization within transmigrant organizations engaged in hometown projects. Certain African ethnic associations in the United States are similarly gender stratified. See "The Gender and Geography of Citizenship in Mexico—U.S. Transnational Spaces," *Identities* 7, no. 4 (2001): 501–537.

29. Henrietta Moore, *Feminism and Anthropology* (Cambridge: Polity Press, 1998), 111.

30. Mark A. Shibley, "Contemporary Evangelicals: Born-Again and World Affirming," *Annals of the American Academy of Political and Social Science* 558 (1998): 67–87.

31. For significant insights on the way in which immigrant religion is practiced in a racialized social context, see the collected volume on Asian American religion by Iwamura and Spickard, *Revealing the Sacred in Asian and Pacific America.*

32. Sarah Coakley, "Kenosis and Subversion," in D. Hampson, ed., *Swallowing a Fishbone? Feminist Theologians Debate Christianity* (London: Society for Promoting Christian Knowledge, 1996), 110.

33. Also see D'Alisera, *Imagined Geography,* 32.

I

Historical and Theoretical Perspectives

1

Communities of Believers

Exploring African Immigrant Religion in the United States

Jacob K. Olupona

Introduction

Despite unprecedented awareness of the importance of new immigrant cultures in contemporary America, modern scholarship has failed to properly document, describe, and analyze the religious activities of African immigrant communities in the United States. It has frequently been assumed, at least in the literature, if not in the consciousness of Euro-Americans, that, since the "cessation" of slavery in America, there has been no African immigration to the United States. Given that the social and economic problems facing African American communities are longstanding and overwhelming, it is not surprising that minimal attention is paid to problems affecting newly arrived African immigrant communities, which are often considered mere extensions of African American communities.

It is partly in response to this lack that we chose to examine African immigrant religious communities in America. We were interested in identifying the scope, range, and varieties of African immigrant religious experience and expression; determining the multifaceted nature of the interrelationships among religion, immigration, and social integration as experienced by African people; identifying the resources and expertise available to African immigrant religious communities; engaging in critical discourse on the construction of cultural meaning and identity formation among new religious and ethnic immigrant communities; and contributing important theoretical and conceptual perspectives to the emerging field of religious pluralism and the dynamics of the immigration process. This essay represents a mapping of our project on African immigrant religious communities.

Historical Background

In the past several decades, African immigrant populations have increased remarkably as U.S. immigration and visa policies assigned preferential status to previously underrepresented African countries. Economic and political crises in Africa escalated to cause the migration of Africans from places such as the Democratic Republic of Congo, Sierra Leone, Somalia, Liberia, Rwanda, Burundi, and the Sudan. Current immigration figures indicate that more than fifty thousand Africans migrate to the United States each year, a substantial population worthy of scholarly and ethnographic study. The total number of African-born immigrants in 2003 was more than 1 million,[1] and more than twice as many Africans were granted legal residency in 2001 as in 1989.[2] The number of African refugees in the United States doubled between 2001 and 2002.[3] The largest group of immigrants entering Minnesota in 2002 was from Somalia. Africans constitute significantly growing populations not only in major urban centers such as New York, Washington, D.C., Chicago, Los Angeles, Houston, and Atlanta but also in small and midsize cities in states such as Ohio and Maine.[4] Religious institutions are providing new immigrants a degree of security in an insecure urban environment and are playing a major role in the processes of adaptation and incorporation. Events in the past few years suggest that these emergent African immigrant communities are already making a significant political, cultural, and social impact on American life.

While several studies have contributed to our understanding of new immigrant religious communities in the United States,[5] no significant scholarship thus far has comprehensively explored African immigrant religions, perhaps because the communities often remain invisible to mainstream society. They are inappropriately subsumed under academic studies of the "Black Church," a term that refers to African American Christian communities. Typically, academic analysis of black religious experience in the United States disregards immigrant blacks, especially Africans, and consequently fails to examine connections between ethnicity and religious beliefs and practices. In addition, ethnic minority churches established by African immigrants during the past twenty years apparently occupy no visible place in American church culture or historiography!

The implication of this study for policy matters is important, especially for public understanding of new immigrant communities. African immigrant religion must be situated within the broader context of cultural and religious pluralism in the United States. Our findings challenge the notion of contemporary American civil religion as an amalgam of beliefs and practices that are essentially derived from Judeo-Christian symbols and expressions. The new American pluralism, partly shaped by the ethos and values of new immigrants, provides a different picture for immigrants from Africa. These immigrants, who have just escaped dire circumstances, suddenly find themselves in exile, having escaped one kind of oppression only to find themselves at the mercy of another. However, with the resources of the religious communities that have adopted them, their integration into American society takes on a less traumatic character, while congregations in turn are making meaningful contributions to the American religious and cultural mosaic.

The study may also have significant influence on the scholarship of religious pluralism and public culture, especially as the debate on the place of values, ethics, and religion in contemporary American society intensifies. As a Nigerian Anglican (Episcopalian) immigrant, I have been surreptitiously thrust into debates on subjects ranging from the ordination of a New Hampshire bishop who is gay to the dominant presence of the Redeemed Christian Church of God in the small Texan town of Floyd. In addition, an African church leader told me a month before the November 2004 presidential election that issues of religion and values would be critical to the election. Moreover, the project raises broader questions of intergroup relations, such as relations between African immigrants and other communities. As a distinct and ever-increasing group, we expect to see African immigrants progressively exercising their expertise, rights, and growing numbers to demand the fair distribution and allocation of community resources.

African religious institutions are pluralistic in that they are simultaneously perceived as sacred and civic institutions. They represent a synthesis of numerous traditions that serve diverse religious and secular functions within the communities. Unfortunately, previous scholars in various disciplines, including religious studies, anthropology, and sociology, have been hindered by obsolete paradigms of assimilation and syncretism and by Eurocentric models of identity that fail to capture adequately either the sense of community integrity prevalent among African immigrants or their sense of the sacred. For these reasons, this project has examined a new population of Africans in the United States through the emerging concepts of transnational identity, African theology, and diasporic studies.

A central finding in our study is that faith-based African immigrant organizations, in addition to serving as sacred places for worship and the social construction of ethnic identity, are creating important opportunities for social and political engagement. Faith-based African immigrant organizations are instrumental in providing a renewed sense of civic values for immigrants and their host communities.[6] For many African religious groups, the idea of "mission" is defined broadly; social engagement encompasses more than evangelism and targets communities throughout the world. We find that African religious communities are closely involved in a variety of social and political issues in the United States and abroad. African religious groups offer creative and critical public roles for African immigrants, especially in relation to issues that affect the wellbeing of immigrants. For example, communities engage in discourse about ethnicity, racism, and violence against immigrants because these issues impinge upon their daily lives. Hence, participation in American civic life is viewed as an integral part of their mission. As one church leader in Miami puts it, "African religious leaders can no longer afford to stand by while Africans are murdered and assaulted by police." This comment was made after recent widespread incidents of police brutality.[7]

In cities across America, faith-based community organizations meet the needs of immigrant communities by offering social services that state and local governments often fail to provide. In the seven major metropolitan areas where we conducted research, we observed that newly arrived African immigrants, like European, Caribbean, and Asian immigrants before them, often face myriad social problems. These include commonplace, nationwide urban social ills created by economic divestment, urban dislocation or "renewal," corporate relocation, the proliferation of low-paid service jobs, gentrification, a lack of affordable housing and adequate health care, two-tiered educational systems, incarceration by the USCIS (INS) (especially of asylum seekers and illegal immigrants), and racial profiling. African immigrant religious groups respond to these social ills by acting as buffers for new immigrants and for the society they encounter at large.

African Immigrant Religious Communities: Variety in Religious Expressions

The African Immigrant Religious Communities Project is concerned with a variety of African religious experiences in the United States. African immigrants have established religious communities and institutions in the

United States that reflect the wide-ranging, sociocultural mosaic of their homelands in Africa. Implicitly and explicitly, African sacred ritual, theology, language, aesthetics, and identity shape the immigrants' institutional structures. Five types of African religious traditions and expressions have informed this project in major U.S. cities: (1) African pentecostal and charismatic churches, (2) African Initiated Churches (AICs), (3) specialized African ministries within major ("mainline") U.S. denominations, (4) African Islamic traditions, and (5) African Indigenous Religion.

African pentecostal and charismatic churches constitute the largest type of immigrant religious group from Africa and are primarily evangelical, born-again pentecostal sects that emphasize holiness, fervent prayer, charismatic revival, proximate salvation, speaking in tongues, baptism of the Holy Spirit, faith healing, visions, and divine revelations.

In contrast to pentecostal/charismatic churches, the second type represents African Initiated Churches (AICs), or indigenous spiritual churches founded by African prophetic and visionary leaders. The AICs often borrow from mainstream European Christian factions, fusing Christian beliefs and practices with African cultural traditions. Distinguishing them from other African churches is their white *sultana* robes that signify purity. They emphasize very traditional African worldviews, using African languages in their liturgy. I should add that my interest in this work began when a *Wall Street Journal* reporter in Atlanta wanted me to tell him about a strange group of African Christians in white sultana robes, walking barefoot in a black church; I knew immediately from his description that he was referring to members of the Celestial Church of Christ.

The third type of African church is formed under the wing of specialized African, ethnic, or national ministries by orthodox U.S. Christian denominations, congregations largely of northern European ancestry. After coming to America, many recent African immigrants switched denominational loyalties by joining the culturally dynamic, savoir-faire pentecostal churches. Trying to prevent the loss of their immigrant members, American denominations responded by creating special outreach ministries that catered to particular ethnic and national immigrants.

The fourth group, African Islamic tradition, is diverse, varying from the Sufi-oriented Mourides of Senegal to more mainstream Islamic sects from Somalia, Kenya, and Eritrea. These diverse groups share the goal of providing mutual aid, cultural renewal, and connectedness. As a response to the profound loss of identity that affects Muslims living in the United States, African mosques have evolved into community centers that provide a sense of continuity with the past as well as avenues for growth and civic participation. As described by a member of a New York community, "The *masjid* is the center of social, political, and spiritual life."

The fifth group, African Indigenous Religion, is the most problematic in that it represents mostly a priestly class of West African *babalawos* (diviners) whose clientele, derived largely from outside the African immigrant community, includes African Americans, European Americans, and Latinos. This group poses the greatest theoretical challenge to scholars because of the interconnection of religion and culture in African society. Traditional religious beliefs and practices often manifest themselves in a variety of ways in African immigrant life journeys: rites of passage, kinship institutions, and community gatherings such as the weekly or monthly meetings of the ethnic associations in which elders act as guardians of traditions, transmitting the age-old beliefs and practices of their lineages and groups to successive generations.

These five categories are ideal types based on a heuristic categorization to enable us to sort out these religious organizations. Because the religious communities are in process, still emerging, and not yet fully formed, we should not assume that the typology is fixed; rather, it is still changing. Indeed, one African clergy in Oakland complained to me that when we ask for statistics on church membership, "We should keep in mind that there are often some fixed members and others who simply go from church to church. At times, I have a feeling that we are just recycling these folks."

Scope and Focus of the Work

This mapping project examined the significance of African immigrant religious communities within the context of American religious landscapes and cultural pluralism. By African immigrant communities, we mean people from Africa who came to the United States as voluntary immigrants, as distinct from people of African origin whose forebears arrived here involuntarily as slaves from the late fifteenth century to the early part of the nineteenth century. In developing this study, we collected data from religious community leaders and members in New York, Los Angeles, Chicago, the San Francisco Bay Area, Atlanta, Miami, and Washington, D.C.

To gather these data, we conducted interviews and participant observation focusing on key research issues and the ways that these play out for the newest waves of African immigrants. Beginning with a social and cultural overview of these seven U.S. metropolitan areas and providing basic data concerning their numbers and the urban space they occupy in each city, our study investigates the African Diaspora and immigrant faith-based organizations, African ethnic and national diversity, and African spirituality and worship style in Christian, Muslim, and indigenous African faith communities. We examine ecumenism and interfaith relations, the independent African Christian church, transglobal ties, new roles for women and men, immigrant entrepreneurs, African cultural identity, and the complex dilemma of the desire to both become "Americanized and to maintain ethnic and national identities." Our study examines concerns for family values and education for children, integration and segregation, immigrant status, and overall African faith-based contributions to American civil society.

Theorizing African Immigrant Religious Communities

How do we conceptualize and imagine these communities of believers? What model best fits their profile and the religious spirituality they espouse?

African immigrant religious communities occupy a large presence in many American urban centers. This physical and symbolic space can be called "junctions between the Diaspora and the homeland."[8] Rey Chow adapted this metaphor to indicate the "marginalized position" of the immigrant. It is a location involuntarily chosen by the immigrant, "one constructed by history."[9] The marginalized African immigrant Diaspora must "master the tactics of dealing with the dominant cultures." Since immigrants and exiles can make no "claims to territorial property or cultural centrality," they learn to "negotiate their cultural identity" as they undergo ordeals encountered in the new place.[10]

African churches, for example, must constantly negotiate their religious identities and their place within two centers of authority: (1) the homeland church that sends "missionaries" to what they imagine to be the "pagan" West and (2) the host's secular and religious centers that consider new immigrants "strange" Christians. When viewed as "strange Christians appearing in white robes"—as the Atlanta journalist described them—members of African churches are imagined and viewed as a minority group "whose existence has been victimized and whose articulation has been suppressed."[11]

However, the marginalized may become central to those who hold onto their ideology and practice as significant, since identity construction has to do "not with being but becoming."[12] "If one considers the opposition of self and other, the other is always to some extent within. That is, what is considered marginal and peripheral is actually central."[13] Sarup's thesis underscores the need to explore the cultural and social significance of African religious institutions, especially when viewed along the two poles of their existence.

Understanding the central role of these emerging communities can also be viewed as a viable scholarly undertaking in the fashionable area of African Diaspora studies. As Lavie and Swedenburg observe, "Diaspora refers to the doubled relationship or dual loyalty that migrants, exiles, and refugees have to places—their connection to the space they currently occupy and their continuing involvement with back home." They add, "the phenomenon of Diaspora calls for re-imagining the 'areas' of area studies and developing units of analysis that enable us to understand the dynamics of transitional cultural and economic processes, as well as to challenge the conceptual limits imposed by national and ethnic/racial boundaries."[14]

Diaspora studies underscore a celebration of a once marginal people who become symbolically central in American society. The relevance to African and to African American religious research is to explore how African religious organizations mobilize their limited resources to move from peripheral status to a central space in American religious landscape. A summary of our findings thus far follows.

African Immigrants' Social and Cultural Life

"Identity" refers to that which we desire to associate with or to be associated with. It is important to understand how identity is constructed and how African immigrants undertake the construction of an emerging identity based on status, role, and behavior. For immigrants, this desire is constituted in memory and consciousness, which span aspects of both the new and the old in the African Diaspora. African immigrants, Africans in the Caribbean, and African Americans are engaged in a common search for sources of being and authority and the quest for truth. Once situated in the Americas, African immigrants do not abandon their African cultural traditions but instead look for ways to reproduce and reinvent culture, often in non-African communities.

Faced with the secularizing trends of modernity and their desire for Americanization, many African immigrants seek to maintain their cultural identities through the development of communal links, religion, new institutions, and social support structures. Contrary to previous assumptions, for some groups, becoming American no longer entails the total abandonment of one's cultural identity. The vernacular American society is changing from a great American "melting pot" to what Sulayman Nyang has termed the "salad bowl," which allows individual components of diversity and ethnic identity to create the existence of the greater whole. This new paradigm of recognizing the role of diverse cultures helps to provide us with a better understanding of the diasporic communities that are developing pluralistic affiliations.

African immigrants are the newest wave of immigrants to enter the United States with inadequate institutions of support. African immigrants must contend with significant issues of racism and tension within the larger American society. Like earlier waves of immigrants, they compete for scarce resources, often leading to social tension and division. These challenges are apparent in questions of identity emerging among African and Caribbean immigrants and African American communities. African immigrants appear to lack visibility and presence in popular culture and are often viewed by Euro-American culture as African Americans.

Parents who emigrated to provide their children with better opportunities in education and employment find themselves enrolling their children in inner-city or substandard schools across the United States, a phenomenon seen in all of our sample cities. In many public schools, immigrant children are exposed to apathy, high dropout rates, large class sizes, and institutionalized forms of segregation and inequality. The response of many African immigrants when faced with this dilemma is to establish religious schools or to encourage youth and Sunday school programs in their churches. It is all an attempt to develop a separate identity quite different from those of the African American and Caucasian communities in an effort to protect their children from the stereotypes and racism present in American society. The fear of these groups is that their assimilation into American culture will constitute assimilation solely into African American culture, which will result in a lower socioeconomic status for their children because of racist attitudes toward this group. The result of this dilemma is a growing tension between African Americans and African immigrants. Many second-generation immigrants strongly oppose cultural markers such as the adoption of "Black English" or "Black Dialect," rap music, and certain forms of dress and style. Many children of African immigrants feel a divided loyalty to two cultures as they grow up. They are exposed to negative opinions voiced by their parents about American blacks and to the apparently more favorable responses of whites to African immigrants, while at the same time they realize that their identifying characteristics link them with African Americans.

An example of tension between African immigrants and African Americans may be seen in a Washington, D.C., interview with a pastor of a Baptist church. Arguing that there are few communities in the United States that open their arms to African immigrants, he observed, "Africans are expected to integrate and 'melt into the pot.'" He cited recent examples of Africans who had been refused membership by white churches and suggested that African American churches have also alienated Africans because members of these churches feel threatened that Africans might take away the little opportunity for upward mobility that African Americans have gained. African Americans view African immigrants in this case as economic competitors.

African immigrant respondents expressed difficulty in dealing with questions of their identity. One pastor and church founder stated, "As Africans in the United States, we have two strikes against us: first we are black, and then we are African." Many African immigrant religious communities also wrestle with the question "How can the United States be both a Christian and a racist nation?" Because of American racism, African immigrants tend to have mixed and contradictory feelings toward their African American associates. They share a common goal in fighting racism, but at the same time, African immigrants also tend to separate themselves from African American culture for fear of facing greater discrimination.

Transglobalism and Cultural Identity

New immigrants are at the center of the emergence of transglobal communities that continue to define their identity with reference to two centers: home and Diaspora. Immigrant communities maintain strong transnational ties between the Diaspora and communities of origin, ties that surpass those with the nation-state of origin. Religious beliefs and practices, including sacred rituals performed through ceremonies, music, and dance, play important roles in forming and developing cohesion in

African communities, serving as avenues for contesting and regulating traditional African cultural practices. Religious affliliation inspires community participation, establishes relationships, and enables communities to orient themselves and to delineate a collective identity and space that traverse national boundaries.

Though transnational ties are forged in political, religious, and economic terms, they are, nevertheless, intertwined. For example, a West African Muslim community in New York City merges the transactions of transnational economics with religious activities. In addition, globalization, the mass media, the information age, and a well-developed communication technology (Internet satellite-broadcasting systems) facilitate ties among communities of origin and the Diaspora.

An important issue for immigrants is the desire to maintain important cultural traditions and identities through transglobal mediums. In particular, African immigrants attempt to preserve their cultural traditions for the second generation. For example, many immigrants feel a strong desire to be buried in their country of origin. In our findings, a New York Islamic mosque and a Christian independent church both placed considerable emphasis on providing collective assistance to pay for the costs of reburial of the deceased in the homeland. Paying for these "repatriation" services is viewed as a community responsibility, as they are of essential importance to African immigrants to the United States. Other examples are present within associations formed across the African Diaspora. In Miami, we see a city with diverse ethnic groups and religious traditions. Many African immigrants to Miami are practitioners of Ifa (Yoruba divination system), whose teachings are very similar to those of Santeria, an Afro-Cuban religion based on the Yoruba religion but with the addition of Catholic saints. Within this pluralistic, tolerant environment, those African immigrants who hold fast to traditional Ifa and Yoruba values are able to function with greater resiliency and cultural integrity.

How will global and local dynamics affect the status of women in new societies? Immigrant women, as Espin has observed, "are expected to preserve culture and traditions, immigrant mothers are expected to be the carriers of culture for their children in the new country."[15] Frequently, gender roles call upon women to provide support that enables the family to function in accordance with prescribed traditions.[16] However, African immigrant churches have largely female congregations that demonstrate a wide variance in religious participation, from assuming very limited "traditional" roles to taking on key leadership positions.

In our fieldwork in some Christian churches in New York, women participate significantly more than men. In some cases, immigrant women may assume a greater role in the leadership. In New York City, three-quarters of the members of the Grace Fellowship for Christian Believers are women. The church declares that any member may hold office, including the positions of president and minister. Similarly, three-quarters of the membership of Vineyard International Christian Ministries is female. Women may be ordained as pastors. In the Ghanaian Presbyterian Reformed Church in Brooklyn, 60 percent of the members are female. The church formed a special women's fellowship active in social support, while males remained less organized and less active in church affairs. In Miami, the building committee that raised more than a million dollars for the construction of a Nigerian mosque was headed by a woman. In many of these communities, immigrant women appear to be assuming a greater role in leadership than they did in their homelands.

Patronage: An American Adaptation

Closely associated with these examples of cultural identity and adaptation are examples of what we term collectively "emerging forms of patronage." To explain this phenomenon, we must first mention that African indigenous religions offer a sense of identity and recognition that are present in the many cultures of the African Diaspora. Historically, the precolonial elite of West Africa were practitioners of African traditions such as Ifa. However, with the rise of the European colonial powers in Africa, many returning ex-slaves and missionaries recruited the misfits and outcasts of African communities, who became the first converts to Christianity. These converts in turn were elevated to the new elite, as colonial governments came to discriminate against the old guard of African chiefs and diviners.

Because of colonialism, many indigenous beliefs were forced to go underground or were practiced in some form of secrecy until political independence was achieved. African slaves who practiced these indigenous beliefs or Islam were further discriminated against in the New World. Many were forced to convert to Christianity or instead chose to disguise their indigenous faiths with Christian elements. As a result, conversion to European Christianity is inexorably associated with imperialism, colonialism, and slavery. Indigenous traditions offer an opportunity for alienated individuals to reassert their membership in and association with the extended African Diaspora and to reclaim ancestral identity through a community.

In this context, we acknowledge that the African shrines and indigenous institutions examined in this survey are usually associated with African elites that take on the role of chief or patron within a community. Often these individuals are the agents of African indigenous religions in America and are related to other chiefs or patrons in African nations. Their shrines and centers take on an Americanized form that does not exist in Africa. In essence, the convergence of the shrine and the chief is an attempt to re-create traditions in an American cultural context and socioeconomic environment. In Africa, chiefs rely upon their structural lineage connections to the state to form their bases of power. In the United States, individuals are unable to associate themselves within the authority of the state, and therefore they have turned to religion within the civil society to establish their authority. Religious contexts have become their forum. As they are unable to rely upon the African state as a source of wealth, status, and power, they have adopted aspects of American evangelicalism to fund and support their efforts through an emerging system of contributions and patronage. Since these new religious shrines and cultural centers are linked with secular and political institutions of chiefs and patronage, their legitimacy is uncertain. It is sometimes unclear whether these shrines represent the indigenous religions they are purported to represent.

Americanization and Modernity

As with the case of patronage, we see examples of African traditions being grafted onto American culture. We loosely call these trends forms of "Americanization" or modernity. In Chicago, for example, some women express a desire to lighten their skin by using special bleaching creams; this practice is found even among Ghanaian women of the African United Methodist Church (AUMC), who, unlike most continental African women, often wear traditional clothing. Moreover, most of their African sisters, especially Nigerians, use these creams. This undue fixation with skin color suggests the possibility that these African women paradoxically retain aspects of their African identity even as they attempt to portray themselves as "light-skinned" African Americans or to be perceived as "American."

Evidence of the desire to become "Americanized" is seen also in the promotion of American "born-again" or Pentecostal practices. As indicated in the Los Angeles data, Pentecostal or "born-again" styles of worship are prominent in African immigrant communities, probably because they are advocated as shaping African beliefs and practices such as spirit possession, divination, or ancestor worship. However, claims by "born-again" adherents must be qualified with the understanding that they themselves place little emphasis on African indigenous traditional values. Often, "born-again" missionaries can be the greatest critics of traditional African beliefs that they view as evil and superstitious. For example, one pastor in Washington, D.C., spoke out against ancestor worship, arguing that we should not place our ancestors on the same plane as God. At another church, a reverend used a handout of weekly "prayer points" called "Breaking the Backbone of Stubborn Witchcraft." According to him, this handout was necessary to allow prayer to change belief in witchcraft (i.e., *babalawos*) to belief in Jesus. To some extent, the claim that "born-again" styles of worship are closer to African styles may represent an attempt on the part of these missionaries to pull African immigrants away from indigenous beliefs and toward beliefs more consistent with the values of modernity.

Urban Space, Location, and Environment

Another curious anomaly we observed in the data relates to the economic use of urban space. In most cities surveyed, African immigrants are attempting to obtain affordable space within economically underdeveloped urban ghettos. Both African Americans and African immigrants have historically have made use of worship space within low-rent inner city areas, and African immigrant churches and *masjids* are often found among decaying businesses and industrial complexes.

The San Francisco Bay Area data are unique in providing overwhelming evidence of a form of reverse "suburbanization." Economic factors have forced African immigrant and African American communities to move out of San Francisco's older ethnic neighborhoods because of gentrification and rising property values. In four interviews held at two churches, an Ethiopian café and a San Francisco community center, respondents indicated, "White people with money are slowly but steadily buying out African American properties." Consequently, almost none of the African immigrant religious communities in the San Francisco Bay Area are located within the city of San Francisco itself. Instead, immigrants have moved to outlying East Bay suburbs such as Pittsburg and Antioch, where one currently finds an abundance of small churches serving these communities.

Religion and Civic Values

For many African immigrants, America has replaced the former colonial powers of England and France as a haven for realizing their economic and political potential. African immigrants in the United States today are involved in diverse and complex forms of political expression that encompass broad issues of culture, identity, and citizenship. One important factor is the high level of education among African immigrants. Almost 90 percent of African immigrants are high school graduates, 75 percent have some college experience, and 25 percent have an advanced degree, making Africans the best-educated immigrant group in America.[17] We suggest that the high educational level of African immigrants, combined with the social context of ethnic pluralism in the United States, expands and broadens opportunities for political expression. In this sense, our work questions the conventional wisdom that the political incorporation of immigrant groups follows socioeconomic assimilation. In the African community, one finds that first- and second-generation African immigrants are highly active in local, state, and national politics, and they can be found advocating for policy change in diverse areas such as immigration, voting rights, civil rights, and foreign relations. Our work is helping us to understand further the social, cultural, and historical context that has enabled the political engagement of these first- and second-generation immigrants.

Political participation among African immigrants takes several important routes, including African religious, cultural, ethnic, and national organizations and associations. As immigrant churches and mosques assume a congregational structure that engenders a spirit of democracy and volunteerism,[18] religious institutions often provide a vital springboard for developing civic and political activity. In the African community, the Friday prayer forum at the mosques and the Sunday church service represent avenues in which the ethos of political participation is disseminated among community members. In some cases, the communication of political messages is quite direct. For example, pastors and Imams may take definite stands in regard to local, state, and national elections, using African rhetorical devises (clever proverbs, traditional narratives, parables, and biblical stories) to influence congregations to vote for candidates who support particular social policies. Religious leaders tend to wield significant influence within their congregations. For example, one week before the U.S. national elections on November 2, 2004, a quick-witted pastor, speaking in parables, cleverly used the story of Moses and the burning bush to insinuate a covert subtext expressing his contempt for the president.

In addition to the influence of political leaders, the religious community provides an informal avenue for the sharing of political views and the distribution of political literature among members. This usually takes place before or after services or in the weekly informal prayer groups (also called "cell groups") that proliferate within religious institutions.

I should also add that African immigrant groups have developed a meaningful voice in the arena of U.S. foreign policy, especially regarding support for democratization movements in their homelands and the administration of development aid. Many topics relating to the African continent draw wide public attention in the United States, such as the AIDS epidemic and ethnic genocide in places such as Rwanda and, currently, the Sudan. Among African immigrants, the wave of democratic transitions in the homeland has served as an energizing source for political expression in the U.S. context.

Networks of Self-Support

African religious communities are developing civic institutions that meet the cultural, social, and economic needs of their communities. These institutions are providing secular services out of both religious and nonreligious centers. They allow networks of communication and support to develop between the immigrant community and indigenous communities in Africa. They are providing language instruction, cultural activities, and access to indigenous healing and religious practices as part of a trans-global identity.

In many cases, the assistance provided by the religious community is indirect. For example, the religious institution often operates as a support network that refers needy members to those members who are capable of offering assistance. In other instances, African immigrant communities are coming together to formalize these "self-help" institutions out of their own distinct identity as a group. Addressing the needs of recent African immigrants, many mosques and churches have developed institutionalized structures to provide secular support with legal assistance, housing, and employment.

Of the fifty-five leaders we interviewed in New York City, forty specifically referred to some combination of services and efforts to assist immigrants. One Imam observed that members gave support to immigrants in the form of counseling, shelter, and employment. In Los Angeles, more than half of the leaders we interviewed reported that they provide networks of support to assist in finding employment, housing, and legal advice. Many of these efforts were cooperative, not only within the religious organization but also among African independent churches themselves. In five interviews, religious leaders were identified as members and participants in the Los Angeles–based African Ministers Association, a pan-African religious organization that attempts to meet and serve the needs of Africans in the greater Los Angeles area.

Like other American cities, Atlanta is home to a number of mutual aid and support networks established by African immigrant religious institutions. For example, members of African mosques contribute to a special sadakat fund that provides financial assistance to needy African Muslims within their community. Additionally, like the data from other cities, the data from Atlanta confirm that assistance for refugees is provided either by individuals, such as prominent religious community leaders, or by groups, such as the Caring Believers Bible Fellowship and the Liberian Community Association of Georgia.

We see many of the same trends in the Washington, D.C., interviews. The Jesus House of the Redeemed Christian Church of God offered its facilities for a presentation by four Nigerian real estate agents, who provided advice to the congregation on buying houses in Maryland. Topics covered included how to establish good credit and how to select the right neighborhood in which to invest. A woman who co-pastors a church in Baltimore with her husband discussed the loss of women's social networks in the U.S. context. She gave a vivid example of a woman who suddenly finds she must "pack the whole family in the car" in order to buy milk at the store. In response, women have organized many activities and services that provide support and promote the health and welfare of the family. An example is the provision of postnatal care for mother and child.

The growth of these secular functions within Islamic and Christian institutions reflects an effort to provide logistical support for African immigrants in American civil society. Throughout our interviews, we found that these social services were conducted almost entirely through volunteer efforts and financial support provided by members.

Conclusion

Although several studies have contributed significantly to our understanding of new immigrant religious communities in the United States, very little scholarship has explored African immigrant religions comprehensively, perhaps because these communities remain largely invisible to mainstream culture and society. Our study is beginning to draw scholarly attention to the cultural and religious distinction of African religious immigrant communities. It also offers comparative materials that inform the emerging discourse on the interface of religion and immigration.

This ongoing work has provided an understanding of the scope, range, and variety of African religious practices in the United States. Particularly significant is the way in which religious practices and cultural norms enable African children and youth to define their identities as Africans living in the United States. These religious and cultural norms serve as a buffer between home and community and the apparently hostile and racialized world in which refugees and immigrants now find themselves. African religious communities continue to participate as American organizations—as citizens in the political economy of the nation. Their upward mobility is a sign of their success, just as their civic engagement indicates their desire to be integrated into the larger American society. Members of African communities, as transnational citizens, can be loyal U.S. citizens and yet maintain their relationship with their native countries. Religion plays a central role in the resiliency of these significant and evolving immigrant communities.

Notes

1. According to U.S. census estimates, the African-born U.S. population totaled 1,147,378 persons in 2004. Data source: U.S. Census Bureau American FactFinder Web site, Table B05006, Place of Birth for the Foreign-Born Population, 2004 American Community Survey, available online at www.factfinder.census.gov (accessed August 2005).

2. Jill Wilson, "African Born Residents of the United States," Migration Policy Institute Web site, 1 August 2003, available online at www.migrationinformation.com.

3. "Historical High Number of Immigrants Move to Minnesota in 2002," Minnesota State Demographic Center Web site, 18 August 2003, available online at www.state.mn.us/ebranch/admin/immigration.html (accessed December 2005).

4. Growing numbers of African immigrants are settling in less populated cities such as Lewiston, Maine, drawn in part by reports of more affordable housing and better schools and services. The large impact of such immigration on these small and formerly homogenous communities has been widely reported in the media. See K. Bouchard, "A Thousand Miles," *Portland Press Herald,* Maine Today Web site, 30 June 2002, available online at http://pressherald.mainetoday.com/news/immigration/020630somalis.shtml (accessed 30 July 2005); S. Miller, "A Lesson in Allaying Immigrant Tensions," *Christian Science Monitor,* 11 August 2003.

5. While there has been a series of articles and reports in the national news media, there are only a few scholarly works that explore the topic of African immigrant religion in the United States. See Paul Stoller, *Money Has No Smell: The Africanization of New York City* (Chicago: University of Chicago Press, 2002); Rogaia Mustafa Abusharaf, *Wanderings: Sudanese Migrants and Exiles in North America* (Ithaca, N.Y.: Cornell University Press, 2003); and JoAnn D'Alisera, *An Imagined Geography: Sierra Leonean Muslims in America* (Philadelphia: University of Pennsylvania Press, 2004). Studies by Eck and by Levitt also make reference to African immigrant religious communities. See Diana Eck, *On Common Ground: World Religions in America* (New York: Columbia University Press, 1997), and Peggy Levitt, *The Transnational Villagers* (Berkeley: University of California Press, 2001). My own research beginning in 1991 played a role in pioneering this field of study, introducing a number of concepts, such as "reverse mission" and "invisible community," that have gained currency in scholarly and public discourse on African immigrant religion.

6. Jacob Olupona (Principal Investigator), "African Immigrant Religious Communities: Identity Formation in America's Pluralistic Society," Report to the Ford Foundation, May 2001.

7. In 1999, New York City police killed an unarmed Guinean immigrant, Amadou Diallo, outside his Bronx home. Police fired forty-one bullets, hitting Diallo nineteen times. One year later, the four officers were acquitted of any crime.

8. Lynn Pan, Sons *of the Yellow Emperor: A History of the Chinese Diaspora* (Boston: Little Brown, 1990).

9. Rey Chow, *Writing Diaspora: Tactics of Intervention in Contemporary Cultural Studies* (Bloomington: Indiana University Press, 1993), 21.

10. Ibid., 25.

11. Ibid., 101.

12. Madan Sarup, *Identity, Culture and the Postmodern World* (Edinburgh: Edinburgh University Press, 1996), 7.

13. Ibid., 6.

14. Smadar Lavie and T. Swedenburg, eds., *Displacement, Diaspora and Geographies of Identity* (Durham, N.C.: Duke University Press, 1996), 15.

15. Oliva M. Espin, *Women Crossing Boundaries: A Psychology of Immigration and Transformations of Sexuality* (New York: Routledge, 1999), 149.

16. R. Stephen Warner, "Immigration and Religious Communities in the United States," in R. S. Warner, ed., *Gatherings in Diaspora: Religious Communities and the New Immigration* (Philadelphia: Temple University Press, 1998), 172.

17. *The Economist* 339, no. 7965 (1996): 27–28.

18. Warner, "Immigration and Religious Communities in the United States," 21.

2

African Immigrant Churches in the United States and the Study of Black Church History

David D. Daniels

The advent of African immigrant churches, specifically denominations, in the United States since 1965 creates a new moment in the history and study of the Black Church in North America. Should African immigrant churches become included in the studies of the Black Church and within African American religious history, or should they be topics only within immigrant studies and studies of new religious movements? Possibly, the emergence of African immigrant churches in United States requires a reconceptualization of the Church. As a conceptual framework, the Black Church might be so tied to the overall history of people of African descent in North America that there is insufficient conceptual space to include the religious experience of recent arrivals from Africa. For the religious experience of post-1965 African immigrants to become incorporated conceptually within the rubric of the Black Church and to be more than a mere addendum, a reconceptualization of the Black Church is required, and this reconceptualization entails a critical dialogue between the historiography of African Christianity and the historiography of African American Christianity in order for the incorporation of African immigrant religion to be performed with intellectual integrity.

This chapter has its origins in a 1992 survey of sub-Saharan African immigrant congregations in Chicago. Until this time, I was unaware of the existence in the United States of African-based congregations beyond the presence of the Ethiopian Orthodox Church. The initial survey was related to preparations for the Parliament of World Religions in 1993. A goal of the African American host committee was to include a representative group of black world religions in the Parliament. So a survey was conducted of African immigrant congregations and religious communities, as well as other religious communities from the Caribbean, in Chicago. In 1993, the survey was shared during the planning phase of The New Ethnic and Immigrant Congregations Project, directed by R. Stephen Warner and Judith Wittner and funded by the Eli Lilly Endowment and the Pew Charitable Trusts. In 1995, a second survey was conducted, this one focusing on sub-Saharan African immigrant congregations in Chicago. In addition to the general survey, three pastors were interviewed. The study results were presented at a symposium sponsored by Butler University in Indianapolis in 1995. In 2000, the research findings, as a paper titled "African Immigrant Congregations in Chicago: A Preliminary Report on a Survey and Its Impact on the Study of Black Church History," were presented at the American Academy of Religion.

Locating African Immigrant Congregations on the Map of U.S. Black Religion

For historians of U.S. Christianity, the initial challenge is where to place African immigrant congregations and denominations on the religious map of the United States. For the most part, African immigrant denominations are invisible to scholars and the general public within the United States. Currently, there are a few dissertations on African immigrant congregations. Yet, the presence of African immigrant denominations in the United States goes undetected.

Publications such as the *Yearbook of American and Canadian Churches* and the *Directory of African American Religious Bodies* include only a few African immigrant denominations. The rare exception among scholarly works is a bibliography authored by Charles Edwin Jones and titled *Black Holiness: A Guide to the Study of Black Participation in Wesleyan Perfectionist and Glossolalic Pentecostal Movements.*[1]

Various African-based denominations have affiliated congregations within the United States. These denominations include:

Brotherhood of the Cross and Star
Celestial Church of Christ
Cherubim and Seraphim
Christ Apostolic Church

The Church of Pentecost
Deeper Life Bible Church
Ethiopian Orthodox Church
Musama Disco
The Presbyterian Church of Ghana
The Redeemed Christian Church of God

Western denominations with missions in Africa are also represented among immigrant churches, including the Roman Catholic Church, the Church of the Seventh-Day Adventist, the International Church of the Foursquare Gospel, and the United Methodist Church.

While the denominations vary, we await future studies to determine whether a particular religious tradition among the African immigrant congregations will become predominant in the United States. In greater Chicago, during 2000, forty congregations were identified. Out of the various denominations, it appears that a significant number (21) belong to the pentecostal/charismatic wing of Christianity. The second largest group (9 congregations) fits within the orbit of the spiritual churches. The third largest sector (6 congregations) is affiliated with mainline denominations. The national origin of congregations reflects the immigration pattern to Chicago: Nigeria (16), Ghana (9), Senegal (1), Ethiopia (1), and Eritrea (1).[2]

Where should these congregations and denomination be located on the U.S. religious map? Are they best categorized and defined as immigrant religion, black U.S. religion, U.S. continental African religion, a new development within the Black Church, or a new religious movement within the United States?

While multiple sites might be identified in order to explore the complexity of African immigrant congregations, conceptual space within the concept of black religious history and the Black Church does exist. Cornel West and Eddie S. Glaude, Jr., craft a minimalist definition of black religious history: "Black religious history involves accounts of the development of black religious institutions and the communities of the faithful that sustain them." Their definition embraces the religious experience and institutions of all people of African descent and conceptually has space to include the insertion of the new black religious institutions founded by post-1965 African immigrants to the United States. The historian James Melvin Washington supplies a definition of the Black Church movement that is as expansive as the West-Glaude definition of black religious history. Washington comments:

> I consider all of the predominately black religious bodies in the United States to be part of the black church movement. I use the word "church" here to mean essentially local groups or congregations organized around various Islamic, Protestant, Catholic, and Jewish beliefs. Black Protestants are by far the largest of the black religious groups in the United States.

Washington's definition of the Black Church as a movement provides as much conceptual space to include African immigrant congregations, for instance, as the rubric "black religion" would. As minimalist definitions, both provide for the possibility of crossing theological boundaries that divide Christianity, black Hebrews, black Islam, African traditional religion, and "synthetic" or spiritual churches. Thus, the concept of the Black Church has been employed to include all black Christian congregations and denominations, ranging from black congregations in white denominations to black denominations themselves.[3]

The Black Church as a concept has demonstrated some degree of elasticity by historically including the U.S. Afro-Caribbean churches within this rubric. The Afro-Caribbean congregations in the United States have retained their distinct identity and profile within a set of denominations: predominantly white groups, such as the Protestant Episcopal Church and the Church of God (Cleveland, Tennessee); racially mixed groups, such as the Church of God of Prophecy; and predominantly black groups, such as the Church Our Lord Jesus Christ of the Apostolic Faith, the African Orthodox Church, and the United Pentecostal Council of the Assemblies of God. While the negotiation of religious space between African Americans with roots in the pre-twentieth-century United States and twentieth-century Afro-Caribbean immigrants to the United States and their descendants is almost invisible within scholarly literature; the social reality is recognized through the concentration of these immigrants in particular congregations and denominations. In some cities, because of the influx of Afro-Caribbean immigrants, congregations that were historically African American now have memberships that are becoming majority Afro-Caribbean. An example is the Concord Baptist Church in Brooklyn, New York.

Migration, both the forced migration of enslaved Africans to the Americas and the internal migration of African Americans within the United States, has been a lively topic within Black Church studies. The immigration of Afro-Caribbean peoples and continental Africans, in contrast, has received little attention. Within the historiography of the Black Church, immigration is bracketed as a subject. The subfield embarks upon on an important new trajectory with immigration as a topic.[4]

How can the inclusion of the recent religious experience of African immigrant congregations and denominations in the United States be achieved within Black Church studies, given the divergent histories of African and African American Christianity—European colonialism versus North American slavery; African traditional religions versus North American "slave religion"; European mission societies versus the black-founded Baptist-Methodist-pentecostal ecclesial orbit; African-instituted churches versus black Hebraic, Muslim, and cultic (leader-focused) groups; strong ethnic identities (e.g., Igbo, Ewe) versus the racial identity of the Negro/African American? I contend that the term "Black Church" is elastic enough to include the experience and recent history of African immigrant congregations. While African immigrant churches and African American churches emerged from distinct historical trajectories, during the mid-twentieth century the trajectories begin to converge as a response to the restructuring of the black Atlantic world and religion that resulted from African and Afro-Caribbean decolonization and U.S. desegregation during the post–World War II era.

Scholars such as the sociologist C. Eric Lincoln argue that during the 1960s, African American Christianity underwent a transformation from the Negro Church to the Black Church. Racial discrimination and segregation proscribed the social context of pre-1967 African American Christianity. According to E. Franklin Frazier, African American Christianity under segregation represented an arena in which African Americans accommodated their subordinated status as Negroes.[5] The Negro Church and a few other institutions served as vehicles through which blacks could achieve social status and provided a key route to respectability. Central to achieving status and respectability was a particular of kind of cultural production that created Negro identity. Negro cultural production lodged itself within the context of elite Western culture, a context that devalued African American folk culture and celebrated European and Euro-American elite cultural expressions. The Negro Church became a site where the dominant ideology of African American inferiority was countered through the creative mastery of elite Western culture and competition with white Americans on their cultural terrain.[6]

As desegregation created new historical and social contexts during the 1960s, African American leaders arose who rejected the privileging of elite Western culture and the ideology of African American inferiority. These leaders supplanted elite Western culture with African and African-derived culture as the context in which African American religion would flourish, producing a shift in African American religion. The shift was characterized ontologically as the "birth of a new 'black being,'" psychologically as the overthrow of "the rule of white men in our [African American] minds," and ecclesially, as the birth of the Black Church.[7]

On the African continent, the African Church also underwent transformation from the mission churches of Europeans to independent churches, African churches. Colonialism and racial subordination proscribed the social context of African Christianity prior to the era of independence. The mission churches in Africa provided an arena in which Africans accommodated their subordinated status as colonized peoples.[8] The colonial mission church served as one of the avenues through which colonized Africans achieved social status and as a key route by which they could gain respectability by graduating from mission schools and/or becoming a church member. Assimilation was deemed central to achieving status and respectability, and certain forms of cultural production were employed to create the colonial African. Colonial African cultural production privileged elite Western culture by devaluing traditional African religion and culture and valorizing elite European culture. The colonial African mission church became a site where Africans mastered elite European culture and competed with Europeans on their own cultural terrain, undercutting the dominant ideology of African inferiority. As decolonization ushered in new historical and social contexts during the post–World War II era, Africans debated the privileging of elite Western culture. Some leaders opted to introduce African culture and cosmology as the context in which African Christianity should be rooted. Thus, the post-1965 era resulted in not only new African immigration to the United States but also promotion by both African Christianity and African American Christianity of a new consciousness and a religious production focused on Africa.

The Impact of African Immigrant Churches on Black Church Studies

How might the inclusion of African immigrant denominations within Black Church studies impact the study of both topics? Black Church history as a discipline takes Africa seriously. However, for the most part, the Africa it prefers is precolonial and colonial Africa. Precolonial Africa is the arena in which scholars explore or reconstruct the roots of African American Christianity, whether in the work of John Thornton and others on Christianity in the sixteenth-century Kongo or in the earlier work of Melville Herskovits and, later, Albert Raboteau on West African religion practices and sensibility. Colonial Africa has been a topic within the rubric of African American missions to Africa in the scholarship of Sandy Martin, for instance. Symbolic or fictive Africa was a focus for U.S. Ethiopianism. Liberia was the focus of the back-to-Africa campaigns and the topic of emigration. There are the comparative studies, such as James Campbell's work comparing the United States and South Africa during the late nineteenth and early twentieth centuries. Yet, as a discipline, contemporary African church life is outside the purview of Black Church history.[9]

If historians of the Black Church initiate a serious study of contemporary African immigrant churches and denominations in the United States, are there classifications currently employed in Black Church studies that could be relevant to such a study? Within the study of the Black Church and black religion, Ernst Troeltsch's distinctions among church, sect, and cult were initially employed by Elmer Clark, Benjamin Mays, and others. Later, during the 1930s, scholars such Raymond Jones offered two typologies. The first typology comprised three groupings: (1) strong, charismatic leaders, (2) "spirit possession" cults, and (3) "utopian, communal, or fraternal" cults. The second typology elaborated on the cult type, proposing seven distinctions: (a) faith-healing cults, (b) Holiness cults, (c) Islamic cults, (d) pentecostal cults, (e) spiritualist cults, (f) cult personalities, and (g) "others."[10] Critics of Jones's elaboration noted that he failed to distinguish between "cults" and other black religious groups such as pentecostals. The term "cult" applies to all non-historic Christian groups (Baptist, Methodist, mainline). Jones separates faith-healing groups from Holiness, spiritualist, and other groups that practice healing without any serious rationale.

Vattel Elbert Daniel, in his 1942 study of ritual and social stratification, focused on expressivity in worship. He established four categories by which to classify congregations: (1) ecstatic sects and cults, (2) semidemonstrative groups, (3) deliberative groups, and (4) liturgical denominations.[11] Among the ecstatic sects and cults, he cited pentecostal churches. Some popular Baptist groups were semidemonstrative; Methodist groups were often deliberative; and the liturgical denominations were the Episcopalians. Daniel was limited by a unitary focus on expressivity in worship that blunted theological differences; thus, a black religious science congregation would be grouped with a black Episcopal congregation, even though their theologies differed.

During the 1970s and 1980s, Hans Baer and Merrill Singer focused on religion, stratification, and racism. They selected two axes: behavior, or the "strategies of social action," and ideation, or "attitudinal orientation." On the first axis, they suggested that the behavior or strategies include instrumental and expressive (cathartic) responses. The second axis, the attitudinal or ideational orientation, includes both positive and negative responses; the positive responses embrace the "values, norms, and beliefs of the dominant group," while the negative responses counter the dominant group.

While Jones elaborated the cult type, Baer and Singer expanded the sect type into five groups: (1) established sects, (2) messianic-nationalist sects, (3) conversionist sects, (4) thaumaturgical/manipulationist sects, and (5) mixed types.[12] Baer and Singer note that the diversity of black religion emerges out of "the issue of alternative strategies" to cope with "the racism and stratification inherent in our sociocultural system." Central to Baer and Singer's framework is the definition of sects as protest movements. In this typology, "established sects" are instrumental in their social strategies and positive toward society, tending to embrace the dominant cultural patterns. They are categorized as reformist in their strategy of social activism. Their instrumental activities include engaging in protest activities, using fundraising to fight discrimination, and sponsoring college scholarships. One classic established sect within the Black Church is the African Methodist Episcopal Church. The "messianic-nationalist sects" are instrumental in their social strategies and negative toward society, rejecting especially key elements of the dominant cultural patterns. Their instrumental strategy develops a counterculture via religious belief, cultural independence, and political/territorial self-determination. Historically, they have posited a new racial identity based on the rejection of the Negro identity as a false construct of whites. Features of their ideology include (a) the myth of the "glorious Black history and subsequent fall," (b) the "adoption of various rituals and symbols from established millenarian religious traditions" (c) the "messianic anticipation of divine retribution against the White oppressor," (d) the "assertion of Black sovereignty through the development of various nationalist symbols and interest in territorial separation or emigration" and (5) the "rejection of certain social patterns in the black community, including family instability, female-headed households, and male marginality." Messianic-nationalist sects include Islamic groups such as the Moorish Science Temple and the Nation of Islam, Hebraic groups such the Church of God and Saints of Christ, and Christian groups such as the African Orthodox Church and the Shrine of the Black Madonna. The "conversionist sects" are defined as expressive in their social strategies and negative toward society, challenging dominant social and cultural patterns through their enforcement of holiness codes. Expressive strategies of social action engage demonstrative and worship behaviors as the "way to effect social transformation." The Church of God in Christ and the Pentecostal Assemblies of the World serve as exemplary conversionist sects. "Thaumaturgical/manipulationist sects" are expressive in their social strategies and positive in their stance toward society. Baer and Singer contend that the expressive strategy of thaumaturgical/manipulationist sects employs magicoreligious rituals or esoteric knowledge such as "burning votive candles," "the use of various occult items, and receiving a 'message' or 'reading.'" Their positive stance toward dominant cultural patterns is reflected in their focus on "financial prosperity, prestige, love, and health." The most famous congregation within the thaumaturgical/manipulationist sects is Chicago's First Church of Deliverance, a member of the Metropolitan Spiritual Churches of Christ Association. The "mixed types" combine both instrumental and expressive strategies and positive and negative stances toward society. The Father Divine Peace Mission exemplifies this category. This group recognizes that the racial reality/condition is only one of many dimensions of African American life. Baer and Singer also note that this typology must incorporate space for change and development, mixing/switching strategies as communities undergo transition.[13]

Gayraud Wilmore proposes a three-part framework: survivalist, elevationist, and liberationist. The survivalist tradition focuses on the everyday living challenges faced by black people. The elevationist tradition engages the self-help activities of black people that uplift or elevate the race. The liberationist tradition involves social activist activities that seek to restructure the society by confronting and eradicating racial injustice.[14]

Are there ways that the typologies of Jones, Daniel, Baer and Singer, or Wilmore might illuminate the contemporary history of African immigrant churches and denominations? Within the Baer/Singer typology, the Redeemed Christian Church of God could be classified as an established sect; the Harrist Church could be classified as a messianic-nationalist sect; the Deeper Life could be viewed as a conversionist sect; and the Celestial Church of Christ could be a thaumaturgical/manipulationist sect. Would these classifications, then, aid in comparing African American and U.S. continental African denominations that are identified as being of the same type? What could be learned from comparing the Celestial Church of Christ to the Metropolitan Spiritual Churches of Christ Association?

Within Black Church studies, scholars have moved from Raymond Jones's complexifying the term "cult" to Baer/Singer's massaging the term "sect." Maybe, to complete Troelstch's trilogy, scholars need to expand his term "church." Of course, the Protestant-Catholic-Orthodox framework is also too narrow to capture the variety of the Black Church and the included African immigrant churches. The categories could be organized according to polity, liturgy, theology, identity, mission, social location, or political orientation. For instance, theologically, Wardell Payne's categories are Baptist, Methodist, Pentecostal/Apostolic, Holiness, Deliverance, Catholic, Disciples of Christ, Nondenominational, Orthodox and Pan African Orthodox, Presbyterian, Spiritualist, Black Hebrews, Islam, and Vodoun.[15]

Borrowing from African Religious History to Widen Black Church Studies

To begin to comprehend the presence of African immigrant congregations and denominations in the United States, scholars need a solid grasp of the historiography of contemporary African religious and church life. With this, they can begin to explore the historical context in which the immigrant congregations were formed in Africa prior to the immigrants' arrival in the United States. Who are these congregants? What defines them? How do they define themselves as different from other groups? With which groups do they identify? What are their historical origins, developments, and transformations? How do they relate to the contemporary religious scene in their home country, as well as in the African region in which they operate? What is the significance of having been classified as Aladura, Zionist, Ethiopian, or Roho[16] in Africa for an African immigration congregation in the United States? How do the experiences of African denominations with congregations in Europe and on other continents shape their U.S. experience? How do we explore these linkages?

The typologies employed within the historiography of African Christianity are not synonymous with the typologies used in Black Church studies. In general, the terminology includes mission-founded churches on one hand and independent, separatist, syncretistic, protest, nativist, tribal, neopagan, spiritist, sectarian, nationalist, Hebraic, cultic, messianic, and post-Christian on the other. Until recently, a major distinction in the historiography of African Christianity has been between denominations derived from Western missions and those that are African instituted. The African Instituted Churches (AICs) include four streams: Ethiopian, Zionist, Aladura, and Roho. The Ethiopian stream consists of congregations and denominations that espouse African religious self-determination and reject domination by European missionaries or mission societies. The Zionist and Aladura streams are charismatic movements that emerge in southern and western Africa, respectively. The Roho stream emerges as a charismatic revival within eastern Africa. An additional typology includes a Kimbanguist stream. Utilizing such typologies within Black Church studies places the African Methodist Episcopal Church, for instance, in the Ethiopian stream; however, the contextual histories of the Zionist and Aladura streams might preclude identifying any African American religious bodies within either of these streams.[17]

These distinctions are currently contested in the scholarly literature. With the advent of African decolonization and independence, the distinction between mission-founded and independent churches has been blurred and sometimes found to be insignificant. For example, "pentecostal" as a term has referred to African denominations that are derived from mission activity sponsored by pentecostal denominations in Europe and North America as well as by AICs. Some scholars classify all AICs as pentecostals, and others make judgments case by case. Consequently, various Zionist and Aladura congregations may be classified as pentecostal. Within Black Church historiography, the term "pentecostal" refers to a set of beliefs and practices and often an historical connection with the Azusa Street Revival and the early-twentieth-century pentecostal movement. The distinction between being mission-derived or non-mission-derived is totally absent, and Black Church studies pursue a case-by-case approach. For instance, although United House of Prayer for All, founded by Bishop Emmanuel ("Daddy") Grace, resembles pentecostal churches, it is not classified as pentecostal because of the messianic or divine attributes assigned to Daddy Grace. Likewise, according to this classification, the Celestial Church of Christ might be excluded from a grouping of pentecostal churches.

Since AICs in African religious historiography are differentiated, can parallel distinctions be made within Black Church historiography. Again, the answer to this question is complex. M. L. (Inus) Daneel has proposed that groups linked with messianic leaders such Simon Kimbangu be redefined as iconic groups. Would "iconic" rather than "messianic" or "divine" be a better lens through which to interpret Father Divine's Peace Mission or Daddy Grace's United House of Prayer for All People? If "iconic" as a concept illuminates these movements, it could inaugurate revisionist studies of Father Divine or Daddy Grace.[18]

Some scholars of African religious history have employed the term "spiritual churches" to refer to a certain set of AICs. While this term has valence in U.S. scholarship, are all scholars using the term in the same manner? How does the Aladura particularity of Cherubim and Seraphim as a spiritual church compare with the particularity of King Solomon's Temple? The typologies employed by Black Church studies/Black religious studies and African religious studies must be interrogated critically in order to develop the best typologies to study black Christianity and religion in the United States since the advent of post-1965 African immigrant churches.[19]

The sociological definition of black religion might require recrafting. Hans Baer and Merrill Singer contended that "the content, structure, and diversity of Black religion derives primarily from three sources: (1) influences from African cultures, (2) influences from religious patterns in Euro-American culture, (3) religious responses on the part of Blacks to cope with their minority status in a stratified and racist society." A post-1965 revised definition that recognizes the presence of African immigrant churches and religion might note that the first influences are from the Atlantic African culture of Africa and the Americas. The second source are the Atlantic influences from the religious patterns of Europe and white North America. And the third source would explore the religious responses on the part of African Americans, U.S. Afro-Caribbean peoples, and U.S. continental Africans to "cope with their minority status in a stratified and racist" U.S. society and global order.[20]

Conclusion

The advent of post-1965 African immigrant churches, specifically denominations, within the United States has inaugurated a new moment in the history and study of the Black Church in North America. By placing African immigrant congregations on the map of U.S. black religion, Black Church studies and religious studies will create new conceptual space so that this phenomenon can be studied with intellectual integrity. Not only is Black Church studies impacted conceptually, but its discourse has been widened by its engagement with African religious studies and history.

Notes

1. Eileen W. Lindner, ed., *Yearbook of American and Canadian Churches* (Nashville: Abingdon Press, 2004); Wardell Payne, ed., *Directory of African American Religious Bodies* (Washington, D.C.: Howard University School of Divinity and Howard University Press, 1991), vii; Charles Edwin Jones, *Black Holiness: A Guide to the Study of Black Participation in Wesleyan Perfectionist and Glossolalic Pentecostal Movements* (Metuchen, N.J.: The American Theological Library and Association and The Scarecrow Press, 1987), 188–204.

2. David Daniels, "Survey of African Immigrant Congregations in Metropolitan Chicago," 2000 (unpublished).

3. Cornel West and Eddie S. Glaude, Jr., "Introduction: Towards New Visions and New Approaches in African American Religious Studies," in Cornel West and Eddie S. Glaude, Jr., eds., *African American Religious Thought: An Anthology* (Louisville, Ken.: Westminster John Knox Press, 2003), xiii; James Melvin Washington, "Jesse Jackson and the Symbolic Politics of Black Christendom," in West and Glaude, *African American Religious Thought,* 922.

4. Reverend Herman L. Greene, *UPCAG—The First 40 Years, Vol. 1: 1919 to 1945* (Sussex, N.J.: Geda Publications, 2005).

5. E. Franklin Frazier, *The Negro Church in America* (New York: Schocken, 1974), 89; Benjamin E. Mays and Joseph W. Nicholson, *The Negro's Church* (New York: Arno Press, 1969).

6. Charles Banner-Haley, *The Fruits of Integration: Black Middle-Class Ideology and Culture, 1960–1990* (Jackson: University Press of Mississippi, 1994), 3–26.

7. Ibid., p. 37.

8. Ogbu U. Kalu, "African Christianity: From the World Wars to Decolonization," in Ogbu U. Kalu, ed., *African Christianity: An African Story,* (Pretoria: Department of Church History, University of Pretoria, 2005), 333–360.

9. John K. Thornton, *Africa and Africans in the Making of the Atlantic World, 1400–1680* (Cambridge: Cambridge University Press, 1992); Sandy Martin, *Black Baptists and African Missions* (Macon, Ga.: Mercer University Press, 1989); Albert Raboteau, "'Ethiopia Shall Soon Stretch Forth Her Hands': Black Destiny in Nineteenth-Century America," chapter 2 in *A Fire in the Bones: Reflections on African-American Religious History* (Boston: Beacon Press, 1995), 37–56.

10. Raymond Jones, "A Comparative Study of Religious Cult Behavior Among Negroes with Special Reference to Emotional Conditioning Factors," *Howard University Studies in the Social Sciences* 2, no. 2 (1939).

11. Vattel Elbert Daniel, "Ritual and Stratification in Chicago Negro Churches," *American Sociological Review* 7 (1942): 352–361.

12. Hans A. Baer and Merrill Singer, "Toward A Typology of Black Sectarianism as a Response to Racial Stratification," in T. Fulop and A. Raboteau, eds., *African-American Religion: Interpretative Essays in History and Culture* (New York: Routledge, 1997), 257–276.

13. Ibid., 272.

14. Gayraud Wilmore, *Black Religion and Black Radicalism: An Interpretation of the Religious History of Afro-American People* (Maryknoll, N.Y.: Orbis Books, 1998).

15. Payne, ed., *Directory of African American Religious Bodies,* vii.

16. Afe Adogame and Lizo Jafta, "Zionists, Aladura and Roho: African Instituted Churches," in Kalu, ed., *African Christianity: An African Story,* 312; Bengt G. M. Sundkler, *Bantu Prophets in South Africa* (Oxford: Oxford University Press, 1961).

17. Adogame and Jafta, "Zionists, Aladura and Roho," 309–329.

18. M. L. Daneel, *Quest for Belonging: Introduction to a Study of African Independent Churches* (Gweru: Zimbabwe, Mambo Press, 1987).

19. Virginia Torvestad, "The Organization of Spiritual Churches," in *The Rise of Independent Churches in Ghana* (Accra: Asempa Publishers, 1990), 34–38; C. G. Baeta, *Prophetism in Ghana* (London: SCM, 1962).

20. Hans A. Baer and Merrill Singer, "Religious Diversification During the Era of Advanced Industrial Capitalism," in West and Glaude, *African American Religious Thought,* 522.

3

The Andrew Syndrome

Models in Understanding Nigerian Diaspora

Ogbu U. Kalu

Who Is Andrew?

There was a time when the Nigerian government resorted to television advertisements to stem the flow of emigration from the country. One of these pictured a burly man called Andrew, who was seen at the international airport with a disgusted, sweaty face, "checking out" of the country in frustration. An avuncular voice could be heard reminding him that "Nigeria is our country, we have no other place." The cajoling worked neither then nor now. The summons to participate in nation building has ceased to be convincing, and the patriotic rhetoric about a jointly owned mother/fatherland has lost its purchase. Much to the contrary, the political elite declares, in Igbo language, "*ana enwe obodo enwe*" (some people own the nation). This is an assertion of power that, like the proverbial he-goat, butts and excludes the weak amid the struggle for dwindling national resources. Once in a while, Nigerian leaders attempt to change hostile public attention by addressing the problem of brain drain with strategies that urge Nigerians abroad to return. Recently, President Olusegun Obasanjo was alleged to have empaneled a committee to travel abroad to recruit Nigerian professionals. Someone quipped that the real plan is to travel overseas and bank the proceeds from the excess oil funds. According to Transparency International, he presides over the third most corrupt nation in the world through the assistance of multinational corporations. The efforts to respond to the Andrew syndrome by containing the level of emigration, hyping patriotic jingoism, or persuading those living abroad to return have met with a cynicism that reflects the distrust bred by the sufferings of professionals at the hands of insensitive Nigerian administrators and worsening conditions of life in spite of the optimism of analysts. If professionals who work abroad constitute the brain drain, it is argued that those who remain at home suffer from brain hemorrhage because of a disabling environment that stultifies.

There is, however, little doubt that many national institutions lack adequate manpower and that the nation spends huge amounts to engage foreign professional experts. Perhaps, universities and the medical field have suffered most from the exodus of educated manpower. It is alleged that more than eight thousand Nigerian doctors work outside the country. Nigerian universities, for instance, are depleted of academics because the situation got so bad that people escaped to all manner of places. Worse, few graduates from foreign universities are coming to replenish the academic culture. The current leaders in the departments are homebred. The problem is continentwide. According to the Association of African Universities, "at the University of Nairobi, only 40 percent of the teaching force holds doctorate degrees: 33 percent at Kenyatta, 32 percent at Moi, and 19 percent at Egerton."[1] In Nigeria, the president explained that the fault lay in poor partnering between universities and the private sector and in overdependence on government funding.[2] On the whole, massive emigration has become a characteristic of the contemporary economic and social environment in Africa. This reflection focuses on its manifestation in Nigeria, with an eye to the continent: its scope, causes, and nature, its impact at the home base, and its character in the Diaspora. We argue that there are four phases of the problem: (1) the home-base conditions that compel emigration, (2) the journey, (3) the diasporic condition, and (4) the prospects of re-entry. Various discourses in the analysis of the political economy explain the first dimension. Quite often, analysts skip the second phase, ignore the complexities of the third, and discuss re-entry with discourses such as brain drain, brain replacement, and brain gain. The perspective here is that all the phases are like the strands of an akwete cloth. A composite, viable tapestry must weave together all strands. The chapter argues that the second phase is a cultural condition by itself, implicating a large swath of the able-bodied population of the continent, and carries much ideological import. It canvasses two models in understanding Nigerian Diaspora: the "exile" and the "crossing Jordan" discourses that are competing models for understanding the diasporic condition. These models weave together the various strands of the Andrew syndrome to explain the impact of emigration on both the Nigerian homeland and the destinations of migration. The two concepts possess a long history in black responses to diasporic experience that stretch back to the debates within the Black Colonization Society and the Back to Africa Movement. Crucial to the re-entry phase is how to curb the dysfunctional potential of migration and reinvent it as a tool to assist the development of the homeland. The morally constructed concept of stewardship shifts the discussion from the sphere of political economy.

The Andrew Syndrome: Anatomy of a Problem

Causes

Nigerians can be found in the most remote regions of Africa, Europe, Asia, Oceania, and America. The Andrew syndrome cannot be restrained from depleting the manpower resources of the nation. Some may argue that the inability of the nation to rise above the disheartening level of poverty is a function of policy failures in mobilizing the human resources. Afro-optimism as a political discourse may point to achievements in the political economy since the late 1990s, but the fact remains that human development indices show that the living conditions have continued to deteriorate and that the scourge of poverty has diminished the potentials for renegotiating the moral culture. For instance, in the universities, one can hardly expect former colleagues who have not been paid salaries to focus on research or to avoid exploiting students. The political elite has become more predatory, corrupt, undisciplined, and violent. Democracy has failed to take hold because there cannot be a viable opposition party when the members can easily be "settled." In the Nigerian parliament, honorable members slap each other freely as they quarrel over money. Basic infrastructure does not exist because corruption ensures that contractors do not perform adequately. The politics of the belly does not inspire patriotism among the ruled. The first phase of the Andrew syndrome has been fully analyzed in the newspapers: a disabling environment in soft states scourged by heavy external debt, under the pressures of asymmetrical power relations in globalization, failed leadership, patrimonial political culture, civil wars, and drought.

Scope and Characteristics

The statistical scope of the syndrome is hard to confirm. The situation is akin to the humorous anecdote about the late colorful Nigerian politician Ozumba Mbadiwe. In 1972, he approached a New York bank to fund a large hotel complex in Lagos. The bank requested a feasibility report. Mbadiwe asked if he could use the phone and called the Ikoyi Hotel, Lagos; it replied that it was full; he called the Federal Palace Hotel, and it was full. He turned to the bankers with glee and muttered, "You see?" The Nigerian university system could be used as a specific example; the U.S. Bureau of the Census report for 1997 shows that of all immigrants to the United States, African immigrants had the highest level of education; in the age range "25 years and above," 48.9 percent of African migrants had a bachelor's degree or higher, whereas 44.6 percent of Asians, 28.7 percent of Europeans, and 5.6 of Latinos had similar educational achievement.[3] It is reported that more than 10,000 faculty members deserted the Nigerian universities in the last decade of the millennium. A generational analysis points to the fact that the first generation of African scholars trained overseas under the ideology of questing for "the golden fleece," returned, and trained others. The second generation that studied for undergraduate degrees at home and traveled out for postgraduate specializations was more likely to stay abroad; if graduates did return, they did not stay long. This shift was driven by limited upward mobility, economic crisis that affected remuneration, and widespread political repression that constrained academic freedom. A third generation has suffered from the stringent limitations imposed by changing immigration policies among Western nations and from lack of scholarships; its members are more likely to be trained in the national universities under extremely difficult conditions, without the guidance of senior scholars and without adequate books and laboratories.[4] Thus, while it may be useful to revisit the stirring examples from the era of Aggrey, Azikiwe, and Nkrumah, it must be recognized that the Andrew syndrome suffers from generational ideological shifts and contexts. Incentives, governance, political culture, and policies on capacity development, quest for meaning, and self-development have triggered the syndrome, or the desire to emigrate.

Some analyses place the syndrome in a wider perspective, arguing that migration is an endemic dimension to human life: interpersonal conflicts and other internal problems have catalyzed migration in the past; external factors such as war, incursion of other groups, culture contacts, and such have forced some people to migrate. Buoyant economies tend to create osmotic pulls on developing economies. Rural-urban pulls always catalyze minor migrations. Paul Zeleza argues that the causes, courses, and consequences of contemporary international migration are tied to complex social networks that have arisen as a result of the long processes of globalization. International migrations have intensified as asylum seekers, refugees, and occupational migrants have moved to the West. *LeMonde Diplomatique* for January 2000 used data from the United Nations High Commissioner for Refugees to describe the rising tide of refugees, especially from Africa, the Balkans, and the Middle East.[5] Skilled migrants have assumed a greater importance. The intensified South-North pattern has generated the racialization of migration, increased the number of illegal immigrants, and even raised the possibility of dual citizenship. Any analysis must balance all these internal and external impulses that lead to emigration.

In this period of human history, it has become an Africa-wide problem. Drought, military coups, and civil wars have created massive population shifts within the continent. We are experiencing *push,* or compelled desertion of homelands, rather than mild *pulls.* It is as if the continent is spewing out its people. Every year, thousands of Africans desert the soft states of Africa, the failed economies, the corrupt political environments. But, sometimes, the reasons are more psychological than economic. From May 18, 2004, to July 18, 2004, the British Broadcasting Corporation ran a five-part series titled *Guinea: Unstoppable Exodus.* The writer Joseph Winters traced an African migrant, Mamadou Saliou Diallo, whom he encountered in Europe, to his village in the lush, picturesque rolling hills of the Fouta Djalon region of northern Guinea. He concluded that "the soil is so fertile, no one is starving but the younger generation is no longer content with mere survival and a way of life which has hardly changed for generations."[6] The ideological slant that portrays the cause of migration as a treasure hunt is incomplete, since this better explains earlier European migratory patterns. The contemporary situation in Africa is complex. Winters pointed to the psychological roots; children were taught that Santa Claus lives in France, and young Africans have internalized images of Europe, its way of life and its material goods. The elite's flaunting of its material wealth encrusts the image and fosters this form of mental slavery.

As Zeleza argued, Africans do not constitute the largest migrant population globally, but they constitute an increasing proportion of migrants, from 10.6 percent in 1965 to 13.1 percent in 1990, and an even greater proportion in the last decade of the millennium. Initially, African migration followed the paths of colonial heritage and linguistic trails; thus, the French assimilation policy attracted migrants from their colonies. In 1990, France had the largest concentration of African migrants: 33 percent of its foreign population. But the pattern became diffused as America became an attractive destination in the 1970s, and Germany, Canada, and northern European countries became friendlier destinations in the 1980s. The vagaries of the developed world's immigration policies have further scrambled the characteristics. Professional Africans are now driving taxis, picking grapes, looking after old people, working in brick-making factories, or packaging chewing gum all over Europe. The professionals who migrate do not necessarily find employment in their fields of specialization. Some can retrain into new professions; others barely survive. We shall return to the Diaspora condition later. Suffice it to argue that the size and the trend of migration are exacerbated by the decimation of both the civil society and the middle class by predatory, authoritarian regimes, whether *prebendary* (the ruler treats the nation as his farm) or *praetorian* (rulers mistake the nation for a military barrack). All employ clientele strategies and manipulate ethnicity and religion in sharing the national resources in the politics of exclusion.

Eating the Crocodile: The Journey Out of Africa

His name is Themba
He lives in Soweto
Every morning he goes to the airport
To watch the planes come and go
He has changed his African name
To a Western one
'Cause he doesn't know how it hurts
To have a name you can't be proud of
He hopes that one day, one day
One of these birds of the sky
Can take him
To a very very far land.

This is a touching ballad on a scorching phenomenon by the South African reggae artist Lucky Dube. As someone ruefully observed, "everybody in my village wants to go to America." Every day, thousands of able-bodied Africans like Themba leave their roots in search of very faraway lands. For many, it is like an odyssey of years of tortured existence spent in transit.

On October 20, 2003, the BBC News reported that seventy Africans (men, women, and children) had died of thirst and hunger after the boat in which they were trying illegally to reach the southern Italian town of Lampedusa from Tripoli broke down and drifted for ten days before it was spotted. Only five were alive when the rescuers reached the corpse-strewn boat. A week earlier, seven Somalis had lost their lives when their boat capsized, and forty-five Egyptians were rescued near Malta. The Nigerian newspaper *The Guardian* reported, on August 10, 2004, that the worsening situation had attracted the attention of the European Union and had become a matter for discussion between the Italian prime minister, Silvio Berlusconi, and the Libyan leader, Colonel Muammar Gaddafi. Italy had participated in the West Libyan Gas Project pipeline, which cost $5.6 billion. Even while exploiting Algerian resources, Berlusconi complained bitterly that Tripoli had become the launching pad for an African migrant invasion of Italy; more than 1,500 people had made the journey to Lampedusa in the past week—with 600 arriving in one night; Italy handcuffed 400 and sent them back to Libya and Tunisia. The Libyan minister for national security, Nasser Mabruk, reassured Berlusconi that Libya had expelled 40,000 immigrants. Much water flows under this bridge.

Discussions about brain drain focus on the professionals and ignore a more disastrous aspect of African migration in which hundreds of thousands use the ancient trans-Sahara slave trade routes to enslave themselves in Europe. In the earlier period, Arabs and Europeans sought the slaves; now Africans torture themselves and offer their bodies to an unwilling Europe that needs cheap labor to maintain certain social services but builds a fortress to avoid the horde at the gates and select only the most desirable. When the migrant beats all odds to arrive at the European destination, he declares victoriously that he has "eaten the crocodile" instead of being eaten! It comes from the Lingala "*alia ngando.*" A culture has been spawned in Africa around this migration pattern that has its own patois, network, and social structures. Much of the migration from contemporary Africa has little to do with skilled manpower or professionals. The fall in school enrollment among Nigerian men reflects the large number of young men from the rural areas of many African countries who are living in the migration routes. It can take years to reach the target destination.

Elie Goldschmidt tells the story of a Congolese who left Kinshasha on August 16, 1996, and crossed the Moroccan-Spanish border in September 2003.[7]

The journey is multirouted: some use old-fashioned air travel to any European country as a stepping stone to other parts of the world. This may require using the services of the so-called visa mafia, which secures genuine visas. Some emigrants fly from Lagos to Spain and proceed to Turkey. This costs about $4,000. Migrants from eastern, central, and southern Africa rely on this strategy. Those migrating within the region, such as within west Africa, may use roads. In the ECOWAS region, visas are not required. Social networks are important, and those who have already settled assist others to come over. Bribery at the borders may turn the journey through the scenic coast of the Atlantic into a harrowing experience.

Sociologists need to study the patterns of visa politics: the locations and procedures of foreign embassies, the fees imposed, screening criteria, and the number of immigrants accepted in the various visa categories. Foreign embassies in Nigeria compete in inventing devices for disgracing the indigenes. The American Embassy turns down the applications of more than 97 percent of applicants after each has paid a fee of $100 (see Appendix). Moreover, the way a person leaves home can be quite important. A few professionals have direct appointments; some win the lottery; others are exchange students and fellowship holders who refuse to return. Some may desert to other countries. For instance, some students who go to Germany for the language course leave before graduation and head to America or other countries. Naturally, sponsors have refused to aid the universities any longer. Fulbright officials are in constant battle with fellows who refuse to return. Thus, any analysis should note that there are different types of migrants: professional, unskilled, and missionary or religious. The typology may determine the route.

The exigencies of leaving home have created a large market for fake passports and visas. As airport security tightens, the most attractive route is the deadliest, especially for the nonprofessional class. It requires migrating through Africa for a long period. This odyssey has four stages: (1) reaching a staging post for the trans-Saharan crossing; (2) crossing the Sahara desert; (3) traveling from Algeria to the Mediterranean shore; (4) crossing either the border to Ceuta or the sea to southern Italy. Each stage is fraught with degrading possibilities. Thousands die. The duration of the journey to North Africa may be determined by financial capability, health, success in eluding the border authorities, and guts. The financial commitment required to cross from Africa to Europe can be enormous. Families sell off their household goods and mortgage family land. Others raise the capital by joining robbery gangs, defrauding banks and employers, or taking loans. One migration route is Douala-Lagos-Lome-Niamey-Agadez-Tripoli-Algiers. From here, the arduous five-day trek through the mountains, the Maghnia Oujda pass, to Fez is the best route. From Fez, the migrant proceeds to Rabat for the final crossing. Another route is Bamako-Tamanrasset-Alger-Bangui-N'Djamena-Kouffra-Benghazi. Several subroutes exist.

Let us join the migrants from the Malian town of Gao, a popular staging depot because the Touareg nomads are expert camel caravan operators across the desert. The trans-Saharan trip to Morocco costs only $430 by van and less by camel. It is nicknamed The Rally after the motor sport across harsh terrains; the vans are nicknamed Marlboro (after the cigarette advertisement in which the Marlboro man rides a camel) and are also used to smuggle cigarettes. Ghanaian and Nigerian smugglers based in Gao run the business and hand over their passengers to the Touaregs or to Arab and Sonrai guides. Indigenes call all the operators "Ghanaians" (perhaps they initiated the smuggling). The Congolese migrants refer to the Nigerians and Ghanaians as "Mongo" (after a Congolese ethnic group, Ba Mongo, who are known for speaking loud all the time). The Arabs are nicknamed "Ndibu" (after a Congolese tribe that first came into contact with the Portuguese). The operators are unionized and tightly organized and sometimes travel by a convoy of utility vans. Many migrants die and are buried in the sand, especially when the vans break down. Fraud is deliberately practiced, and some guides abandon the passengers in small villages as Kidal and Menaka and disappear after collecting their fees.

Migrants are dispersed along the route, and colonies of migrants along the way aid with mobility and expedite transit. The colonies of migrants comprise people who ran out of money and have to work, those who have been abandoned, and those became too ill or were caught and repatriated. They provide hospitality and information. But there is a social network of people from certain regions who assist others who speak the same language. There are also networks maintained by gangs that operate along ethnic lines. For instance, the Igbo groups keep strictly away from the Yoruba. Business competition, secrecy, and security of turf hold sway. Each group cooperates with indigenes to provide transportation across the desert to the coast or across the sea to Europe.

The feminine dimension to migration is a sordid story of its own. There was a time when Nigerian smugglers used migrant women's bodies in the transportation of illicit drugs. Today, women constitute a significant portion of immigrants on this route. These women are called commodities, just as they served as troop comforters during the civil war. Many survive by linking themselves to a group of men who protect and provide for them or to a pimp who uses them to fund his own trip. Others pay their way through prostitution. But there is another sex trade route that goes directly by air to Italy. A number of women go on that adventure willingly; pimps recruit others for prostitution in Europe. Stories abound about the networks that recruit from Edo State, especially Benin City, for the Italian market. The early ones came home with lots of money. Nicknamed "*Italos*," they flaunted their wealth in a manner that made them the envy of village girls. A popular singer, Ohahen, wrote a hit song celebrating the exploits of a wealthy *Italos* named Dupay, who was a philanthropist, sank boreholes for her community, and "sponsored" many girls who went to Italy. Since those halcyon days, the Italian authorities have deported many women, each of whom had invested more than $45,000 to outfit herself. In 2003, the Nigerian Embassy in Rome was nearly burned by aggrieved pimps. A number of NGOs have intervened to assist the women: Girls Power Initiative, the International Organization for Migration, the National Agency for Prohibition of Trafficking in Persons, and the Committee for the Support of Dignity of Women all help the repatriated women.

The third segment of the journey is within North Africa to the coast. Harassment from Algerian and Moroccan officials forces the migrants to hide in camps, where they live according to their nationalities and language groups in incredible squalor. Without baths and personal hygiene, they look like a group of mad people. Clandestine existence can prolong the transit even longer. Indeed, these transit camps have spawned an entire culture of their own where one learns to survive the worst forms of hardship. Each ghetto has its own bylaws. Penury is major problem, because by the time they arrive in North Africa, many lack even a penny. From Tindouf in Algeria, guides assist the migrants to trek twenty kilometers through the mountains into a village in Morocco. A bus ride gets the survivors into Casablanca. Transport from Casablanca to Tangiers on the coast costs $6,000. Northern Morocco has for a long time served as the center for smuggling cannabis to Europe. A number of gangs operate here and have simply diversified their business to include smuggling people. They compete with Nigerian gangs that operate in this sector.

There are three ways of making the final lurch into the land of promise: fake papers, wire cutting, and boat ride. The untoward events of September 11, 2001, meant the end for fake-paper agents. The cheapest mode is by cutting wire. A taxi ride from Rabat to Tetouant costs about $500. One then hides in the bush for as long as it takes to risk cutting the fence wire into Europe. But the chances of being caught and deported are very high. Many fail on the first attempt and return to the bush for further attempts. This explains why Water Airways (a boat ride) is popular in spite of the obvious dangers of boat wrecks and arrest by officials. For those heading for southern Italy, the boat trip remains the fastest route even if one dreads that Mami Wata might be lurking in the water and might capsize the boat.

Tangiers is one crossing point. People smugglers charge 1,000 euros for the short journey by inflatable boats or Water Airways into the Spanish enclaves of Ceuta and Mellila. In Ceuta, the triumphant migrants who have eaten the crocodile spend months waiting for their applications for asylum to be processed. The chances of working and recovering the years of investment remain elusive. A new sea route uses dinghy boats to reach the Canary Islands. It is estimated that in 2004, more than 7,000 migrants arrived in Fuerteventura, a journey of 100 kilometers, at a cost of 700 euros.[8] The perspective here is that the mode of the journey determines the pattern of the diasporic condition. The slum conditions that face Africans in Residence Prealpino, in southern Italy, are worse than those in the slums the migrants left at home. The poor quality of life and the lack of access to sustainable earnings diminish migrants' capacity for realizing their dreams. The hope of returning may vanish like a mist confronted by the harsh sunshine of survival. Many are stranded because they arrived having paid high fees; unable to find the vaunted wealth, they survive on very little, working long, tedious hours. I met a formerly successful barber who sold even his clippers to undertake this quest for "foreign exchange." He, like many others, could no longer afford to return home to Nigeria. But those he left at home believe that he has gone "overseas"; they wait for money transfers through Western Union. Migrants include children. Boatfuls of children are smuggled daily into Gabon, in West Africa, and from there into Europe.

From the Cape Verde Islands to the Sunnyside slums of Pretoria, the criminality of Nigerian immigrants has elicited public outcry and murderous vengeance. Many prisons in Europe are filled with Nigerian drug smugglers. From Seoul to Singapore, posters warning of Nigerians decorate airports and embassies; it becomes difficult for other Nigerians to travel with dignity. The Nigerian embassy in Seoul is constantly besieged by the duped. In Eastern Europe, a frustrated man shot a Nigerian embassy official. The survival instinct has created a plethora of devices. Some pay indigenes for fake marriages to secure the proper documents. Marrying a white woman pays more dividends in Germany than in America. Thus, we are faced with a unique condition at the turn of the twenty-first century. How do we conceptualize this condition?

Metaphors of the Diasporic Condition: Exile and Crossing Jordan

Africans are in the midst of a complex migration pattern that scatters rather than consolidates. The success of a small group of professional migrants should not blind us to the larger realities. Many migrants are numbed by the impact of broken dreams. The diasporic condition is complex. The perspective here is to identify four dimensions: economic, identity, associational life, and religious solace, using the United States as an example.

The Economic Dimension

The first problem that confronts an immigrant in America is the need for documentation of status. The person is an alien, and this status alienates the person from access to sustainable life. It may take years to move from this penumbra zone to a green zone, that is, to obtain a green card. Some migrants resort to creative fraudulent ways to respond to the system. Next, the migrant discovers that the economic structure has an ethnic formulary. Africans are low in the ranking because there is a regional character to the increase in global migrations, and the African case differs from other forms of Diaspora. The numerical strength of Latinos in the United States has risen so sharply that they are now the second largest racial minority group. Demographically, they have overtaken blacks and appear to be more unified because of similarities of language and culture. This has immense political consequences as political parties court their votes and listen to their demands. The percentage of Latinos in unionized trades has risen, whereas the percentage for blacks has declined. Asians (Indians and Koreans) control certain businesses in America such as dry cleaning, environmental maintenance, and gas stations. Africans compete with Haitians over the control of taxi business, while the Polish own the luxury limousines.

More important, there is an unarticulated ideology in the Diaspora culture that is based on certain indices: the source and style of migrations; the presence or absence of compelling reasons for migration; educational and skill level; and experience in the new home. For instance, when Koreans pool money to sponsor a family to migrate to Canada, the family is accorded landed immigration status up front because it has brought funds for investment. The migrant family merges into a large community with its own banks, imported industrial goods, and so on. Such a family enters its new home at a different socioeconomic level than one not so well prepared and is cushioned by a strong network. There is no pressure to speak a foreign language because the signboards are written in Hangu. The only Nigerians who enjoyed this kind of Canadian privilege are those who stole from new-generation banks and escaped after the banks failed! African migrants must struggle hard to gain access to good-paying jobs, to secure valid documents, and to pay the cost of retraining. They suffer racism and sexism like any other black person; many immerse themselves in strenuous work just to live. However, African migrants have made enormous contributions. Moreover, their children are doing well in schools. In August 2004, the *New York Times* reported, "In the 1990s the number of blacks with recent roots in sub-Saharan Africa nearly tripled while the number of blacks with origins in the Caribbean grew by more than 60 percent. In recent years, black immigrants and their children have become more visible in universities, the workplace and politics." The article added that the trend has been "accompanied in some places by fears that the newcomers might eclipse native-born blacks. And they have touched off delicate musings about ethnic labels, identity and the often unspoken differences among people who share the same color."[9]

Exile and Crossing Jordan: Identity Crisis, Associational Life, and Survival

The *New York Times* story just quoted uses the example of Abdulaziz Kamus, an Ethiopian-born activist who was confronted with rejection by fellow blacks; though he is an American citizen and is black in color, he was told that he is not an African American. During the 2004 elections, Alan Keyes spelled it out on the ABC program *This Week with George Stephanopoulos:*

> Barack Obama and I have the same race—that is, physical characteristics. We are not from the same heritage. My ancestors toiled in slavery in this country; my consciousness, who I am as a person, has been shaped by my struggle, deeply emotional, and deeply painful with the reality of that heritage.[10]

The ambiguous relationship between African Americans and Africans is an old one. W. E. B. Du Bois described it with the famous concept of "double consciousness." It frustrated Wilmot Blyden and has forced African migrants to nurture a wealth of associations that serve as survival networks. In addition to religious organizations, these networks may be based on profession (as among physicians), nationality, ethnicity, state of origin, clan, Old Boys/Old Girls, and so on. It appears that the smaller the boundaries, the more effective the group. Enthusiastic participation in these may depend on a core ideology or self-perception—whether one feels like an exile or like a person who has crossed Jordan into the Promised Land. Experience may compel a shift; some sit on the fence totally confused, willing to participate but unsure about the possibilities of ever returning to settle in the homeland. The two models may explain how individuals survive in the Diaspora. At the root is the attitude toward the homeland viewed through the prism of fate once one has reached the destination.

The exilic concept is old. The Jews perhaps made it famous, and their survival strategies have attracted attention. The British perfected the idea. Sir Walter Raleigh could go out and steal in the high seas and return home to be knighted. He and his men spent brief periods in self-willed exile and brought the dividends back home. European cities are still decorated with trophies from such sallies. They created trading companies that governed foreign peoples on behalf of their nations. These were short-term migrant exiles. But most of the migrations from Europe to North America, for instance, went beyond short-term exile and, in fact, ceased to be conceived as exilic. Potato famine in Ireland in the nineteenth century triggered a massive population shift. The first direction was to the south, and soon English cities, such as London, were bursting at the seams. East London still bears the raw marks of this phenomenon. A secondary process started as the migrants moved out of England and across the Atlantic Ocean. The effort to develop the new homelands into extensions of England collapsed. With invented histories and stirring ideology, a new world emerged, and the inhabitants celebrated a new identity. This explains the July 4 holiday, the victory parades and the fireworks. From these emerged the concept of the melting pot, a shared American dream, and the requirement that newcomers blend into the culture. The Italians and the Polish modified their names as soon as they stepped off the ships and reinvented themselves. Frantz Fanon, in his book *Black Skin, White Mask,* caricatured an image of a young African who stood for hours in front of a mirror to learn how to roll French words with his tongue in a desperate effort to assimilate. Albert Manonni returned to this idea in *Prospero and Caliban* to demonstrate how the dependency syndrome is created and internalized.

Exile contains the notion of leaving and returning. The hope of an exile is to return. It says something about the manner of leaving, perhaps unwillingly; perhaps deliberately to go out in search of the "golden fleece," but always with the intention of returning to share the resources. I could hear one of the doyens of the Back-to Africa movement, or the American Colonization Society, Bishop Henry Turner. He intoned that he knew why God allowed the massive slave trade. It was to bring Africans in contact with the gospel so that they could return to develop the motherland through Christianity. This inspired Alexander Crummell to go to Liberia after studying in England. Among the black Americans, the exilic metaphor was very powerful. It moored their sense of identity and carried the hopes, aptly articulated in Psalm 68:31, that "Princes shall come out of Egypt; Ethiopia shall soon stretch out her hands unto God." Numerous exegeses appropriated the passage to prophesy the return of the glory of Africa through her scions, who will come back from across the ocean, from the lands into which their captors had sold them. Black manifest destiny designated the Africans in Diaspora as the agents to fulfill God's counsel for Africa.[11]

This ideology combined with the activities of mosquitoes spurred a massive missionary enterprise by blacks who came from North America and the West Indies to Africa until about 1920. The high mortality rate among Europeans on the West African coast compelled a search for black missionaries who could survive the conditions. White churches scoured through black colleges to recruit missionaries. Thus, the Presbyterian Church in Nigeria was founded by someone not from Scotland but from Jamaica. So was the Baptist Church in Cameroon. Indeed, the Methodists, Basel Mission, and Anglicans sent out delegations to recruit from the West

Indies. Hope Masterton Waddell and his compatriots spent years trying to convince the reluctant Scots to assist them in their mission to Calabar. While the Scots were dilly-dallying, the Primitive Methodists reached Fernando Po. Happily, they got stuck there, and the United Free Church mission passed them to reach Calabar in 1846. The irony was that while the whites spawned concepts such as manifest destiny, social Darwinism, white man's burden, and the idea of progress to legitimize colonization and imperialism, the blacks in Diaspora countered by insisting that they were exiles who must return home to regain control of their homelands. In 1891, Wilmot Blyden gave a lecture in Breadfruit Street Church in Lagos titled "The Return of the Exiles." He acknowledged the sacrifices of missionaries but intoned that Africans must evangelize Africa! Or, as Mojola Agbebi told a weekly newspaper in Sierra Leone, the sphinx must solve its own riddle.[12]

This explains the hostility and fear that faced African Americans in white-settler regions of Africa. These blacks disproved the notion that Africans lacked the capacity to rule. Marcus Garvey's political rhetoric created the rumor during the First World War that African Americans would invade and rescue Africans in Malawi and Kenya. When Ethiopia defeated the Italians at Adwa in 1896, the propaganda value for Africans in the Diaspora could only be imagined. Whites were not invincible! The exilic concept could be a powerful, antistructural, subversive ideology.

Admittedly, the returnees faced opposition from many blacks who had rejected the exilic idea and who argued that the back-to Africa ideology was a white subterfuge to deprive those on whose backs the economy had been built. They had decided that they were going nowhere. In spite of the sufferings in the middle passage and what followed, they had crossed Jordan and arrived at the Promised Land. The idea of crossing Jordan replaced the exilic metaphor of the black nationalists. On closer examination, both used the powerful symbol of the covenant. Both resorted to the Bible for a motivating concept. For the exile, the covenant holds out the hope that, one day, there will be a return. God will not abandon His people in a foreign land and permit the homestead to rot. Exiles agonized at the possibility of singing the Lord's song in a strange land. This is why Old Testament figures such as Daniel, Ezra, and Nehemiah stand out as imposing figures who had the opportunity of relaxing in the exiled land but refused to do so.

But when one crosses Jordan, the covenant idea can be deployed to urge that one start afresh, forget the past, and pay attention to the future, which is pregnant with great possibilities. One's attitude to the past is crucial in the crossing-Jordan metaphor. It is expressed by the success to develop the land, plant, marry, and prosper, without looking back. It is built on the principle of assimilation. One does not forget where one came from. Indeed, the pride of one's heritage makes one demand respect from the new homeland. A Coptic Egyptian in Germany said that he expected the Germans to know that he came from the cradle of civilization and deserved respect as he became integrated into Deutschland. He did not know that the Germans read history differently and presumed that the pyramids and discoveries in medicine were the achievements of Greeks or fellow Europeans who had occupied Egypt! The typical migrant who has crossed over to Jordan does not bother to read the newspapers from his country or retain much contact with fellow migrants.

The various forms of associational life in the Diaspora enable migrants to maintain links to the homeland, cushion the rough edges of sojourn, and provide the occasional opportunities to dance the "native" dance, eat indigenous food, and celebrate the rites of passage. These nurture immigrants' cultural roots. In the 1960s, before the floodgates opened, most migrants were students. They gathered to celebrate those who had graduated and nostalgically trooped to the airport to bid them farewell as they returned home. The religious dimension to the exilic experience had not fully emerged. Nowadays, Africa's contribution to the world is African spirituality.[13] The migration route is full of religious agents acting as missionaries for their denominations, supervisors of international branches, and evangelists who tour the northern hemisphere ministering to either migrant communities or mixed congregations. Religious communities assist new immigrants to secure roots; they provide a network of social and economic transactions, spiritual solace, and link to the religion of the homeland. Thus, Diaspora must be studied with an eye to periodization and typology.

Given the enlarged scale and wide differentiation in the character of migrant population, even the character of national and ethnic associations has changed. Many discard the exilic ideology and adopt the mentality of those who have crossed Jordan. Their children who are born in "Jordan" may not even speak any Nigerian language. They internalize the raw images of Africa purveyed by white media. Parents become helpless to control, discipline, or teach their children about the values of the homeland. It may not matter whether the migrants are married to Nigerians or to the inhabitants of the new homeland. At the social level, the bond of nationalism may be replaced by competition, hostility, quarrels, trickery, and mutual suspicion. Ethnicity has become a more virulent force in Diaspora since it grew teeth during the civil war when the calabash of blood broke on our heads. The two ideologies, exile and crossing Jordan, jostle for preeminence among immigrant communities. People may be unconscious about them because their preoccupation with survival on daily basis, with paying mortgages and other looming bills that keep many occupied in dealing with the realities of the culture.

Another dimension is the impact of Diaspora on the family. Many migrant families find that women access service jobs faster than the men, who may lose respect by being unemployed for long periods until they have retrained and found work in new professions. The impact of migration on the family, on values, and especially on the inherited patriarchal values system soon creates the paradox that some pretend to have crossed Jordan but deep inside are agonized exiles. Still others pursue the almighty dollar with such vengeance that they do not have the time to think about the homeland and the "nonsense people are doing there!" To narrow the scope of one's vision could be useful; to absorb the American individualization concept may be economical. To disappear into the new culture is safe. After a long period of hibernation, one young man could no longer resist making contact with his mother in the village even though he still gave only a postal box address located in central Manhattan. The psychological bonds remained enduring.

Reinventing Diaspora Experience: Stewardship in Exile

A major dimension to the Diaspora discourse is the possibility of return. The perspective here is that the question is wrongly posed. There are many reasons. The conditions at home must first change. Moreover, there are many tales of woes among those Nigerian professionals who have ventured to invest at home. More crucial is the importance of remembering the motherland, as Bishop Turner did, and yet struggling for success in the new home, as Turner's opponents urged. Both sides of the debate have merits that can benefit us in our own contemporary struggles to weave a sustainable ideology in the midst of galloping migration from Africa. The question still pulsates: how can the migration pattern aid African development?

The discussions about Nigerian Diaspora have been dominated by two ideas, brain drain and the call for the exiles to return. The development of the nation is said to have suffered by the depletion of highly qualified human resources. Meanwhile, the country pays a high price to import foreigners. It has been argued that migration out of the continent is not restricted to HQPs (highly qualified personnel). The more serious matter is the reopening of ancient slave routes by Africans who sell themselves. The fraud, abuse, corruption, inhumane conditions, and avoidable deaths of hundreds of thousands deserve the urgent attention of African leaders and the international community. The image of the continent is at stake. The number of Nigerian or Mongo operators tarnishes Nigeria's already battered image. More cogently, what is needed is to "fully assess the extent of the damage and enormity of the task of redeploying existing capacity, rebuilding old capacity, and creating new capacity," mitigating the effect in the short to medium term and substantial reduction in the long term.[14] This is to reinvent Diaspora as a tool of hope.

Discussions begin with brain drain because the International Labor Organization estimated that, in 2000, one-third of the most highly qualified African nationals lived outside their country of origin, mainly in the Western world. Analyses, however, diverge widely on brain drain, defined as the movement of high-level experts from developing countries to industrialized nations.[15] Some concentrate on the effect on donor countries and portray migration as the source of underdevelopment and another variety of the exploitation by industrialized nations. This perspective bemoans the effect on local institutional capacity, the flight of human capital, the vicious cycle of human capital depletion, and the dire effects on healthcare delivery and education. The short response is to curb outflow and urge the HQPs to return home. Home means "Hope On Me Eternally." Asi Ansah aptly dubs the option as the nationalist perspective.[16]

A second discourse regards this effort as an incomplete answer because emigrating professionals are less likely to return only out of patriotism. Constraints on return include the jealousy of former colleagues, the hostility of the bureaucracy, the politics of ethnicity, and the lack of jobs. An internationalist perspective argues that migration of HQPs results in creating a brain bank in developed countries that the nation can draw on at will; that brain gain does not occur when an HQP returns. That does not add anything; it maintains the status quo ante; therefore, there is no gain. Gain occurs only when additional skilled people are attracted to a country, and value added. This view pretends that the donor has a surplus to bank outside; it understates the causes, courses, and character of migrations. The migrant may be so disgusted with the homeland that he might be crossing Jordan to a new land of promise with no intention of looking back.

A third global discourse argues that the world is in an era characterized by mobile, urban forces that erode barriers and transfer knowledge at high speed. These reshape work spaces and locations and create networks that enable all countries to benefit from brain circulation. Migration brings Africa's voice into the global marketplace. The feedback potentials are to interpret Africa to the world and vice versa, promoting the globalization of Africa and the Africanization of globalization in productive ways that enhance cultural flow. The flaw is that many nations of the southern hemisphere are not fully implicated in the technological development; thus, the asymmetrical power relations ensure that the northern hemisphere will benefit more from these conditions. However, this option is buttressed by a comparison with the history of British and Jewish migrations. The core argument is the emergence of a purposeful, unified, and dynamic transnational bourgeoisie with a congruence of interests that is not state-centered; dispersed Africans could form a strong network of communities around the world, imbibing knowledge and skills and transferring these to their homelands. This requires a strong identity, a sense of mutual dependence, a global network anchored in mutual trust, an open mind, and a passion for new ideas. These qualities enabled the British to spread their influence. George Sefa Dei and Alireza Asgharzadeh emphasize the possibility of a viable solution that is ideologically driven. They urge that African migrants exercise agency by being apologists and propagandists for the southern hemisphere, using their knowledge and resources against the Western monopoly on interpretations and forging partnerships with progressive forces and institutions in Africa.[17]

A number of prescriptions deal with specific actions that nations may undertake. African countries must endeavor to build viable conditions for utilization of HQP resources: first, by developing centers of excellence that could attract high-level manpower, develop training programs, grant writing workshops, and support short specialized studies abroad as measures for rebuilding local capacity. As Augustine Oyewole argues, this is the fastest way to attract HQPs, who will, in turn, make substantial contributions.[18] The next set of measures links local institutions with international networks, collaborates with indigenous professionals, and initiates the short- to medium-term return of HQPs. For instance, the Nigerian government recently initiated the Nigerian Experts and Academics in the Diaspora Scheme (NEADS). According to the newspaper *This Day* for November 16, 2004, the major objectives of this program target the educational base of development and are:

> To encourage the movement to Nigeria on short basis of academics and experts of Nigerian origin in the Diaspora to contribute to national development through engagement in teaching, research and community service activities in the Nigerian university system;
>
> To tap from the huge human resources of Nigerian origin based within and outside the country but located for the purpose of work outside the Nigerian university system for the improvement of the delivery of university education.[19]

This type of program achieves the transfer of technical knowledge; it creates brain networking exchanges without demanding that migrants pack their bags for home. However, for the daring ones, there are helpful organizations such as the Migration for Development in Africa (MDA), which collaborates with Organization for Migration (IOM) to cushion the re-entry impact.

Finally, the word "steward" in its Greek form, *oikonomos,* is derived from *oikonomia,* the management of the household (*oikos*). It would appear that the task is not just for economists. The steward is a manager and organizer of the resources of the household. The work demands self-discipline, leadership ability, and the ability to make informed choices amid competing wants to enhance the capacity of the household to prosper. In our schools, the regimen was designed to nurture young people, to recognize their innate abilities (intellectual and other skills), and to help them learn the disciplined development and management of such resources in order to serve God and society. The social-activist dimension explains our pride in the many African migrants who have achieved in the various diasporic contexts. Stewardship shifts the discourse from the economic sphere or the government's propaganda to a moral appeal to maintain a racial covenant, sharing in the management of the homeland by contributing through philanthropy, investment, networking, capacity building, and buttressing activist civil society and community development projects.

Appendix

"The Line of No Return," by Chimamanda Ngozi Adichie

Lagos, Nigeria. I watch dawn split open.[20] The ashy darkness separates and light creeps over all of us standing in line outside the United States Embassy. For the first time, I see the blues and pinks of the *buba* the woman in front of me is wearing. And the hawkers and touts walking around are no longer shadows; I see their scarred faces, their calculating smiles. I have been in line since 4 A.M. Some of the people in front of me spent the night under a tent opposite the embassy.

I feel a strange kinship with them, and yet I am not particularly friendly. I do not start a conversation with anybody: perhaps because my eyes are still cloudy from lack of sleep, perhaps because I feel resentment at the inconveniences of having to be here so early. I wish I had not come back to Nigeria to renew my American student visa, I wish I had done it in England or Canada. Then I chastise myself. This is my country. The reason I did not bother to go to another country was that I knew I would be asked to return to my "home country."

I buy a Maltina from a hawker, and drink it while I listen to the people around me exchange stories, forming friendships that will dissolve with the visa line. The touts swarm around. "I have serious connections inside the embassy, Auntie," one of them tells me. "Just 1,000 and you will enter today for sure."

I would not give him 1,000 naira even if I had it to spare. The 12,000 naira visa fee is steep enough. As the sun rises, I estimate how much the embassy will make from the people in line today. They will give visas only to a fraction of these people but will take almost $100 worth of naira from each of them. Perhaps $40,000 for today. Conservatively.

When I finally get to the entrance, the Nigerian guard looks through my passport. He is upset that I travel to England often. "Why?" he asks. I want to tell him that he is working for the United States Embassy, not the British, and that his job is simply to make sure I have the right documents. But I say nothing. He puffs his shoulders and grunts with self-importance. "Passport photos?" he asks.

I hand them to him.

"Use your right hand!" he says.

I transfer my files to my left hand and then hand him the photos with my right. He notices they are the same photos I have used in my British visa. "Get back!" he says. "Go and take another picture and come back! You cannot wear the same dress in two passports!"

I stare at him. "What does it matter as long as the photo is not more than six months old?"

"Are you insulting me?" he asks. "Are you insulting me, eh?"

I turn and leave. Insult means many things to us Nigerians. Our self-confidence is so fragile that anything—a challenge, a correction, a question—could well become an insult.

I come back the next day, with new photos in which I look ridiculous because the photographer—his signboard said, "*Expert in American Visa Passport Photos*"—stuck little balls of paper behind my ears. The Americans want to make sure your ears show, he told me. He didn't listen when I said that my ears don't need to stick out like lettuce leaves, that the Americans simply don't want your hair to cover your ears.

I am relieved to finally get into the cool embassy building, with garish paintings on the wall: an American girl holding a Nigerian flag, a Nigerian holding an American flag. The room is crowded. Preening and smirking, guards walk around, with comical jaunts to their gaits. Once in a while, they call out names and people rise eagerly, nervously, and walk to the interview booths. Babies cry. There are many children here, because the Americans do not believe you when you tell them how many children you have; they have been known to give visas to only four out of five children in one family. Next to me, a little boy, about 4 years old, is telling his father in a high voice, "We will bring a gun and shoot Mummy today!" He points at his mother as he speaks. She ignores him, carefully going through files to make sure they have everything the Americans want.

The man beside me watches them, appalled. "What is happening to our children?" he asks me. "And see how the father is laughing!" He says that he is a philosophy professor and teaches at a college in Atlanta. There is a steady hum of talking around the room, but it dies down when a white woman comes in, with short hair that sticks up on her head like brush bristles. She is the director of the visa section, the philosophy professor tells me. She holds a loudspeaker to her mouth: "Raise your hands if you are here to renew a student or a work visa! Raise your hands high! I can't see! High!"

Her tone makes me feel like I am in primary school again.

"Keep the hands up! O.K., down!" She is wearing a multicolored caftan with jagged edges—the sort of thing a foreigner will wear to look African but an African will never wear. A child has walked up to her and is holding onto the caftan, looking up at her and smiling. He wants to play.

"Get this kid off me! Get this kid off me!" she says. She gestures wildly and for a moment I am afraid she will hit the child with the loudspeaker. The little boy is laughing now; he thinks it's some sort of game. There is the rumble of laughter through the room. "Oh children," someone says.

But the woman is not amused. "Who has this child?" She shakes her caftan as if to shake the child off until his mother goes and picks him up. "He just likes you," she tells the woman. The woman glares at us. "You think it's funny? O.K., I won't tell you what I wanted to tell you about the interview process. Go ahead and figure it out for yourselves."

She turns and walks away. The room is immediately mired in worry. "We should not have laughed," somebody says. "You know white people do not see things the way we do."

"White people don't play with children," another says. "She was angry." "Somebody should beg her not to be angry." "I hope they will still interview us." "Please, somebody should go and beg her."

The philosophy professor is incensed. "Can you imagine her talking to people in America or Europe like this?," he says. "She wouldn't dare."

I nod. I am as angry as he is—because of the collective humiliation of being in this soulless lounge, but also because of how quickly my people have forgiven her, have created different rules to excuse her unprofessional rudeness, her infantile tantrum.

I am acutely aware of the complex layers of injustice here. The first is the larger injustice of our history, the benignly brutal colonialism that spawned vile military regimes—events that made this scene possible. Then there is the injustice of this glaring power dynamic: our government cannot demand that we be treated with dignity within our own borders. And, saddest of all, the injustice that we perpetrate on ourselves by not giving ourselves any value, by accepting it when other people strip us of our dignity.

When it is my turn to present my case, the young American who interviews me says that she grew up in Philadelphia, where I lived for a short time during college. She has hazel eyes and is friendly and warm. She tells me that my new visa will be ready the next day. Later, when I tell my friend about this woman, I am told how lucky I was to get one of the few good ones.

As I leave the building, I hear the philosophy professor yelling at a man behind a glass screen. "How can you say I am lying?" he asks. "Why don't you call Atlanta and verify? How can you say I am lying?"

He has not been as lucky as I have been.[20]

Notes

1. Association of African Universities, *Strategic Plan, 2003–2010, Final Draft* (Accra: African Universities House, 2003), 1.

2. *This Day,* 24 November 2004, available online at www.thisdayonline.com (accessed December 2004).

3. See Paul T. Zeleza, "Contemporary African Migrations in a Global Context," *African Issues* 30, no. 1 (2002): 9–14.

4. See the conference proceedings "African Scholars and the African Humanities: A Symposium," African Studies Program, Northwestern University, Evanston, Ill., 3 June 2004.

5. See Philippe Rekacewicz, "The Rising Tide of Refugees," January 2000, *Le Monde Diplomatique,* available online at http://mondediplo.com/maps/refugeesmdv49 (accessed December 2004).

6. "Guinea, Unstoppable Exodus," BBC News, 18 May 2004, available online at http://news.bbc.co.uk/1/hi/world/africa/3568329.stm (accessed December 2004).

7. Elie Goldschmidt, "Facing the Strait: Congolese Migrants in Transit to Europe," seminar paper, Anthropology, University of Chicago, 2004.

8. "Migrants Flock to Canaries," BBC News, 26 October 2004, available online at http://news.bbc.co.uk/1/hi/world/Europe/3950701.stm (accessed December 2004).

9. "African American Becomes a Term for Debate," *New York Times,* 29 August, 2004, available online at http://www.nytimes.com/2004/08/29/national/29african.html (accessed December 2004).

10. Ibid.

11. See O. U. Kalu, "Ethiopianism in African Christianity," in O. Kalu, *Clio in a Sacred Garb: Christian Presence and African Responses* (Pretoria: University of South Africa Press, 2007).

12. Hollis Lynch, *Edward Wilmot Blyden: Pan-Negro Patriot, 1832–1912* (London: Oxford University Press, 1967).

13. Stephen Ellis and Gerrie ter Haar, *Worlds of Power: Religious Thought and Political Practice in Africa* (New York: Oxford University Press, 2004).

14. Soumana Sako, "Brain Drain and African Development: A Reflection," *African Issues* 30, no. 1 (2002): 25–30.

15. Ibid., 25.

16. Asi Ansah, "Theorizing Brain Drain," *African Issues* 30, no. 1 (2002): 21–24.

17. G. J. S. Dei and A. Asgharzadeh, "What Is to Be Done? A Look at Some Causes and Consequences of the African Brain Drain," *African Issues* 30, no.1 (2002): 31–36.

18. Augustine Oyewole, "Brain Drain: Colossal Loss of Investment for Developing Countries," *The Courier ACP-EU,* no. 159 (September–October 1996): 59–60.

19. *This Day,* 16 November 2004, available online at http://www.thisdayonline.com/nview.php?id=2049 (accessed December 2004).

20. The *New York Times,* 29 November 2004. Reprinted by permission.

II

Reverse Mission

Faith, Practice, and the Immigrant Journey

4

Non-Western Christianity in the Western World

African Immigrant Churches in the Diaspora

Akintunde E. Akinade

Introduction

Immigration is changing the religious configuration of the United States. The 1965 Immigration Reform Act contributed to an unprecedented wave of American immigrants in the twentieth century. These immigrants have inevitably contributed to the new religious reality in the United States. The American religious tapestry is no longer a monochrome but a rainbow of many religions and congregations from all over the world. Bruce Lawrence has rightly described the epicenter of American identity as "piebald and plural."[1] One fascinating phenomenon within "a new religious America"[2] is the rise of African churches. The U.S. 2000 census put the number of African immigrants living in the United States at about a million. This number will continue to rise.[3] Today, as in the past, Africans migrating to the United States bring their religions with them, and gathering religiously is one of the ways they make a life in this country.

This chapter examines what African churches (especially the ones belonging to the Yoruba charismatic/pentecostal movement) are doing in the United States and how they have been able to maintain their religious identity in a new cultural context. I argue that we have to see this religious movement as an integral part of world Christianity whose new resurgence and renewal defy simple categorization and facile generalizations. This chapter underscores the importance of non-Western Christianity in a Western context. African churches in new cultural milieu boldly confirm the radical deterritorialization of Christianity. Border crossing and itinerancy are essential characteristics of the Christian faith. These factors continue to transform the face of Christianity in the twenty-first century.

The New Face of World Christianity

The veritable explosion of Christianity in non-Western societies and culture—Africa, Asia, Latin America, and the Pacific—has presented us with a compelling story of Christianity as an authentic world religion.[4] This remarkable shift of the center of Christianity took place in the second half of the twentieth century. For instance, in 1900 more than 80 percent of professing Christians lived in Europe and America. In our contemporary world, 60 percent of professing Christians live in the non-Western world. This radical demographic shift has led to the dismantling of Eurocentric presumptions, as a result of which the West has ceased to be the culture of location for the Christian world. In non-Western societies, the reference point for the gospel was not the originating culture of Europe or America but the culture of the receivers. Christianity was inevitably adopted within an appropriate local framework and reshaped by indigenous genius, sagacity, worldview, and ethos. The subject of the new shift in Christianity has been vigorously pursued by Philip Jenkins in *The Next Christendom*. In this book, Jenkins expands on the position of scholars like Lamin Sanneh, Andrew Walls, and Kwame Bediako and laments that this new shift in world Christianity is still ignored or treated with disdain in the United States.[5] He points out that even someone as perceptive as Robert Wuthnow did not mention this new phenomenon in world Christianity in his influential book, *Christianity in the 21st Century*.

Whether acknowledged within the Western magisterium or not, the new centers of vitality and importance in theological construction and world Christianity are in Asia, Latin America, and Africa. The old centers of theological influence are becoming the new peripheries.[6] In order to fully understand the dynamic nature of world Christianity today, it is very important to have serious engagement with the Christian movements in the Third World. This is the only way to fully understand the amazing diversity of the world Christian movement. The Kenyan theologian John Mbiti once remarked that many Christian scholars in Europe and America have more meaningful "academic fellowship with heretics long dead that with living brethren of the Church today in the so-called Third World."[7]

No serious study of Africa can ignore Christianity and the role it has come to play in Africa. Let us take a quick look at statistics. David Barrett, the editor of *The World Christian Encyclopedia* and widely regarded as the guru in this subject, claims that in 1900 there were about 10 million African Christians out of a continental population of 107 million—about 9 percent of the total. In 2000, the number had changed dramatically; there were 360 million Christians out of a population of 784 million. This represents 46 percent of all Africans.[8] This percentage is likely to continue to rise because African countries have some of the world's most dramatic rates of population growth. It is estimated that by 2025, 50 percent of the Christian population will be in Africa and Latin America, and another 17 percent will be in Asia.[9] As Andrew Walls affirmed:

> This means that we have to regard African Christianity as potentially the representative Christianity in the twenty-first century. The representative Christianity of the second and third and fourth centuries was shaped by events and processes at work in the Mediterranean world. In later times it was events and processes among the barbarian peoples of Northern and Western Europe, or in Russia, or modern European, or the North Atlantic world that produced the representative Christianity of those times. The Christianity typical of the twenty-first century will be shaped by the events and processes that take place in the Southern continents, and above all by those that take place in Africa.[10]

This is an important affirmation. It compels us to look beyond naïve skepticisms and examine how the explosion of Christianity in Africa has transformed the world's largest religion. John Mbiti once remarked that as the axis of Christianity shifts southward, it may justify consideration of shifting the headquarters of the World Council of Churches from Geneva to Kinshasha. While this may be too grand an idea, I agree with him that in the twenty-first century, the center of the church's universality will not be Rome or 475 Riverside Drive in New York, but Brazil, Lagos, Manila, or the Congo.[11] Hilaire Belloc's bold declaration that "Europe is the faith" is now anachronistic. The salient issues within world Christianity are being determined from multiple centers.

Old Wine in a New Wineskin: Aladura Churches in the Diaspora

Immigration, transnationalism, and globalization have contributed to the radical alteration of the georeligious reality all over the world. In the United States, immigration and religious diversity have shattered the belief that the United States was, as described by the sociologist Will Herberg, a "three-religion country"—Protestant, Catholic, and Jewish. By the 1990s, there were Muslims, Hindus, Buddhists, Jains, and Sikhs in many American cities and towns. In 1991, Diana Eck inaugurated the Pluralism Project at Harvard University to study the rapidly changing religious landscape of the United States. The New Ethnic and Immigrant Congregations Project (NEICP) was established in 1993 by Stephen Warner at the University of Illinois at Chicago. The findings of this three-year interdisciplinary research have been published in *Gatherings in Dispora: Religious Communities and the New Immigration.* It is quite interesting to note that a study of African immigrant churches is conspicuously absent in these two projects. This religious movement remains, by and large, terra incognita to many well-informed people in the West. The amazing growth of Aladura religious movements in the Diaspora demands careful investigation and attention. The most robust and enduring initiatives at establishing viable congregations in the United States have been carried out by these churches, which include the Christ Apostolic Church, the Celestial Church of Christ, The Cherubim and Seraphim, and the Church of the Lord. They belong under the rubric of African Initiated Churches (AICs), and they have an enduring religious legacy within African church historiography. These churches made their debut on the American scene in the 1970s, and today they can be located in all the major cities in the United States. Many Yoruba Christians in the United States strongly believe that these churches provide the right context for enduring fellowship and worship. They believe that their pastors are more accessible and extremely helpful as they adjust to the vagaries and challenges of American life and culture. It is interesting to note that while mainline African churches are always clamoring for their ministers who have come to the West for professional training to return home, Aladura churches have made concerted efforts to send their pastors to the United States to establish viable congregations. These churches have always maintained that the world is their parish. They are very bold in their ministerial vocation and unrelenting in reaching out to the Western world. In recent times, the Anglican Church of Nigeria has demonstrated a keen interest in following the example of Aladura churches in reaching out to people in the West. The ordination of an openly gay bishop in the diocese of New Hampshire gave the Anglican Church of Nigeria the auspicious opportunity to send a message to Christians in the West. Archbishop Peter Akinola of Nigeria is now a household name within the Episcopal Church, U.S.A. Today, when Akinola sneezes, a majority of people in the Episcopal Church get a cold! Whatever criticisms one may have about Akinola's modus operandi and his blistering denunciations of homosexuality, his project is telling testimony that the strident voices from the so-called underside of history can no longer be ignored or taken for granted by churches in the Western world.

I believe that the formidable presence of immigrant churches constitutes a *kairos* movement in American Christianity. Christian communities formerly served by Western missions are now proclaiming the good news and introducing a new grammar of faith to the West. They possess sound contextual theologies, a vibrant church life, and dynamic memberships. Many Africans describe these churches as their "home away from home." Immigrants are interested in a community they can call home in spite of what the Department of Homeland Security says about their status in the United States. Pastor Abraham Oyedeji, the founder of Christ Apostolic Church, First in the Americas, in Brooklyn, New York, says that immigrants are attracted to a church that understands their story and that can provide both material and spiritual resources for dealing with their pain and predicament.[12] The Cherubim and Seraphim Church, the International House of Prayer for All People, founded by the Reverend Dr. Fred O. Ogunfiditimi, has many branches all over the United States. The Church has been very active in providing Africans with the resources of dealing with the tremendous challenges of living in the United States. Stephen Warner has described this important dimension as the "settlement function of congregations."[13] In addition to fulfilling this function, these charismatic churches also provide a context for experiencing God here and now in the midst of urban chaos, poverty, racism, confusion, anomie, and alienation. Karla Poewe has observed that charismatic Christianity has a global relevance because it provides a holistic religious experience that integrates mind, body, and spirit.[14] This holistic dimension plays a major role in the incorporation of immigrants into the civic life of American culture.

Aladura Christianity has a long tradition as a grassroots religion. This legacy is demonstrated in the way these churches have become the voice for the voiceless and the bastion of hope for the hopeless and marginalized. In the United States, the congregational context within these churches engenders a fraternity that helps to ameliorate the dangerous hierarchies and principalities of the outside world. Within the confines of a sacred canopy, members can develop veritable resources that will ease their civic incorporation into the American life. The network of support and fraternity within church circles help immigrants to deal with the social challenges and the overwhelming challenges of American culture. The story and odyssey of church members who have "made it" or have established their own small businesses become living testimonies for new immigrants. Such testimonies provide rhyme and reason to the otherwise chaotic circumstances that face new immigrants in urban settings.

Aladura spirituality is deeply rooted in the African understanding of the Christian community. The New Testament concepts of fellowship (*koinonia*) and the church as a called-out assembly (*ekklesia*) are taken seriously by these churches. Aladura churches generally assume the form of a community relatively small for members to cultivate and maintain enduring relationships. It also provides a spiritual haven where enduring cultural values are cherished and valorized. Culture is the basis of the creativity of any group of people. It is also the foundation of their collective identity. It expresses their worldview, their understanding of the meaning of human existence, and their concept of the transcendence. Aladura churches in the Diaspora have persistently maintained that it is possible to be "Christian" and "African" at the same time. In these churches, African Christians can express their faith in their own traditional languages and cultural idioms.

The precarious political and economic situations that are manifest in many African countries today have contributed to the large number of immigrants in the United States. African charismatic churches support immigrants' identities as Africans and at the same time offer the opportunity to experience the mystery of the transcendental *mysterium tremendum et fascinans* of God. Church services and fellowship meetings bring people together as one under God to create an outflow of joy and renewal. This experience is analogous to what Emile Durkheim described as "moments of effervescence." Such instances have enabled immigrants to cope with an array of problems, including culture shock, anxiety, paranoia, unemployment, racism, and the distress of a new situation and environment. There is no gainsaying the fact that these churches have contributed immensely to the incorporation of African immigrants into the American sociocultural and civic life.

The Integrity of the Good News

The beauty of the gospel lies in the fact that it has been appropriated in multiple ways all over the globe. African Christianity was received outside the enlightenment framework or paradigm. Its configurations, institutions, and concerns have been largely shaped by indigenous sensibilities. The capricious burden of "Afro-pessimissm" often provides the legitimacy to gloss over some of the unique contributions of African religious experience. It is imperative to move beyond paternalistic presuppositions and demeaning reductionism to a deeper understanding of African religious experience and its potential to contribute to a deeper understanding of charismatic Christianity. The West can no longer be the sole arbiter of what is right or wrong in matters of faith. The intense skepticism about the resurgence of African Christianity and some of its concomitant credentials must be jettisoned in order to fully appreciate the nature of Christianity in the world today. African Christianity in this new millennium is enriched by sound polymethodic approaches, and it is unencumbered by any serious debilitating patrimony. It has come of age and is poised to contribute to the global ecumenical banquet. Aladura churches in the Diaspora do compel us to grapple with the significance and contributions of African spirituality to this ecumenical project.[15]

On the Question of Identity

The question of identity is a perennial theme in any Diaspora. In anthropological parlance, identity is a social concept about groups of people who think of themselves, or are thought of by others, as alike and unique in some significant way. The identity issue revolves around a distinctive trait of a person or a group of people. This understanding of identity inevitably places an emphasis on cultural identity, of which religion is an integral part. The development of an African identity is very important for African people in the United States primarily because of the constant efforts made in the past to undermine the African identity. In an important theological study, Engelbert Mveng examined the problem of "anthropological poverty" that has bedeviled African peoples for centuries. According to Mveng, anthropological poverty consists in "despoiling human beings not only of what they have, but of everything that constitutes their being and essence—their identity, history, ethnic roots, language, culture, faith, creativity, dignity, pride, ambitions, and right to speak."[16] Religion has continued to play a significant role in the acculturation process of Africans in the Diaspora. Many Africans believe that their religious affiliation and identity are the antidote to acute deracination. It is interesting to note that immigrant churches are still very concerned about maintaining their cultural identity in spite of being confronted with the metaphor of the American melting pot. I argue for a death-refusal stance of African spiritual sensibilities even when they are being open up to an intrusive, and corrosive, wider world. This resilience has enabled African churches to flourish in new cultural environments. Karen McCarthy Brown has correctly argued that "African religious retentions in the New World, like Christian borrowings, are neither random nor fragmentary, but systematic and thoroughly understandable in terms of history and circumstance."[17] Immigrants are in most cases more religious than they were before they left home primarily because religion is one of the important identity shapers that help them preserve individual self-awareness and cohesion in a group. Religious affiliation is one of the significant strategies that allow immigrants to maintain self-identity, achieve communal acceptance, and incorporation into the civic community.

Implications for World Christianity

This is an exciting time in world Christianity. It does not take a prophet to see that we are living in an extraordinary age. In fact, the twenty-first century will be marked by a vast missionary movement from the South to the North. The lands that a century before were considered the ends of the earth will have the opportunity to witness to the descendants of those who had earlier witnessed to them. This calls for the need to rethink old assumptions within the ecumenical movement. It is a time to learn about theological voices from the Third World and to initiate an agenda for theological mutuality and reciprocity. Churches from the South are inexorably moving to the North. They come with a bold missionary agenda. Speaking about African churches in Europe, Gerrie ter Haar writes,

> Just as European missionaries once believed in their divine task of evangelizing what they called the dark continent, African church leaders in Europe today are convinced of Africa's mission to bring the gospel back to those

> who originally provided it. Thus, many African Christians who have recently migrated to Europe, generally to find work, consider that God has given them a unique opportunity to spread the good news among those who have gone astray.[18]

Church leaders from the South also consider it utterly outrageous and are deeply affronted that so many Christian scholars in older Christendom know so little about the churches of the Third World. These church leaders are saying: we have learned to theologize with you, from you, and about your concerns. Now if you wish, we would like to share our spirituality with you. Only in that way can the universality of the church be meaningful.[19] Kosuke Koyama once said that Christianity cannot be a one-way-traffic religion. According to him, this type of Christianity is an ugly monster, and one-way-traffic human relationship is ugly.[20] The new configuration in world Christianity calls for continuous self-critical analysis and mutual reciprocity. It also requires two-way-traffic that is deeply rooted in the crucified Christ. Lesslie Newbigin has argued that Western Christians need African, Asian, and Hispanic Christians in order to have a rigorous analysis of some of the elements within Western culture. He was deeply concerned about the need for a mutual give-and-take structure within the ecumenical circle. According to him,

> We need their witness to correct ours, as indeed they need ours to correct theirs. At this moment our need is greater, for they have been far more aware of the danger of syncretism, of an illegitimate alliance with the false elements in their culture, than we have been. But . . . we imperatively need one another if we are to be faithful witnesses to Christ.[21]

Orlando Costas has written:

> Third World Christians may not be able to provide money or an overwhelming amount of missionary personnel, but they can provide models of a critical insertion in their culture and society that have given prophetic depth to their life and witness. To see and hear what is happening in the churches of Africa, the Middle East, Asia, Latin America, the Caribbean, Oceania, and in Asian, Black, Hispanic, and Native American communities of the United States should be a top priority of main-stream American Christianity.[22]

Christianity in the twenty-first century is a multicentered reality, made up of interconnecting networks and communities.[23] Peter Beyer says that "glocalized multi-centredness is a defining feature of the religions that dominate the structure of the global religious system."[24] Robert Schreiter has also written about the importance of global theological flows of discourses, ideas, rituals, and practices for connecting local churches to one another across borders.[25] Everywhere we go, we find peoples and cultures crossing borders, coming into contact with one another, affecting one another in new and unexpected ways in our new global village. In spite of its shortcomings and pitfalls, globalization continues to reshape and redefine many nations in the world. We have been ushered into a brave new world of borderless boundaries and new paradigms in interpersonal connections. Roland Robertson has rightly described globalization as a process of "compression of the world." The constant denominator of contemporary religious geography is that no single religion dominates the world. It is pretty impossible to show a world map in which each country is exclusively assigned to one particular religion. Churches of the world are diverse, as the cultures of the world. Border crossing is a permanent aspect of Christianity in the twenty-first century.[26] Borders are often conceived as limits,[27] but they are also avenues for connection and dialogue. Churches across the ages have crossed historical borders of experience and culture in many ways. Since the Apostolic period, Christianity has been crossing different borders and moving into new geographical areas. Right from its beginning, Christianity has been a migratory religion. It has moved into new regions and uncharted territories with remarkable speed and stupendous gusto. The initial shift in the center of gravity of Christianity occurred within the first century of the Christian era. Within a short period, Christianity ceased to be an isolated phenomenon. Rather, it crossed over into many parts in the Hellenistic world, moving with considerable ease across the Mediterranean and beyond it. Andrew Walls has even suggested that "a threatened eclipse of Christianity was averted by its cross-cultural diffusion. Crossing cultural boundaries has been the life blood of historic Christianity."[28] The radical deterritorialization of Christianity on our present age is not something new. It is a testimony to Jesus' audacious injunction that "you shall be my witnesses in Jerusalem and in all Judea and in Samaria and to the end of the earth" (Acts 1:8). The vital responsibility within this new situation is to find ways to pursue continuous constructive dialogical engagement among churches. This dialogical engagement will contribute to the vitality and integrity of Christianity in the twenty-first century.

Conclusion

The unprecedented alteration in the geography of Christianity has created an increasing urgency to reassess the needs and opportunities of world Christianity. One of the implications of this demographic shift in world Christianity is that people from diverse cultures have redefined Christianity on their own terms and within their own local framework. Christianity has become a multicultural world religion, blossoming in many cultures, unburdened by any subversive hegemonic control, and galvanized by new missionary impulses criss-crossing the globe in new and creative ways. African Christians continue to adjust to new sociocultural conditions in the Diaspora. They have the potential to contribute to new charismatic renaissance and renewal in the West. It is apposite to add here that Christians should be home everywhere because of the mystery of the incarnation and nowhere because of the eschatological emphasis that is geared toward the longing for Christ's return. The genius of the Christian faith is the ability to maintain the delicate balance between these two tendencies. Mark Noll has observed that "a religion invigorated by that kind of tension is exactly the kind needed to nourish public life—both where Christianity has long been resident and in the many places around the globe where it has only recently found a home."[29] In declaring the West the new "Macedonia," African Christians are claiming that they have something substantial to contribute to the public life and spiritual awakening in the West. Immigration and cross-cultural fertilization will continue to engender new religious paradigms in world Christianity.

Notes

1. See Bruce Lawrence, *New Faiths, Old Fears: Muslims and Other Asian Immigrants in American Religious Life* (New York: Columbia University Press, 2002), xvi.

2. See Diana L. Eck, *A New Religious America* (New York: HarperCollins, 2001). Stephen Warner has also described the American context as "an open religious market, constitutive pluralism, structural adaptability, and empowering opportunities." See his 1997 Presidential Address, *Sociology of Religion* 59 (Fall 1998): 199.

3. See Emmanuel Akyeampong, "Africans in the Diaspora: The Diaspora and Africa," *African Affairs* 99 (2000): 183–215, for a comprehensive analysis of the nature, complexity, and composition of the African Diaspora.

4. Walbert Bühlmann coined the term "the Third Church" to refer to the shift of Christianity to the South. See *The Coming of the Third Church* (Maryknoll, N.Y.: Orbis Books, 1978).

5. Another important article is Philip Jenkins, "The Next Christianity," *The Atlantic Monthly,* October 2002. *Newsweek* magazine has also written a report on the changing trend in the Church. See Kenneth Woodward, "The Changing Face of the Church," *Newsweek,* 16 April 2001.

6. See Dana L. Robert, "Shifting Southwards: Global Christianity Since 1945," *International Bulletin of Missionary Research* 24, no.4 (April 2000): 50–58; Kwame Bediako, "Africa and Christianity on the Threshold of the Third Millennium: The Religious Dimension," *African Affairs,* no. 99 (2000): 303–323; and Wilbert Shenk, "Toward a Global Church History," *International Bulletin of Missionary Research* 20, no. 2 (April 1996): 51–56.

7. John S. Mbiti, "Theological Impotence and the Universality of the Church," in G. H. Anderson and T. F. Stransky, eds., *Mission Trends No. 3* (Grand Rapids, Mich.: William B. Eerdmans Publishing Co., 1976), 17.

8. See Jenkins, "Next Christianity," 55.

9. Ibid.

10. Andrew F. Walls, "Africa in Christian History: Retrospect and Prospect," *Journal of African Christian Thought* 1, no. 1 (1998): 2.

11. In his book, Lamin Sanneh argues that it is still a territorial complex that identifies Christianity exclusively with its Western domains. The new paradigms in world Christianity have contributed to "the dissolution of Christendom, the shattering of the territorial European shell of religious identity." See *Encountering the West* (Maryknoll, N.Y.: Orbis Books, 1993), 185.

12. Personal interview, 20 May 2004.

13. See Brian Steensland, "Exploring Religious Diversity and Immigration: A Conversation with Stephen Warner," *Regeneration Quarterly* 3, no. 2 (Spring 1997): 16.

14. See K. Poewe, ed., *Charismatic Christianity as a Global Culture* (Columbia, S.C.: University of South Carolina Press, 1994).

15. Aladura Christians emphasize the efficacy of prayer. Aladura worship and rituals are geared toward the spiritual diagnosis and treatment of personal problems. Within the worship context, the Holy Spirit is also invoked as the veritable fire from heaven that consumes all the machinations of the devil and all malevolent spiritual forces. This vibrant pneumatological paradigm has tremendous theological significance.

16. See V. Fabella and S. Torres, eds., *The Irruption of the Third World* (Maryknoll, N.Y.: Orbis Books, 1983), 220.

17. Karen McCarthy Brown, "Women in African American Religions," in J. Carman and S. Hopkins, eds., *Tracing Common Themes: Comparative Courses in the Study of Religion* (Atlanta: Scholars Press, 1992), 242.

18. Gerrie ter Haar, *Halfway to Paradise: African Christians in Europe* (Cardiff, U.K.: Cardiff Academic Press, 1998, 92. Her article "Strangers in the Promised Land: African Christians in Europe," *Exchange* 24 (February 1995): 1–33, is also very useful.

19. This is one of the claims made by Orlando Costas in his "Christian Mission in the Americas," in J.A. Scherer and S. B. Bevans, eds., *New Directions in Mission and Evangelization* (Maryknoll, N.Y.: Orbis Books, 1994).

20. Kosuke Koyama, "Christianity Suffers from Teacher Complex," in G. H. Anderson and T. F. Stransky, eds., (*Mission Trends No. 2* (Grand Rapids, Mich.: William B. Eerdmans Publishing Co., 1975), 73.

21. Lesslie Newbigin, quoted in Andrew F. Walls, *The Cross-Cultural Process in Christian History* (Maryknoll, N.Y.: Orbis Books, 2002), 69.

22. Orlando E. Costas, *Christ Outside the Gate: Mission Beyond Christendom* (Maryknoll, N.Y: Orbis Books, 1982), 82.

23. It is very important to understand that world Christianity is not just about chronology. It is imperative to understand the way the Christian message has been appropriated and reshaped in different contexts. This is the genius of the Christian message. African responses to Christianity are multilayered. Aladura Christianity is one of the responses.

24. Peter Beyer, "De-Centering Religious Singularity: The Globalization of Christianity as a Case Point," *Numen* 50, no. 4 (2003): 382.

25. Robert J. Schreiter, *The New Catholicity: Theology Between the Global and the Local,* Maryknoll (N.Y.: Orbis Books, 1997), 15–21.

26. Several scholars have used this idea within postmodern discourse. See Walter D. Mignolo, *Local Histories/Global Designs: Coloniality, Subaltern Knowledges, and Border Thinking* (Princeton: Princeton University Press, 2000); Homi K. Bhabha, *The Location of Culture* (London and New York: Routledge Press), 1994; and Edward Said, *Culture and Imperialism* (New York: Knopf, 1993). I am very grateful to Dale Irvin for introducing me to these books and to the language of border crossing.

27. For instance, the anthropologist Mary Douglas speaks of borders and boundaries in human experience as places of danger and trepidation. See her *Purity and Danger: An Analysis of the Concepts of Pollution and Taboo* (London: Routledge and Kegan Paul, 1966).

28. Walls, *Cross-Cultural Process in Christian History,* 32.

29. See Mark A. Noll, "Andrew F. Walls: The Missionary Movement in Christian History," *First Things 101* (March 2000): 55–56.

5

Portable Faith
The Global Mission of African Initiated Churches (AICs)

Elias K. Bongmba

African Initiated Churches (AICs) had been part of the global community for nearly half a century when the first African churches were established in Europe. In this chapter I argue that the portability of faith by members of AICs reflects a global mission project of the Christian tradition. The discussion draws from ongoing studies of Christians in the Cameroonian and Nigerian Diaspora in Houston, Texas, focusing on the sense of global mission that characterizes one religious community, the Brotherhood of the Cross and Star. The discussion is a meta-theological exercise that explores the ongoing theological development of this AIC.[1] This theological reflection should be situated alongside theoretical issues in the study of AICs in Africa and the African Diaspora. These issues include the stability and the processes of stabilization of the AIC, the routinization of charisma, ecumenism, millenarianism, and, more recently, diasporization and globalization. It is not possible within the limitations of this chapter to engage in a detailed analysis of these issues, but they provide a theoretical framework for a theological discussion of the sense of global mission claimed by the Brotherhood of the Cross and Star. Of these theoretical concerns, one could argue that the question of stability has run its course because many AICs have survived, thrived, and continue to expand globally. The routinization of charisma has not reached its full potential because leadership in many churches remains in the hands of second- and third-generation leaders who have family ties to the founder of AICs. The stability of the churches not only holds promise for the future of the church but may in a way signal the inevitability of the routinization of charisma. On ecumenism, many of Africa's new churches have played a visible role on the international scene with some joining ecumenical groups. The Kimbangu Church, the Aladura churches, the African Church of Israel Ninevah, and the African Church of the Holy Spirit have been active in the World Council of Churches.[2]

The other theoretical issues that expand the context for the study of AICs are the ideas of Diaspora and globalization. Both concepts speak to transnational movements, particularly at a time when the escalation of marginalization and misery validates the appeal of AICs. Thus, diasporization and globalization offer researchers new tools for the phenomenological analysis of the religious experience of AIC members who now call different Western cities home. By globalization, I refer to the growing interconnectedness of people across national and regional boundaries through information, money, goods, and culture. Religion has been at the forefront of globalization even before the idea was conceptualized with the present emphasis on information technology and economic activities.[3] Both Christianity and Islam have been worldwide movements, defined themselves as such, and set out on a proselytizing project that has linked different parts of the world in a spiritual, economic, social, and often political alliance. New religious movements have also transplanted their faith in different parts of the world and are working hard to gain new members. James Beckford argues that the new movements, which have made contact with other cultural forces, are adapting and actualizing new forms of "global consciousness."[4] Although the new movements have "global aspirations," their "transnational mode of operation" emanates from one country.[5] This is certainly the case with the churches I discuss in this chapter, such as the Brotherhood of the Cross and Star, the Eternal Sacred Order of the Cherubim and Seraphim, and the Redeemed Church of God, which have churches in Houston, Texas, but are all directed from their world headquarters in Nigeria. We can therefore understand their claim that they are merely spreading the word of God as part of a divine mission in light of the global forces that have facilitated movements of ideas, materials, and people around the world.

African presence in the West goes back a long time.[6] As Emmanuel Akyeampong argues, "The exigencies of global capitalism have sucked Africans into a global labor market for the past five centuries: from the slave-worked plantations of the New World to the transitory black laborers who built railroads and other infrastructural developments like the Panama Canal . . . to the African soldiers who fought in both World Wars to the contemporary brain-drain of African professionals and academicians to the West."[7] In recent years, economic difficulties and political violence have intensified the new diasporization of Africa.[8]

Current discussions on the new African Diaspora focus on the departure of intellectuals and highly skilled workers who now provide professional services overseas and teach in universities. The United Nations Development Program (UNDP) reported in 1992 that by 1987 nearly one-third of skilled African workers had moved to Europe, with the Sudan losing 17 percent of its doctors and dentists, 20 percent of its university teaching staff, and 30 percent of its engineers. During the same period, the UNDP report stated, "Africa as a whole is estimated to have lost up to 60,000 middle and high-level managers between 1985 and 1990."[9] Since the 1990s, about 20,000 educated and skilled Africans have left the continent every year.[10] Recent literature on the Diaspora continues to map out trends in African migrations since the publication of *Global Dimensions of African Diaspora*, in 1982.[11] The new migrations have enlarged and expanded the African Diaspora by increasing the numbers in the Black Atlantic as well as by opening up new destinations, such as Australia, Israel, Japan, and New Zealand.[12]

Writing in the special edition of *African Issues*, Uwem E. Ite reports that an estimated 300,000 African professionals live and work in Europe and North America, and figures from the United Nations Educational Scientific and Cultural Organization (UNESCO) indicate that about 30,000 Africans with doctorates live and work outside the continent. It is estimated that about 700 Ghanaian doctors practice in the United States, and about 10,000 Nigerian academics work in the United States.[13] In the same issue, Anthony Barclay argues that the movement of scholars away from Liberia has handicapped the University of Liberia to the extent that in 2001 "70 academic staff members held bachelor's degrees, 107 held master's degrees, and 10 held doctorates."[14] All of this has had a negative effect on stability in Africa.[15] Furthermore, the brain drain has taken away not only intellectuals but also potential politicians and future leaders. This talent cannot be replaced easily, and this loss will have a negative effect on attempts to institute good governance in Africa. In addition to these studies, which highlight the flight of the professional class, other studies demonstrate that the African Diaspora in Europe and the Americas is growing because many ordinary citizens who cannot make it in their home countries are also moving to the northern hemisphere.

The determination of youths in Africa to escape poverty and other sociopolitical problems can be understood only through a comprehensive study of the complexity of international migration networks that have been established recently in most of Africa. These networks promise to take people to the land of their dreams. Nantang Jua has argued that these networks, which offer the many unemployed people in Africa the promise of fulfilling their dreams in Europe, are also part of an ongoing power game that is already familiar to many of the participants who choose to undertake the risk and pay huge sums of money to get to their destination.[16] Promoters of the recent immigration, seeking clientele among youths who are eager to leave, have established a new lucrative industry—demanding large sums of money up front from their clients before embarking on a journey that may not even be successful. The business is also riddled with sexual exploitation, and many of the women end up as sex workers in brothels. The level of desperation is so high that many people I talked to in Cameroon during the summer of 2003 consider this engagement an investment in the future of the women and their families. Jua states that one neighborhood in Geneva is called Evodula, after the village in Lekie Division in Cameroon from which most of the sex workers came. As Jua argues, these recent developments in migrations to the north are indicative of the destructive power relations and consumer culture that have dominated the postcolonial state.

The religious dimension of the new African Diaspora is receiving new attention today, but African Christians have established a presence in the West for several decades. The early churches were started in the United Kingdom in the 1960s, largely by Nigerians. Ter Haar has studied the more recent phenomenon of African churches in the Netherlands, where increasing numbers of immigrants, largely from Ghana, have founded churches.[17] Most of these churches are in Amsterdam, where an estimated forty such churches had been established by 1997. As Africans have moved to Europe in search for a better life, their religious imagination has played a central role in the search for meaning and the construction of identity. Ter Haar problematizes the concept of Diaspora as it is used to describe Africans in Europe, arguing that it is part of an ideological project that has involved a new form of othering and isolation based on contemporary understandings of the term Diaspora itself and related identity labels such as ethnicity and fundamentalism.[18]

Ter Haar states that early African dispersion was forced during slavery, but the recent migration of people out of Africa has largely been voluntary.

As Africans have moved overseas, they have tried to maintain their identity, and religion has played a central role in that process. While many Africans in the new Diaspora identify themselves first as Christians, then as Africans, the public in Europe insists on highlighting the Africanness of their congregations for European racial projects. Since the notion of Diaspora includes a feeling of homesickness and a longing for the homeland and a plan of return, one ought to raise the question of a longing to return in the context of recent debates on the meaning of the African Diaspora. The Africans in Houston may not be going home soon. Ter Haar argues that the future for the African immigrants in Europe, where they have settled and found employment and are raising their families, is not back in Africa. She states, "African Christians in Europe, as far as I have been able to detect, do not look back to the African past while spiritually and physically preparing for their return to the continent of their birth. On the contrary, they are generally forward-looking people who use all their physical and spiritual resources to secure a better future in Europe for themselves and their families."[19]

In my conversations with Cameroonians and Nigerians in the greater Houston area, the comment I hear often is that they came to the United States to get an education and then planned to return home and work to build their own countries, but things changed and soon they realized that they had started families and are now not only attending high school graduations but working hard to send children to college and see them graduate and get into professional schools. Many do not think that they can be very useful at home, largely because they will not be able to provide and support their families as they are able to do now in their new homes. They have settled in their new homes, and many have become citizens. This is not an indication that they have decided to abandon Africa, because there is still a longing for the homeland. First, there are personal ties that they cannot break from easily. Second, they maintain economic ties with their home countries. Third, the new immigrants have also maintained political ties with their home countries. Some of the immigrants are in the United States in exile from their home countries and have remained active as political dissidents.

Although Africans maintain close contact with their home countries, identifying the churches they have established in the Diaspora mainly as "African" ignores other aspects of the mission of the church. My own research in Houston demonstrates that labels are indeed not helpful. There is no doubt that a number of issues converge. The case of Houston-area churches confirms the concerns raised by ter Haar but also highlights dynamics that reflect the local situation in Houston. First, the establishment of immigrant congregations does reflect trends in the recent diasporization of Africans. Many of the members arrived in the United States in the late 1970s following the global economic crises caused by the oil crises of 1973. The financial crises unleashed by the oil crises, in addition to internal dynamics such as political corruption and the decline of the state, forced many Africans to remain in the United States and encouraged a large majority of professionals already in Africa to move to the West. In the wake of this relocation, Africans continued to search for meaning and turned to their religious roots. A large majority of the new immigrants were Muslims and Christians. They brought their faith with them and established Mouride communities in New York and Los Angeles and Christian congregations in New York, Washington, D.C., Dallas, and Houston, among other places.

The rise of African immigrant congregations must be studied in light of the fact that many members of the congregations see their relocation as part of a divine plan that allows them to move with their faith and plant new churches in the West. In this respect, the North is seen not only as offering relief from economic deprivation but also as a place to take a message of hope, and alternative forms of religious expression. The emphasis on missions is not an attempt to deemphasize the "Africanness" of the church or to remove the label AIC. What is involved here is a complex contextualization that calls attention to the historical distinctiveness of AICs, yet points to the universality of the idea of "church" that members of the AIC share with other Christian communities. It is this commitment to universal claims that legitimizes the immigrants' sense of mission, because they see themselves as part of the salvation history and as carriers of a message that is relevant to the whole world. The members of the churches I have studied so far see themselves as part of the church of God because they are committed to Jesus Christ. They do not see themselves as primarily a social agency established to cater to the needs of immigrants from Cameroon or Nigeria. The fact that most of their members come from a particular country or a specific region within a country reflects historical circumstances. Here we must be careful to avoid racializing the religious identity or denying the positive contributions that difference brings to the expression of the Christian faith.

Ebaugh and Chafetz have raised the question of ethnicity by arguing that immigrant congregations employ certain strategies to "reproduce ethnicity." Ethnicity is reproduced when the congregations replicate physical aspects of their religious institutions in their home country or incorporate ethic practices such as holidays and religious ceremonies.[20] In the Nigerian and Cameroonian congregations, there are several reasons one must be cautious when generalizing about ethnicity. First, some of the congregations with a large proportion of Nigerian members do not describe themselves as Nigerian churches, instead presenting themselves as Christians. Evidence for this includes the fact that the two branches of the Eternal Sacred Order of the Cherubim and Seraphim have adopted very general names that reflect their history and the centrality of their ministry rather than the official name of the home churches. The first is called the Mount of Healing, and the second is called the Mount of Salvation. The members of the Brotherhood of the Cross and Star refers to their church by the biblical name Bethel. The Cameroonian congregation is called the Omega Ministries. Several other congregations with a large number of Nigerians call their congregations by general names, such as Our Savior's Church, founded by Dr. Awe.

Second, no strong nationalist sentiments are displayed in the sanctuary or celebrations of the congregations. These congregations do mark the independence days of the respective nations, but they are careful that they do not give the impression that they are politicizing their time of worship. During the 2003 anniversary of Cameroon National Day, immigrants from Cameroon organized a day of prayer and invited speakers to address the political situation in Cameroon. Some of these congregations tend to ignore some cultural celebrations on grounds that these conflict with their faith as Christians. My contention here is that these are conscious attempts to promote a Christian image, rather than an ethnic image. Every time I have visited these congregations, they have stressed the oneness of humanity. They do not see their task as promoting ethnicity. Even when they sing songs composed in Nigerian languages, it is clear that they are only singing hymns that have been part of their faith from the beginning in Nigeria. It is therefore important we also explore theological and missiological categories as we seek to understand AICs in the Diaspora. Both the Eternal Sacred Order of the Cherubim and Seraphim and the Brotherhood of the Cross and Star see the establishment of their churches in the West as promises made to their founders. The branches of well-established churches in Nigeria see their task as a mission enterprise because they have been called to preach the gospel in every corner of the world.

Let us take the example of the Brotherhood of the Cross and Star in Houston, a messianic religious movement that started in Nigeria, to illustrate the argument that AICs in the Diaspora see themselves as part of the global mission of the church. The Brotherhood of the Cross and Star is a controversial case study because its detractors often criticize the church for being more devoted to their founder, Olumba Olumba Obu, than to Jesus of God. [21] My concern here is to address not issues of orthodoxy but their sense of Christian mission.

The Brotherhood of the Cross and Star in Houston

The leader of the Brotherhood of the Cross and Star, Olumba Olumba Obu, sent pastors to start churches in North America in 1972. One of the earliest schisms in the movement resulted from conflict between two pastors fighting for control of the congregation in the United States.[22] The Houston Bethel was established in 1988 and currently rents a facility in the southwest area of Houston.[23] In keeping with the traditions of the Brotherhood, the doors of the Bethel are always open for worship, prayer, and fellowship. Most members fast, maintaining a vegetarian diet in accordance with the teachings of the Holy Father, Olumba Olumba Obu.[24]

The first members of the Houston Bethel came to the United States as students on student visas. Today, most of the members of the Houston Bethel hold bachelor's degrees or advanced degrees, and some currently attend professional schools. The beginnings of the movement in Nigeria are a subject of interest because the precise life story of the founder, Olumba Olumba Obu, is not well known, as Friday Mbon relates in his sympathetic account of the movement.[25] Olumba Olumba Obu was born in 1918. His father, Olumba Obu, was a member of the Presbyterian Church.[26] This was the year of the epidemic, which Olumba Olumba interprets as the cleansing movement of the Spirit. Many do not know very much about his early life because he moved from his birthplace, Biakpan, to Calabar. Biakpan, the city of his birth, has since become an important place and is called by some "the New Jerusalem."[27] Olumba Olumba Obu received revelation when he was only five years old, at which time he began to lead prayers and teach his age mates to love one another. Also early in life, he performed his first miracle by resuscitating a woman. He attributed his powers to the one who sent him, God.[28] Amadi reports that he predicted things that would happen to people in the future.[29] We have only sketchy information about his early education, which included only four years of formal schooling. He received no formal theological training. Mbon indicates that Olumba remembers only a relative teaching him a song from the Efik hymnbook, titled "Breathe on Me Breath of God."[30]

Olumba continued to preach about love, a practice that has been a hallmark of his movement in Calabar. He was an honest businessperson and won the respect of many people in this Nigerian town. In 1942, at age 26, he gave up business to answer a call to full-time service and thus started what would become the Brotherhood movement in Calabar. He has consistently pointed out that the movement has no specific beginning or end, thus emphasizing the eternality of the movement. His first meeting and ministry space was located at number 35 Wilki Street in Calabar—a house that belonged to one of his followers. Olumba Obu participated in development projects with members of his hometown but faced opposition and left the organization, and he has not returned to his place of birth since January 1956. He devoted his time to preaching, registered his movement, and was granted a certificate of incorporation in 1964 by the Federal Government of Nigeria. The movement was known as "Christ's Universal Spiritual School of Practical Christianity" but was later renamed the Brotherhood of the Cross and Star. The Brotherhood stands for the oneness of all created by God. It signifies love of and for all people.[31] The cross symbolizes the sufferings of Jesus for humanity, and the star stands for Christ's victory over death and sin as well as being a symbol of the reward that will be given.[32] On August 6, 1980, the Movement relocated to its present home at 34 Ambo Street in Calabar.

The Brotherhood Movement has an organizational structure that resembles African hierarchies.[33] Despite this fact, Olumba Olumba Obu insists that there is no hierarchy in the movement because no one is superior in the service of God. The leadership structure has at its helm Olumba Olumba Obu, called "The Father," as the Sole Spiritual Leader. The rest of the leadership structure consists of the Leader's representatives, appointed with the approval of Olumba Olumba Obu, to represent him in different Bethels.[34] Bishops are ordained and preside over a diocese that has about ten districts. They are identified by a purple girdle worn on their official vestments. Very few people have been ordained as bishops, and Mbon and Amadi suggest that this points to the significance of this office. I should also point out that all the ordained bishops are men. Women hold offices, preach, and teach in the Houston Bethel, but it remains to be seen if women will be ordained as bishops in the movement.[35]

The local Bethels have elders who are appointed with the approval of Father Obu, who then sends a representative to ordain the newly appointed elder. The elder is in charge of the physical wellbeing of the local Bethel. The Brotherhood leadership also includes two groups of prophets and prophetesses, divided according to seniority. They wear girdles made of different colors, and they hold office for life and function in that office everywhere they go. Their main task is itinerant evangelism. The movement also has senior pastors, as well as pastors, who wear black girdles and carry out the pastoral functions of the Bethel. The movement has a pastoral hierarchy organized as follows: state pastors, divisional pastors, district pastors, area or zone pastors, and local Bethel pastors. Other offices include senior and junior apostles, deacons, deaconesses, and evangelists, all of whom wear red girdles. Their task is the proclamation of the gospel.[36] If one were to construct a hierarchy, it would look like this. At the top, we have the Sole Spiritual Leader (also called Father), Olumba Olumba Obu, followed by the Leader's representatives, bishops, and elders. These are followed by the senior prophets and prophetesses, prophets and prophetesses, senior pastors, pastors, senior apostles, senior deacons, senior deaconesses, senior evangelists, apostles, deacons, deaconesses, and evangelists. One might then add below the spirited children, choristers, congregation, and children.[37]

Mbon points out that "Leader Obu occupies a special position as the movement's main and infallible interpreter of values. Members' belief in the effectiveness of his prayers and healing, and their conviction of his deity and consequent purity of life add up to legitimize Leader Obu's central position in the movement. . . . Leader Obu is the movement and the movement is Leader Obu."[38] Others argue that this centrality is clearly demonstrated by the fact that Leader Obu is taken to be God the Father incarnate; the title "Father" "define[s] his role as the cosmic leader, and teacher of everything in heaven and earth, with no deputy or assistant."[39] Local Bethels have within them fellowships and associations to coordinate the activities of the movement. The highest policy group of the movement is the Spiritual Council, which was instituted December 24, 1966.[40] The future structure of the movement will depend on the way the routinization of the leader's charisma evolves.[41] However, Mbon points out that the leader has jurisdictional authority and has transferred functional authority to local Bethel leaders such as the Houston Bethel, where local leaders make decisions on their activities in consultation with the U.S. hierarchy and Father Obu.[42]

The central teachings and doctrines of the Movement include a strong emphasis on love, which the Leader considers to be the basis of the movement and its teaching around the world.[43] Adherents regard the Bible as primary revelation, but there is more emphasis on the New Testament, and, even here, one gets the impression that it is the gospels and the book of revelation that are most important.[44] Mbon argues that Father Obu teaches that God is human and spirit and holds to a complicated pantheism that is often mistaken for polytheism.[45] He professes a dualism of good and evil but subordinates evil to good because he believes that behind every evil, there is an opportunity for something good and that God will always enable believers to overcome evil. Olumba Olumba Obu teaches that Christ is the only path to salvation and insists on this. However, as Mbon points out, Obu also teaches that Christ became a sinner in taking on himself the sins of the world.[46] It is a complicated teaching because the incarnation of God on earth also includes Obu's presence here on earth.[47] He teaches a holistic salvation that includes deliverance from all infirmities and sins.[48] Olumba Olumba Obu recognizes the Holy Spirit as the third person of the Trinity, but that third person has now come to the earth to reside among people in the person of Olumba Olumba Obu. This has prompted a debate about the deification of Olumba Olumba Obu. Mbon argues that in many ways Father Obu and members believe that he is the incarnation of God here on earth.[49] This brings up the issue of millennialism and messianism.

Olumba Olumba Obu's millennial vision is tied together with his mission on earth, which is to transform this world to usher in the reign of God.[50] Mbon points out that Father Obu predicted that the new reign of God could occur sometime between 1999 and 2001. Leader Obu's role is messianic because he is the one who would usher in this reign of God. "My mission is to establish the new Kingdom of God on earth, so that the will of God may be done on earth as it is done in heaven."[51] His vision is more of a transformation rather than a catastrophic end of times. Olumba Olumba Obu's millennialism falls into a second-stage category described by Bryan Wilson, who argues that "when the dream of a transformed social order, a millennium that will come into being by magic gradually undergoes mutation to become a new world to be planned, to be discussed by rational procedures, and to be worked for . . . one sees the secularization of the revolutionist worldview."[52] In the case of Olumba Olumba Obu, what we see is not an overt secularization or a programmatic and structured control to bring about the millennium. Instead, the transformation to the millennial age will be marked by a reign of love, and all who do not posses this love will not participate in the life of this new community. Obu states, "The reign of our Lord Jesus Christ begins fully in 2001. . . . From 2001, all different governments of the world will surrender their governments to our Lord Jesus Christ."[53] According to the beliefs of the movement, the headquarters of the new order will be Biakpan, the birthplace of Olumba Olumba Obu.[54]

Although I have not provided a detailed discussion of his eschatology, Obu's teachings are similar to, but different from, some of the millennial movements studied by Catherine Wessinger and scholars who see millennialism as movements that express "human hope for achievement of permanent well-being, in other words, salvation." Wessinger argues that, in general, catastrophic millennialism hold that this present order will be destroyed either by human or divine agents and the elect will be saved, while progressive millennialism proclaims that the kingdom of God will be ushered in gradually as humans collaborate with a divine or superhuman agency. What is different here is that the Brotherhood does not advocate violence in any form. The Brotherhood is more of a progressive millennial movement whose leadership combines what Wessinger describes as ideological, charismatic, and prophetic powers. [55] The movement's position is close to what in systematic theology is described as postmillennialism.

Daily life in Houston is a spiritual and existential engagement for members of the Brotherhood. Elijah, another member of the Houston Bethel, views his life in the Diaspora as a member of the Brotherhood in these terms. Brother Elijah knows that he cannot be put in one box because of his various identities. He is a Nigerian who is dedicated to keeping some of the best traditions of Nigeria. He is an active member of the Umunnabuike social club, whose members are drawn from Imo State. The group emphasizes unity, service, love, mutual support, and help for one another in this "wilderness." Their name means that one tree cannot make a forest. Elijah also switched college majors from architecture to healthcare. His wife, Maria, is a nurse. He is proud to be a Nigerian, and he believes that all that is wrong with Nigeria today can be changed by the grace of God. Brother Elijah is not bothered by the false images that people have of Nigerians. "I know a lot of good Nigerians who have proven themselves to be good and decent people."[56] Brother Elijah thinks that there is something about Nigeria and Nigerians that fuels such false stories: "The Nigerian character has a zeal to accomplish something. Many times this makes them work hard to achieve their aspirations so that they can be the best. Many of them will not rest until they accomplish their goal and human tendency being what it is, some tend to do it by any means." He reflects on the relationship between Africans and African Americans, pointing out that both communities are victims of uncritical assumptions.[57]

Brother Elijah says that the Brotherhood is at the *core*[58] of an individual's experience: "It helps you come to grips [with] the fact of your existence as a human being." He describes the Brotherhood as a journey that has started, continues daily, and will take one to his ultimate goal in life. This is a teleological perspective that underscores the view that the Brotherhood is a way of life. Furthermore, he argues that the Brotherhood is the energy that is at the center of one's life and journey. It is deep inside and provides a sense of purpose. One cannot be tired because of the knowledge that one is working and walking with the Supreme Being who is here to bestow this energy. One relies on the power that is in the spirit of the Brotherhood to do all the tangible and intangible things of life. "The Brotherhood experience is a gradual, dynamic movement" that each one of us has to undertake. He continues,

> It is a concrete experience because you can always feel the energy that is there with you, at home, work, school, and everywhere you go. If this experience were with you only in the Bethel, there will be nothing different about The Brotherhood. It will then just become another religion like all the others.

The reference to religion is an important issue for Brother Elijah because he was raised in the Seventh-Day Adventist Church in Nigeria. He was active in the church and in his secondary school days, serving as the president of the Scripture Union. He heard about the Brotherhood and the Father. He heard all the miracles and saw the work of the Father. Brother Elijah attributes his decision to join the movement to the miracles of Olumba Olumba Obu, but, more important, to the theological consistency in the teachings and actions of the Father. He was surprised at the visions of the Father, the fact that he can heal and knows all about a person before the person comes to see him. But the critical theological issue for Brother Elijah and his litmus test for the movement was that the Father did all of this in the name of Jesus. The Father testifies that Jesus is the Son of God. Brother Elijah argues that this is the test set by the apostle

Paul. Some core issues bind members of the Brotherhood together as a diasporic community. The issues that they all seem to deal with as individuals and as members of the community include the question of borders, the quest for economic success, and concerns about the fate of Nigeria and Africa. In the sections that follow, I discuss these common concerns and the Brotherhood's theological vision, which provides an orientation for members to respond to these issues.

The Brotherhood and Its Universal Message

The development of the mission phase of the Brotherhood has grown with the church. Several years ago, Rosalind Hackett argued that migration, development projects, and active evangelism had helped spread the teachings of the church to other states in Nigeria, as well as neighboring countries such as Gabon, Cameroon, and Liberia. Branches were also established in the United States, Britain, Germany, India, Trinidad, and the former Soviet Union.[59] In addition to evangelism, Obu has engaged in an active social ministry in Calabar and has won the hearts of many. However, his most distinctive claim is that he sees the community as a new kingdom, which was to be fulfilled in 2001. Members of the Brotherhood demonstrate an attitude toward borders that is in keeping with their vision of the world and theology. Their Spiritual Father has made it possible for them to cross all borders for his glory. A key issue for members of the new African Diaspora who have crossed borders is one's visa status in the United States. Most people do not talk about their status; however, members of the Brotherhood do not have a problem talking about it, emphasizing that they always keep their records up to date.

In an interview I conducted with Sister Miriam in 1998, she indicated that she believes that the Father intervenes in all her travels and passport issues. She went to England in 1981 and remained there for four years. When the time came for her to renew her travel papers, the authorities asked her to submit letters from her religious leaders in Nigeria. She wrote a letter, sent it in the morning, and late that evening received a response from Leader Obu, who reassured her that she would get her papers because God has chosen the foolishness of Africa to confound the mighty and wise people of the world.[60] She eventually obtained her visa, and it was later renewed, permitting her to stay indefinitely. "The Father himself was there with me, opening the doors." She subsequently traveled to Holland and Germany before returning to Calabar. She thought she was done, but the Father told her that America needed to have the same spirit. "America needs you. My children in America are writing to me about it." Sister Miriam found herself in Washington, D.C., in the early 1990s. Since her mission was clear, she did not need an attorney to work out the details of her travels and stay in the United States. Instead, she believes, the Father opened the door again for her. Other members of the Brotherhood in Houston similarly express a lack of difficulty dealing with borders and papers.

The theological vision that helps members deal with life in a new society is that of the Brotherhood as a universal fellowship.[61] They believe that they have a mission to communicate the incarnation of God on earth today in the person of Leader Obu, who has come to fulfill the promise of Christ and bring peace on earth. Writings from the church are often dedicated "To the sole Spiritual Head of the Universe, Leader Olumba Olumba Obu, the entire Holy Family and the true believers of the physical manifestation of the supreme God Head on earth."[62] This universal (global) perspective is different from that of some of the new religious movements in Africa. Most of Africa's initiated churches have been engaged in a contextual praxis aimed at incarnating Christ and the Christian church for their African locality. The Brotherhood of the Cross and Star has a different vision. Its leader is referred to as the sole representative of God on earth, and 34 Ambo Street is the location of the world headquarters of the Brotherhood of the Cross and Star. Members claim that the light that has come to the world in these last days radiates from there to all places in the world.

The Brotherhood has embarked on a vigorous missionary program to spread the teachings of the Father, which it emphasizes calls people to faith in Christ around the world.[63] Members of the Houston Bethel see themselves as part of this worldwide movement and for that reason say that they do not think that they are in a strange place or land. On the basis of this teaching, they would object to the designation of the Brotherhood of Cross and Star as an African Initiated Church. Such a geographical restriction is not consistent with the revelation that their Holy Father has received. They feel at home here. It does not mean that they do not find aspects of American culture strange. Daily routines such as managing schedules, family, community activities, and services at and for the Bethel are demanding and challenging. Members have been subjected to police power. Hence, they joke with each other about traveling safely and not being stopped by the "cops." They are keenly aware of the gun violence that is ever-present in a city like Houston. Some of them have had coworkers killed by gun violence. However, the Father enables them to overcome these challenges.

We have in the Brotherhood of the Cross and Star a unique response to globalization and transnational identities. Members of the Brotherhood say their critics who suspect that a Christian movement with a global impact cannot come out of Africa are wrong. It is too early to gauge the impact of this mission because one has to wait for the movement to routinize. However, the critique that a grandiose message that claims that God has been incarnated in these last days in Africa cannot be taken seriously for now seems to be made in haste. Regardless of one's views about the movement, the Brotherhood promises to develop a vision and staying power.[64]

The Message to the World Is Love and the Coming Theocracy

In a world where all people face the temptation to grasp power and wealth, what is the proper action by believers, especially as they struggle in the Diaspora? The Holy Father guides his followers in these last days to live in peace, and this will come if people love one another. The community takes interpersonal relationships seriously. When I first arrived at the home of one of the members, Sister Miriam, Sister Genevieve was there, and both of them greeted me with the greeting "The peace of the Father be with you." This is a standard greeting of the Brotherhood, which is extended to all people. In my conversations with them, it has become very clear that they believe that peace begins when individuals receive the love of God through "our Lord Jesus Christ" (another standard expression of the Brotherhood) and that such love (*ima*), demonstrated in the Father's actions, must be passed on to other people.[65]

The call to love is spelled out in the Father's teachings, published in a collection of sermons titled *The 3rd Covenant*.[66] In the section titled "The Reign of Love by 2000 A.D.,"[67] Obu argues that followers of the Brotherhood should let love engulf the entire universe. All things in the world amount to nothing without love. Anyone who claims to love God and does not have love is false. He argues that Jesus introduced love to the world and manifested it better than any other person. The Father's statement here is one with which many Christians would concur because the teaching of the Christian Church has been that Jesus is love. According to

Obu, then, to follow Christ is to practice love, and "the only existing law in the kingdom of God is brotherly love."

Drawing from the first lesson, the Father argues that love is fragile and will break if it falls on the ground. Love is also light, and "without it you cannot see. You become decomposed and useless anytime you in indulge in falsehood."[68] Love is the only key to the kingdom of God, where distinction based on sex, age, or race is ruled out. The Father uses military images to convey the power of love: "Love is the supreme commander of heaven and earth. . . . Love is God. . . . What we call the world is an overflow of the love of God arranged in artistic perfection." The Holy Spirit has come down to fulfill, and teach people about, the love of God.[69]

Obu tells his followers that God who is love requires that his children be faithful and avoid theft, fornication, hate, and other malicious acts. God's love cannot be manifested in the world today because people refuse to follow God's truth. He restates his authority by arguing that, regardless of what the critics say, the Brotherhood of the Cross and Star presents direct teaching by the Spirit himself, who has come down in our day: "The Brotherhood of the Cross and Star is the last hope of man. . . . The Brotherhood of the Cross and Star is the center of love. It is a place where the Almighty God dwells and where judgment shall be delivered to all creation. . . . The Brotherhood is the new ark of Noah, and it is the last opportunity for you to save yourself."[70] Obu states that those who lack love will be eliminated, regardless of their religious persuasion, and at the time of writing he predicted that those who refuse to show love would not exist by the year 2000 A.D.

The Brotherhood of the Cross proclaims that a theocracy is needed today to change the destructive course of the world. Members of the new African Diaspora have ongoing ties at home, where their interest in social transformation begins. Members of the Houston Bethel stand in a dialectical relationship with their new home, Houston, and their respective places of origin in Nigeria. In addition to the ties with their headquarters in Calabar and the songs that they sing in the Ibo and Efick languages, this generation of the Brotherhood in Houston maintains close relationships with families in Nigeria. Members often travel back and forth between Nigeria and Houston. Several are associated with Nigerian community organizations in Houston. They often reflect on the crises of corruption in Nigeria and Africa, which has forced many of them into exile. In response to the growing crises in Africa, the Holy Father teaches that theocracy is the only solution to the problems the world faces today.

In *Theocracy: The Only Way Out,* Olumba Olumba Obu proclaims that the world needs one leader, government, currency, belief, and kingdom. This bold statement responds to the crises in Nigeria, Africa, and the so-called New World Order declared by former U.S. President George H. W. Bush.[71] The preface shows clearly that because the human project, democracy, which falls under the permissive will of God, has failed, it is time for humankind to surrender and give God the chance to rule.[72] Introducing the message, Brother Udoaka Ekepeanang states that Jesus came into the world to teach that God expects humans to love one another and to start a new renaissance.[73] Before returning to heaven, Jesus promised that the Holy Spirit will reconstruct the world and build God's kingdom on earth. The Holy Spirit is now present in a morally barren world to teach universal love to people of all races so that a new world will emerge. This introduction also gives a sketch of this new rule, which I quote in its entirety because it is an encompassing project.

> There will be nothing like democracy or politics. The government of the world will be under the Father, and the new world ideology will be theocracy. Theocracy is the government of god by god and for the elect of God. Man will kill and make war no more and so there will be peace everywhere . . . there will be no passports, visas, immigration or customs. There will be no more wars. Everybody will be law abiding and peaceful. Thus there will be no military, police or paramilitary units anywhere in the world. You will have a European mayor in Kenya, a Nigerian as Governor in America, an American as President anywhere in Asia, an African as head of State in Europe or America and so on. In essence when you talk about the New World Order you talk about love and Oneness of the human race, a new order with one faith, one hope, one love and one people with no division or barriers, strife or discrimination, one language, one currency, one mind, sharing everything in common, living in righteousness and perfection, one baptism. and one God the Father who is in all and through all and above all.[74]

The outline of the new theocratic government is introduced by a sermon titled "Change of Baton: From Democracy to Theocracy," which highlights faith. The Centurion had faith and believed that Jesus needed to say just a word for his child to be healed. The application for the world today is "Salvation is not a matter of seeing before believing, it is a matter of faith. There is no need for anyone to want to come to 34 Ambo Street to see the Father, to have audience with Him or for Him to place His hands on one's head and pray. Stay where you are, whether in your house or inside a hole, and you will feel His impact only if you believe."[75]

Olumba responds to his critics this way:

> The world vilified The Brotherhood of the Cross and Star calling us various names ranging from a vampire organization, worshipers of mammon, a group of infidels and anti-Christs. But today the truth has uncovered . . . that [the Brotherhood] is the only source of salvation. God himself being all-knowing and powerful has known the rebellious nature of man towards the truth . . . all we need to do now is to believe in Him for our salvation.[76]

At first one has the impression that the Brotherhood attributes the mighty works of God unfolding in the world today to Olumba. But one also has to consider this disclaimer before one reaches that conclusion: "It is not Olumba who is doing the works in this kingdom but the Father."[77] Olumba Olumba Obu proclaims that there will be a reign of peace. The example that is cited is that Father Obu has "decreed" that there will be no more military coups in Nigeria. "Ever since the Father made the pronouncement all coup attempts have been abortive and those involved crushed. The soldiers themselves are marching back to their barracks once and for all and never to rule Nigeria again."[78] Olumba Olumba Obu is critical of the situation in Nigeria, where greed has led to the proliferation of local and state government and weakened a nation that was once united and strong. "The story of local government councils is even more pitiable. There is corruption and looting of the sick and homeless. . . . Nigeria, and indeed Africa is so richly blessed by God. But the administrators of those resources squander and destroy them."[79] The preacher then argues that America has not succeeded in creating democracy around the world. Peace will come only when God's appointed people who are righteous, truthful, and obedient rule the world. Building on the text "Except the Lord build the house, they labor in vain that build it, except the Lord keep the city, the watchman waketh but in vain," from Psalm 127:1, the preacher argues that "it is the responsibility of the Father to install the right candidate for His choice."[80] This section of the sermon closes by arguing that Jesus Christ is the way, the truth: "The rulership of the Holy Spirit brings peace, joy and prosperity. No government run by man will ever work well. In God's case, there will be one government under one rulership and one people. We are all one. Live and let others live too is the golden rule."[81]

There is no doubt that the Church sees itself as an agent of the coming theocracy. The leader urges all people not only to pay their tithes but, more important, to "rush for baptism into the Brotherhood of the Cross and Star. Any country that wants to survive must take directives from the Holy Spirit now on Earth."[82] At first reading, this might sound like the appeals of televangelists who, after indicting the present generation, close their sermons by inviting listeners to join or stand with them in this mission to change the world by sending in a gift. Evangelists also often promise to send to the givers by return mail their own recipe for solving the problems of the world. However, it is also possible to consider this teaching of the coming theocracy in light of the Brotherhood's message of love and practical Christianity. The Father claims to be the Holy Spirit on earth. He has been sent not to condemn anyone who claims to be Christian but to point the path to the truth. All the things people attempt to do on earth will be worthless if they do not take this path. There is no doubt that the members of the movement think that the crises of the world today can be solved only through a spiritual renewal in which the Brotherhood will be at the center. It is this teaching that provides a sense of focus for the members of the Houston Bethel.

Conclusion

I have argued that members of AICs in the Diaspora see themselves as part of the Christian Church's global mission agenda. The Houston Bethel of the Brotherhood of the Cross and Star, which considers itself a universal school for practical Christianity, demonstrates this sense of mission by preaching a gospel of love and proclaiming the coming of a theocracy as the only solution to the current global crisis of leadership. The Houston Bethel continues to practice the teachings of its founder, Olumba Olumba Obu, and to use his teachings to survive and thrive under new circumstances in Houston. Members believe that their Leader is God's only representative on earth, who enables them to deal with daily issues such as border crossings. He teaches them to love one another because love is the only thing that will outlast all that one achieves in life. Finally, they believe that the institution of a theocracy is the only thing that will solve the crises that the world is going through today. Their Leader, Olumba Olumba Obu, has come into the world in these last days to prepare the world for such a transformation. The implications of this teaching is something that can be worked out only in the future, but, for now, we can point out that clearly the new African Diaspora includes people who seek comfort from the teachings of Olumba Olumba Obu, who founded the Brotherhood movement as a universal school for practical Christianity.

Members of the Houston Bethel carry out Father Obu's teachings in various ways. First, they emphasize love among people. In the three years that I have attended services with them, the preachers have talked of love, pointing out that believers should love one another. They have urged members to forgive one another in the spirit of love and put away judgmental spirit from their midst. They do not have a communion as other Christian groups do but do have a "love feast," food that has been prepared by members of the group, which they share at the end of the service. This feast creates and solidifies their love and bonding with one another. Second, they count on the leader of the Brotherhood, Father Olumba Olumba Obu, to protect them every day. They believe that he is with them, even here in Houston, and that nothing can stand in their way. All they need to do is to continue to serve him faithfully and be prepared for him to lead them, because he can appear to an individual at any time. Third, consistent with their belief that human beings have corrupted this world and that only a theocracy can rescue the world today from decay, they talk constantly about the economic situation in Nigeria and other African countries, emphasizing that Olumba Olumba Obu has come in these last days to proclaim repentance and faith in Jesus so that all people can turn to God, who will establish the theocracy. There are millennial overtones in this message, but it points to a worldly peace and justice. Last, members of the Houston Bethel believe that they are at home wherever their Holy Father, Olumba Olumba Obu, has sent them. They may have been born in Nigeria and have relatives there, but they consider that they are at home wherever the Father sends them to go and preach.

The fact that people who were born in Nigeria and have immigrated to the United States consider such a move the work of God and an act of obedience to their Spiritual Father can be interpreted in several ways. First, this is a theological statement, which transforms the movement from a regional spiritual organization in southeastern Nigeria into a worldwide movement. Their members can settle anywhere in the world to carry out the mission of the movement. The presence of God and their Spiritual Father is with them. Second, to be away from home and remain engaged with things happening at home in Nigeria, yet feel at home in the new country because it is God's will and the will of the Father could also be interpreted as a political statement that calls into question artificial boundaries. Although many of the members deal with an enormous amount of paperwork to regulate their status as immigrants in the United States, they believe that it is just a matter of time until all boundaries are eliminated. Third, feeling at home in a new land expresses a new eschatological attitude. The millennial era, according to Olumba Olumba Obu, will be ushered in soon. It will be a theocracy, and, since God will rule, national boundaries will not be important. All of the children of God who practice love are part of this millennial reign, and they can live any way they choose to live. Finally, the view that it is God's will for them to feel at home here in Houston is, in essence, a missiological statement. The members of the movement are here on a mission—to carry the will of the Father in evangelizing the world in preparation for the new millennial order that will usher in God's reign.

Notes

1. One of the first studies of the theology of an AIC was done by Gerhardus Oosthuizen in his study of the theology of the Nazareth church of Isaiah Shembe. See Gerhardus Cornelis Oosthuizen, *The Theology of a South African Messiah: An Analysis of the Hymnal of "The Church of the Nazaritese"* (Leiden: E. J. Brill, 1969).

2. Marie France and Perrin Jassy, *La Communauté de Base dans les Eglises Africaines,* Series II, vol. 3 (Bandundu, Zaire: Centre d'Etudes Ethnologiques, 1970), 86–77.

3. See the early serious attempts to link religion to globalization by Roland Robertson, "Globalization, Politics and Religion," in J. A. Beckford and T. Lackmann, eds., *The Changing Face of Religion* (London: Sage, 1989), 10–23; Roland Robertson and J. Chirico, "Humanity, Globalization and Worldwide Religious Resurgence: A Theoretical Exploration," in *Sociological Analysis* 46 (1985): 219–242; Roland Robertson, *Globalization: Social Theory and Global Culture* (London: Sage, 1992); Peter Beyer, *Religion and Globalization* (London: Sage, 1994); A. Geertz, ed., *New Religions and Globalization: Theoretical and Methodological Perspectives* (Aarhus, Denmark: Aarhus University Press, 2003); J. A. Beckford, "New Religious Movements and Globalization," in P. C. Lucas and T. Robbins, eds., *New Religious Movements in the 21st Century: Legal, Political, and Social Challenges in Global Perspective* (New York: Routledge Press, 2004), 253–264.

4. Beckford, "New Religious Movements and Globalization," 255.

5. Ibid., 257.

6. Ivan van Sertima has argued that blacks arrived in the New World before Columbus. Ivan van Sertima, *They Came Before Columbus: The African Presence in Ancient America* (New York: Random House, 2003).

7. Emmanuel Akyeampong, "Africans in the Diaspora: The Diaspora and Africa," *African Affairs* 99 (2000): 186.

8. Elisha Stephen Atieno-Odhiambo, "Hegemonic Enterprises and Instrumentalities of Survival: Ethnicity and Democracy in Kenya," in *African Affairs* 61, no. 2 (2002): 228. There are several examples where this has taken place in Africa. For example, in 1982, when political activists planned to launch a new political party in Kenya, President Daniel Arap Moi pursued activists, imprisoning some, declared some university professors subversive, and rushed through an amendment in parliament declaring that Kenya was a one-party state. Moi accused the professors of teaching the "politics of subversion majoring in violence. The president vowed to root out plotters from within the Kenyan nation." For an account of this incident see B. A. Ogot, "The Politics of Populism," in B. A. Ogot and W. R. Ochieng,' eds., *Decolonization and Independence in Kenya 1940–93* (Athens: University of Ohio Press, 1995).

9. United Nations Development Programme (UNDP), *Human Development Report 1992* (New York: Oxford University Press, 1992), 56–57.

10. Paul Tiyambe Zeleza and Cassandra R. Veney, "Editor's Introduction," in "The African 'Brain Drain' to the North: Pitfalls and Possibilities," *African Issues* 30, no. 1 (2002): 1–2.

11. Joseph E. Harris, ed., *Global Dimensions of the African Diaspora* (Washington, D.C.: Howard University Press, 1982). In addition to conferences, there are now journals that address issues affecting members of the growing African Diaspora.

12. Ibid., 183.

13. Uwem E. Ite, "Turning Brain Drain into Brain Gain: Personal Reflections on Using the Diaspora Option," *African Issues* 30, no. 1 (2003): 76–80.

14. Anthony Barclay, "The Political Economy of Brain Drain at Institutions of Higher Learning in Conflict Countries: Case of the University of Liberia," *African Issues.* 30, no. 1 (2002): 42–46.

15. Samuel Atteh, "The Crisis in Higher Education in Africa," *African Issues* 24, no.1 (1996): 36–42.

16. Nantang Jua, "Differential Responses to Disappearing Transitional Pathways: Redefining Possibility Among Cameroonian Youths," *African Studies Review* 46, no. 2 (2002): 23–25.

17. Gerrie ter Haar, "African Churches in the Netherlands," in G. ter Haar, ed., *Religious Communities in the Diaspora* (Nairobi, Kenya: Acton Press, 2001), 156.

18. Ibid., 42–43.

19. Ibid., 51.

20. Helen R. Ebaugh and Janet S. Chafetz, *Religion and the New Immigrants: Continuities and Adaptations in Immigrant Congregations* (Walnut Creek, Calif.: Alta Mira Press, 2000), 385–407.

21. Elias K. Bongmba, "The Brotherhood of Cross and Star: Houston Bethel," unpublished paper, 2001.

22. Essien A. Offiong, "Schism and Religious Independency in Nigeria: The Case of the Brotherhood of the Cross and Star," in Rosalind Hackett, ed., *New Religious Movements in Nigeria* (Lewiston: Edwin Mellen Press, 1987), 180.

23. Another African Initiated Church, the Cherubim and Seraphim Movement, which started in Nigeria, also rents property in the same business complex.

24. The Father tells members in *The 3rd Covenant* that a true vegetarian diet is a mark of spirituality. Olumba Olumba Obu, *The 3rd Covenant* (Calabar, Nigeria: Everlasting Gospel Center, 1997), 39.

25. Mbon argues that the biographies of other religious founders in Nigeria, such as Josaiah Oshitelu, Moses Orimolade, and Captain Mrs. Christinah Abiodun Emmanuel, are well known to scholars. See Friday Mbon, *Brotherhood of the Star and Cross: A New Religious Movement in Nigeria* (New York: Peter Lang, 1992), 20. See Harold Turner, *African Independent Church, Vol. 1: History of an African Independent Church, The Church of the Lord Aladura* (Oxford: Clarendon, 1967); J. Akinyele Omoyajowo, *Cherubim and Seraphim: The History of an African Independent Church* (New York: NOK Publishers, 1982); G. I. S. Amadi, "'The New World Order': The Brotherhood of the Cross and Star's Perspective," in Christopher Fyfe and Andre Walls, eds., Christianity in Africa in the 1990s (Edinburgh: Centre of African Studies, University of Edinburgh, 1996), 149–160.

26. I am indebted to Mbon for this account of the early beginnings of the movement. See Mbon, *Brotherhood of the Star and Cross,* 24.

27. The name of this town is cloaked in mystery because people use the Efik derivation of it, "Obio Akpan Abasi," to refer to it as "the city of the first Son of God." See Mbon, *Brotherhood of the Star and Cross,* 21.

28.Ibid., 25–27.

29. G. I. S. Amadi, "Power and Purity: A Comparative Study of Two Prophetic Churches in Southeastern Nigeria," Ph.D. dissertation, University of Manchester, 1982. Olumba Olumba Obu has a unique ability to predict political events in Nigeria. During periods of political crisis, many people, including politicians, have sought his opinion and advice.

30. Mbon, *Brotherhood of the Star and Cross,* 30.

31. Ibid., 39; Rosalind Hackett, *Religion in Calabar: The Religious Life and History of a Nigerian Town* (Berlin and New York: Mouton de Gruyter, 1989), 186.

32. See the sermon delivered by Olumba Olumba Obu titled "What Is the Brotherhood?" in Olumba Olumba Obu, *What Is the Brotherhood? What Is Cross? What Is Star?* (Calabar, Nigeria: Brotherhood Press), 2.

33. Olumba Olumba Obu has stated: "As the secular government is hierarchically arranged, so is the government of the Kingdom of God arranged. In the house of God the same system of government is adopted." See Brotherhood of the

Cross and Star, *The Elder's Handbook,* vol. 30 (Calabar, Nigeria: Brotherhood Press, n.d.), 31.

34. Mbon describes the office this way. "A Leader's representative may be appointed to be in charge of a Bethel, a district, a division, an area, or a zone, as those territories are defined in BCS organizational structure. In all cases, all other officers in each of those territories are under the Leader's representative in that territory and are accountable to him or her." Mbon, *Brotherhood of the Star and Cross,* 55.

35. Women play a more significant role in the African Initiated Churches in which they were cofounders. See Akin Omoyajowo, "The Aladura Churches in Nigeria Since Independence," in E. Fashole-Luke, R. Gray, A. Hastings and G. Taasie, eds., *Christianity in Independent Africa* (Bloomington: Indiana University Press, 1978), 96–110; See also K. A. Opoku, "Changes Within African Christianity: The Case of Musama Disco Christo Church," in Fashole-Luke et al., eds., *Christianity in Independent Africa,* 111–121; Tim Allen, "Understanding Alice: Uganda's Holy Spirit Movement in Context," *Africa: Journal of the International African Institute* 61, no. 3 (1991): 270–299. However, it must be pointed out that the role of women in most of these independent churches remains marginal. When the churches started to grow and expand, the men usually took over the important leadership positions from women. For further analysis see Mary Farrell Bednarowski, "Outside the Mainstream: Women's Religion and Women Religious Leaders in the Nineteenth Century," *Journal of the American Academy of Religion* 48 (June 1980): 207–231; Catherine Wessinger, *Women's Leadership in Marginal Religions: Explorations Outside the Mainstream* (Urbana and Chicago: University of Illinois Press, 1993); Cynthia Hoehler-Fatton, *Women of Fire and Spirit: History, Faith, and Gender in Roho Religion in Western Kenya* (New York: Oxford University Press, 1996), 97–107.

36. Mbon, *Brotherhood of the Star and Cross,* 59–69.

37. Hackett, *Religion in Calabar,* 189.

38. Mbon, *Brotherhood of the Star and Cross,* 44.

39. Founders of other movements, such as Isaiah Shembe, who started the Nazareth Church in South Africa, and the Prophet Harris, who started the Harrist movement in Ivory Coast, were also divinized by some of their followers. See A. Vilakasi, B. Mthethwa, and M. Mpanza, eds., *Shembe: The Revitalization of African Society* (Johannesburg, SA: Stocktaville Publishers, 1986); Sheila Walker, *The Religious Revolution in the Ivory Coast: The Prophet Harris and the Harrist Church* (Chapel Hill: University of North Carolina Press, 1983).

40. Brotherhood of the Cross and Star, *Prophet's Handbook,* vol. 2 (Calabar, Nigeria: Brotherhood Press, n.d.).

41. See Max Weber, *The Theory of Social and Economic Organization,* trans. A. M. Henderson and Talcott Parsons (New York: Free Press, 1964).

42. Mbon discusses the notion of jurisdictional and functional authority first articulated by Jim Kiernan. See Mbon, *Brotherhood of the Star and Cross,* 68; see also Jim Kiernan, "Authority and Enthusiasm: The Organization of Religious Experience in Zulu Zionist Churches," in J. Davis, ed., *Religious Organization and Religious Experience* (London: Academic Press, 1982), 177–179.

43. See Mbon, *Brotherhood of the Star and Cross,* and Hackett, *Religion in Calabar,* for a summary of the central teachings of the Brotherhood of the Cross and Star.

44. Mbon points out that it is the only movement that does not emphasize the importance of the Hebrew Bible as a resource for liberation. Mbon, *Brotherhood of the Star and Cross,* 75–76.

45. Ibid., 79.

46. Ibid., 95. Mbon points out that Olumba Olumba Obu also emphasizes that Jesus showed favoritism to the Syropheonician woman who asked Jesus for help.

47. See James Umoh and Asuquo Ekanen, "Olumba Oluma Obu: The Mystery Man of Biakpan," in Olumba Olumba Obu, *Brotherhood of Cross and Star: Facts You Must Know,* vol. 1 (Calabar, Nigeria: Brotherhood Press, 1979), 33.

48. Mbon, *Brotherhood of the Star and Cross,* 102.

49. Ibid., 107.

50. Ibid., 138.

51. Ibid., 139–141.

52. See Bryan Wilson, *Magic and the Millennium: A Sociological Study of Religious Movements of Protest Among Tribal and Third-World Peoples* (New York: Harper and Row, 1973), 7.

53. Quoted in Mbon, *Brotherhood of the Star and Cross,* 142. See "A Special Message from Leader Olumba Olumba Obu: Towards a New Generation," *Daily Times* of Lagos, 16 February 1985, 11.

54. See detailed analysis of this in Mbon, *Brotherhood of the Star and Cross,* 144.

55. Catherine Wessinger, ed., *Millennialism, Persecution, and Violence: Historical Cases* (Syracuse: Syracuse University Press, 2000), 6–12. See also Catherine Wessinger, *How the Millennium Comes Violently: From Jonestown to Heaven's Gate* (New York: Seven Bridges Press, 2000).

56. Personal interview, 18 September 2000, Houston Bethel.

57. Brother Elijah tells me that many people make assumptions about Nigerians that are false, just as many in the American society make assumptions about African Americans that are not true.

58. He called attention to this word by the inflection of his voice and by his gestures, so much so that I pointed out to him that I understood that he wanted to highlight the word *core,* and he said that he was doing precisely that.

59. Hackett, *Religion in Calabar,* 190.

60. Personal interview. This interview was conducted at the residence of Sister Miriam, who lived here in Houston for several months and actually led worship services.

61. Although I use the word "universal" in this chapter in a general sense to mean "worldwide," it is important that I inject a theological caution. The Brotherhood's universal mission is not universalist according to that theological tradition that goes back to the early church and the teaching of Origen. This position, generally called *apokastastasis,* expresses the view that in the end all humankind will be restored to God. While the Brotherhood stresses that God is a forgiving God, it does not stress divine love as defined by Karl Barth—the belief that, in the end, the grace of God will triumph. Rather, the Brotherhood followers believe that each one must come to God through Jesus Christ and that God is in our midst today through his only appointed representative, Olumba Olumba Obu.

62. See Olumba Olumba Obu, *Theocracy, the Only Way Out* (Lagos: Trumpet Readers Family, 1999).

63. See Hackett, *Religion in Calabar,* 190–191.

64. Some of the new religious movements of Africa no longer exist. A good example is the Jamaa movement, which was founded by Placide Tempels in Katanga in the Democratic Republic of the Congo. A seminal study of the movement was undertaken by Johannes Fabian, *Jamaa: A Charismatic Movement in Katanga* (Evanston, Ill. Northwestern University Press, 1971). See also Johannes Fabian, "Jamaa: A Charismatic Movement Revisited," in T. Blakely, W. van Beek, and D. Thomson, eds., *Religion in Africa: Experience and Expression* (London: James Currey, 1994), 257–274.

65. Hackett, *Religion in Calabar,* 186.

66. Olumba Olumba Obu, *The 3rd Covenant* (Calabar, Nigeria: Everlasting Gospel Center, 1997).

67. I do not believe this teaching has been revised now that we have passed the year 2000.

68. Olumba Olumba Obu, *The 3rd Covenant,* 4.

69. Ibid., 5.

70. Ibid., 35. In one of the rare uses of the Hebrew Bible, Father Olumba Olumba Obu proclaims that the Brotherhood today fulfills the promise of Nebuchadnezzar's dream and that God is now dwelling here with people on earth. This is the claim that underlies their opponents' suggestion that they are divinizing Father Obu.

71. The term "new world order" refers to President George H.W. Bush's perspective on the world in the aftermath of the collapse of the Soviet Union at the end of 1989. He also used this notion to justify the Persian Gulf war. The Brotherhood of the Cross and Star publishes a magazine titled *New World Magazine.* Wessinger points out that the Bahai's use the expression and may have originated it in its present form (personal communication).

72. Olumba Olumba Obu, *Theocracy, the Only Way Out,* i.

73. Since President Thabo Mbeki's call for an African renaissance, the idea has become a buzzword. This brief reference to it here could be an indication that the movement is attuned to the latest ideological pronouncements on the continent. Mbeki made his call for an African Renaissance in Cape Town, 27–28 May 1997. His statement is available online at http://www.html.africanews.com (August 1997); see also Thabo Mbeki, "On African Renaissance," *African Philosophy* 12, no. 1 (1999): 5–10.

74. Olumba Olumba Obu, *Theocracy, the Only Way Out,* 2–3.

75. Ibid., 5.

76. Ibid., 7–8.

77. Ibid., 13.

78. Ibid., 15.

79. Olumba Olumba Obu, *Theocracy, the Only Way Out,* 17. For the argument that Africa has many resources that have been wasted, see George B. N. Ayittey, *Africa in Chaos* (New York: St. Martin's Press, 1998), 5.

80. Ibid., 19.

81. Ibid., 20.

82. Ibid., 25.

III

Gender, Ethnicity, and Identity

6

Gender, Identity, and Power in African Immigrant Evangelical Churches

Regina Gemignani

Introduction

This chapter explores the relationships among religion, gender, and ethnicity in the African immigrant churches. It aims to understand the complex negotiation of gender as women and men newly arrived to the United States adjust to transformational changes in education, work opportunities, and marriage and family structures. Feminist theorists have pointed out the "hierarchies of difference" embedded in ethnic, national, and religious ideologies and the way in which identity discourses both unite and exclude.[1] In relation to Diaspora studies, Anthias suggests that while the concept of Diaspora focuses attention on transnational and dynamic processes that "recognize difference and diversity," there is still a tendency to undertheorize the ways in which "boundaries of exclusion" reproduce class and gender hierarchies.[2]

This chapter addresses both accommodation and resistance to gender hierarchies in African immigrant churches in the United States. Very few studies of immigrant religious communities examine women's agency in shaping gender relations at the level of household and community. Much of the existing research on gender in these communities simplifies the relationship between ethnic and gender ideologies and neglects women's agency in challenging gender hierarchies. (Notable exceptions discussed in this chapter include studies by Kim and by Rayaprol.)[3] For example, Ebaugh and Chafetz describe ethnicity in immigrant religious communities in static and bounded terms, as "native culture" or "'old country' cultural traditions" that are carried along into the U.S. context, largely serving to reproduce patriarchal cultural forms.[4] Even in the broader literature on gender and immigration, there is a tendency to view immigrant women as victims, or conscious supporters, of patriarchal ethnic structures. Pessar states that most immigrant women "have only nibbled at the margins of patriarchy" and that they rarely challenge patriarchal domestic ideologies and practices, instead choosing to "defend and hold together their families" in the face of disruptive Western influences.[5] This chapter suggests an alternative view, in which women are not in an either/or position with respect to their ethnoreligious identity and their struggle against patriarchy. Instead, it investigates the polyvalence of ideals such as family, domesticity, and the ideal of women's submission itself and shows how women are able to negotiate these meanings as they simultaneously challenge gender hierarchies and construct religious community.

This study explores shifts in the gender division of labor in the African immigrant household and the role of the pentecostal churches in shaping responses to these changes. In African Christian as well as Muslim communities, there is a great deal of flux, ambiguity, and conflict around gender issues, as members adjust to the freedoms and opportunities and, from another perspective, the anomie, individualism, and moral latitude of American life. This is true for both the Christian and the Muslim communities. The focus of this research is on the pentecostal churches, where a significant number of women are finding employment in the skilled professions and where there is a pronounced attempt on the part of these women to reconcile conservative gender values with transformations in their income, autonomy, and status.

Methodology

This analysis is based on research conducted between February 2004 and June 2005 as part of the African Immigrant Religious Communities Project at U.C. Davis. This research focused on the rapidly expanding African-led pentecostal communities in Northern California, including Sacramento and the San Francisco Bay Area.

As part of my efforts to research the growing phenomenon of African immigrant churches, as well as engage in a more specific analysis of gender relations within these institutions, I conducted twenty-four open-ended, in-depth interviews with seventeen men and seven women. These interviews were conducted in seventeen Christian churches, of which sixteen are pentecostal/charismatic churches (one church is a Lutheran immigrant mission). Pentecostal churches represent the majority of African-led Christian churches, making up more than 70 percent of the institutions (others include mainline and African Initiated Churches). Of the individuals who were selected for interviews, eighteen were pastors in their community, and the rest held other formal leadership positions within their church. Interviews were conducted in two phases. The first phase (sixteen interviews) involved in-depth questions about a broad range of topics—the history and mission of the church, the relevance in immigrant lives, gender issues, and forms of civic participation. The second phase (eight interviews) provided an opportunity to follow up on some of the findings from interviews and participant observations and to focus more specifically on gender issues in the churches, the most important of which was women's work opportunities, gender conflict in the household, and the perceived benefits gained through the community and the practice of their faith.

For six months from March 2004 to August 2004, I attended weekly services and special events held at the churches. Attending the intensive four days of fellowship and worship during the national conventions of two large pentecostal churches also was helpful in gaining knowledge about gender discourses in the Christian community. Other key insights were provided by Dr. Jacob Olupona and his ongoing research on the topic of African immigrant religion in the United States, as well as by the many scholars and religious practitioners who have collaborated on the project, especially the invaluable contributions of a diverse and dynamic group of women leaders who attended our 2005 conference, "African Religious Community Leaders in the U.S.," at U.C. Davis.

Gendered Employment Patterns: New Opportunities in the Skilled Professions

As pointed out by Kofman, few scholars have recognized the extent of immigrant women's involvement in the skilled professions in the European and the U.S. economies. She suggests that their invisibility is a result of the fact that these women fail to conform to the dominant image of immigrant women in the work force (e.g., as the unskilled "trailing wife"). In reality, developed countries are experiencing an expanding demand for skilled female labor in sectors such as education, health, and social work.[6] Nursing is one important area in which immigrant women, most notably women from Africa and the Caribbean, are finding work both in Europe and the United States, and "nurses have become a truly globalized and portable profession."[7]

One of the most obvious employment patterns among African immigrants is the large number of women working in the nursing profession. Women respondents who were trained as nurses in Africa describe their journey to enter nursing in California as one that involved a considerable but manageable degree of effort.[8] One woman nurse who moved to the United States from Nigeria in order to seek out a position states:

> It took roughly four months to get to the point of authorization for the [RN board exam]. . . . To take the board exam was not a big deal. Our medical education is basically the same, but we have a lot of differences, too, and I needed to go for a preparatory class to take the board. The class was between five hundred and six hundred dollars. That was kind of expensive for a new person who has come. . . . Then I took the test. About five months after coming. And then, to God's glory, I passed it. After I passed the board, I went all around, the employers were interested to take up the sponsorship because [after board certification] it is all right, so I got a position. Although some institutions declined, because it is not an easy thing for a facility to sponsor a client. It takes forever, it takes a lot of paper work, and they have to declare a lot in the process. So some shy away from it.

The most difficult part of the process is often the time spent waiting for work authorization after finding a sponsor. The relationships formed in the religious community are an essential means of support during the year-long waiting period. She explains:

> That first year is the hardest time because you can't work. You depend only on the support and help of brethren. And you find people even giving you monetary assistance, giving you assistance food-wise, and accommodating you, almost free of charge. . . . It was like a community thing. And I think you may not get that outside the church, even if it's a Nigerian community. Because the binding force is the teaching and the belief and the love of Christ and the Christian virtues that we take care of one another. Outside the church, outside Christianity, you may not find that comfort and that support. So that went on and even during those periods that I was missing my family, not having enough money to call, the Christian environment was a big support. I would go to prayer meetings on Wednesdays and the

> prayer points would be for those with immigration needs. And after the prayers, everybody lifting up your problems and everything, you go back home strengthened and determined. Despite all the worries and anxieties of family, you find out that you start receiving that internal peace. You start toughening your spiritual muscle; you pray with them; you are at peace. So, after that length of time, finally the authorization papers came.

Most African women with prior training as nurses are ultimately successful in securing remunerative positions as nurses in the United States. And many who were not previously trained successfully work their way through nursing school, often receiving assistance from more established relatives and fellow church members.

Through their perseverance, immigrant women in nursing and other skilled service professions can independently achieve upward socioeconomic mobility, often beyond what was attainable at home. Many purchase homes and invest for their children's education. In contrast to these highly employable women members of the immigrant community, African men often have difficulty transferring their degrees in fields such as medicine and business to the U.S. context. They are rarely trained as nurses before coming to the United States, and most do not feel comfortable entering this feminized profession. Among the practical few who do decide to pursue nursing, the road is a difficult one, as they fear the perception in the community that they are doing "women's work." One finds male nurses conducting their professions in secret, concealing the nature of the work from members of the community and even their own friends.[9] Women with advanced degrees in areas such as business describe the difficulties that they, too, have faced in finding a position, and some state their plans to enter the nursing field in the future. They point out the irony that the highest valued degrees in Africa, such as a master's degree in business or public administration, are often the least likely to be recognized in the United States. It is also important to note here that some of our respondents felt that the greater employability of women was a result less of the transferability of different degrees than of the racial discrimination in the job market that affects men in the immigrant community more than women.[10]

The gendered employment trends in the African community contradict the view that women immigrants are less likely than men to convert their education into high status positions. Pessar, citing recent studies showing that relatively few highly educated immigrant women are able to find prestigious professional positions, concludes that "'making it' in America may sadly, yet, be a story about men despite the inclusion of women."[11] In contrast, in most African immigrant homes, women's incomes have increased substantially compared to men's. This has not only served to elevate women's status and autonomy but has also led to a great deal of intrahousehold conflict as husbands and wives adjust to a new gender division of labor. Within the Christian communities I visited, leaders and members expressed concern about the impact that shifting gender roles are having on families and on the community at large. The following are quotes from several women church members and community leaders:

> There's a shift in that role from what it is in Nigeria. . . . In Nigeria, the husband has the sole responsibility of taking care of the wife. You could be working, but you don't have to work if they don't want you to work. But when you come into America, there's a shift in the breadwinner role. Basically because nursing in America is an easy-to-find job, a good paying job . . . and women are the greater population of nurses. So even those who are not nurses from Nigeria, when they come into this country, they started training as nurses and when they get trained, they make more money than their husbands. And you'll find a change that starts affecting the relationships in the family. That is more common with people who are outside church. When I say church, I mean a relationship with God. Those who don't have any relationship with God, they find it so hard. A lot of homes are broken, a lot of relationships torn, because the wives make more money than the husbands.

> I think our problem here is because our society is based in Africa, where women are supposed to be mothers. They take care of the kitchen, the clothing, the *everything*. The men are the sole providers. They are supposed to be the head. So when we come to this culture, our men are not used to that. They find it very difficult, to stoop down—they look at it as stooping down and doing the woman's role—to cook, to clean up, to take care of the children. They find it difficult.

> In this society, I have seen families that have struggled. Because the men still cannot see themselves as primary child care providers. So even when they are not working, the average African, when he's not working, he's going to school, he's still out there struggling, hustling to see what he can bring to

> the table. So, yes, I have seen very few of them who have accepted to care for the children while the mothers are working.
>
> Men, you know, are difficult to change. . . . And they are not changing to what is prevailing here. The women are easily changing to the system and saying, "You have to help me in the house." And that is strange to the men. They are saying, "What's wrong with you, what are you becoming? Are we not coming from home? We were both at home together and you knew what to do." They don't want to know that the system has really changed here. Some men want to sit down and have the women serve them like at home. Some cannot even microwave their food!

For pastors, marital conflict is a concern for a number of reasons, not the least of which is the increasing rates of divorce in the immigrant community. Two male pastors express their view about the growing prevalence of these conflicts:

> Here women are out of the house. Of course in Africa, women were also out of the house, but the difference is that, back in Africa, if the woman is doing business that takes her away or she's working for the government that takes her away from home, she had house help. Here there's nothing like that, so the pressure is now on both, the husband and the wife. And yet the husband realizes, "If my wife stops working, how can we live on one income?" So these issues are always there, and sometimes the husband still expects that the woman should come home from work and cook and do the laundry and all that and all the guy has to do is just to sit back and relax like an African chief.
>
> It depends on the orientation. Some people are not used to the wife having a job, some are used to the wife staying at home. . . . What is the role of a woman? If the role of a woman in the family is nurturing in type and the role of the man is the provider, as specified in the Bible, the woman does the nurturing at home, the man does the providing. But now, economically, things have changed. So it's becoming difficult for some men to accept that, "Now my wife has to go to work. She's going to be bringing in the bacon as well as I bring in the bacon." And sometimes the woman brings more bacon than the man.

In many Christian communities, pastors, and especially women church members, are actively engaged in addressing these conflicts through the reinterpretation of "traditional" gender ideals and practices. The following sections explore some of the ways in which the churches provide an opportunity for the expression of multiple and contested meanings regarding gender, work, and power.

Gender Relations in the African Immigrant Evangelical Churches

The factors mentioned earlier—skilled migration patterns, shifts in the gender division of labor and increasing gender conflict among church members—are interesting in light of recent studies of gender and immigrant religion. As pointed out, this work tends to emphasize the reproduction of patriarchal values inherent to religious and ethnic identities. However, as suggested by Kim, immigrant religious communities are also organized to minister to the varied needs of their members, including and perhaps especially in terms of the difficult adjustments that immigrants, both men and women, must make to adapt to U.S. life.[12] The African churches in this study are highly oriented toward community work, offering programs, advice, and psychological and spiritual solace to both men and women members. In addition, they are perhaps unique among immigrant communities in the degree to which women are engaged as leaders, both informally and in formal church positions, and to which they actively express their concerns and interests through this involvement in community activities and programs.

The dual roles of immigrant Christian communities as both "patriarchal and effectively liberating"[13] are evident in the context of African immigration, and the construction of gender in these arenas is a dynamic and contentious process. The following sections illustrate some of the ways in which women negotiate gender by drawing upon the rich symbolic and social resources of their church communities.

Religion and the Reproduction of Patriarchal Values

The work of Anthias and Yuval Davis describes some of the linkages between gender and the construction of ethnic and national identities. As they point out, gender is instrumental in the biological and social reproduction of ethnicity and nation. Of particular interest to this chapter are

(1) the role of women in the ideological reproduction of the ethnic, national, and religious collectivity and (2) the role of women as signifiers of difference.[14]

One of the most important ways in which gender differences are promoted in the immigrant churches is through women's role in the ideological reproduction of the African Christian community. Women's responsibility for transmitting traditional beliefs and values is largely an extension of women's domestic roles, for example, their responsibility for the socialization of children and food preparation.[15] In many African churches, one finds women responsible for a multitude of activities that aim to transmit the cultural heritage to the youth and community. Examples include baby naming ceremonies, engagement practices, and wedding celebrations. These are variously described as national, ethnic, or "African" practices. However, Christianity serves as an important filter in the ongoing invention of tradition, since only a select group of values, beliefs, and practices are viewed as important to the church community and to the cultural education of the second generation.

Food preparation is a particularly important arena illustrating women's involvement in the transmission of cultural practices. As pointed out by Ebaugh and Chafetz, food practices are highly relevant to the construction of ethnicity in immigrant religious communities.[16] Many fellowship activities in the communities that we have visited are oriented around the preparation and enjoyment of shared meals. As suggested by the respondents, these occasions serve as a central means to unite the community. For example, one Liberian pastor stated, "Women get together and they cook. And we come together and we eat together, and that promotes fellowship." He explained that the African meals that they share create a "homey" atmosphere in contrast to the alienation of U.S. society, where "your next door neighbor won't speak to you." In the Ethiopian church, a pastor similarly explained, "Our activities within the church, the singing we do in Amharic, the coffee fellowship that we have, bonds us together. . . . If you tell my kids we're going to another church, another what we call 'foreign church' or 'American church,' they won't like it. They prefer to be within their group; 'birds of a feather flock together!'" One Liberian pastor recruited by an immigrant community described his surprise at learning how central food was to his congregation's fellowship activities. Upon learning that his wife and extended family were expected to organize a large meal for the congregation every week, something that he "really did not plan for," he decided to introduce a sign-up sheet so that members could rotate the responsibility among themselves. At one very small gathering after the Sunday service at this church, I found women members serving an elaborate, multi-course Liberian meal.

An interest in variety and authenticity in the culinary experience is widely evident in these church communities. In a Nigerian-led church, a deacon of Yoruba ethnicity described some of the hard-to-find foods that they enjoy during fellowships, including *egusi* (melon soup), *iyan* (yam flour porridge), and *amala* (plantain porridge). When I asked whether eating these foods was important to people, he exclaimed, "Ah! People come only because of that! People will come a hundred miles or any long distance to eat this food because it has been a long time since they tasted it and they don't know when they will eat it again." In a cooking class for women that I attended, which was led by the visiting Nigerian mother-in-law of a women church leader, there was a great deal of discussion about the various ingredients, their characteristics and uses, and where they could be purchased. As in other aspects of church services, there is a simultaneous attempt to appeal to non-Africans by offering standard "American" dishes, which include "Chinese food." One pastor states:

> Now if we have a celebration, of course you will see the Nigerian food. That's what mostly we eat, rice, a lot of *jollof* rice. But we as a local assembly, because we are trying to attract anybody, whenever we have celebrations we do try to incorporate some menus that are typical of this society—fried chicken, potato salad, tossed salad, or Chinese food, for those people who won't eat all that we have. At least Chinese food is receptive anywhere and anytime.

In all cases, cooking in the church is the exclusive domain of women and is marked as such. For example, when I was guided through a new church building, the pastor pointed to the kitchen and stated, "That's where women do their thing." Women cook for fellowship times, family celebrations, holidays, and special events and to welcome new members into the community. They are also often responsible for purchasing the necessary supplies, decorating, and cleaning.

In addition to their responsibility for organizing meals and cultural events, women are also responsible for instructing the youth about cultural values, such as respect for elders. These lessons require sensitivity to the interests and needs of the youth as they negotiate their own way in

U.S. life. One woman pastor explained that she must always balance her own values with those of Western society, and that it was important to recognize the limits to which one can "make them continue the African way." As pointed out by D'Alisera, the transmission of identity from parent to child is another important way in which women accommodate change "while resisting their "ultimate incorporation . . . into the American 'melting pot.'"[17]

Women's involvement in the reproduction of ethnicity through food preparation and cultural transmission may direct them toward the sphere of homemaking and childcare and may act to strengthen and legitimize divisions between men's and women's work. Women, viewed as responsible for social reproduction, are assigned the double burden of managing a career and performing domestic duties. Moreover, to the extent that women's role in the home is subordinate to men's leadership in the public sphere, women's contributions may be devalued, thereby marginalizing women as a group and reinforcing gendered dichotomies such as public/private, production/reproduction, and reason/emotion.

Women, of course, are agents in the processes of identity formation and the construction of gendered divisions of work. In our interviews, a number of respondents expressed the view that men are the household leaders and that women nurture and care for the family and community.[18] The following are similar views held by two women respondents:

> The man is the head of the house. That's God's command in itself. That's another teaching that the group tries to project to its members: keep your husband as the head of the house no matter where you are. I mean, no matter what degree you have, your husband is still the head. We kid around and we say M.R.S. is a degree you get in the kitchen, that's where you are. We don't care if you have a—I have an MBA. It doesn't matter. Your husband is the head of your house.

> [If you are the major wage earner] you will still have to submit. That you are assisting the family is not a thing to think that you are the head. You know there's no controversy in the head seat in the family. The man is the head of family and you have to submit. And whatever you are contributing, you contribute it to the family.

As suggested by Anthias and Davis, "The roles that women play are not merely imposed upon them. Women actively participate in the process of reproducing and modifying their roles as well as being actively involved in controlling other women."[19] Difference, however, does not automatically imply hierarchy, and one must be careful not to automatically equate "tradition" or "ethnicity" with women's subordination. This point is elaborated much further in the next section of this chapter.

The second point drawn from Anthias and Yuval Davis, women's role as a marker of collective boundaries and difference, represents another critical factor shaping gender in the immigrant churches. Again, both Christian and ethnic/national identities come into play. The image of women as the virtuous and nurturing mother/wife (a feminine ideal commonly found in the African churches) is linked to ethnicity as well as to the religious ideal of the Christian home. In the context of U.S. immigration, this symbolic ideal is often emphasized as the religious community defines its identity in contrast to a morally flawed American society.

Recent studies suggest that among immigrants living in the United States, feminine ideals become symbols for collective identities. Espiritu, for example, in her work on gender relations in the Filipino immigrant community, shows how womanhood is "idealized as the repository of tradition. . . . The norms that regulate women's behaviors and boundaries become a means of determining and defining group status and boundaries. As a consequence the burdens and complexities of cultural representation fall most heavily on immigrant women and their daughters."[20] She cites the history of colonial, racial, class, and gender subordination as important factors shaping the construction of ethnicity and gender, as immigrants "stake their political and sociocultural claims on their new country." In the context of immigration, the "margins imagine and construct the mainstream in order to assert superiority over the latter."[21]

In the African community, there is a similar tendency for wives and daughters to be represented as "paragons of morality" that differentiate the "family-oriented model minority" from mainstream society.[22] When asked to describe the characteristics of the ideal woman, respondents most often mentioned virtuousness, including temperance, modesty, sexual morality, piousness, and dedication to one's family. One woman responded to the question with reference to the name of the women's group at her church:

> Well, the way we call ourselves, we call ourselves the Women of Honor. And, being a women's leader, the ideal way I would like to carry myself outside because I want to lead by example, would be as somebody who is honorable. Dress modestly, react reasonably, exhibit patience in my reactions and

> attitudes, be respectful. . . . If we want to present the ideal woman from this church, of course we are going to pick a woman who can speak our "language," who can speak honorably. . . . Her mannerisms, the way she carries herself, will attract respect, they will say, "Ooh that woman, she has an air about her." And it's all about God. A Godly air, not being stuck up, your nose being stuck up in the air as "I am it and a bag of chips," no we are not talking about that. We are talking about being modest in your dress, in your outlook. Even when you wear make-up, you are not going to wear a wild lipstick that will be loud everywhere. We are praying that that is what we will be.

In the quotes that follow, two other women respondents describe the way in which an ideal woman dedicates herself to her family and community.

> I mean you talk about successful marriage; a marriage comprises a whole lot of things. As the Bible says, it's about a virtuous woman who keeps her home and keeps her family and things like that. And that's what the group [church] is trying to promote. I mean it's just trying to make sure that the women are virtuous women in their homes. And that's a very central aspect of keeping a home and a marriage together.

> Those who are not Christians, who are not committed to God, I don't know how they pass through the pressures of marriage. There's a lot of pressure, a lot of sacrifice in marriage. So my definition of an ideal woman is a God-fearing woman. A woman that knows her God, a woman that respects and fears God. And when that is in your heart, it produce a good relationship with your husband, it produce a commitment to your community. It will produce every other thing that makes you good.

Respondents were quick to contrast their community values with the elevated divorce rates and "broken families" of Western society. Women church members were portrayed as nurturing wives and mothers and were credited (or blamed) for the degree of happiness and stability in their homes. In one church that I visited, women hold an annual dinner banquet that celebrates women's role in the family. The two most recent gatherings were titled "Destroyers of a Christian Home" and "Building Blocks of a Christian Home." I was told that the events are designed as part of a public outreach service that aims to show the wider community the strengths and differences of a church in which the gospel is not "watered down." The outreach event serves as an opportunity to perform gender roles that symbolize, and naturalize, the moral standing of the religious community.

Bowie has drawn on Mary Douglas's theories on ritual purity to illustrate the power of religious dress in reproducing, contesting, and transforming social identities.[23] Understanding the complex, polyvalent qualities of dress in the African churches is beyond the scope of this chapter. However, I suggest that one important reason that dress is emphasized in so many of the churches is that it foregrounds the ideal of the virtuous woman, thus defining group morality and integrity. One example found in the African immigrant religious communities is the Deeper Life Ministry, started in Nigeria but now established across Africa, North America, and Europe. In this church, women's adherence to very strict dress codes requires covering the head, wearing modest clothing in muted colors, and avoiding all jewelry, makeup, and hair adornments. One participant at a nationwide conference in Chicago stated that women's clothing and appearance are now so central to the group's identity or "Being Deeper Life" that some women are becoming focused on the external, to the detriment of their inner religious experience. Women's lack of adornment contrasts sharply with the tendency toward elaborate and colorful fashion in both African and African American churches,[24] not to mention the stark differentiation from materialist values in the United States. In other churches, where one finds much more embellishment in dress styles, it is still very common to hear discussions about the need for women's modesty in appearance. Muted shades of makeup, especially lipstick, are often mentioned, as well as the need for adequate coverage of women's bodies.

The purpose of this discussion has been to illustrate the gender differences promoted in the church communities and to suggest some of the ways in which gender ideologies that extol male leadership and women's role in the family and home *may* contribute to patriarchal power. Gender hierarchies may be promoted both at the level of the household and within the structure of the church organization. Regarding the latter, women in most of the church communities hold positions of authority (e.g., pastor, deacon, heads of various church ministries). However, with the exception of the Redeemed Christian Church of God, it is rare to find a woman pastor who leads a church on her own rather than serving as co-pastor with her husband.[25] Moreover, women report that men make many of the central decisions in the church and that women are still struggling for an equal voice in the leadership.

Women in many of these communities are limited by patriarchal relations, especially involving the gender division of labor in which women are viewed as primarily responsible for the home and men hold a position of authority in the household and community. At the same time, some of the most interesting aspects of the Christian communities are the way in which they are supplying a space for women to contest dominant gender ideologies and relations, not by rejecting ethnicity and tradition but by revising the gendered meanings inherent to ethnoreligious belonging.

The Wisdom of Submission: Religion and Resistance to Patriarchy

Although the evangelical Christian churches seem on the surface to uphold gender hierarchies, a closer look at the gender discourses and practices found within these groups shows both accommodation and resistance to patriarchal values. Beckford has suggested that religious movements encourage change and experimentation in gender and social relations. He contrasts the "free space" or "quasi-laboratory" in which experimentation takes place in religious communities with the "increasing stranglehold of the state and transnational corporations over wide swaths of social and cultural life."[26] He points to women's agency within a number of movements and their active negotiation of gender.[27] Evangelical Christianity, in particular, has been shown to encompass a wide variety of beliefs and practices related to gender, and Shibley points out that, contrary to popular stereotypes, this form of Christianity often serves as a site for reconstituting gender.[28] In his study of a Mexican American evangelical church, Lyon similarly describes the "malleability" of pentecostal theology, which can be "pragmatically molded to fit the needs of very different constituencies."[29]

The African pentecostal communities are a cogent example of this, as illustrated by the unique and creative responses to social transformation experienced in the context of immigration. One of the important ways in which gender hierarchies are contested in the African pentecostal churches is through the value assigned to the private sphere. Popular discourse about the family and home challenges conceptions of this sphere as one of subordination and passivity. For example, metaphors used to describe women's work in the home contrast with a feminine ideal of passive nurturing—they are said to "defend" the home and to "build" and "construct" family and community. As Brusco states of evangelical communities in Colombia, the private realm of home and family is placed at the center of both women's and men's lives. She states that "conversion entails the replacement of an individualistic orientation in the public sphere with a collective orientation and identity in the church and home."[30] Additionally, public/private divisions are redrawn as the private realm is made public through events such as the community dinner banquets discussed earlier. Rayaprol reports similar findings from the Indian immigrant community where women migrating to the United States have made the private goals of socialization of children and cultural reproduction the central aspect of the public agenda of their temple.[31]

In a community where home and family are accorded such a central place in public and private life, "the husband may still occupy the position of head, but his relative aspirations have changed to coincide more closely with those of his wife."[32] This brings us to a second, related point concerning the negotiation of gender in the African evangelical communities, the way in which a unidimensional form of household authority is downplayed in favor of a more complex understanding in which women use their "wisdom" and favor with God to wield power and influence in their homes. Griffith's work is highly relevant here. Drawing on her work with Women's Aglow Fellowship, a U.S.-based association for evangelical women, she shows how women's understanding of the biblical notion of submission balances compliance and strength and has multiple layers of meaning ranging from the act of yielding to men's power to "a strategy of containment" that celebrates women's power to influence their husbands to their own ends.[33] Of particular interest in her work is the way in which "women retain a kind of mediated agency through their reliance on the omnipotent God.[34] She cites Coakley, who describes "power in vulnerability . . . the willed effacement to a gentle omnipotence which, far from 'completing' masculinism, acts as its undoing."[35]

Griffith's illustration of the linkages between submission and "women's capacity to release divine power and effect change" is pertinent to the negotiation of gender in the African immigrant churches. Here there is a similar emphasis on the power of submission. Women with whom I spoke emphasized the fact that submission to their husbands did not imply recognition of their unqualified authority but instead represented submission to the will of God. As stated by one woman, "It's not like you have to take anything a man says hook, line and sinker. Submission means to God, 'as unto God.'" In turn, God is viewed as being favorably disposed toward these sacrificing women. There is a subtle pressure upon the husband to acquiesce to his wife's will, which, as suggested in conversations with women, could imply anything from a general show of patience and kindness to more specific issues that are being negotiated between spouses, such as the division of work in the home. Submission for many of the women becomes a means of guiding and persuading a husband by respecting and recognizing a certain kind of participatory and nonauthoritarian leadership. In this way, the linkages between identity and gender are reinterpreted to suggest the interdependency between husband and wife and their shared responsibility and accountability in the home. A woman respondent stated:

> See, that's the thing. It is the woman's role to help the husband to guide him in the way of the Lord, too. And that's why these women are so active in the churches. And then the husbands see this, all these good attributes, and then they get attracted to the church also and they come, they hear the word of God, and they know they have to act right. It's a two way thing. If you're good to your wife, you wife is good to you, and vice versa.

One finds that in many discussions of wifely submission, there is a simultaneous reference to the mutual submission of husband and wife or, in some cases, to a more specific mutuality between a husband's "love" and a wife's "submission." In one example, a dynamic woman pastor visiting from London addressed a church gathering in Sacramento. During her sermon, she told the group that "men lack in love and women lack in submission." She described the need for men to love their wife as Christ loves the church, enough to give his life to the church. In expanding on the topic of women's submission, she stated only that men and women should "submit themselves one to another" and that women "should submit to their husband not to someone else's husband!" Male pastors, responding to the concerns of their women congregants as well as their own concerns about divorce, are often found promoting similar views. A pastor who is a highly popular marriage therapist in one urban community describes his message to husbands:

> We have so many verses in the Bible that helps us. One of them is First Peter 7:2 that says, to paraphrase, "Men we need to treat the woman as if they are co-head to Kingdom of Heaven." There is no difference. The man is the head of the woman just as Christ is the head of the church. Christ said, the

> man is to love the woman as Christ loved the church. Because when Christ loved the church, he died for the church. . . . Submission is lesser in my opinion than love. Love is so great that if there's love, you don't worry about submission. If you love a woman, she would treat you like a king. But when there is no love, it's difficult for the opposite sex to be submissive. So we use the book of Ephesians, the book of Luke, even the entire Bible, we do that a whole lot to be able to help people understand that husband and wife are co-head to the kingdom of the Lord, even though you are the head of the house.

Later in the conversation he described how his teachings suggest that men must maintain a positive relationship with their wives in order to gain God's favor:

> We are being told to love our wife if we don't want our prayer to be hindered. I run praying to God, "Please Lord help me," but if I'm not doing well with my wife, my prayer will be hindered. That's what I teach.

Considering the central role of prayer in these churches, as a direct link to God's greatness and benevolence, such beliefs and teachings wield significant power in men's and women's lives.

Also central to women's negotiation of power in these communities is the notion of wisdom. In conversations with African pentecostal women, I found that wisdom was portrayed as the key for transforming submission into power. When women speak of their wisdom, they always do so with a sense of pride and self-awareness, often using examples that illustrate the positive effects of the application of women's wisdom in their own lives or in those of their family and friends. There are many examples of the way a woman's submission can be combined with wisdom, to "turn around" an authoritative husband. One woman respondent related her own personal experience:

> As a woman you are still supposed to keep your marriage, and the best way you can keep that is to try to stay as humble as you can. And try to be submissive but at the same time try to use wisdom into turning that machismo around. Because you can win a lot of that, you can turn that around, out of love and what not. For instance, I will use my own example, you know when I came here I got a better job and my husband was not working when he came here. But finally he got a job. But while he was home for couple of

> months, even though he was a doctor in Liberia, here it was difficult for him to get to that. . . . I used wisdom. And the wisdom I used was, "Oh honey since you're home, just get connected with your kid, you all stay together and bond." He said, "Oh, okay." After doing that, looking and waiting for a job, waiting, waiting, waiting . . . I would come home and then I would just say, "Okay, this is the check that we made." So, it's a we, there was no more I; I stopped with the I and I took that out of my vocabulary right there. So when I came in I said, "Oh look at it, here's the check that we just made. Do you want to deposit it? Do you want to write the check for the bills?" So he took control of that. Wisdom. I used that wisdom.

Another woman stated:

> Now, when you submit unto your husband, it means that you pay allegiance. It's hierarchical; we have God, we have our husbands, and then we have our children. When you submit to a husband, it means obedience unto your husband, respect unto your husband, following your husband. [*pause*] Now, did the Bible say we should also be wise?

Ideals such as submission and women's wisdom are drawn from the Bible and are freely interpreted in these churches as women assign their own meanings to the sacred text. The views, teachings, and interpretations of pastors are highly regarded in these communities. However, it is important to point out that church members, including women, actively interpret the gospel for themselves and for others, in ways that at times are quite independent of, and sometimes in conflict with, a pastor's teachings. One woman who had made a decision largely on her own to separate from a physically abusive husband described to me the importance of a "radical, pentecostal" approach in which each person is made to understand that reading the Bible is "an individual work between you and the Lord." Men and women are brought to understand "that they have the same access as the pastor has to the Holy Spirit and to God Himself. Relating her own personal experience, she elaborated:

> If I am abused to that point that my life is threatened physically, I can move away from that situation. But does God allow for divorce? No. Now, even ministers have different views. Some ministers will say you move on with your life, and God is the God of second chances. Other ministers will say no. But, to God be the glory, I came to a point where I could read the Bible

> myself. I could seek the face of the Lord concerning issues that are very dear to me; Father, what do I do concerning this? I pray and hear from God concerning myself. So even if the minister has given me advice contrary to the way I feel, it behooves me to do what I have to do because it is me. . . . Nobody, no minister taught me this [that a woman can separate from a husband if she remains celibate]. I was, one day, I don't know what I was doing, I was reading the Bible. I don't even know if I was using the daily devotional that addressed that issue, but I was reading the Bible and, "What, God said *this?* God said *this?* I can!" It was like my entire life I thought, "OK, there is no separation." First Corinthians, I found it myself, 7:10. I read the whole thing over and over.[36]

Bible studies and marriage seminars offer an important opportunity for women to publicly share their views and interpretations. The woman just quoted currently has her own informal marriage ministry that focuses on sharing her experiences with women suffering domestic violence. It is perhaps this sense of human agency in communicating, understanding, and forming a relationship with God that is so central to the way in which religion serves as a "flexible ideological resource" for the negotiation of gender in evangelical churches.[37]

Conclusion

> Everything has a time and everything is how you focus it, how you continue to press in. The more we press in, the more we focus, we are going to come to that point. Now you see on television women are now televising, women are *pushing* all over the world. Because from the history of the church, a woman was supposed to be a saint and a sinner. They were even supposed to sit at the back of the church, in the days of Paul. But this age has eliminated all that—this generation. Because God Himself said that this generation will be a new generation. It will be a generation of wisdom. The wisdom of people has caused things to change. And women are now seeing that they can be in leadership and do just as well as men. The women are now stepping up. It's left to us.
> Woman leader, Bethel World Outreach Ministries

Women in the African pentecostal communities in the United States reproduce gender hierarchies as they promote their role as nurturing defenders of the family in a community which defines itself, and its existence in the United States, largely in moral terms. They willingly acquiesce in the authority of their husbands as they reproduce the ideals of the African Christian family. At the same time, men's power in the household and community is mediated by God's authority as understood and lived in these communities, an authority that exacts mutual love, respect, and humility.

In many African churches, it is common to hear reference to the gendered meanings of the power of submission. For example, one pastor states, "No matter how powerful a man is, if his wife follows biblical injunction, that man will be under the power of the woman." And a very popular expression among women is "You must stoop to conquer." Such statements demonstrate the ambiguous nature of woman's power and the blurred boundaries between submission and control. Such concepts are central to the construction of gender in the immigrant churches and to the teachings, lessons, and advice that, as reported by many respondents, are instrumental in shaping relations between men and women. Respondents often remark on dramatic changes, often referred to as "breakthroughs," that they have seen in the relationships between husbands and wives as a result of church involvement. They describe the efficacy of counseling and marriage seminars provided through the church and the transforming effects of advice and prayer that takes place during phone calls with pastors and between members of a fellowship. Several church members pointed out that the private nature of marital conflict makes it difficult to discuss these issues with others; it is only within the trusting relationships of the church fellowship that members freely give and receive advice and counseling. As one woman stated:

> We are more receptive because of the work Christ is doing in our lives. There is the humility that comes with knowing Christ. We are humble, we're open to one another. My daughter can talk to me in a way that I will never be able to talk to my mother. She knows that as a Christian, the way I will handle those things will not be "Oh, how dare you, you are just my child." No. We are more receptive to one another because of the mindset, the training that comes from the pulpit . . . Not that we sit down and say, "Men, because your wife is more trained or she has a career that is more lucrative in this environment, oh, please, stay at home." No, no, no. That is not what we are being trained to do. We are being trained primarily to be Christ-like. And one of the very, very, primary issues—there is love for one

another. When you love somebody, you're willing to meet the person halfway. So to speak, you're willing to lay your life down to accommodate that person. And when you are in that state, you can work with the person.

Before concluding, it is important to mention that the question of who and what women are "conquering" as they humbly attend to the desires and needs of their husbands, families, and communities is also of great significance. While this chapter focuses on patriarchal structures and intramarital struggles over the division of labor, one must also recognize the interaction between multiple and interconnected forms of domination experienced by women of color.[38] African women immigrants are certainly not divorced from the attacks on the black family as a result of public policy and institutionalized racism in America[39] or from the view of women of color as either perpetrators or victims of social ills. As "defenders of the family," they also challenge the hierarchies of class and race pervasive in their host society.[40]

Notes

1. As described by Yanagisako and Delaney, "ideologies of ethnicity, sexuality, nation, and religion are all hierarchies of difference in which power relations are embedded. All draw on notions of gender, sex, reproduction and descent. It is the common basis of these processes of identity-making which makes it highly productive to read across them, to understand each in relation to the others." S. Yanigisako and C. Delaney, eds., *Naturalizing Power, Essays in Feminist Cultural Analysis* (New York: Routledge, 1995), 20.

2. Floya Anthias, "Evaluating 'Diaspora': Beyond Ethnicity," *Sociology* 32 (1989): 557–580.

3. Jung Ha Kim, "The Labor of Compassion: Voices of 'Churched' Korean American Women," *Amerasia Journal* 22, no. 1 (1996); Aparna Rayaprol, *Negotiating Identities: Women in the Indian Diaspora* (New York: Oxford University Press, 1997).

4. Helen Ebaugh and Janet Chafetz, "Agents for Cultural Reproduction and Structural Change: The Ironic Role of Women in Immigrant Religious Institutions," *Social Forces* 78, no. 2 (1999): 585–613. Also see H. Ebaugh and J. Chafetz, "Reproducing Ethnicity," in their edited volume, *Religion and the New Immigrants, Continuities and Adaptations in Immigrant Congregations* (Walnut Creek, Calif.: Alta Mira, 2000).

5. Patricia Pessar, "Engendering Migration Studies: The Case of New Immigrants in the United States," in P. Handagneu-Sotelo, ed., *Gender and U.S. Immigration: Contemporary Trends* (Berkeley: University of California Press, 1999), 31.

6. Eleonore Kofman, "Gendered Global Migrations: Diversity and Stratification," *International Feminist Journal of Politics* 6, no. 4 (2004): 656.

7. Ibid., 655. In addition to African and Caribbean women working as nurses, Kofman cites numerous other examples of immigrant women in Europe and the United States who have found opportunities in professional and managerial fields. Kofman's work challenges gendered theories of globalization and the idea of a knowledge society that is driven solely by technology and in which "care, social reproduction and women are evicted from the narrative" (ibid., 653).

8. Significant state-to-state differences may exist regarding the ease with which immigrant women enter the nursing profession. For example, Aderemi describes the struggle of African women to become credentialed nurses in certain U.S. states where discrimination is more pronounced and their relocation to "liberal" states where they are better able to negotiate the system and pass the nursing board exam. These women often return to work as nurses in the "hostile" states (Pastor Thomson Aderemi, "African Immigrant Religious Communities in America," paper presented at the African Religious Leaders Conference, U.C. Davis, April 21–24, 2005).

9. Jacob Olupona, personal communication.

10. For a recent study on the dramatic decline in employment experienced by black and Hispanic males during the recent economic turndown, see "A Crisis of Black Male Employment," available online at the Community Service Society Web site, www.cssny.org/pubs/special/2004_02labormarket.pdf (accessed July 2005).

11. Patricia Pessar, "Transnational Migration: Bringing Gender In," *International Migration Review* 37, no. 3 (2003): 812–847.

12. Kim, *Labor of Compassion*, 97.

13. Ibid., 94.

14. Floya Anthias and Nira Yuval-Davis, eds., *Woman-Nation-State* (London: Macmillan Press, 1989), 9.

15. Anthias and Yuval Davis also point out that ethnic minority women may be less assimilated socially within the wider society and thereby become responsible for maintaining ethnic traditions. However, this social isolation does not seem to be particularly evident among African immigrant women.

16. Ebaugh and Chafetz, "Reproducing Ethnicity," 396. Rayaprol also discusses the symbolism of ethnic food among Indian immigrants attending Hindu temples. See Rayaprol, *Negotiating Identities*, 67.

17. JoAnn D'Alisera, *An Imagined Geography: Sierra Leonean Muslims in America* (Philadelphia: University of Pennsylvania Press, 2004), 152.

18. Also see Pessar, "Transnational Migration," 32.

19. Anthias and Yuval Davis, *Woman-Nation-State*, 11.

20. Yen Le Espiritu, *Home Bound: Filipino American Lives Across Cultures, Communities and Countries* (Berkeley: University of California Press, 2003), 160.

21. Ibid., 159.

22. Ibid., 60.

23. Fiona Bowie, *The Anthropology of Religion: An Introduction* (Oxford: Blackwell, 2000), 73.

24. For example, see Gwendolyn O'Neal, "The African American Church, Its Sacred Cosmos, and Dress," in L. Arthur, ed., *Religion, Dress and the Body* (New York: Berg, 1999).

25. The Redeemed Christian Church of God is one of the more progressive African pentecostal churches in terms of women's leadership opportunities. The church has at least ten women head pastors in various states, including California, Ohio, New Jersey, Georgia, and Florida, and also has very high-ranking women administrators based in the Nigerian headquarters (Pastor Dotun Kukoyi, personal communication).

26. James Beckford, *Social Theory and Religion* (New York: Cambridge University Press, 2003), 173.

27. Ibid., 180.

28. Mark A. Shibley, "Contemporary Evangelicals: Born-Again and World Affirming," *Annals of the American Academy of Political and Social Science* 558 (1998): 67–87.

29. Luis Leon, "Born Again in East L.A.: The Congregation as Border Space," in R. S. Warner and J. G. Wittner, eds., *Gatherings in Diaspora: Religious Communities and the New Immigration* (Philadelphia: Temple University Press, 1998), 190.

30. Elizabeth Brusco, "The Reformation of Machismo: Asceticism and Masculinity among Colombian Evangelicals," in V. Garrard-Burnett and D. Stoll, eds., *Rethinking Protestantism in Latin America* (Philadelphia: Temple University Press, 1993), 149.

31. Rayaprol, *Negotiating Identities,* 98, 137.

32. Brusco, "Reformation of Machismo," 149.

33. R. Marie Griffith, *God's Daughters: Evangelical Women and the Power of Submission* (Berkeley: University of California Press, 1997).

34. Ibid., 183.

35. Ibid., 185. Coakley, who writes about the biblical concept "power in vulnerability" from the insightful perspective of feminist theology, describes how humility and vulnerability in Christian ritual are experienced as a yielding to divine power. She suggests that "vulnerability" should be interpreted not as female weakness but as "a (special sort of) human strength." See Sarah Coakley, "Kenosis and Subversion," in D. Hampson, ed., *Swallowing a Fishbone? Feminist Theologians Debate Christianity* (London: Society for Promoting Christian Knowledge, 1996), 101.

36. Here she refers to the biblical passage that states, "To the married I give this command (not I but the Lord): A wife must not separate from her husband. But if she does, she must remain unmarried or else be reconciled to her husband."

37. Shibley, "Contemporary Evangelicals," 74.

38. Chandra Mohanty, "Introduction: Cartographies of Struggle," in C. Mohanty, A. Russo, and L. Torres, eds., *Third World Women and the Politics of Feminism* (Bloomington: Indiana University Press, 1991).

39. For example, see Twila Perry, "Family Values, Race, Feminism and Public Policy," paper presented at the Conference on the Future of the Family, Seoul, Korea, 24 August 1995, available online at http://www.scu.edu/ethics/publications/other/lawreview/familyvalues.html.

40. bell hooks, *Yearning: Race, Gender and Cultural Politics* (Boston: South End Press, 1990).

7

Gender and Change in an African Immigrant Church

An Anthropologist and a (Former) Prophetess Reflect

Deidre Helen Crumbley
and Gloria Malake Cline-Smythe

> According to the Founder and First Primate of the Church—Prophet Dr Josiah Ositelu, God told him from the beginning of his ministry that He . . . has called both men and women into his ministry and should therefore not refuse or reject female disciples. Ministerial hierarchy in the Church therefore has men and women at parity. Both women Ministers and Laities are actively involved in the activities of all the diverse ministries and councils.
>
> "Women: The Church of the Lord Organisation."[1]

The African Diaspora in the New World has occurred in two major waves of migration. The first, shaped by the trans-Atlantic slave trade, was a consequence of forced migration to supply labor to expanding European nation-states. The recent African migration is a voluntary response to turbulent change in contemporary postcolonial Africa.[2] Both have entailed more than the movement of human bodies from one geopolitical space to another; both have entailed the movement of ideas, values, traditions, and institutions.

The slavery context of the first wave of Africans constrained the New World transfer of religious practices to varying degrees. The current transfer of African religious practices to American soil, occurring more than one hundred years after the Emancipation Proclamation, demonstrates greater exercise of religious autonomy and agency. African religious institutions are arriving whole and intact—open to adaptation, but on their own terms.

The decade between 1992 and 2002 saw half a million Africans immigrate to the United States. More than 75,000 of these were Nigerian, the largest group of Africans to immigrate in that period.[3] Some Nigerians have brought their religious institutions with them, further diversifying the already pluralistic religious landscape of twenty-first-century America. One of these is the Church of the Lord (Aladura) (CLA), an indigenous expression of Christianity that emerged among the Yoruba people of southwestern Nigeria. CLA is also part of a larger phenomenon of African Instituted Churches, discussed later in this chapter.

The Church of the Lord (Aladura) was founded in 1930 in Nigeria by Josiah Olunowo Ositelu, a Yoruba man from the town of Ogere and a former Anglican catechist-in-training before his vision and "call" to a new ministry. Like other Aladura or "owners of prayer," CLA selectively combines Yoruba and Christian religious traditions, but, unlike many Aladura churches, the Church of the Lord (Aladura) ordains women. This Church was not destined to remain a purely African phenomenon. Within twenty years of its founding, it had expanded beyond Nigeria into Anglophone Liberia and Sierra Leone.

In the 1960s, CLA spread to its first non-English speaking African country, Francophone Togo, then to South London, in Britain, and to Atlanta and Philadelphia, in the United States. In 1975, the Church of the Lord (Aladura) became a member of the World Council of Churches (WCC), and twenty years later, in 1994, the Church was formally registered in Germany. The German mission of CLA has flourished through the endeavors of the youngest son of the Church founder, the current CLA Primate Dr. Rufus Okikiolaolu Olubiyi Ositelu, who has earned two doctorates, one in computer science and the other in religion and theology.[4] Today, CLA has "stations" or branches in the United States, the most active ones located in Wooster, Massachusetts and Providence, Rhode Island. There are also two branches in New York City, one of which is located in Brooklyn, on Munro Street, the same street on which one also finds an "assembly" of Christ Apostolic Church (CAC), the first major Aladura church to emerge in Nigeria.

The Church of the Lord (Aladura), then, has become an international phenomenon. Further information about its beliefs, practices, history, and mission can be accessed globally at its World Wide Web Internet homepage, which states:

> Through the Internet, God has made a way for the Gospel of Christ to go out quickly around the world. We are honoured to be included among His messengers.[5]

The Church of the Lord (Aladura) Web site serves as a source of general information and a medium of evangelism. It is also a window on CLA gender practices.

Aim, Approach, and Methods

This Web site provides the point of departure for pursuing the threefold aim of this study. The first is to explore gender dynamics of CLA in its American context. The second is to incorporate into this investigation the female experience of CLA faith and gender practices. The third is to consider the implications of our findings for the study of gender in African Immigrant Religion (AIR) in the United States.

The rational for privileging the female voice in this study is that while Western intellectual categories help to critically assess social phenomena cross-culturally and to analyze gender categories within particular ethnographic contexts, the perspectives of actual culture bearers are crucial for developing nuanced interpretative frameworks, categories of analysis, and alternative research designs.[6] Thus, this article is coauthored by a Western-trained academic and an African faith practitioner. The resulting interpretative framework reflects social-scientific concern with structures and protocols of power, as well as valued perspectives of meaning and motivation shared by believers.

Deidre Helen Crumbley is a sociocultural anthropologist whose work has focused on religion and gender in Africa and, more recently, in the African Diaspora.[7] Gloria Malake Cline-Smythe, originally from Freetown Sierra Leone, rose to the level of senior prophetess in the Church of the Lord (Aladura) and was made supervisor of the East Coast CLA, except for the New York branches. Still, the anthropologist is not without her own faith and cultural background, and the prophetess is lacking neither in academic credentials nor in critical intellectual skills. Deidre Crumbley was raised in a female-founded African American "holy-sanctified" storefront church in the inner city of Philadelphia, and, in addition to her doctorate in anthropology, she holds a master of theological studies degree from divinity school. Gloria Cline-Smythe graduated with honors from Fourah Bay University, with a major in English and literature and a minor in theology. She has long aspired to expand her rich spiritual life to include formal theological training in a master of divinity program to better prepare for her ministry. In her secular profession, she has pursued successful careers in local and federal government on both sides of the Atlantic.

The first contact between the two women occurred through e-mail on 10 August 2003. Primate Rufus Ositelu referred Dr. Crumbley to the prophetess when the anthropologist expressed her desire to conduct research on gender dynamics in the CLA mission in America. Electronic media have continued to be central to the interaction between these two women, for whom the CLA Web page served as a point of departure for discussions about gender and church expansion. They also speak regularly by telephone, discussing and debating the collection and interpretation of data. Lengthy quotations from the prophetess are taken directly from her written notes.

Apart from the incorporation of twenty-first-century information technology into data collection methods, this investigation employs a conventional social-scientific case-study approach. Furthermore, at its inception, the interaction between the two women conformed to the traditional anthropologist-informant model. The prophetess enjoyed the "the opportunity of brain teasing" that "got me working on something I had not given thought to for some time." She delights in the intellectual banter between them and responds to the anthropologist's role of devil's advocate with grace, despite the directness of some rather personal questions.

As the research project proceeded, it became clear that, because of her university training and familiarity with social-scientific models of religion, Gloria Cline-Smythe was a source not only of rich data but also of analysis and critique. Thus, one of the first statements she made to Dr. Crumbley was that she wanted to make one thing perfectly clear: the Church of the Lord (Aladura) does not consist of uneducated people without resources, adding, "We have passed that." Prophetess Cline-Smythe pointed out that CLA's parishioners possess the wherewithal to emigrate from the continent and arrive in the United States able to compete successfully in the American context. Many have arrived with professional training and degrees that can stand them in good stead anywhere in the world. She insisted that her African church not be represented as the faith of backwards people from a backwards continent. Once convinced that this research project would avoid stereotypic representations of Africans and reductionistic interpretations of their faith, she agreed to be interviewed and eventually became coauthor of this essay.

The research contributions of Cline-Smythe required the anthropologist to change her view of the prophetess from informant to consultant and eventually to colleague. These shifts produced new perspectives on gender in African immigrant religion in general, and on menstrual blood avoidance in particular. Gender has been a research focus since Dr. Crumbley began her study of Aladura churches in Nigeria. For her, gender represents a conceptual problem; however, it is not "an issue" for her coauthor. Indeed, the anthropologist worked hard to retain the gender focus of this research project before realizing that the topic of gender and menstrual taboos would have to be approached as more than a matter of power relations if the collaboration was to be fruitful.

This research project, then, blurs conventional methodological and interpretive boundaries between the researcher and the researched. Furthermore, the inception and evolution of this study over its two-year duration highlights the interactive and constantly changing nature of knowledge production, in at least two ways. First, as is elaborated in the epilogue to this chapter, shifts took place in the prophetess's institutional relationship to the Church of the Lord (Aladura). These shifts reflect the challenges facing an African Instituted Church when it becomes an African Immigrant Church in America; these shifts also reflect the intersection of the personal and public, while underscoring the fact that academic research occurs within everyday human existence. As such, academic research is vulnerable to the unpredictable imponderables of life.

Second, the cyberspace point of departure for this study grew directly out of an encounter between the anthropologist and the primate of the Church of the Lord (Aladura). In part, the CLA link titled "Women" came into existence as a response to a criticism of the Web site made at the Third International Interdisciplinary Conference of the African Christian Diaspora in Europe, held at the Hirschluch Conference Centre near Berlin, 11–15 September 2003.[8] At this conference, Deidre Crumbley made the comment that the Church of the Lord (Aladura) Web site had failed to address one of CLA's most outstanding features, the ordination of women. Given the public nature of this criticism, the primate might have stood on his dignity and merely taken offense. Instead, his response was one of concerted constructive action, for, the month after the Hirschluch Conference, a new link titled "Women" had been added to the CLA homepage.

Concepts, Categories, and Language

The Church of the Lord (Aladura) is an institutional expression of the Aladura movement, which emerged out of an early-twentieth-century prayer and prophet-healing movement among the Yoruba people of southwestern Nigeria. CLA members, like other Christians, believe that Jesus Christ is the Son of God, that the Bible is the "Word of God," and that the Holy Ghost is the Spirit of God that guides and dwells with believers. In addition, Aladura also believe that witchcraft is real but is rendered ineffective by Christian faith and Holy Ghost protection, that Holy Ghost power can be evoked to address life's vicissitudes, and that fervent prayer, holy water, vigils, fasting, the burning of candles, and recitation of particular psalms can heal human bodies and situations. Aladura also celebrate and express the presence of divine spirit through holy dance and glossolalia, that is, speaking in unknown tongues.

As an Aladura church, the Church of the Lord (Aladura) is a Yoruba expression of the continentwide phenomenon of indigenous Christianity known as African Instituted/Initiated Churches.[9] African Instituted Churches (AICs) throughout sub-Saharan Africa selectively incorporate African and Christian cultural and religious traditions into their religious beliefs, practices, and organizational processes. In its U.S. diasporan context, the Church of the Lord (Aladura) is a "religion on the move";[10] it is also an example of African Immigrant Religions (AIR), which includes not only AICs but also African Islam and African traditional religions.

To avoid the interpretive baggage of terms such as "menstrual taboo" and "ritual pollution," these phrases have been intentionally replaced in this essay by "menstrual rites" and "ritual menstrual practices." Rejecting commonsense associations of menstrual blood with unhygienic dirtiness, classical anthropological interpretation associates "menstrual taboo" with the symbolic reassertion of gender rules in socially ambiguous situations.[11] To understand the coexistence of CLA menstrual rites with female ordination and office parity requires attention to notions of the sacred and the profane in the particular culture context, as well as the nuances of performance through which women specialists negotiate their identities as women and as leaders of their faith.[12]

CLA Gender Rules and Structures

The Church of the Lord (Aladura), from its early history, placed women in positions of explicit leadership. In 1966, the ordained female ministry was established by the founder as a divine injunction; the founder added, "And as long as the church exists it shall not cease." The second primate, Adeleke Adejobi, writes:

> We firmly believe in the doctrine of the Priesthood of all believers (male and females alike). . . . We believe that God calls men and women who surrender their lives to Him and obey His Divine calling. . . . In this new life one's nationality or race or education or social position is unimportant; such things mean nothing. Whether a person has Christ is what matters, and He is equally available to all.[13]

The schema of CLA offices explicitly identifies offices of equal rank for men and women:

Primate (unitary office)
Provisional head (unitary office)
Apostle/Reverend Mother Superior
Bishop/Reverend Mother
Archdeacon/Archdeaconess
Senior Prophet/Senior Prophetess—Senior Evangelist/Senior Pastor
Prophet/Pastor/Prophetess—Evangelist/Pastor/Lady Evangelist (Grades I)
Prophet/Pastor/Prophetess—Evangelist/Pastor/Lady Evangelist (Grades II)
Probationary Ministers (male and female)
Disciples (male and female)

Only the primate and the provisional head are unitary offices, and, to date, these offices have been held by male clergy. However, as Primate Adejobi pointed out, there is nothing in the Church constitution that forbids a woman from becoming primate, so, theoretically, a woman may hold any CLA office up to and including the primacy. Male and female clergy holding the same office are assigned the same duties and responsibilities.[14] For example, section 6 of Article V, "Ministers and Officers," describes the duties of the senior prophet/senior prophetess as follows: "In addition to his/her pastoral functions, he/she shall perform some other administrative duties as may be assigned to him/her by the Primate or Provisional Head or the Diocese Overseer."[15]

Having a female body, however, places at least three constraints on women's access to holy space and ritual objects. First, ordained women may not perform the four sacraments of communion, marriage, baptism, and funerals until they reach the age of sixty and no longer menstruate. The explanation for this policy, provided by the current primate, Dr. Rufus Ositelu, is that when women are postmenopausal, the effect of menstrual blood on the elements of the communion—the bread/flesh and wine/blood of Christ—is no longer problematic. It should be noted that the prohibition against performing the four sacraments also applies to "Probationary Ministers" who "shall not perform Baptism, Holy Communion, Holy Wedlock and funerals."[16] Second, as expressed in the Church constitution, women must sit outside the church sanctuary during their menstrual cycles.[17] Third, Primate Adejobi writes, women are excluded from arbitration of doctrine: "We opine that, when St. Paul said, "I do not permit a woman to teach" (Timothy 2:11–14) . . . this is not an absolute denial of a woman's chance to preach, but it forbids a woman to be the ultimate arbiter of doctrine."[18] Primate Adejobi explained that the basis of the prohibition against women arbitrating doctrine is that Jesus and the twelve disciplines, founders of the Christian faith, were male.

CLA members who have female bodies, then, each month, must avoid holy things and spaces; are not able to perform the four sacraments until they no longer menstruate; and are excluded from doctrinal arbitration. Still, their access to formal "political" power is in sharp contrast to their ritual or "ceremonial" leadership. Other studies have emphasized the latter among AICs in general and Aladura churches in particular.[19]

Cyberspace Images of Gender

As the 6,177th visitor to the Church of the Lord Web site, http://www.aladura.de/, on Wednesday, November 15, 2004, Dr. Crumbley encountered a site that was available in several Western languages, including Spanish, German, and French. The home page has ten links that introduce visitors to CLA beliefs, practices, national and international organizational structures, ecumenical affiliations, youth activities, contact information, outreach ministries, and the annual Mt. Tabieorar pilgrimage, held in the hometown of the founder. There is also a link that connects to the World Council of Churches Web site, attesting to the "ecumenical outlook" of CLA, which has been a WCC member since 1975. Another important link reflecting the global mission of CLA is an article on "missions in reverse," that is, the role of African Instituted Churches not only in propagating the gospel worldwide but also in revitalizing Western Christianity.[20]

Other than the "Women" link, there are no direct references to gender issues or women's place in the life and history of CLA, with the exception of contact information for Spr. Mother Barbara Ositelu.[21] The "Women" Web page begins with the quotation that opens this chapter, followed by a list of the various church bodies on which CLA women sit. These range from the highest executive bodies, such as the Supreme Council of Prelates, the Primate in Council, and the Board of Trustees, to ministries such as Teaching, Social, Music, and Drama. Also included are organizations solely for women, such as Mother's Union Band and the Council of Deaconesses.

Prophetess Cline-Smythe responded to the Web site, generally, by commending the primate for expanding it to include a link that addressed the place of women in the Church of the Lord (Aladura). Her response to its treatment of the topic was that, had there been time and space, there was so very much more that could have been written about women in church history and current affairs. She would love to see the inclusion of stories about the women who had been instrumental in spreading CLA to Liberia, Sierra Leone, Britain, and the United States.

In sum, the Church Web site reiterates CLA's women-inclusive structures that not only support the ordination of women but also explicitly assign women the same rank and responsibilities as men. But how are CLA gender rules experienced in the everyday institutional life of the Church, especially in its American context? This question is addressed by documenting the lived-reality of CLA gender practices through the life and work of a senior clergywoman who has participated in CLA organizational processes on both sides of the Atlantic.

Sierra Leonean Beginnings

The prophetess was not always a member of the Church of the Lord (Aladura). She was raised in the Methodist Church at a time when Aladura churches were not an established part of the Sierra Leonean religious landscape. The transplanting of this Nigerian Church was effected through the joint mission of Primate Adejobi and his ordained wife, Reverend Mother Superior Olive Adejobi, when they were young and in the early stages of their clerical careers,

> In 1948, Apostle Adejobi took the bold step of venturing out from Nigeria with his beautiful young bride, Olive; later she was to become the Reverend Mother Superior and also Vice Provost of Aladura Theological Seminary and Prophets/Prophetesses Training Institute. The inclusion of his wife in his ministry brought a different light to the Church's acceptance of women in the work of the mission. They became partners, and, in this way, many women were brought into the fold of the Church, first in Freetown and later in other major cities and towns of the Republic of Sierra Leone.
>
> The mission was first based at Dove's Cot, a little area in the east end of the city. Later, land was acquired, first at Wilberforce for the setting up of a seminary and later, on Williams Street, where the headquarters were established. To complete the early acquisition of property, bearing in mind the growth and development of the mission, land was bought on the hillside of Freetown that could accommodate the Church's own Holy Mount as well as a mini-cathedral. The Mount became the base for the spiritual development of ministers and, later, of laity found ready for such training. Regular meditation, Bible study, and ["spiritual exercises" that include] rolling and praying, as well as time for seclusion for preparation of ordination or anointment, are all carried out there.

Gloria Malake Cline-Smith was raised in the Methodist faith, and came to the Church of the Lord (Aladura) as an adult, after visiting the church during a lunch break one afternoon in Freetown at a time when her ex-husband was having a problem at work:

> It was the first time I had had anything to do with a church of "the praying people" (Aladura). I was captivated by my first experience of just walking into the church . . . to find someone who never knew me nor had ever had the opportunity to talk to me . . . to tell me the reason for my coming to the church that day. I found it bewildering, [but] as each of the prophecies came true, my faith in the God of the Church of the Lord (Aladura) became stronger.

Not only did she join the Church of the Lord (Aladura), but she began to ascend its national and international hierarchies.

> Time saw me grow through the ranks of laity to the position of international deaconess as well as assistant secretary to then Primate Reverend Dr. E. O. A. Adejobi. . . . [Being] the assistant secretary to the primate afforded me the opportunity to learn more about the Church, its administration, and its relationship with other church bodies like the World Council of Churches in Geneva, and others. I became a part of the local planning sessions for international forum . . . arranging our own international assemblies held once every three years in any country which felt like hosting it. In my national church, I served on the Education Board, the Board of Trustees, various Unions, and organizations of the church.

These various roles allowed her to interact with the clergy of other denominations, including Aladura denominations, causing her to realize that in many of them, because she is female, she never could be ordained or hold high office.

As an ordained CLA minister, she found her spiritual life in Sierra Leone further enriched by evangelical outreach, extended periods of prayer, and Bible study. She also supported parishioners as they drew on their faith to negotiate life's vicissitudes.

> I loved to pioneer branches—a challenge that not many people are cut out for. The planting of new branches of the Church took a lot of time and patience to get it operational. I found the practice of fasting and midnight struggles, beach prayers and struggles, most effective, as much as outside preaching from street to street within an area. The Bible had to be the basis for everything preached because a new convert had to have something tangible he could fall back on. The support demonstrated by the congregation, which is generally divided into Bands or Unions, is commendable. They fasted with whomever needed special prayers and equally shared in the outcome. If it turned out to be negative, they were quick to give encouragement and lend their committed time and support.

The female members with whom she worked had special needs, which the Church of the Lord (Aladura) in Sierra Leone addressed directly:

> The common needs, which brought many women together, kept them in groups within the Church. Childbearing, being a very important aspect of an African woman's life, stable homes, dedicated husbands, peace in one's home, astute business attributes, and the success of one's profession or

> career were some of the reasons that brought women and kept them together until their prayers were heard. As more women proved the power of prayer through God's miracles in their lives, so word of the work spread. It was and has continued to be that men were brought into the Church through their wives. Some [women] have stayed and nurtured their families through the years, and become formidable pillars where others have moved on to other things but still remember the blessings derived from their years within the walls of the [CLA].

While becoming increasingly involved in CLA, the prophetess held prestigious posts in Freetown's local government.

> At the time I came into the mission, I was a local government officer, serving as Secretary to the Mayor of Freetown. I had professional British training . . . as a secretary, and as the years progressed, I pursued a degree program [at] the University of Sierra Leone, majoring in English language and literature with a minor in theology. I graduated with a Second class in 1987 and returned to my local government position, but this time in an administrative position serving as city manager. Several foreign governments gave me the opportunity of receiving training to equip me for this position including the U.S.A. government through Operation Crossroads Africa. . . . I combined my church work with my regular work without problems, and from time to time invited my colleagues to attend functions at our church at which I preached.

Coming to America: CLA's American Mission

Prophetess Cline-Smythe observed that, for reasons of history and contemporary circumstances, many of the first Church of the Lord (Aladura) branches in the United States were founded by Liberians. CLA was planted in Liberia about the same time it arrived in Sierra Leone through the missionary efforts of Apostle Samuel Oduwale and his wife, Delicia. Together they worked to spread the faith in the capital, Monrovia, and eventually in America, in part because of the close relationship between Liberia and the United States. Liberia was founded in 1822 to repatriate freed slaves from the United States, and it has maintained strong links with the United States and enjoyed special political and economic concessions. Unsurprisingly, many Liberians came to the United States for further studies and because it offered better prospects. Among African immigrants, Prophetess Cline-Smythe observed, disproportionately large populations of Liberians are found in Philadelphia, Pennsylvania; Providence, Rhode Island; and Worcester and Roslindale, Massachusetts. Those who were CLA members in Liberia wanted to worship in the traditions of the Church of the Lord (Aladura) in this new American context. As in Liberia, the husband-and-wife missionary team of the Oduwales was central to the spread of the CLA in America. However,

> after the death of her husband, Samuel, in the early 1960s, the Reverend Mother Delicia Oduwale moved to Philadelphia, where she founded the St. Samuel Chapel. Another Liberian, Archdeaconess Marie Cooper, of CLA Bronx, New York, also with her husband, provided spiritual nurturing for many who came to their church on Monroe Street, in the Bronx. The years have taken their toll on these female pioneers, but the churches, no matter how few their members, stand as a testimony to their hard work.

Because of the unrest associated with the civil war in Sierra Leone, the prophetess immigrated to the United States in 1991. Before leaving Freetown, she made a solemn vow that if her emigration was successful, she would pioneer a CLA branch in America.

> The payment and fulfillment of vows is taken as a sacred trust between a member and God, particularly when that vow is made under very trying circumstances. Such was the situation I found myself in when I arrived in this country [after] a ten-year [civil] war and an abusive marital relationship, which I had regularly committed into God's hands. I had fallen ill on the flight here. My recovery took a very long time, and when finally I fully recovered, I realized something was missing in me. I had been regularly attending church services near where I lived, but it was never fulfilling. I started looking around for a church with drums and clapping and a real pentecostal flavor but could find none. Then, one day, I bumped into an old school friend who had migrated to this country in the late sixties and . . . she invited me to her church.

This church was very far from her home, and with limited funds and transportation, she found it difficult to be an active participant. The prophetess, along with a few of the women living in her area, began praying and worshipping by phone, which "meant we all tied up the lines of the various homes we lived in and offended, in no small way, the various family members we were living with." Then, one night, she had a dream "in which I was reminded of my vow that if the Lord got me out of my troubles and I set my feet in this white man's land safe and sound, I would plant a church for His glory." Thus, her CLA mission in America was born, and as overseer of her region she would be intimately involved with the planning and development of not one but several congregations. Though the work was "fraught with difficulties from its inception," it was a "joy to see all the paperwork taken to Ogere, the International spiritual headquarters of the mission in Nigeria, and to be proudly received by the late third primate, Dr. Gabriel Ositelu."

Challenges to CLA in America

The prophetess identifies six challenges that face the Church of the Lord (Aladura) clergy in the American mission—none of which relate to CLA gender dynamics. First, she describes CLA in America as not only a "church of immigrants" but also a "church of migrants." Many CLA members are recent arrivals to the United States and are in the process of regularizing their immigration status. They are often "on their way elsewhere," and they want to relocate for several reasons, including wanting to live in a less urban setting, wishing to compete for jobs where there are fewer Africans with similar qualifications, and wanting to start their own "white-garment church" in an area where such African churches are few and far between. Regardless of their reason for leaving the Washington, D.C., area, the impact of such departures on the CLA mission is the same; when parishioners are "on their way elsewhere," it is difficult for clergy to develop a faith community that is financially self-sustaining, socially cohesive, and institutionally loyal.

A second challenge is a utilitarian approach to the Church. For example, worshippers visiting the parish in May, fasting and praying that their visa be regularized, by January may have relocated to Tennessee with green card in hand! The prophetess notes sadly:

> I found, to my disappointment, quite a few episodes which regularly reminded me of the Parable of the Ten Lepers. As soon as issues were resolved, they were gone—no forwarding address, no telephone number,

nothing. In other words, the Church became used for the fulfillment of desires, and it was dropped subsequently as hot potatoes.

A third challenge facing the clergy is the experiential and communication gap between mission clergy in the Diaspora and clergy policymakers back in Africa. In the prophetess's CLA province back in Sierra Leone, clergy are required to minister full time and cannot hold another job; however, in America, where stations are financially unreliable, if CLA clergy do not hold a secular job, they cannot keep a roof over their head. Thus, CLA mission clergy in America can find their finances stretched and their lives stressful as they work full-time jobs while trying to spread the gospel in a strange land. Representatives of the primate, who serve as mentors to CLA clergy, are similarly constrained in their duties by a lack of time and financial support.

CLA clergy in the American mission are pioneering churches far from the support of extended family networks, in a society where they are lumped into a racial minority and perceived as a religious oddity. They also face the challenge of finding a way to make this experience "real" for church leaders who live in African nations under familiar laws, within traditional kinship networks, and in socially familiar contexts where their culture and their faith traditions are normative. The experiential gap between mission clergy in the Diaspora and clergy policymakers in Africa is keenly felt when clergy are expected to comply with the policy of sending one-third of church income to the Nigerian headquarters. This is difficult to do when the stability of fledgling parishes is so financially unpredictable. Add to this the task of staying on top of annual income tax remittances to the Internal Revenue Service, and the financial pressure on clergy is further exacerbated.

A fourth challenge involves interaction with local authorities. These include compliance with municipal codes, fear of immigration enforcement, and the effect of these on church attendance and quality of worship.

> Fear of law enforcement, in whatever form, keeps people away, particularly when the issues they are praying for are related to their [immigration] status being regularized. . . . Fear of reprisals, if people go into spirit and start shrieking or praying in a loud voice, is also a problem area. In the past, it was easy to godfather a church in the basement of homes, a school room, et cetera, but now there are basic requirements which must be provided; they [include] being in compliance [with] the Americans with Disabilities Act, having parking lots demarcating space for physically challenged persons.

A fifth problem is that stable and loyal communities tend to consist of older members. While the Rhode Island CLA branch is the most active and loyal, the average age of its members is sixty-five. Many of the children of leaders of CLA members in Africa join other Churches when they come to America. Just because someone was CLA in Africa does not mean that he or she can be depended upon to join and support CLA in America. The challenge is how to build on the stability of established elder members, retain younger CLA members once they have come to America, and attract other immigrant Africans and nonimmigrant Americans.

A final concern is about passing on valued gender practices to young men in the American mission of the CLA. Cooperation between female clergy and a trustworthy male is essential: "Tradition . . . dictates that during a female minister's monthly cycle, she cannot go into the inner altar to light up the candles and set the altar up for service. Therefore, she needs a Deacon or a Curate to ensure that, at that time of the month, the cleanliness of God's house is maintained." This requires a close and mutually respectful relationship between the presiding female priest and the man who works with her. The problem is twofold. First, the number of young men who attend CLA churches here in America is low. Second, many have grown up in America and not in Africa, where, as CLA members, they would have been regularly exposed to male and female clergy ministering together. This observation implies that the parity and inclusivity of CLA gender rules, though not perfectly enacted, nonetheless provide ideals to which one can aspire and to which one can be held accountable. It also implies that such ideals are not normative in American gender practices in either secular or religious institutions.

Negotiating CLA Gender Practices in America

The issue of gender was not mentioned among the problem areas just described. Only when the anthropologist pressed the matter did the prophetess address it. On these occasions, she graciously complied by offering richly nuanced insights and humorously related anecdotes. These provided a valuable window into the lived experience of being female in the Church of the Lord (Aladura) in America.

Women in leadership positions in African Immigrant Churches, such as the Church of the Lord (Aladura), are faced with the challenges of tradition and culture in the discharge of their duties as female ministers:

> Tradition dictates that in the presence of men, women are supposed to be submissive and obedient and to play a subservient role. However, the [Church of the Lord] empowers women to be leaders and gives each of us the same administrative powers . . . given to men; but, in reality, a woman needs to draw a fine line between being the effective minister . . . yet a respectful woman, who does not disregard the societal position of a man who many need chiding for infractions done.
>
> Our mothers in the church, such as retired Reverend Mother Olive Adejobi, wife of the second primate of the church, the late Dr. Emmanuel O. A. Adejobi, was hardly ever known to publicly administer punishment to male ministers when once they were out of seminary and in the field. She had to find recourse of meting out whatever deterrents through other means such as disciplinary committees, et cetera. She . . . was always committed to upholding the tradition of a woman's place to that of a man in whatever she did but at the same time respecting [one's] anointing as an ordained female minister of God.

Not all CLA female clergy have successfully negotiated the subtleties of CLA gender practices. Catherine Kamara, the first Sierra Leonean woman to train for the CLA ministry, the first CLA archdeaconess, and CLA representative to the World Council of Churches, was a role model to CLA women in Sierra Leone. Today, however, she heads her own church in England and is no longer affiliated with the Church of the Lord, due to irreconcilable differences associated with her strength of personality. Here, when the anthropologist asked how the prophetess, also a strong personality, handled this situation, Prophetess Cline-Smythe, in keeping with her ability to look reality squarely in the face and laugh at it, chuckled as she related that she, and women like her working in the United States, have been referred to as "these recalcitrant American women" who are "no more African women." Nevertheless, because "it is the women who stick" and see things through, changed male attitudes were inevitable, no matter the difficulty.

Honoring the Menstrual Rites in America

The prophetess values the menstrual rites of CLA and continues to practice them here in America, not only at CLA parishes but also when she visits American churches. She did the same when growing up in the

Methodist Church in Sierra Leone, where her parents did not permit her to take communion when menstruating. This practice was common in "established" churches when she was growing up. Even today, she observes, some female members of Anglican churches in Africa do not approach the altar area, or even the sanctuary itself, when menstruating. In her home in the Washington, D.C., area, when she menstruates, she has a male household member drape her personal altar with a white cloth; then, after her menses, she "reconsecrates" her altar using Psalm 24. She observed, "As educated as I am, at this time of the month, I think of my self as unclean"; yet, she made it clear that this sense of being "unclean" does not diminish her sense of value to herself or her anointment.

She admits that it will require Holy Ghost guidance to communicate the value of CLA menstrual practice to non-Africans. CLA menstrual rituals are not a matter that clergy immediately broach with non-African newcomers, because, if they are put off by what is too culturally alien, they may "miss the religious experience of a lifetime"—namely the profound intimacy of "communing with God as friend to friend," an event full of "power and beauty." The prophetess has not had such experiences in the mission church of her youth or in contemporary mainline churches. She is quick to add, however, that such intimate encounters with God are not limited to CLA, but they do require "correct parameters"—namely a community of faith that regularly and fervently fasts, prays, and studies scriptures "together and on one accord."

Conclusions and Implications

While the case-study approach of this study does not lend itself to generalizations, its findings help to advance the threefold aim of this study. Regarding the first aim of exploring gender in the Church of the Lord (Aladura) in the American context, the case of the Oduwales in America suggests that married ordained partnerships continue to be a missionary strategy. At the same time, being a single clergywoman did not prevent the prophetess from being assigned as regional overseer for the East Coast of the United States. Future research should explore the translation of women-inclusive CLA organizational structures into the American mission field, as well as subtler gender expectations that women should be discreet about disciplining male clergy in public. Tension between the need to show deference to men and the desire to be true to one's anointment could give rise to frustrations that lead women, like Catherine Kamara, to leave CLA when they have so much to contribute to its future expansion in Africa and abroad.

The second aim of the investigation was to incorporate into the research project the female voice from within the faith community. The voice of a senior clergywoman enriched the study with unique perspectives on female roles and symbolic life in CLA. The anthropologist had followed menstrual rites while conducting fieldwork in the Church of the Lord, but her cultural background did not prepare her to see menstrual rites in terms other than compliance. Menstrual rites "stood out" for her, becoming a major intellectual problem and research focus. Menstrual rites did not "stand out" for the prophetess. For her, they are part of a life of faith that also includes a highly valued life of devotion, duties, and status of ordained clergy on a par with those of men and a committed life of evangelical outreach. As such, gender is not a concept to be lifted out and analyzed separately but a daily reality to be lived and negotiated within the context of faith and mission. While remaining committed to the analysis of power and inequity, the anthropologist has expanded her understanding of menstrual rituals as more than a measure of power and control. The menstrual rites in the Church of the Lord are best understood in light of meanings and values associated with Church doctrine, its vision, and the cultural legacies of its members.

Prophetess Cline-Smythe is neither oblivious to nor in denial of the challenges that face her as a CLA clergywoman; however, she has directed her limited time and resources to honoring her "anointing" and to keeping her vow to propagate the gospel in America, which she has exceeded by being an area supervisor. Of course, one might argue that this response is the consequence of false consciousness fostered by internalized sexism. This explanation, however, suggests a lack of intellectual self-awareness and human agency on the part of the prophetess that the anthropologist, after working with her over the past two years, finds unacceptably inaccurate.

Regarding the third aim of this study, its larger implications for studying gender in African Immigrant Religions (AIRs), a methodological approach that incorporates the voices and collaboration of women can yield enlightening perspectives and productive applications. These include refined intellectual categories of knowledge for future academic research and fostering dialogue among CLA women and men about issues that could fester and explode if left unaddressed. Another application is the role of women's voices in establishing an information-based dialogue between immigrant communities and American institutions as they struggle to understand and appreciate each other's gender practices in religiously plural twenty-first-century America.

Epilogue

When this essay was first conceived, its subtitle was "An Anthropologist and Prophetess Reflect." By the end of the two-year research period, the qualifier "former" had to be added to it. Gloria Malake Cline-Smythe insisted on this revision because she had ceased to serve in her capacity as a regional overseer in the American mission of the Church of the Lord (Aladura). This decision was neither sudden nor made lightly; it has entailed soul searching, a strong sense of loss, and still unresolved sentiments. The "prophetess"—still referred to this way because she continues to speak forth the gospel and prophesy to those seeking spiritual guidance—is clear about her new direction. She has become active in the Lutheran Church, which she initially visited out of ecumenical curiosity, having had little exposure to this denomination in Africa.

She came to love the Lutheran liturgy, and, coming from the CLA experience, where clerical gender parity is normative, she was at ease with Lutheran gender practices. The Anglican liturgy is also beautiful, she observed, but while it has finally ordained women, it has unresolved issues about accepting women in higher posts, such as bishop. Additionally, the Lutheran church she attends has a "praise and worship" devotional service, during which she plays African drums, sings, and claps, reminiscent of enlivened CLA worship. When asked to describe the exact nature of her relationship to CLA, she responded, "I just don't know." When describing what it is like to be estranged from CLA, she says, "I feel in my very bones . . . a part of myself is missing."

What, then, could have led to such extreme measures, and what are the implications of this outcome for both the mission of CLA in America and the study of African immigrant religion? The reasons, in the end, come down to three points, two of which are addressed in the earlier "Challenges to the CLA in America" section. These two are the instability of local congregations and the communication gap between mission clergy in the Diaspora and those in the African headquarters. The "migrant immigrants" who make up these churches cannot be depended upon to provide the financial support needed to maintain the church, especially after one-third of its income is sent back to CLA headquarters in Nigeria. The prophetess made commitments of time and resources willingly and aggressively pursued the building of the CLA Church in America until CLA headquarters decided that she should relocate and start a mission in the state of Texas. At this point, the communication gap became unbridgeable.

In Nigeria, there is no social security to fall back upon, but there are traditional extended family structures and land tenure practices that make it possible for elders to have housing and food when they no longer can work. In the United States, such traditional social practices have given way to state and corporate structures so that, without a solid retirement plan and social security benefits, most American workers cannot be sure of meeting their basic needs in their old age. The prophetess was unable to communicate these contingencies to the Nigerian headquarters, where the response to her hesitation was to refer her to the biblical model of Abraham faithfully following God's command to leave his home and family in Haran for "a land that I will show thee."[22]

The America imagined by people outside the country is often a land of milk and honey; outsiders seem to be unaware of America as a land of working poor where many middle-class professionals are just a couple of paychecks away from being homeless and without medical coverage. A government job with the income, benefits, and security like that now held by the prophetess is very difficult for an immigrant African woman with dependents to find in America. It took her a long time to secure this post, after an extended period of temporary secretarial assignments.

Additionally, she is just a few years from retirement, and, as indicated in her narrative, she has had health challenges since her arrival in this country. While coauthoring this article, she was diagnosed with a life-threatening disease. Though her spirit and her faith are strong, such realities are sobering, and they reinforce what she has come to realize, namely that "This is my life we are talking about." She had to find a way to answer her call and still find a way to survive as a recent African immigrant in America.

She is happy in the Zion Evangelical Lutheran church, and Zion appears to be happy with the expression of African Christian spirituality she brings to this community of faith. The congregation is located in Tacoma Park, on the border between Washington, D.C., and Maryland, in the heart of an immigrant neighborhood "where Africans abound." About 70 percent of the approximately 250 members of Zion are of African descent, mainly Africans, with some West Indians and a few African Americans. The remaining members are white Americans, of whom a few are originally from Germany. Zion also has an African Outreach program, and through the Lutheran Church the prophetess may be able to realize a longheld dream of attending seminary and thereby better serving the propagation of the gospel.

It should be noted that no formal letter of termination from CLA headquarters has been presented to her, but then she was never "posted from Africa." She had already immigrated to America when she was asked to oversee the CLA churches in her region. Thus, her work with the CLA mission in America had as much to do with the completion of a personal vow as the performance of a clerical assignment.

The implications of this turn of events are important for future growth of the Church of the Lord (Aladura) in America. No matter how much CLA missionaries in America love the CLA faith and spirituality, as does the prophetess, they need support to do the work of church-building. This includes concessions based on a realistic appreciation of the institutional, financial, and personal challenges that face CLA clergy as Africans immigrants in America. If these realities are not taken into consideration, these frontline warriors for African Instituted Churches in the Diaspora could be lost to other denominations. This is especially the case when, as with this Lutheran congregation, other denominations sincerely welcome cultural diversity and provide its bearers with support and security.

The turn of events in the church life of the prophetess raises conceptual and methodological questions in the field, as well. How are scholars to address the religious practices of African immigrants who join established American denominations? Do their lives of faith cease to be of scholarly concern because they are not in African religious institutions? Finally, what methods are to be followed to access and interpret their religious contribution to American religious pluralism today? Although she is no longer active in the Church of the Lord (Aladura), the Aladura spirituality that Gloria Cline-Smythe brings to the Lutheran Church will impact this mainline denomination from within. As such, her story provides an important vehicle for interpreting Africa immigrant religion in America on the level of individual faith.

This article is dedicated to those African men and women who have selflessly dedicated their efforts and resources to establishing the Church of the Lord (Aladura) in America, Britain, Germany, and throughout the CLA Diaspora.

Notes

1. This quotation is taken from the Church of the Lord (Aladura) Web site, available online at http://www.aladura.de/women.htm (accessed 8 November 2004).

2. Roswith Gerloff, "Africa as the Laboratory of the World: The Africa Christian Diaspora in Europe as Challenge to Mission and Ecumenical Relations," in R. Gerloff, ed., *Mission Is Crossing Frontiers: Essays in Honor of Bongani A. Mazibuko* (Pietermaritzburg: Cluster Publications, 2003), 343.

3. U.S. Department of Homeland Security, *Yearbook of Immigration Statistics 2002* (Washington, D.C.: U.S. Government Printing Office, 2003), 12–14, 17–18.

4. Rufus Okikiolaolu Olubiyi Ositelu, *African Instituted Churches* (New Brunswick, N.J.: Transaction Publishers, 2002), 200.

5. "Partner in Progress (PIP): The Church of the Lord Organisation," Church of the Lord (Aladura) Web site, available online at http://www.aladura.de/pip.htm (accessed 18 November 2004).

6. I. Amadiume, *Male Daughters, Female Husbands: Gender and Sex in an African Society* (Atlantic Highlands, N.J.: Zed Books, 1987), 15, 28–29, 31–68, 89; I. Amadiume, *Reinventing Africa: Matriarchy, Religion and Culture* (London and New York: Zed Books, 1997), 110, 119, 123–130, 191–192; N. Nzegwu, "Gender Equality in a Dual Sex System: The Case of Onitsha," *Canadian Journal of Law and Juris Prudence* 7 no. 1 (1994): 84–95; O. Oyewumi, *The Invention of Women* (Minneapolis: University of Minnesota Press, 1997), ix–xiii, 13–15, 29, 31, 46–49, 58–62.

7. Deidre Helen Crumbley, "Also Chosen: Jews in the Imagination of a Black Storefront Church," *Anthropology and Humanism* 25, no. 1 (April 2000): 6–23. See also Deidre Helen Crumbley, "On Being First: Dogma, Disease, and Domination in the Rise of an African Church," *Religion* 30, no. 2 (2000): 169–184; Deidre Helen Crumbley, "Patriarchs, Prophets, and Procreation: Sources of Gender Practices in Three African Churches," *Africa* 73, no. 4 (2003): 584–605.

8. "Women: The Church of the Lord Organisation," The Church of the Lord (Aladura) Web site, available online at http://www.aladura.de/women.htm (accessed 18 November 2004).

9. Allan Anderson, *African Reformation: African Initiated Christianity in the 20th Century* (Trenton: African World Press, 2001), 10. See also Ositelu, *African Instituted Churches,* 74–75.

10. Gerloff, "Africa as the Laboratory of the World," 365–367.

11. Mary Douglas, *Purity and Danger: An Analysis of the Concepts of Pollution and Taboo* (London: Routledge and Kegan Paul 1966), 1–5, 113.

12. For example, in the Igbo traditions of southeastern Nigeria, Professor Ogbu Kalu observes an association of menstrual blood with a sacred and powerful "other." Here, the phrase "*ifu nso*" is used to refer to menstrual blood. Literally it means "seeing" (*ifu*), "a holy or sacred thing" (*nso*) (personal correspondence, 8

December 2004). Abraham Akrong describes how similar beliefs prevent female religious specialists in Ghana from engaging in ritual activity when menstruating. These beliefs suggest that a god, on coming suddenly upon menstruating women in his or her shrine, might mistake the power in menstrual blood for an unknown force. Striking out against the trespasser, the god might accidentally kill the menstruating women. Interview with Abraham Akrong, University of Ghana, Legon, interviewed in Hirschluch, Germany, 13 September 2003. Also see Thomas C. T. Buckley and Alma Gottlieb, "A Critical Appraisal of Theories of Menstrual Symbolism," in T.C.T. Buckley and A. Gottlieb, eds., *Blood Magic: The Anthropology of Menstruation* (Berkeley: University of California Press, 1988), 23–50.

13. E. O. A. Adejobi, *The Observances and Practices of the Church of the Lord (Aladura) in the Light of Old Testament and New Testament* (Nigeria: Enterprise Du Chez, 1976), unpaginated preface.

14. *Year 2000 Revised Constitution of the Church of the Lord (Aladura) World Wide* (Shagamu, Nigeria: Grace Enterprises, 2001), 10–18, 60–61.

15. Ibid., 17.

16. Ibid., 18.

17. Ibid., 62.

18. Adejobi, *The Observances and Practices of the Church of the Lord (Aladura)*, preface.

19. B. Jules-Rosette, "The Arcadian Wish: Toward a Theory of Contemporary African Religion," in B. Jules-Rosette, ed., *The New Religions of Africa* (Norwood, N.J.: Ablex, 1979), 219–229, B. Jules-Rosette, "Women in Indigenous African Cults and Churches," in F. C. Steady, ed., *The Black Woman Cross-Culturally* (Cambridge: Schenkman Publishing, 1981), 185–207; Deidre Helen Crumbley, "Impurity and Power: Women in Aladura Churches," *Africa* 62, no. 4 (1992): 6–23.

20. "Artikel: The Church of the Lord Organisation," Church of the Lord (Aladura) Web site, available online at http://www.aladura.de/artikel.htm (accessed 18 November 2004).

21. "Info: The Church of the Lord Organisation," Church of the Lord (Aladura) Web site, available online at http://www.aladura.de/news.htm (accessed 18 November 2004).

22. Genesis 12:1.

8

West African Muslims in America
When Are Muslims Not Muslims?

Linda Beck

Introduction

The subtitle of this chapter may be somewhat misleading, if not offensive. The religious identity of Muslims is after all invariable, as is the case with Christians, Jews, Hindus, Buddhists, and members of other any religious (or atheistic) group. Nevertheless, it has been argued and commonly accepted that identity is multifaceted and situational, with a single group identification becoming particularly salient depending on the context. The salience of one aspect of our identity, however, does not negate the presence or importance of other facets that continue to influence the fluid boundaries between groups and the way we relate to others with overlapping identities who share one or more elements of our identity. Moreover, the salience of a dimension of our identity is often external, a product of the way others perceive or do not perceive us. This does not, of course, change who we are or who we believe ourselves to be in general terms or in any particular context or situation.

This chapter examines the multifaceted identities of West African Muslims in the United States, specifically in metropolitan New York City, to investigate the alleged situational nature of identity and its impact on group membership and relations. As with any other group of individuals, there are many dimensions to the identity of West African Muslims, including race, ethnicity, nationality, class, age, gender, immigration status, and, of course, religion. In conversations with West African Muslims in New York City, I found that the various aspects of their identities undoubtedly influenced their assessment of the place of West African immigrants in American society and their relations with the larger "black

American" and Muslim communities.[1] As it is beyond the scope of a single chapter to discuss all the dimensions of the identities of West African Muslims, this chapter focuses solely on three aspects of their identity that they share: race, religion, and recent emigration from West Africa.

Although I have been working in and with African immigrant communities in New York City for a number of years, the analysis presented here is based largely on a series of interviews conducted in the summer and fall of 2005 with West African immigrants and representatives of the broader black American and Muslim communities as part of a larger research project on West African Muslims. The questions posed were based on prior knowledge of the historical relationship between these communities as well as of various contemporary events, some of which are discussed in the chapter. Having watched the African immigrant communities grow and transform over the past decade, I recognize that this chapter is a snapshot of a "moving target" that can provide us with insights into the experiences of West African Muslims in America and their relations with the broader communities in which they live. It is, therefore, likely that subsequent research, including my own, may reveal that some aspects of what is presented here may no longer hold true. Nonetheless, the views of these informants at this point in time provide critical information about the early experiences and adaptation of West African Muslims to life in America.

West African Muslims in New York are considered and consider themselves to be "foreign," not only in terms of their immigration status but also in sociocultural terms, as African and Muslim. To analyze their dual *Fremdheit* or foreignness, this chapter focuses on how the formation of West African Muslim communities, which has been well documented by other researchers,[2] has influenced and been influenced by the communities' relationship with two marginal groups in the United States: the largely foreign-born Muslim communities and autochthonous African Americans. The tension and confluence among these communities with overlapping identities are a product of not only their interactions but also the conceptions of the dominant "autochthonous" population (i.e., white Christian Americans) as to what it means to be African, Muslim, and foreign. Within the global city of New York, these interactions (or lack thereof) influence the mobility of West African Muslims in spatial and economic terms, as well as their "integrative" mobility, that is their ability to undergo, control, or resist integration into American society that may transform individual identities and/or sociocultural categories (e.g., African American, Muslim, and foreigner).

Intra-Muslim Relations in New York City

West African (WA) Muslims clearly see themselves as part of a larger *umma* (community) of Muslims, both worldwide and specifically within New York City. For most WA Muslims in New York City, however, daily contact with Muslims from other regions of the world is relatively limited. The notable exception is often African American Muslims, relations with whom are discussed more fully in the subsequent section on the interactions between WA Muslims and African Americans of all religious faiths.

In New York City, WA Muslims are well aware of their status as a numerical minority within the Muslim community, as well the perception held by some other Muslims that they are either only "half Muslim" or not Muslim at all for religious and/or racial reasons. Since 9/11, however, there have been increasing efforts to bridge the gap within the diverse community of Muslims in New York City as a result of "racial" or, more accurately, "religious profiling" by U.S. government officials, as well as increased prejudice, bias attacks, and allegations of discriminatory acts perpetrated by non-Muslim Americans. After briefly discussing the diversity and divisions among Muslims in New York, this section focuses on the dynamic relationship between WA Muslims and other "foreign" (immigrant) Muslims, specifically the Arab and South Asian communities, and the impact of 9/11 on these relationships in light of racial stereotyping by non-Muslim Americans, as well as among Muslims.

Diversity and Divisions Among Muslims in New York

The division of the Muslim community into discrete communities is most evident in the creation of neighboring mosques that serve different subgroups of Muslims.[3] Although there are a number of multiethnic mosques in New York, mosques are commonly referred to by an ethnonational or geographic adjective rather than by their official Islamic names; thus, there is the Bangladeshi mosque, the Nigerian mosque, or, more generally, the African mosque in a neighborhood.

While WA Muslims, particularly those who drive livery and taxi cabs, may pray in different Muslim communities wherever they find themselves during the week, an Ivorian Imam explained that on Fridays, African immigrants pray in an "African mosque." Drawing a secular comparison to the president of the United States as president of all Americans, he asserted that in theory "an Imam is an Imam of all the people." In practice, however, "African people pray with their own people who have an African Imam." Of course, the same may be said of other immigrant and African American Muslims, as well as other religious communities.

According to a leader of a secular association of Senegalese, this is not surprising, because "immigrants tend to travel with their cultural baggage. Wherever you go, you get along with the same community; you replicate what you did back home." He offered the example of Senegalese who "don't have connections with Nigerians or Ivorians [in Africa], so they don't here, either." He noted that "these are neighboring African states; Pakistan and the rest are even farther away."

Self-segregation into discrete religious communities may be attributed in part to language barriers. This is particularly true of Muslims from francophone West Africa. While those who came to the United States with a western-style education are typically more comfortable with French than English, a large percentage of WA Muslims—if not the majority—have never been to school and thus prefer to use their maternal language or an African lingua franca both inside and outside the mosque. Other than prayers in Arabic, Imams in predominantly African mosques speak in one or more African languages to communicate their Friday sermon and other information to their membership. In fact, the fluency of an Imam in an African language can be as important as his religious credentials in terms of his ability to draw members to a particular mosque.

Beyond language, WA Muslims have repeatedly referred to "the desire to go where [their] friends and family are." According to a Mauritanian Muslim who works with a nongovernmental organization that provides social services to the African immigrant community, WA Muslims—like other immigrant groups and New Yorkers in general—work "long hours and have little time to socialize." As is the case for churches and synagogues, prayer in a mosque attended primarily by other members of one's particular ethnic group, nationality, and/or geographic region of birth provides people with an opportunity to connect with and feel a sense of belonging to a community in a city reputed for its isolation and alienation, especially for recent immigrants who lack fluency in English.

WA Muslims have also spoken of other sociocultural differences that have led them to create their own religious space, some of which are tied to religious differences. As one self-identified "secular" Gambian Muslim explained, "we are all Muslims, but customs and traditions interfere with religion." His views were echoed by an Afro-Caribbean Muslim with close ties to a Senegalese Sufi *tariqa* (order or brotherhood) who stated that there is "only one Islam, but it is like light through a prism that is blocked by African culture."

The most common example offered to illustrate these differences was whether Muslims must pray with their arms folded or leave them by their side.[4] While from the perspective of a non-Muslim this may seem to be a relatively minor difference, it allegedly has been the source of frequent consternation and derision directed against WA Muslims.[5] This perhaps reflects the deeper religious differences between the largely Sufi WA Muslims and the broader Muslim community that follows the *Sunna* (path), varyingly referred to by WA Muslims as "Wahhabists," "conservative" Muslims, or, as some Senegalese informants refer to them, "Ibadous," in reference to followers of Ibadou Rahman who adhere to a form of reformist Islam that has become popular in Senegal, particularly among urban youths and women.

While the Ibadou movement reflects the progressive though slow spread of reformist Islam among predominantly Sufi Africans on the continent, immigration appears to have reinforced or even propelled this religious transformation. The rise of a more conservative form of Islam can be a source of tension among WA Muslims, as well as between African Sufis and other Muslims. While "conservative" Muslims are highly critical of some Sufi beliefs and practices—often challenging adherents' identity as Muslims—WA Sufis are often critical of what they perceive to be the narrow-mindedness and intolerance of "conservative" Muslims. The president of one WA mosque, for example, objected to the way "Wahhabists" view innovation, arguing that "there is a need to distinguish between things that are new and those that the prophet opposed."

Among WA Muslims, the tensions between Sufi and reformist Muslims have resulted in the splintering of various communities and led to the formation of splinter groups among the Senegalese community of Murids ("Mourides"). These largely young and typically educated Murids embrace the Islamic message of Sheikh Amadou Bamba, the founder of the Muridiyya Sufi order, but object to the hierarchy of the *marabouts* (spiritual leaders) who inherited their religious title and benefit financially from their relationship with Murid *talibes* (adherents, literally students). In praising an Imam as "a good guy," one such Murid described him as being more of an "Ibadou" like himself in that the Imam "does not send all his money to the *marabouts* and leave his family unprovided for."

The Gambian community has experienced similar factionalism as the result of religious differences between Sufi Muslims and those who follow the *Sunna.* Composed primarily of adherents to the Tijaniyya, the members of the Gambian Society in New York opened their own mosque on the Grand Concourse in the Bronx, within walking distance of the borough president's office and Yankee Stadium. Despite the small size of the community (several hundred), a second mosque was constructed shortly thereafter, on neighboring Fordham Road by the Gambian Islamic Society, composed of a group of Gambians who follow a more strict variant of the *Sunna.*

Some WA Muslims who have embraced the *Sunna* and broken away from WA mosques dominated by the Sufi *taruq* have joined other Muslim communities that practice a more "conservative" form of Islam or, as a leader in the Murid community disparagingly described it, an Islam that comes "out of Mecca" as opposed to Africa.[6] For the most part, however, WA Muslims in New York City—Wahhabists and Sufis alike—remain relatively isolated from other Muslim communities not only because of religious differences but also because of sociocultural and racial differences.

Racial Tensions and Isolation Among Muslims in New York

The common refrain repeated by WA Muslims when asked about their relationship with the broader Muslim community was that there is little or no interaction. Typically, this larger community of Muslims was identified with the numerically (and, arguably, ideologically) dominant Arabs and South Asians, particularly the former, although African American Muslims were often lumped in, as well.

Some informants commented that there may be connections between WA and other Muslim communities but that this presumably occurs "among the Imams at the top level." Their assumptions were confirmed in interviews with Imams in the three boroughs of New York that have a large number of WA Muslims (Manhattan, especially in Harlem, the Bronx, and Brooklyn). Various Imams referred to their participation in the Imam Council and *Masjid Shura* (the Mosque Council), as well as to invitations they accepted to lead Friday prayer at other mosques and to similar invitations they extended to others.

From the perspective of the WA Imams, however, these intra-Islamic organizations are dominated by other Muslim communities. For example, after declaring that there are no problems between his community and the broader Muslim community, an Ivorian Imam was critical of the Imam Council for being composed "exclusively" of Arab Muslims. He described the Manhattan *Masjid Shura* to which he belongs as being led by Arabs, South Asians, and African Americans, all of whom are contending for its leadership. Another Senegalese Imam, who claimed that few WA mosques belong to the *Masjid Shura,* described this leadership struggle as a fight by African Americans, who "have been kept out for so long," against Arab and South Asian Muslims who "can't get over the idea of former slaves serving as leaders."

There were reports of similar ethnoracial tensions within the *Masjid Shura* in the Bronx, as well. One prominent member of the Gambian Muslim community in the Bronx asserted that "whenever West Africans go [to the *Masjid Shura*], there are always problems." Insisting that the problem is based on ethnicity and race, not religious differences, he noted that "most West Africans will tell you everything bad about an Arab in the first five minutes you speak with them."[7]

Although typically not within the first five minutes of our discussion of intra-Muslim relations in New York, WA Muslims repeatedly referred to racial bias among "Arab" Muslims against "Africans" or "blacks" in general. In some cases, their views were based on experiences in Africa; a black Mauritanian informant asserted that Arabs think "black people can't be a good Muslim." He offered an example of a mosque built in Mauritania by the Moroccan government, after which an Imam was selected on the basis of a series of tests of the candidates' religious knowledge. When a black Mauritanian was selected, the Arab-controlled Mauritanian government allegedly tried to impose someone else and gave up only when the Moroccan government intervened. Interestingly, the Arab identity of the Moroccans was never considered in his analysis of this example of racial tensions between Arab and black Muslims.

Other WA Muslims recounted personal confrontations with Arab Muslims prior to their arrival in the United States. A Gambian Muslim illustrated the racial prejudice of Arabs, which he generalized to the Arab community in New York, with an encounter he had in Iraq while serving on a merchant ship. He was approached by an "Arab" (presumably an Iraqi) while praying on his ship's deck with a fellow Muslim and shipmate from Indonesia. The "Arab" man indignantly asked him why he was bothering to pray, as his black skin indicated that he was "in hell already . . . that it is too late to pray."

Even those who have had more favorable personal experiences with Arab Muslims claimed that racial bias prevents a unified Islamic *umma* both in New York and globally. An Imam from the Cote d'Ivoire, who had spent a decade in Saudi Arabia and traveled widely in North Africa, asserted that "Arabs look at blacks as slaves," though he himself is not treated this way because he speaks Arabic.

The linguistic component of the racial tensions between Arab and African Muslims was also evident in an exchange between a Pulaar-speaking Muslim from Senegal and a Yemeni shopkeeper in Brooklyn. After the Senegalese Muslim greeted and thanked the Yemeni Muslim in Arabic, the shopkeeper proceeded to engage him in a conversation in Arabic. The Senegalese Muslim recounted:

> When I explained that I do not speak Arabic, he asked me indignantly whether I am Muslim. When I responded yes, he retorted that "then you must speak Arabic as that is the language spoken in paradise." I responded that "as Mohammed was an Arab, I respect you, but in paradise Pulaar and all other languages spoken by Muslims will be spoken and mutually understood."

In the end, he let the matter drop, but not before telling the Yemeni man that "according to the *hadith,* Mohammed asserted that a black servant (Bilan) would be the first to paradise because he had suffered the most." After relaying the encounter, the Senegalese Muslim criticized the Yemeni's attitude as "nationalist rather than religious," adding that the religious discourse of Arabs is characteristically one of nationalism, while Muslims in sub-Saharan Africa have a religious discourse of "tolerance" (liberalization).

The contrast that he drew between these two groups of Muslims extended to differences in the discourses of "Arab and African mosques." He described the former as "more political" and the latter as "more poetic." African Muslims, he claimed, do not talk about politics "unless there is a real crisis."[8] As an illustration, he asserted that following the attacks on the World Trade Center and the Pentagon on September 11, 2001, there were politically charged sermons in Arab mosques but not in West African mosques. While there were many Arab Muslims in the United States who vehemently denounced the bombings, the perception of this and other WA Muslims of the differences between "Arab" and African Muslim communities has led WA Muslims to distance themselves from Arab Muslims, who are typically perceived by American popular culture (and often U.S. government officials) as "radical Muslims" associated with Islamic terrorism. In contrast, many leaders of the Arab and South Asian Muslim communities have begun to reach out to other Muslims, including WA Muslims, in search of allies after 9/11 and, according to some cynical West Africans, in search of "a façade of moderation."

"Distancing" from Other "Arab" Muslims

WA Muslims in New York were nearly unanimous in their condemnation of the terrorist acts of violence that took place on 9/11. There were few if any dissenting opinions and certainly none stated in public. WA Muslims quickly distanced themselves, as did other Muslims in the United States, from the Muslims who perpetrated these acts in the name of Islam. Vividly remembering that the attacks took place on a Tuesday, the president of a WA mosque in the Bronx proudly noted that on Friday of that week, the Imam gave a sermon "about the fact that we are not like them." He publicly stated that this community of mostly Senegalese Muslims was deeply sorry for what had happened and offered its condolences to the American people. Like many other communities of Muslims in New York—West African and others—it collected money and did fundraising to help the victims and their families.

While the president of the mosque added that Muslims in general are not like the terrorists involved in 9/11, conversations with some WA Muslims revealed prejudices against Arabs that led them to embrace ethnoreligious stereotypes similar to those held by non-Muslim Americans. Describing the 9/11 attacks as a "killing of innocents," one black Mauritanian Muslim claimed that West Africans are "strict about abiding by the [Islamic] rules regarding not killing, but for Arabs the killing is easy and justifiable by the Koran."

The stereotyping of Muslims as Arabs, and to a lesser degree as South Asians, by non-Muslim Americans has made WA Muslims largely invisible. As an Afro-Caribbean Muslim explained, there were "few African faces on the media talking about 9/11; the focus was on one geographic location as representing 100 percent of the Muslims in the world." Ironically, this has meant that WA Muslims have been largely spared from the biases and abuses other "foreign" Muslims have suffered since 9/11. In relation to his view that the "Arab community is paranoid," an Ivorian Muslim noted that "African immigrants do not identify with this [because] they don't have the same problems."

Consequently, some informants claimed that 9/11 has had little impact on the WA Muslim community. Instead, WA Muslims see themselves largely as "bystanders." According to a WA journalist based in New York, neither they nor African American Muslims see 9/11 as "their event." Nor have they seen the anti-Muslim backlash as an attack on them. This perspective was supported by a consensus among black Muslims that "they [i.e., the U.S. government and/or the non-Muslim majority] know that we are not terrorists."

Nevertheless, there have been some repercussions for WA Muslims. The leader of a West African association in Brooklyn noted that, while relatively minor and seemingly insignificant when viewed in isolation, various forms of harassment and discrimination have intensified for the WA Muslim community since 9/11. Numerous black Muslims (African American, Caribbean American, and West African immigrants) have complained that their readily identifiable Muslim names have made them a target for U.S. immigration officials, landlords, financial institutions, and government agencies. For example, many WA Muslims have had difficulties renewing their visas or gaining U.S. citizenship. In one case, a WA man with a clearly Muslim name has not been able to become a naturalized citizen although the rest of his family has obtained U.S. passports, despite the fact that he has lived here several years longer than they and that he has been legally employed since his entry over a decade ago. While the Department of Homeland Security may be considering other, undisclosed factors, he and other WA Muslims attribute the discrepancy to the fact that none of the other family members has a name commonly associated with Islam.

When WA immigrants have been identified as Muslim, either by the clothes they wear or by self-identification, they have often been subjected to ridicule and verbal abuse. A WA Imam recounted his experience shortly after 9/11 when walking in his Harlem neighborhood dressed in a caftan and cap with Muslim prayer beads in hand. Someone shouted out, "Osama bin Laden is here" in a clearly derogatory and accusatory manner. On another occasion, a merchant told him, "When you leave here take everything with you, including the bombs." Attributing such comments to ignorance, each time the Imam just smiled and said, "Peace be with you." Fortunately, he noted that that "this sort of thing has faded," which he attributed to Americans' having "found out the truth about Islam that it is not about violence but peace."

Interestingly, non-Muslim WA immigrants—fellow "foreigners" and Africans—have also engaged in the stereotyping of Muslims as terrorists, creating or potentially deepening a divide within WA immigrant communities. A Gambian Muslim described how an African American friend asked a Ghanaian if he was Muslim. The Ghanaian's response was, "I am not a terrorist. Do I look like one?!" The Gambian Muslim retorted that there are many Ghanaian Muslims, yet "have you ever heard of them blowing up things in Ghana?"

This argument as a defense against the characterization of African Muslims as "Islamic terrorists" may have been weakened by the bombings in Kenya and, more recently, in London in which African Muslims were involved, causing concern among some WA Muslims. Most of the West Africans interviewed thought that these events are unlikely to change the distinction made "between Arabs as terrorists versus African Muslims" because the involvement of African Muslims in terrorist attacks happens "just once in a blue moon." Others, however, predicted that it is just a matter of time until there is an expansion of terrorist activity in sub-Saharan Africa, which will lead to biases against all African Muslims. There are "Wahhabists everywhere in Africa," observed a member of the Hal-Pulaaren community in Brooklyn, although he acknowledged that they are a small minority.[9] Shortly after the London bombings, a Senegalese Muslim in the Bronx noted that up until now the "racial" or, more accurately, "religious profiling" of Muslims in the United States has been limited to Arabs, the only ones being searched by U.S. police, "but that is going to change." He warned that the involvement of Somalis in the London bombings might mean that Africans will be "put in the same package" as Arab and South Asian Muslims.

The only prominent case to date of a WA Muslim detained in the United States on charges related to terrorism was the arrest of a sixteen-year-old Guinean girl in March 2005. In the country illegally, she and another sixteen-year-old girl, from Bangladesh, were formally charged with immigration violations after the Federal Bureau of Investigation asserted that they might be recruited for a suicide mission by a suspect in an ongoing terrorism investigation. The accusation was denied by their lawyers and families, with leaders of the American Muslim community, such as Adem Carroll, of the Islamic Circle of North America, claiming that the investigation had "gotten out of hand, like a lot of other so-called terror investigations" (*New York Times,* 7 April 2005). According to the *New York Post* (8 April 2005), both girls had reportedly "visited an unidentified mosque known to have been the site of anti-American and extreme fundamentalist rhetoric," leading one leader of the WA Muslim community to note that "these days if you speak with or visit someone who is on a list, you are on the list, too." Nonetheless, he quickly added that "the state has the right to defend itself," a view that many other WA Muslims shared.

Despite other, more minor examples of WA Muslims having been victimized or harassed because of "religious profiling," a leader of the Senegalese community noted that "there has been no attempt by black Africans to denounce" bias acts against Muslims. "They just tell everyone to be careful, to not get involved, and to stay away from those interpreting Islam this or that way," he explained. "Basically, they are 'distancing' themselves' from 'radical' Muslims, reinforcing the division between 'good' and 'bad' Muslims created by the U.S. to fight the War on Terror," as Mahmood Mamdani describes in his popular book *Good Muslim, Bad Muslim.*[10]

Moreover, WA Muslims have been largely successful in distancing themselves because of the racial stereotyping of Muslims by the dominant American culture of white Christians. Relations between African immigrant communities and the police have not been problem-free, as the deaths of Amadou Diallo and Ousmane Zongo at the hands of the New York Police Department indicate. Nevertheless, WA Muslims generally attribute these incidents not to religious discrimination but to language barriers and a lack of knowledge of their culture among the police; they have largely ignored the racial issues emphasized by African Americans who have spoken out on the deaths of Diallo and Zongo.

While not sensing a reaction in the immediate aftermath of 9/11, WA Muslims, like other largely undocumented immigrant groups, have felt keenly the impact of policies that have been put into place in response to the attacks. For example, there have been complaints about the new policy instituted by the Metropolitan Transportation Authority of randomly checking backpacks and large packages on subways and public buses. This has been problematic for WA vendors who travel on public transportation with large packages of their wares. Nevertheless, this is generally seen by WA immigrants as an inconvenience, rather than as an infringement on their rights. As one WA Muslim noted, "Americans are more concerned about infringements on civil liberties. The Africans tend to feel that the police have the right to look and that the loss of two to three minutes isn't a big deal" in light of security concerns.

A Senegalese journalist suggested that WA immigrants are more concerned about changes in governmental policies regarding driver's licenses.

He described this as part of the "delayed effect" of 9/11 that has made WA immigrants feel they are being victimized by the government's reaction to the attacks. He referred to a pending court case in which the plaintiffs claim that the New York State Department of Motor Vehicles does not have the right to enforce immigration laws, which are within the domain of the federal government, when they detect a violation. Other West Africans complain that, in general, "where officials would close their eyes before now, there is less tolerance for infractions." Consequently, they are concerned that the slightest violation may result in their deportation.

These "delayed effects" may in fact result in strengthening WA Muslims' relations with other immigrant groups, including other immigrant Muslim communities in the United States. Many of these have reached out to African Muslims in order to unite and strengthen the *umma* in the aftermath of 9/11 and the responses of the U.S. government and the American public.

Improving Intra-Muslim Relations Post-9/11

While most WA Muslims reported no change in their relationship with other Muslims since 9/11, a significant minority claimed that 9/11 had a positive impact. One WA leader in the Bronx noted two positive repercussions of 9/11 for the WA Muslim community. First, there is now a better understanding of Islam because of intense media coverage and various programs to educate the American public. Second, he asserted, Arabs and South Asians have been forced to reach out to WA Muslims and to form alliances since they are now under siege.

Moreover, he claimed that greater scrutiny and restrictions on the use of charitable contributions in the United States have created an unanticipated windfall for WA Muslims. For example, the Islamic Development Bank (IDB) is now funding a school project submitted by WA Muslims based in the Bronx. Judging from my conversations with representatives of the IDB's parent organization, the Organization of the Islamic Conference, it appears quite likely that, in the past, the IDB simply received few if any applications for project funding from WA Muslims in the United States. Nevertheless, at least from the perspective of these WA Muslims, difficulties associated with the political affiliations of Middle Eastern and South Asian Muslim groups have made "apolitical" WA immigrant groups ideal conduits for investments in Muslim communities in America.

More locally, some WA Muslims described how 9/11 has "actually brought the Muslim community together." An Imam in Harlem described how the various Muslim communities have "sat down and talked about their differences but also their need to come together or always be a victim of this society." He, along with various other WA Imams, described how they have been asked to give prayers at other mosques, in particular the Islamic Cultural Center (more commonly referred to as the 96th Street mosque), which is the most prominent mosque in metropolitan New York. But, once again, all the examples of bridge building have taken place at the elite level within the Muslim communities.

Furthermore, many WA Muslims voiced their skepticism about recent efforts by Arab and South Asian Muslims to reach out to their communities. A Gambian Muslim complained that 9/11 merely resulted in public displays of Muslim brotherhood "that should be happening in private as well but aren't." Another black Muslim, this one from the Caribbean, observed that "all of a sudden they became our brothers" but that such fellowship is based on "false premises." He maintained that the relationship between Muslims "should be unconditional. You shouldn't need a crisis to find out that we're brothers." He added wryly, "Now they draw you closer when shaking your hand."[11]

On the other hand, several WA Muslims described improving relations and "greater tolerance" between African American and WA Muslims, despite differences in their religious practices and tensions between the broader African American and African immigrant communities, which has been widely reported in the media and some academic writings.

African American Relations with West Africans in New York City

In contrast to the limited interaction between West African Muslims and other "foreign" Muslims, WA immigrants have frequent contact with African Americans because they typically live in predominantly African American neighborhoods in Harlem, Brooklyn, and the Bronx. Despite the frequent portrayal of tensions between these communities, their relations are more complex, with increasing bases for finding common ground and increasing cooperation. Before discussing their interactions, however, it is important to consider the various explanations of how they came to have shared spaces in New York City and other urban areas in the United States.

In his doctoral thesis, Professor Zain Abdullah, of Howard University, maintains that the recent wave of African immigrants was drawn to Harlem as a "black Mecca."[12] While this may have been true for a handful of African intellectuals who had previously been exposed to the history of the Harlem Renaissance, most African immigrants, who have limited if any formal education, are unaware of the historical significance of their new residence before their arrival. This was repeatedly confirmed in interviews with Harlem-based African immigrants from all walks of life. Furthermore, initially, most African immigrants did not migrate to Harlem, preferring communities in the Bronx and lower Manhattan, where large numbers of immigrants who arrived in the 1980s worked as taxi drivers, mechanics, and street vendors.

WA Muslims reportedly began moving to Harlem in the 1990s for several reasons. After a fire destroyed a hotel in lower Manhattan that housed a large number of francophone WA Muslims, they moved to Harlem because, according to a New York-based Senegalese journalist, it was easier to get from there to the downtown shopping district where they sold their wares than from the Bronx.[13] According to this journalist, Harlem at that time was seen as dangerous, not as a Mecca: "Taxi drivers did not want to leave their cars on the street. But then, in the early 1990s, there was a government program to renovate Harlem housing and provide rent control." As a result, many West Africans began moving to Harlem.

As with all immigrant groups, economic considerations have influenced the location of WA neighborhoods in each of New York's boroughs, as well as in other cities, such as Washington, D.C.; Atlanta, Georgia; Columbus, Ohio; and Memphis, Tennessee, where there are significant concentrations of African immigrants. In New York, the large communities of WA immigrants in the south Bronx and in the Bedford-Stuyvesant area of Brooklyn, both known for their poverty and crime, are the result of inexpensive housing and employment opportunities. For example, the Hal-Pulaaren community in Brooklyn was formed when a neighborhood of Pulaar-speaking Mauritanians, Senegalese, and Guineans became implanted along Fulton Street, in Bedford-Stuyvesant, after a member of the community found a job at a factory in the area and moved there from the increasingly overcrowded multiethnic community of West Africans in lower Manhattan.

These explanations are incomplete, however, as there are other neighborhoods in these boroughs that are not predominantly African American but that are in close proximity to employment opportunities and where rent is low. The fact that West Africans chose specifically to live among African Americans may be explained by a cultural or racial affinity, though this was not verbalized by WA informants. Instead, a leader of the Association des Sénégalais d'Amérique (ASA), headquartered on 116th Street, in Harlem's "Little Senegal," described African immigrants as being attracted to predominantly African American neighborhoods because they are not as "visible" in these areas of the city. While the wish not to be visible may be related to the undocumented immigration status of many West Africans, the ASA leader explained that, regardless of immigration status, "one doesn't want to be visible when it is negative visibility." He suggested that West Africans "don't move to Little Italy [in lower Manhattan] because they are not expected to be there." To live there would bring "negative" attention from the current inhabitants. When asked if this is attributable to the state of American race relations, he agreed but added that it is also a reflection of an international racial hierarchy. In his native country of Senegal, for example, the nationality or economic class of white foreigners is not important; what is "seen is that they are white and this is associated with beauty and wealth, as [being] positive. Even lighter-skin Senegalese are seen in the same light"; higher status is associated with lighter skin. Both he and other WA informants have, nevertheless, indicated that poor race relations between "white" and "black" Americans in the United States do not reverberate in the same manner among WA immigrants, which is a source of tension between them and African Americans.

Issues of Race, Class, and Culture Between African Immigrants and African Americans

When I first arrived in New York City, almost a decade ago, an African American friend and colleague at Columbia University commented to me that when Africans first arrive in the United States they feel a greater affinity to white Americans (presumably white liberals) than to African Americans, but the longer they stay here, they grow increasingly closer to African Americans as they are forced to confront the racial, if not racist, nature of American society. I remember, as a "white liberal," being concerned not so much that my personal and professional relationships with recent African immigrants might be fleeting but that the continuing divide between white and black America is likely to reverberate with African immigrants and their descendants rather than lead toward a resolution of (or at least a reduction in) racial tensions in the United States.

I have, therefore, been an interested observer over the years of how WA immigrants have negotiated race relations in American society. I have listened with interest when a colleague born and raised in West Africa described himself as "voluntarily becoming African American" and when the daughter of African immigrants described her social circle as including only people of color—African, African American, and Latino. She was, nonetheless, highly critical of African Americans who "look out for and keep to their own group." Declaring that she does not "know what is wrong with black people" (in reference to African Americans), she praised white Americans for being "more willing to allow others to enter their group."

Similarly, a leader in the Senegalese immigrant community described African Americans as "foreign averse." When West Africans came to Harlem, he explained that there was

> a realization that we were different and at the same time the same. This is a source of tension. [African Americans] think we are the same. They identify with Africa and yet they realize that we are different and it is a shock. . . . They see us as clumsy—our English, our food, how we carry ourselves. All this combined together is a source of tension, conflict, misconceptions. and negative labels placed on us.

As an illustration of how "foreign averse" African Americans are, he offered a personal story about a time when he brought some white American college students to a jazz club in Harlem. Afterwards, he was told by African Americans in no uncertain terms, "Don't bring them into our community." While he was taken aback by this and might not have agreed with American racial segregation turned on its head, he clearly understood that "the fear of bringing whites into the community is very real" among African Americans.

Evidence of the threat posed by "foreigners" is most apparent in the gentrification of the area around "Little Senegal" in Harlem, which has led not only to a growing number of white residents but also to skyrocketing real estate prices and rents for residential and commercial properties. This poses a threat not only to the area's "original" African American inhabitants but also to the West Africans residents and merchants in the neighborhood. Sensitive to the position of African Americans, an ASA leader explained that "now they don't know who is with the devil. They are quick to put us [Africans] with them [white Americans]"—the ones who are intruding on their neighborhood. On the other hand, he claimed that African immigrants "don't feel the same fear of whites coming into the community."

A fellow Senegalese active in the Muslim community in the Bronx offered his own views on race relations in the United States today, claiming that racist "thoughts are at the source of most [African Americans'] problems, constraining them" and their ability to succeed in life. He offered as an illustration people who do not work because, he alleges, they "refuse to work for a white person." His response to this is "that was then and this is now," in a clear reference to the history of racism in the United States. When asked if this causes friction between him and others in the community, particularly African Americans, he responded, "Every day and everywhere," but he maintained that usually it is a temporary friction until African Americans learn that he is "not all talk," that he is seeking to change things through his work with both African American and African immigrant youths.

Other African immigrants have reported teasing one another about being "welfare," a reference to the large number of African Americans receiving government assistance. The irony of reciprocated biases between African immigrants and African Americans is that they largely reflect the racial prejudices of white Americans and have deep historical roots in imperialism and the slave trade. For example, West Africans commonly distinguish themselves from African Americans because African Americans are descendants of slaves, although one young woman from West Africa charitably noted that "perhaps some of them came from my family." Nonetheless, she went on to describe African Americans as "corrupted by American culture," specifically consumerism, which has led to a mentality of "got to get it now and don't care how." She distinguished between African Americans who "look out for themselves" and African immigrants who are "more collective, committed to helping their family," attributing the difference to "how they were raised."

These commonly held views may explain why a leader of the Gambia Society described most African immigrants as not interacting with their African American neighbors. He claims, however, that he does so because he is not offended by the frequent comments by African Americans that

Africans have "come here from the bush" or by references to their "climbing out of trees," which he attributes to the "ignorance" of some African Americans. There are others whom he has befriended, and he insists that it is necessary to distinguish between them and the African American "guys who are standing at the street corner when [he goes] to work at 7 A.M. and are still there at 7 P.M." when he comes home. He asserts that one should not pay attention to "these guys who dropped out of junior high."

The tensions between African immigrants and African Americans are clearly tied to class and other economic issues, such as the conflict between African street vendors and African American merchants along 125th Street (before the vendors' move to the Shabazz market). When asked about relations between the communities, several WA immigrants mentioned that "African Americans cannot accept the fact that Africans are doing well," while others referred to the shooting deaths of African taxi drivers during robberies by African Americans. More recently, however, there have been attacks in which Africans are believed to have been targeted by African American assailants because of their identity as immigrants rather than for economic reasons.

Unfortunately, anti-immigrant attitudes among African Americans are not limited to a lower class that comprises the undereducated and/or unemployed. Several WA Muslims discussed tensions in their relationships with African American Muslims. Some attribute these tensions to differences between their Sufi beliefs and the "Wahhabist teachings" of African American Muslims, although there are African Americans—in particular, women—who have joined WA brotherhoods. Other WA Muslims have argued that the tensions with African American Muslim communities are not about religion but rather reflect anti-immigrant attitudes among some, though certainly not all, African Americans.

One example of these anti-immigrant sentiments is found in Harlem and concerns the relationship between WA Muslims and the leadership of an African American mosque. When West Africans first began moving into this neighborhood, they were welcomed by the Imam of this mosque, whom one WA Muslim described as "accommodating us as guests in the U.S." After the Imam passed away, however, tensions mounted as the new leader of the mosque began to express anti-immigrant sentiments during Friday prayer, according to various WA sources. He allegedly preached about the need for African immigrants to "return home," allegedly making accusatory statements such as "We know you come here and marry our sisters." Although African immigrants continued to rent the mosque for various religious and secular events such as public meetings with visiting *marabouts*, government ministers, and other West African dignitaries, in the mid-1990s they began to pray in other mosques, such as the Mosque of Islamic Brotherhood on 113th Street, and to create various other places of worship in the neighborhood.[14]

On the other hand, the strong relations between the WA Muslim community and the African American Imam of the 113th Street mosque is indicative of the role that religious as well as racial brotherhood plays as a basis for common ground and confluence among WA Muslims and African Americans.

Building Bridges Between the Communities of WA Immigrants and African Americans

While religion may be a source of tension between Sufi African Muslims and more "conservative" African American Muslims, it also serves as common denominator linking the two groups. As one WA Muslim indicated, "Relations are best between African Muslims and African American Muslims, as there is more of a bridge" between them than between WA Muslims and other Muslims or non-Muslim African Americans. This is particularly true among the African Americans who have joined WA brotherhoods, in particular the Senegal-based *tariqa* of the *Muridiyya* (Murid). As described in various publications by Victoria Ebin, the initial Murid house in Brooklyn during the 1980s attracted many African Americans, particularly women.[15] *Sereigne* Moustapha Mbacke, a great grandson of the Murid founder Sheikh Amadou Bamba, was instrumental in establishing the house. He described how dozens of African Americans flocked to the Murid house each weekend. Within the Murid community, there continue to be prominent African Americans, including a New Jersey-based businessman who helped them purchase the group's current House of Islam, in Harlem, along with a large number of followers who are highly visible during the various events surrounding Sheikh Amadou Bamba Day, held each July in New York City.

In addition to African American converts to Muridism and other WA expressions of Islam, there are the efforts of the Harlem Islamic Leadership to unite the *umma* of all ethnic groups, nationalities, and sects. The main goal is to have a single *umma* in Morningside Park, along the southwest border between Harlem and Columbia University, while maintaining individual community centers. Although some Muslim leaders have refused to join, the Harlem Islamic Leadership is indicative of the growing formal and informal relationships between African immigrant and African American Muslim communities.

Beyond the religious communities, West African immigrants are also developing stronger ties with African American and Afro-Caribbean politicians, meeting with and campaigning for them and providing them with forums through their associations and media programs. While leaders of the African immigrant community have been reaching out to African American politicians such as Congressman Charles Rangel, former City Councilman Bill Perkins, and former Manhattan borough president Virginia Fields, as well as her Afro-Caribbean counterpart in the Bronx, Aldolfo Carrion, politicians have also become increasingly interested in African immigrants. The growing political alliance is tied to the naturalization of undocumented Africans under the 1996 collective amnesty and to the general increase in the size of the population of documented and undocumented African immigrants in metropolitan New York.

During the 2005 mayoral race, for example, various West African associations supported candidates and invited them to speak to their groups. Many West Africans, especially Senegalese, supported Ms. Fields's unsuccessful bid for the mayor's office, citing not issues of race but the presence of a well-placed compatriot on her staff. As one WA leader explained, "The point is to support someone who can provide political access, so that a Senegalese is appointed to their administration." He was critical of others in the WA community who supported the re-election of Mayor Michael Bloomberg, "not for racial reasons but because [Africans immigrants] need to be united behind a single candidate." He offered as proof the fact that his association could not get Mayor Bloomberg to speak to the community "because we don't have anyone in his office."

Various leaders of the WA community referred to the need to be politically active and to develop a bloc vote in order to gain influence in American politics. A WA Muslim leader in the Bronx offered the Jewish community as a model he seeks to replicate in terms of how Jewish voters "use their money and knowledge to get what they want." Acknowledging that the WA Muslim community is small now, he noted that he is "well aware that it only takes 5,000 votes to get a borough council member elected, 20,000 for a state assemblyman, et cetera."

The splintering of West African support during the recent mayoral race, however, indicates that the political views and interests of West African Muslims, like Muslims in the United States in general, cannot necessarily be neatly categorized or represented by either of the two major parties. Like African Americans and other minorities in the United States, WA immigrants may have a natural affinity for the Democratic Party, given its historical support of civil rights and social welfare programs. On the other hand, the socially conservative agenda of the Republican Party, as well as its support for another immigration amnesty, is also attractive to WA Muslims. In this sense, a moderate republican such as Bloomberg had a certain ideological appeal to WA Muslims, who praised him despite evidence of what his democratic opponent, Fernando Ferrer, described as the growing economic disparity between the "two New Yorks," with most African immigrants falling in the category of "have nots." While support for Bloomberg among some West Africans may have been based on a realistic assessment of his almost inevitable re-election and a desire to gain political access, others praised his "can-do" philosophy, in contrast to Democrats, who "want everyone on welfare." Critical of social ills such as "children having children," WA supporters of Bloomberg blamed the Democratic Party for producing or at least tolerating such social problems by providing financial support through welfare. In a reference to affirmative action, which has been championed by the Democrats and criticized by Republicans, one WA Muslim expressed the view that "regardless of what happened to your parents or grandparents, you have to work hard."

Aside from Bloomberg, however, WA immigrants clearly see African Americans, not the immigrant Muslim community, as their "natural" political allies. When asked why, a leader of the Hal-Pulaaren community in Brooklyn noted that, despite differences between African immigrants and African Americans, the children of WA immigrants grow up with, and become, African Americans. This may be the greatest basis for confluence between the communities in the years to come.

Conclusion

West African Muslims in New York are undoubtedly *always* Muslim, regardless of how they are perceived by fellow immigrant Muslims, white Christian Americans, or even African Americans of all denominations.

Nevertheless, racial prejudices felt by Arab Muslims against black Muslims, racial stereotyping by white Christians (and the U.S. government) in its "religious profiling" post-9/11, and racial politics among African Americans and Afro-Caribbeans often give greater salience to the ethnonational and racial identities of WA immigrants, whether or not this is either desired or advantageous. These issues of identity politics are not inconsequential to the WA Muslim community, as they are likely to influence—and have already shown evidence of influencing—the community's spatial, economic, and integrative mobility. Researchers would be well advised to consider also how the integration of WA Muslims into American society is likely to influence the possibility of upward or downward mobility for their children and grandchildren.

Notes

1. The term "black Americans" is used here to refer to all members of the African Diaspora—new and old—who self-identify as Americans on the basis of their place of birth or long-term residence in the United States. When referring specifically to descendents of Africans who were forcibly brought to the United States during the trans-Atlantic slave trade, the term "African American," which has current currency in the United States, will be used. Other members of the African Diaspora, such as immigrants from the Caribbean and their offspring, will be referred to by their region or country of origin, such as Caribbean or Jamaican American. These terms are employed to avoid confusion. The appropriate terminology is still being debated among the diverse subgroups that share both an African heritage and a common racial identity as "black" in America.

2. See Cheikh Anta Babou, "Brotherhood Solidarity, Education and Migration: The Role of the Dahiras Among the Murid Muslim Community in New York," *African Affairs* 101 (2002): 151–170; Mamadou Diouf, "The Senegalese Murid Trade Diaspora and the Making of a Vernacular Cosmopolitanism," *Political Culture* 12, no. 3 (2000): 679–702; Sylvianne Diouf-Kamara, "Senegalese in New York: A Model Minority?" *Black Renaissance* 1, no. 2 (1997): 92–115; Victoria Ebin, "Commerçants et missionaires: une confrèrie sénégalaise à New York," *Hommes et Migrations* 1132 (1990): 25–53; Victoria Ebin, "Les Commerçants Mourides à Marseille et à New York," in E. Grégoire and P. Labazée, eds., *Grands Commerçants d'Afrique de l'Ouest* (Paris: Karthala, 1993), 101–123; Victoria Ebin, "Making Room versus Creating Space: The Construction of Spatial Categories by Itinerant Mouride Traders," in B. Metcalf, ed., *Making Muslim Space in North America and Europe* (Berkeley: University of California Press, 1996), 92–109; Donna L. Perry, "Rural Ideologies and Urban Imaginings: Wolof Immigrants in New York City,"

Africa Today 44, no. 2 (1997): 229–260; Paul Stoller, "Spaces, Places and Fields: The Politics of West African Trading in New York City's Informal Economy," *American Anthropologist* 98, no. 4 (1996): 776–788; Paul Stoller, "West Africans: Trading Places in NY," in N. Foner, ed., *New Immigrants in New York* (New York: Columbia University Press, 2001), 229–249; Paul Stoller, *Money Has No Smell: The Africanization of New York City* (Chicago: University of Chicago Press, 2002).

3. Although the Arabic term *masjid* is quickly replacing the anglicized French term "mosque," I have chosen to use the term "mosque" to refer to a place where Muslims worship as there is some controversy over whether particular "mosques" in New York are indeed *masjids* or merely Islamic centers. This is directly related to the prohibition in Islam against dividing the *umma* into numerous communities of worship on the basis of nonreligious identities or groupings.

4. One informant offered an intriguing explanation for the different positioning of arms during prayer that accommodates both practices as equally appropriate or "Islamic." He attributed the origins of folding one's arms during prayer to a period of time when the Prophet was wounded, making it uncomfortable for him to pray without holding his arm. He added that some now argue that they must follow this example, while others say it was circumstantial and that Muslims should pray with their arms by their side.

5. Other differences mentioned by WA informants include the manner in which the ritual of washing before prayer is performed and how long a Muslim must remain in a prone position after saying "Allah Hakbah" during prayer.

6. Interestingly, his reference to the Islam that comes "out of Mecca" was not intended to suggest a "purer" form of Islam but rather one that is alien to or adopted by Africans.

7. The leader of the *Masjid Shura* in the Bronx is a Pakistani, but WA Muslims seldom make the distinction between Arab and South Asian Muslims.

8. He later acknowledged that the other exception in West Africa occurs during electoral campaigns, when Muslim leaders often become politically active in support of a particular party or candidate.

9. He sighted the example of Mamou Fall, a Senegalese national who had been living in Italy and was deported after making public statements about his support for al-Qaeda. When he made similar pronouncements in Dakar, adding that Osama bin Laden would take over Senegal in ten years, he was arrested.

10. Mahmmod Mamdani, *Good Muslim, Bad Muslim: America, the Cold War and the Roots of Terror* (New York: Pantheon Books, 2004).

11. Several informants discussed how various "Arab mosques" have allegedly attempted to put a "black face" on their community by making black members more prominent. Interestingly, this follows the example of many white-dominated American institutions, public and private, that have sought to demonstrate to the public the minority of African Americans or blacks among their members in general to demonstrate their commitment to diversity.

12. Zain Abdullah, "Islam, Africa and the Black Encounter: Boundary Shifting among West African Muslims in Harlem," doctoral dissertation, New School University, New York.

13. Later, the WA street vendors were forced out of the posh Fifth Avenue shopping district in lower Manhattan and set up their stands along 125th Street in Harlem before being relocated to the Malcolm Shabazz Market on 116th Street. See Stoller, "West Africans: Trading Places in NY."

14. One WA Muslim claimed that the new Imam of the Shabazz Mosque traveled to Senegal in the interest of strengthening ties with the local community. While he was there, he complained to the Murid *marabout* Sereigne Mortada Mbacke that his followers should not participate in the Shabazz mosque only during the *marabout*'s annual visits to New York City (for Sheikh Amadou Bamba Day). Although this allegedly led to increased attendance initially, the Murids now have their own "House of Islam" on 135th Street, in Harlem.

15. Ebin, "Commerçants et missionaires"; Ebin, "Les Commerçants Mourides à Marseille et à New York"; and Ebin, "Making Room versus Creating Space."

9

African Religious Beliefs and Practices in Diaspora

An Ethnographic Observation of Activities at an Ethiopian Orthodox Christian Church in Los Angeles

Worku Nida

Introduction

The proliferation of African religious communities in Diaspora is increasingly emerging as an important area of research for both African and Africanist scholars of various disciplinary backgrounds (including religious and cultural studies, history, anthropology, sociology and theology, to mention just a few). Some recent studies with a focus on "globalization" (which I understand as the historical flows across boundaries of peoples, goods, and ideas, cultures and religions included) have reconceptualized the nature of such flows by paying due attention to the dialectic relationship between the local and the global and by rectifying the major perspectives from earlier studies on the topic, which overemphasized the global North (i.e., the Western) end of the continuum. Drawing on such current topical studies,[1] Jacob K. Olupona has pointed out the new trends in research on globalization as follows:

> Scholars are beginning to reject the former paradigms of globalization as a pseudonym for modernity in recognition of the transnational elements of globalization. . . . It [globalization] is part of a process of forming overlapping identities that transcend the nation-state. . . . Utilizing a trans-global paradigm, we can examine the resiliency, adaptation and even expansion of the traditions of African Christianity, Islam, and indigenous traditions. . . . Already we have seen a number of major U.S. cities such as Washington,

> D.C., Atlanta, and New York begin to undertake a fundamental transformation. Unlike earlier waves of immigration, these new immigrants retain an ability to utilize modern technologies of communication and travel which serve to both expand and strengthen these communities in what some scholars have come to refer to as the age of postmodernism or multiple modernities. . . . As a consequence, we see a reformation and adaptation of the local into a new cohesion that retains a non-Western memory within a Western environment. These trends are nowhere more prominent than within the African immigrant religious communities.[2]

My ethnographic study of religious activities among Ethiopian immigrants in Los Angeles corroborates Olupona's observation. My research examines globalization as a transnational identity-making process, pointing to the performative and border-crossing characteristics of cultures, including religious beliefs and practices. In this chapter, I discuss aspects of this research, which allows me to join these ongoing discourses about the relationship between African religions and African identities in Diaspora. To participate in these ongoing conversations, I tell a story about diasporic religious activities as people's ways of crafting personal and collective identities. In doing so, I aim to contribute to the topical studies by examining the ways in which African immigrants use religious beliefs and practices to create transnational and/or translocal spaces in and through which they (re)fashion their diasporic identities. On the basis of my ethnographic observation of specific church-related services and activities, this chapter portrays the ways in which Ethiopian Christian immigrants have used their religion to carve out an institutional space (which is at once sociocultural, diasporic, and transnational) in and through which they (re)define themselves in relation to others within the diasporic contexts in the United States and the world over.

In particular, the chapter deals with how aspects of Ethiopian cultural and religious traditions have changed through diasporic experiences, focusing on a story about a situation where Ethiopian traditional, liturgical chanting known as *kidase* was taught at Virgin Mary's Ethiopian Orthodox Tewahedo Church, at Compton, in South-Central Los Angeles. This story of chant education is based on my observation of the situation in October and November 2000 to fulfill a requirement for a linguistic anthropological course on language and culture at UCLA's Department of Anthropology. Since this situation is about education and the teaching-learning process, it deals with communication, language, and the meaning-making process. Thus, in analyzing my data, I have used some perspectives from linguistic anthropology and religious discourses and interjected my personal and family experiences.

Following Duranti's argument that there are linkages between linguistic forms and specific cultural practices,[3] and using the ethnography of communication framework,[4] I provide a linguistic anthropological portrayal of the actual *kidase* chant teaching-learning process. The chapter is divided into four sections. In the first section, I set the context by providing brief background information about the church in Los Angeles in specific, and about the Ethiopian Orthodox Christian Church as related to its traditional chanting, in general. Then, I describe the chanting class and provide an ethnographic analysis of the meaning-making (communication) process in the second and third sections, respectively. Finally, I make some concluding remarks about my observation of diasporic cultural practices and discourses as related to issues of (trans) locality and (trans) nationality.

The Setting: The Church in Los Angeles and Its History

The religious services and education on *kidase* (Ethiopian traditional chanting that I observed) took place at Virgin Mary's Ethiopian Orthodox Tewahedo Church, located at southern Compton Avenue, South-Central Los Angeles, California. Like many other diasporic communities settled in the United States, and particularly those in southern California, Ethiopian immigrants have longed to establish a house of worship in Diaspora. This desire has marked an important rite of passage for Ethiopians as they struggle to preserve their language and religious identity and pass those traditions on to their children. However, achieving these goals was not an easy task for these Ethiopian Christian immigrants in Los Angeles. For more than a decade, Ethiopian immigrants had to hold their services at different places, renting space from other churches, until they found their own place of worship at Virgin Mary's Ethiopian Orthodox Tewahedo Church. Fifteen years ago, the Ethiopian immigrants' dream of finding a spiritual home was fulfilled when members bought this church in South-Central Los Angeles. The church is one of the four orthodox churches that have been established by Ethiopian immigrants who are living in Los Angeles. It is important that the Ethiopian Diaspora in North

America, particularly the United States, has taken form only in the past thirty to thirty-five years. Compared to some other immigrant groups (including other Africans), Ethiopians have not been in the States for very long. Among other factors, this Ethiopian exodus was caused by political turmoil, famine, and drought in Ethiopia during the 1970s. It has been assumed that there are about 70,000 Ethiopian immigrants in the Greater Los Angeles area, while the total number of Ethiopian immigrants in the United States is estimated at 300,000.

The Virgin Mary's Ethiopian Orthodox Tewahedo Church is said to be the first of its kind to be established by Ethiopian immigrants in the United States. According to Abune Zena Markos (who is the patriarch of Ethiopian orthodox churches located in West Coast cities such as Los Angeles, San Diego, Oakland, Seattle, San Francisco, and San Jose), this is a pioneer institution in North America. "You know, and we all know, this church is the first and then everything started from here, and then the one in Dallas was established," said the Abune at the church's Sunday services on November 28, 2004, which I attended. The other three Ethiopian orthodox churches in Los Angeles are St. Mary's Ethiopian Orthodox Tewahedo Church, Abune Gebremenefisqidus, and Medahinalem (which was created by Eritreans), all of which are said to have been established by members who split away from the congregation of Virgin Mary's Ethiopian Orthodox Tewahedo Church. The split was said to have been caused by, among other things, competing political interests of individuals and/or groups that initially were all members of Virgin Mary's Church. Such political divisions are, and have always been, informed by political developments and change in government back at home in Africa.

In 1991, the Ethiopian People's Revolutionary Democratic Front (EPRDF), led and dominated by the Tigrian People's Liberation Front (TPLF), took over national political power, overthrowing the Derge (the military regime led by Mengistu Haile-Mariam) in Ethiopia. The TPLF-dominated EPRDF's government has introduced and implemented ethnic-based politics and facilitated the separation of Eritrea from Ethiopia, actions that have been bitterly opposed by the majority of Ethiopians both at home and in Diaspora. However, some individuals and groups have supported the actions of the EPRDF government. Thus, some of my respondents believe that such political developments in Africa have affected the Ethiopian diasporic Christian congregations negatively, leading to division and the formation of several congregations and churches, such as Virgin Mary's Ethiopian Orthodox Tewahedo Church and St. Mary's Ethiopian Orthodox Tewahedo Church.

Moreover, in 1990, some members of the two congregations mentioned were engaged in bitter disputes over the name "Saint," a category each disputing group wanted to use to designate its own church. Such disputes led to a long lawsuit that resulted in only one of the congregations being able to use the name "Saint," hence St. Mary's Ethiopian Orthodox Tewahedo Church, located in the Ladera Heights neighborhood of West Los Angeles and established in 1999 on a property purchased by its members. The other Ethiopian Orthodox church in South-Central Los Angeles, which is the subject of this chapter, has been renamed Virgin Mary's Ethiopian Orthodox Church. This lawsuit reportedly caused considerable expense and created animosity between the members of the two congregations, although some of the members of both churches are reported to have started healing their differences and establishing a relationship between the two congregations as sister religious institutions. As a result, the two churches have been participating in some common services for annual Ethiopian festivals such as Timiket, Epiphany.

Interjecting Personal/Family Experiences

As an Ethiopian immigrant and a person who was raised as an orthodox Christian, I often visit Virgin Mary's Ethiopian Orthodox Church for Sunday services and prayers. I currently attend this church more for social and cultural reasons than religious ones. For instance, I had my son, who is now five years old, baptized there when he was forty days old, according to the Ethiopian orthodox traditions. My American wife and I negotiated to do this because we want our son to stay in touch with the Ethiopian side of his cultural roots, his other culture being American through his mother. Therefore, we viewed baptism as one of the mechanisms through which our son will grow up accessing Ethiopian cultural and social resources that are being organized and mobilized by the Ethiopian Orthodox Church in Los Angeles. That is, his baptism perhaps will enable him to interact with other Ethiopian children during church activities, although this may not guarantee that he will stay in touch with the church (given that when he grows up he may decide not to keep going to the church).

In addition, baptizing my son in traditions similar to those in which my parents and I were baptized, and attending the Ethiopian church, gives me a great deal of satisfaction. In doing so, I have felt that I am still connected to my Ethiopian roots, despite the fact that I am living in the United States, a world apart from Ethiopia. At the church, I meet fellow Ethiopians, interact and talk with them in Amharic (the Ethiopian national language), as well as in Guragegna, and observe the Sunday liturgical services and rituals. All these activities make me feel less lonely (culturally and socially speaking) in the strange and racialized American social and cultural environment.

Concerning this project, initially, I was interested in observing closely the weekly Sunday services and rituals (chanting included) in formal liturgical settings and exploring why people come to the church so often, despite their busy schedules and long working hours. However, I decided to focus just on the chanting education because it was more manageable, informal, and interactive than the entire Sunday services performed for a big congregation of people in the formal setting of a two-story church.

Situating the L.A. Church in Its Historical Context

Before I describe the chanting education and other religious activities that I observed, I would like to place Ethiopian traditional chanting in its historical context, that is, in relation to the history of Ethiopian orthodox Christianity, which goes back to the fourth century A.D. A brief general history will enlighten our understanding of the development of Ethiopian traditional chanting in general and its diasporic form at Virgin Mary's Ethiopian Orthodox Tewahedo Church in Los Angeles, in particular. Christianity was first introduced to Ethiopia by two Syrian missionaries in 330 A.D. Then based in Egypt, the missionaries came to Ethiopia and converted the ruler of the Aksumite Empire, King Ezana, in the historic town of Aksum, in the present Tigrai region, in northern Ethiopia. Ezana's rule represented the peak of Aksumite civilization in Ethiopian history, when the Aksumite Empire was considered one of the four biggest world powers (along with the Roman Empire, China, and Persia) of the time. After Ezana's conversion, one of the Syrian missionaries, Freminatus, was appointed by the Egyptian pope as the first bishop for Ethiopia, and since then Christian churches have been built in various parts of northern Ethiopia.

However, it was after nine Syrian priests came and undertook extensive missionary activities during the sixth century A.D. that Christianity spread widely in Ethiopia. The nine priests are known for the expansion of monasticism in the country.[5] As a result of the interactions among internal historical, political, economic, and social forces, orthodox Christianity took its Ethiopian shape over time. Thus, during the imperial expansion of the Ethiopian rulers, from the fourteenth to the nineteenth centuries, orthodox Christianity expanded throughout the country. In its long history, Ethiopian orthodox Christianity has served as a state ideology for the government as church and state have coexisted, supporting each other. The state-church relationship (far from being conflict-free itself) has always disfavored other religions such as Islam and the traditional beliefs of the eighty-six or so different ethnic groups throughout the country. However, despite this, Ethiopia represents an example of a long religious syncretism where the followers of Christianity, Islam, and traditional religions have coexisted peacefully for centuries.[6] The current population of Ethiopia (which is now estimated at 72 million) is half Christian and half Muslim.

This religious diversity is mirrored among the Ethiopian immigrants in the United States, as well. Muslim immigrant Ethiopians have established mosques known as Bilal Ethiopian mosques in many major cities such as Los Angeles, Washington, D.C., and Dallas. Bilal is known in Islamic history as the Prophet Mohammed's servant and the first man who said *hazan,* the prayers at Kabba in Mecca, and he happened to be an Ethiopian. Thus, Muslim Ethiopian immigrants named their mosques in the United States after Bilal. This reflects Islamic history and the long-established Islamic relationship between Ethiopian and the Arab worlds (beginning during the seventh century A.D., when followers of the Prophet escaped persecution in Arabia and sought asylum under the protection of the Ethiopian Christian government in Axum). Ethiopia is the first country in the world outside Arabia where Islam was practiced.

The tradition of Ethiopian liturgical chanting, *kidase* (mass), has evolved within the general historical contexts I have outlined and needs to be understood accordingly. There are two more fundamental points to be made in relation to the history of Ethiopian liturgical chanting. First, Saint Yared of Aksum, who lived in the sixth century A.D., is considered the founding father of melody for the Ethiopian liturgical chant and for church music in general, locally known as *zema. Zema* (Ethiopian notation) may be defined as "song" (but is different from *zefen,* which also means "song" in Amharic) or "melody," or "a pleasing sound." Thus, Yared created the notation for Ethiopian liturgy, *zema* genre. However, Ethiopians from different regions have improvised on *zema* and used it in various ways, resulting in the development of regional styles such as the Qoma and Achaber schools of vocal style.[7]

Another important aspect of Ethiopian liturgical chant is its language. The Ethiopian churches' literature and liturgy are written in classical Ethiopic, Geez, which is a Southwest Semitic language. The initial translation of the Bible (including the canonical and apocryphal books of the Greek Old Testament and New Testament, as well as others) into Geez was completed during the seventh century A.D. Geez continued to be the official language of state and church until Amharic replaced it during the eighteenth century. However, Geez is the Latin of Ethiopia (Africa, for that matter), because it continued to function as an ecclesiastical and liturgical language, as Latin does in the West. Because of the development of Geez language and literature, Ethiopia stands out as the only African country with a long history of literary traditions as related to Christianity and Islam.

The Kidase Class at Virgin Mary's Ethiopian Church

Drawing on the rich history of orthodox Christianity, Ethiopian liturgical chanting, including *kidase,* is usually performed by highly trained singers (such as deacons called *depteras* and priests) who from boyhood spend decades learning the chant. The liturgical chant learning process in the Ethiopian traditional setting requires complex pedagogical performances involving both music and texts. The *kidase* class that I observed at Virgin Mary's Church in Los Angeles also follows essentially similar procedures, employing both melody and books. However, there are significant differences between the local and the diasporic forms of training and socialization the members into Ethiopianess through chanting.

The *kidase* class at Virgin Mary's Church was taught by a priest and two other men. These three men have training and experience in liturgical chanting in general, and *kidase* in particular. The priest was among the persons in charge of the church's liturgical services and activities and was thus a religious leader. The other two men were volunteering to help the priest in his instruction for *kidase* class, which took place weekly on Tuesday evenings between 6:00 and 9:00 P.M. I observed several such classes in October and November 2000, and it is these classes upon which my analysis of the chant-learning process is based.

Attendance and the Classroom Situation

According to the attendance list, there were a total of forty enrolled students (almost half women and the other half men) for this class, although when I attended the class on October 10 and November 21 and 28, there were only twenty-seven, nineteen, and twenty-six students in attendance, respectively. The majority of them were young, maybe in their late twenties, and I estimated that the senior members were in their late forties. Despite the fact that the participants seemed to differ in terms of education, social class, and profession, they all share orthodox Christianity and Ethiopian identity. However, it is quite possible that these identity markers might be understood differently by different members of the community both in Los Angeles and back home in Africa. Some of the class members are professional. For instance, one of the participants I talked to after the class is an engineer. The majority seemed to be involved in minimum-wage jobs, and one young woman told me that she had two low-income jobs. I have been surprised that people who live on minimum wages such as this young woman manage to make time to come to the church for services and classes.

Like other classes in this church, the *kidase* class was taught in a hall next to the main hall (where formal liturgical services and rituals are performed) in the church structure. This hall is a multipurpose space, and it is used as a classroom, as well as a dining and living room during both regular Sunday services and church holidays such as the Ethiopian New Year, Timiket (Epiphany), and Christmas. At the *kidase* chanting class, students sat on chairs arranged in row behind several rectangular tables that faced the teachers, that is, the priest and his two assistants, who themselves sat behind one rectangular table in front of the students. The priest was in the middle, while his two assistants were to his right and a student-coordinator was to his left. These spatial arrangements tell us a lot about power relations among the participants, both reflecting and (re)creating their social organization. Thus, the priest's seat indicated that he has a central role in the process and that he is the most powerful person in the group, with his assistants and the student-coordinator ranking next, and the students coming last.

On my first visit, on October 10, 2000, I was invited by the priest to sit next to him, but I thanked him for the offer and sat next to one student, whom I know very well from Ethiopia and who had earlier introduced me to the two assistants. On the teachers' table, there were different objects, such as containers, clothes, hand-crosses, canes, and umbrellas, which are used in formal church liturgical services. Next to this table, there was a drum lying on the floor. During my subsequent visits, the spatial arrangements remained the same, except for the fact that some students changed seats and there were no material objects used for the class.

Before the actual *kidase* chanting class began, the student-coordinator stood up and asked one of the students to lead the prayer in Amharic. Then the volunteer led, and all participants prayed along. On my first visit, after the prayer, the priest asked me to tell the class why I was there. Accordingly, I told them that I am a graduate student at UCLA, doing a research project on the chanting class for a course on language and culture, and that I would like to study this aspect of our (Ethiopian) culture more closely. I also told them that I would like to share my observation of the class with others in my graduate program and asked permission to take pictures and use a tape recorder, which, fortunately, I was granted.

The Class in Action

After my introduction, the actual class began. Each of the classes I observed had two sections. The first part was about liturgical objects that were displayed on the instructors' table, while the second part dealt with the actual *kidase* chanting. However, the classes I observed on November 21 and 28, 2000, focused solely on chant recitations.

The priest began teaching about the liturgical objects with an Amharic proverb, "*beje yale worqe indemedabe yeqotera,*" which may roughly be translated as "you consider the gold you own as bronze" or "people do not appreciate the value of what they have." He used the proverb to mean that the students have an important culture, the Ethiopian Orthodox Church and its activities, and that they are not appreciative enough of its value. He then asked, "How many of us know what these [pointing to church items on the table in front of him] liturgical objects are for, what their meanings are, who uses them, you see?" Then he said that everything has meaning and significance in the church services and went on describing each object, picking up one item at a time and telling the students its functions and symbolic meanings. The following transcript is one of his descriptions of the objects:

> Look, watch me, this is called *aklil* [i.e., crown]. It is not a hat. But this one is a hat [pointing to the special hat he wore]. The crown was brought to this church for social things, for weddings. However, its function in our church is different. In our Ethiopian [orthodox Christian] culture, a crown is worn by deacons. When? . . . They wear it when deacons are chanting *kidase* during church services. This is what they put on their head [showing them by putting the crown on his head]. [Also,] a priest who has a wife can wear the crown and chant *kidase.* But not allowed for a monk. A monk like me cannot wear crown and perform kidase chant. . . . That is not allowed. Only a secular priest is allowed to do so, and of course deacons are, too. . . . In short, here I am teaching about what the procedures are, and these are the meanings of church objects, clothes, bells everything. You have to know all this. It is not just the *kidase* chanting that you have to learn. If you [the students] do not know the meanings of all this, you would not be able to tell if I had wrong clothes on, if I had performed it appropriately, if I had chanted the wrong chant for the wrong ritual. . . . You have to learn all the procedures and the meanings of things so that you would be able to correct things in our church. You would know what is what, who is doing what during [the formal liturgical] services.

In addition, the priest described the symbolic meanings of the material artifacts and their colors in particular. For example, he said that the red color of liturgical items such as clothes and hats for deacons and priests represents the crucifixion of Christ, and the sad moment of this important event is signified by dark color. He also used stories and metaphors from the participants' daily lives to explain the power of God and to convey his messages about the relationship among prayer, loyalty to God, and rewards for good behavior from God. He said:

> God is an iron. When you have cloth that is wrinkled, what do you do? You use an iron to straighten your clothes. [Likewise,] if you want to solve your life problems, ups and downs, do good thing, you obey God's rules, pray to Him, and follow his roads. God is your iron. . . . Do not wait until you come to the church to pray, to recognize God. Pray wherever you are, while working, eating, and driving, always.

During this instruction, the two assistants helped the priest by complementing what he said and giving additional examples, and particularly by singing the *kidase.* The students were very active, following attentively, asking questions, and seeking further clarifications about the liturgical objects.

The Ethnographic Analysis of the Communicative Process of the Chant

The *Kidase* Recitation

Traditionally, *kidase* was performed by highly trained singers who from boyhood spent decades learning the chant (note that it was very unusually for girls to learn *kidase* in Ethiopia, because of gender bias). Likewise, the priest and his two assistants at Virgin Mary's Ethiopian Church who taught *kidase* were well versed in the liturgical chant of the Ethiopian Orthodox Church. In Ethiopia, such classes are taken gradually, because there are different stages through which young men train their voices with repetitive practices. According to the priest, when he learned *kidase,* he had to take several introductory classes, which he calls *dimiste meselekia,* that is, "voice training classes," before he began the actual *kidase* chant. In addition, he stated that there are four major kinds of vocalizations, which in turn are classified into a number of categories and portions depending on when and by whom (priests or deacons, or both as a group, or both with the congregation) they are performed. Accordingly, the teachers (and the singers in formal liturgical settings) employ different kinds of vocalizations that are appropriate to specific *kidase* types/categories/portions. They "draw upon distinct expressive resources and configure them differently in their expressive vocal styles to achieve distinct social (and religious) ends."[8] Moreover, the priest said that "here in the U.S., we do not follow the pedagogical rules of the Ethiopian orthodox Christian church. . . . These students do not have any background in liturgy and they have never taken voice-training classes. We do it this way because we are not in Ethiopia." This shows that culture is dynamic and that the diasporic experiences of Ethiopian immigrants have affected the pedagogical principles and styles of the Ethiopian Orthodox Church at home. Even the *kidase* chant has taken its diasporic shape through immigrants' experiences.

As in Ethiopia, the language of *kidase* (and all liturgical performances of the Ethiopian Orthodox Christian Church) class at Virgin Mary's Church was Geez, ancient Ethiopic. Interestingly, unlike the priest and his two assistants, who were versed in ancient Ethiopic, the participants did not speak or understand Geez. However, the *kidase* recitation was performed in Geez, and all the instructors and students used a textbook of *kidase* in Geez, with translations in Amharic. In Ethiopian liturgical chant tradition, the systematic use of texts, words, and melody is a long-established tradition (dating back to the sixth century A.D.), evidenced in thousands of surviving Geez manuscripts, handwritten on parchment.

The *kidase* class represented a communication event in which people used different resources such as verbal and nonverbal signs, bodily movements, and various language registries. Also, it was a multilingual event in that several Ethiopian ethnic languages (such as Guragegna, Oromogna, Tigrigna, Walyatigna, and Hadiyigna), Amharic, and Geez were spoken by the participants and teachers at different levels. Thus, a lot of code-switching took place. For example, when the teachers performed in class, they recited in Geez, whereas when they explained the text or when they answered students' questions, they spoke in Amharic. Similarly, when students repeated the chants loudly following their instructors, they performed in Geez (although they did not understand it), but they used Amharic when they asked questions and communicated with the teachers and when they spoke to one another. In addition, in dyadic and small-group interactions, people employed their respective ethnic languages.

In class, the teachers chanted portions of a *kidase* category sound by sound, word by word, phrase by phrase; and the students repeated them, imitating the teachers. However, I noticed that some students had difficulty imitating their teachers' vocal styles, given that the students had not trained their voices and that intonation is an essential aspect of *kidase* performance and training. Ethiopian chant tradition has oral, musical, and textual (as it relies on notated manuscripts) aspects, and the mastery of its notation requires a lot of memorization and recitation.

A chant portion called *tezekerene* from the *kidase* class I recorded on October 10, 2000, signified this process. After the students recited several portions, the priest suggested that *tezekerene* be the next portion recited and performed, and this was accepted. According to the priest, *tezekerene* is a special chant that is usually sung by priests in memory (and on the day) of crucifixion. As usual, the priest and his assistants started singing *tezekerene* in its typical melody; and then they asked the students to repeat it. They did so, repeating it twenty-four times. Still, it was not easy for the students to imitate the melody. In fact, one of the priest's assistants admitted as much, saying, "We understand this [melody] is a bit difficult. It takes repetition, and repetition, and repetition. We will come back to it later. Don't worry about it now. Let's go ahead and do *namen* [another *kidase* category]." Finally, they gave up on *tezekerene* for that day.

I am interested in this portion because it represents a typical example of the use of a range of resources in a communicative, meaning-making event such as the *kidase* chant class. Also, of all recitations I observed, this one was the most difficult for students seeking to imitate the vocal styles of their teachers. As a result, in his efforts to help the students, the priest (along with his assistants) used his words, intonations, and gestures (the movement of his body parts: hands, fingers, head, face, and eyebrows), in addition to jokes and examples from his training.

An Analysis of the Chant Education as Meaning-Making Process

Following Dell Hymes, Bonvillain argues that an examination of the different characteristics of setting, participants, topics, and goals and their relationships constitute the major part of the ethnography of communication.[9] Dealing with communication in specific institutional settings such as courts, Bonvillain also points to the issues of "formal" and "informal" in discursive processes.[10] Using this framework, I will provide a descriptive explanation of the formal and informal aspects of *kidase* chant class at Virgin Mary's Ethiopian Orthodox Church. I will highlight its institutional setting to demonstrate that the interaction between the formal and the informal aspects of *kidase* shapes the meanings of the communicative event and that the boundaries between the two are porous and elastic.

Issues of Formality and Informality in Communication

On the one hand, the fact that this event took place in the church makes the process formal. According to the Ethiopian Orthodox Christian tradition, church is considered not only a formal but also, and more important, a sacred and holy institution of social, cultural, and political significance. Similarly, Ethiopian churches in Diaspora such as Virgin Mary's in Compton carry these meanings and importance. All activities that are carried out in churches need to be viewed accordingly. The *kidase* chant class is no exception, for *kidase* is a corpus of chants that praise God and His deeds. As regards this, before the class began on November 28, 2000, the priest at Virgin Mary's Church said:

> The fact that you [the students] are here to learn *kidase* means that God likes you, that God gave you a heart that helped you come here. . . . This is

really, a very good sign. I am serious. It is true because by learning *kidase* you are becoming the singers [preachers] of God's words.

Thus, he communicated his message to the students that they were dealing with something very serious and important, invoking formality.

Despite this, and on the other hand, the *kidase* class was not really a formal event in that it was performed outside the contexts of actual liturgical performances for various church services. Unlike the formal liturgical rituals that take place in a special part of the building where the tabbot is kept, the chant class is given in a dining and living room, which makes it less formal. Moreover, in the chant class, a priest and two volunteering assistants teach *kidase* to a very limited number of mainly young people. In the formal setting, *kidase* is performed by highly trained deacons and priests for a large congregation of people. Also, in *kidase* classes, both the teachers and participants did not follow the dress codes that would be observed at formal church services. One finds that in the *kidase* class, the boundaries between the formal and the informal are blurred, which is even more evident in participants' interactions, in topic selection, and in setting goals.

Participants

On the basis of my observation of the interactions of the participants, I found the teaching-learning process in the *kidase* class to be both formal and informal at the same time. On the one hand, the relation between the students and the priest (and his assistants) carried a formal connotation. As a religious leader, teacher, and elder (the priest and both of his assistants were older than other participants in class), the priest was highly respected by the students, both men and women. This was reflected in the participants' (both the teachers' and the students') use of terms of address. For example, students used a special title, *Abba,* in addressing the priest. *Abba,* which means "Father" in Amharic, is a title that people use to address men (I use "men" because there are no women priests in Ethiopia) who are highly educated in Ethiopian liturgy. In the Ethiopian Orthodox Christian tradition, it is used to address a priest, a pope, or a patriarch. *Abba* signifies both social status and respect related to the priest's position as a religious leader and thus a spiritual father. Also, students used the honorific *antu* (the polite "you" in Amharic), which is the second-person plural pronoun, in addressing the priest. *Antu* in Ethiopian culture signifies special status (social political and religious), seniority, and unfamiliarity. In contrast, *ante* and *anchi* for men and women, respectively, are the second-person singular pronouns and do not imply differential power relations; rather, they signify equal power relations and intimacy.

Furthermore, students addressed the assistants of the priest using the Amharic *Ato* (which may be translated as Mr. in English) with their given names, implying the formers' respect for the latter. It is worth mentioning here that Ethiopians use titles and/or honorifics in their address only when speaking to someone of a higher social status. They address them by their given names because, according to Ethiopian naming traditions, Ethiopians do not have a family or second name that is generic for all members of a given family. Rather, they take a first (given) name and use their fathers' names as second names. That is why the students use the *Ato* title and the given names (instead of the second names) of the priest's assistants. However, the priest and his assistants addressed the students by their given names, using the nonhonorific pronoun *ante* for male and *anchi* for female, which were also used by students in addressing one another. These language-usages implied differential power relations between the teachers and students, both distinguishing the former from the latter and characterizing their relationships. They also showed the intricate relationships between language and culture (society), as the participants' use of carefully selected linguistic forms implies their knowledge of the roles of social factors such as age, gender, social status, class and ethnicity in communication and their participation in activities as cultural members.

Topic Selection and Setting Goals

In contrast to their terms of address, the participants' interactions in terms of selecting topics and setting goals seemed less formal, and more coparticipatory. Although the priest and his two assistants guided the participants in the recitation, they did not decide what should be recited for a specific class by themselves. Rather, the entire class (students and instructors included) negotiated in order to decide on the topics for each day. Usually, such negotiations took place before the actual class began. Accordingly, the instructors and students agreed on a topic, section, or specific category of chant on a particular day. For example, in the two of the classes I observed, amazingly, topics were decided according to the suggestions of two young women. This was surprising to me because, in Ethiopia, this kind of participation by women in church education is very uncommon, because of the existing male-biased gender ideology. In addition, students took an active part in class by asking questions and performing the *kidase* rituals. However, when a part of a category of *kidase* was taught, it was chanted by the teachers—the priest and his two assistants—and repeated by the students. As a result, the teachers and the participants, as speakers and audience, respectively, alternate roles, since sometimes, when the students performed the recitation, the teachers became the audience.

Likewise, the goals were commonly set at the congregational level. The stated goal of the *kidase* class was to produce competent members for the church by educating them about the orthodox Christian rituals, *kidase* included, in particular, and about Ethiopian histories and cultures as related to orthodox Christianity, in general. Not surprisingly, the cultures and histories being taught emphasize orthodox Christianity and leave out other significant aspects of Ethiopian cultures and histories, especially those linked to Islam and traditional religions. However, on the basis of my observation of some of the dyadic and informal small-group (two to five people) discussions that took place before and/or after the actual *kidase* class, it seems to me that there were other, unstated (personal, political, and social) goals that the participants wanted to achieve.

In such micro-arenas, discourses about issues such as famine, politics, relations between between the countries of Ethiopia and Eritrea, and issues of human rights in Ethiopia dominated the discussions. Some people supported the current Ethiopian government, while others opposed it strongly. Moreover, there were people who reflected the views of some Ethiopian opposition political parties, of which some are ethnically organized, while others are multiethnic parties fighting against the EPRDF government in Ethiopia. Since participants represented views of different political and ethnic groups, their interactions were characterized by both tensions and solidarities that are prevalent within the church congregation, as well as in Ethiopian immigrant communities in Los Angeles and other cities in the United States, and throughout Ethiopian society.

Furthermore, it is important to note that these components of communication are in dynamic relation with one another. Their relationships and structuring are underscored by the cultural/social knowledge shared by the participants as reflected in their recognition of social factors such as age, gender, and social status. This confirms Duranti's argument that there are important links between linguistic forms and specific cultural practices such as liturgical chants.[11]

Conclusion

This event was a communicative and meaning-making process in which the priest both socialized the participants through language into Ethiopian church culture and socialized them into the language of church culture. The priest and his assistants used language in its varied forms—verbal; embodied, such as in gestures, facial expressions, different body positions (e.g., movement of hands and heads); and material (i.e., the displayed liturgical objects) in (re)creating and conveying cultural meanings based on Ethiopian church traditions. They also employed jokes, proverbs, and space. The priest was particularly effective in moving the participants along with his descriptions of the church items, by using gestures and space, especially stretching his arms into the empty space around him to explain sizes of different church objects that were not displayed on the table.

This event confirms the power of the linguistic anthropological definition of language as a cultural resource and "speaking" as a social practice.[12] This is the case because the instructors used the Ethiopian church language (and material artifacts, such as the liturgical objects displayed in the *kidase* class on October 10, 2000) to socialize the participants into being competent members of the Ethiopian church community in Los Angeles. As a result, the participants will be more effective at interacting within their new social worlds. Also, the speech process was essentially social, as it involved interactions of different individuals, who share certain cultural backgrounds, and reflected some political tensions among themselves at the same time.

In addition, in their interactions, the participants and the teachers have both reflected and co-constructed social organization, a process that represents both continuities and change. In some ways, such as in the use of terms of address and honorifics, we see the reproduction of social relations representing the larger entity (i.e., Ethiopian society), of which this religious community at Virgin Mary's is a part. In contrast, we also see some social relations being recreated and redefined. For example, I have observed two new developments in this socialization process, developments that have evolved in the diasporic version of Ethiopian liturgical culture. First, the participation of women in liturgical education is new. In Ethiopia, it is, and has always been, very uncommon for women to attend liturgical education. This gender-biased view of the Ethiopian church is depicted by one Amharic proverb, "*set atkedise atkeises,*" which translates as "a woman cannot perform *kidase* chant, and neither can she become a priest." Although the purpose of *kidase* chant education at Virgin Mary's Ethiopian Church in Los Angeles is not to produce priests and/or priestesses, the fact that half of the participants are women represents an impressive change in the history of Ethiopian liturgy that has resulted from the lived diasporic experiences of Ethiopian Christian immigrants in the United States. Second, the nature of the interactions between the instructor (the priest in particular) and the students at Virgin Mary's church's *kidase* class was fundamentally different from the traditional interactions back home in Ethiopia. Here in the United States, students, including women, feel freer and more comfortable asking any questions about the Bible, Ethiopian liturgy, and church practices than do students in a similar setting in Ethiopia.

This ethnographic case study illustrates that, through the interaction between formal and informal aspects of the communication process, the *kidase* class offers an important opportunity for students to explore and redefine cultural values and social relations in their new social context. It points to the ways in which Ethiopian immigrants reconstitute themselves and their self-other configurations in Diaspora. The study also has broader implications in that it demonstrates that, through their diasporic religious and ritual activities such as *kidase* chant class, African (and other) immigrants reconstruct their transnational/translocal identities and maintain as well as recreate patterns of society and culture in their new life-worlds.

Notes

1. M. Kearney, "The Local and the Global: The Anthropology of Globalization and Transnationalism," *Annual Review of Anthropology* 24 (1995): 547–556; Robert Hefner, "Multiple Modernities: Christianity, Islam, and Hinduism in a Globalization Age," *Annual Review of Anthropology* 27 (1998): 83–104; F. Jameson and M. Miyoshi, eds., *The Cultures of Globalization* (London: Duke University Press, 1998).

2. Jacob K. Olupona, "Globalization and African Immigrant Religious Communities," in: Jennifer I. M. Reid, ed., *Religion and Global Culture: New Terrain in the Study of Religion and the Work of Charles H. Long* (New York: Lexington Books, 2002).

3. A. Duranti, *Linguistic Anthropology* (Cambridge: Cambridge University Press, 1999), 84–85.

4. Nancy Bonvillain, *Language, Culture, and Communication: The Meaning of Messages*, 3rd ed. (Englewood Cliffs, N.J.: Prentice-Hall, 2000), 78–102.

5. Taddesse Tamrat, *Church and State in Ethiopia: 1270–1527* (Oxford: Clarendon Press, 1972).

6. Worku Nida, "The Waq Cult of the Gurage," in *Proceedings of the 11th International Conference on Ethiopian Studies* (Addis Ababa: Addis Ababa University Press, 1993); Nida, *JEBDU: The Culture and History of the Gurage People* (in Amharic) (Addis Ababa: Bole Printing Press, 1991); Nida, "The Traditional Beliefs of the Gurage with Particular Emphasis on the Bozha Cult," in *Proceedings of the 1st National Conference on Ethiopian Studies* (Addis Ababa: Addis Ababa University Press, 1990).

7. K. Shelemay and Peter Jeffery, eds., *Ethiopian Christian Liturgical Chant: An Anthology*, vols. 1–2 (Madison, Wis.: A-R Editions, 1993).

8. Laura R. Graham, *Performing Dreams: Discourses of Immortality Among the Xavante of Central Brazil* (Austin: University of Texas Press, 1995), 65.

9. Dell Hymes, *Foundations in Social Linguistics: An Ethnographic Approach* (Philadelphia: University of Pennsylvania Press, 1974); Bonvillain, *Language, Culture, and Communication*, 78–102.

10. Bonvillain, *Language, Culture and Communication*, 364–383.

11. Duranti, *Linguistic Anthropology*, 84–85.

12. Ibid.

IV

Civic Engagement and Political Incorporation

10

Transnationalism, Religion, and the African Diaspora in Canada

An Examination of Ghanaians and Ghanaian Churches

Wisdom J. Tettey

Introduction

Increasingly, a lot of people are being compelled to leave their countries of origin to settle in other places as a result of socioeconomic problems wrought by global forces and/or political turmoil in their home countries.[1] These developments, combined with the constriction of "time-space distanciation"[2] made possible by advances in technology, have led some observers to argue that the distinction between temporary and permanent migration is becoming increasingly blurred, if not unsustainable. Richmond, for example, contends that "globalization has facilitated worldwide network linkages with friends and families in the former country, and with the international labour market."[3] This, he points out further, has resulted in the phenomenon of *transilience,* that is the ability to move back and forth between two or more countries and cultures. A corollary to these processes of shifting locations and attachments is the reconfiguration of people's identities in ways which are anti-essentialist and transcend fixed notions of self, location, culture, ethnicity, and citizenship.[4]

The simultaneous occupation of multiple locations is the basis for the concept of hybridity, which allows us to examine migrants' experiences in ways that overcome the tendency toward "victimology of transnational migrants, empowering them, linking the past with the present."[5] To capture the multiple complexities that characterize immigrants' "in-between" status[6] and to give the concept of hybridity a more encompassing essence vis-à-vis issues of belonging, otherness, and identity, it is important that we explore other dimensions of the immigrant experience, beyond the traditional focus on culture and cultural difference. In order to do this, Anthias puts forward an analytical framework premised on the idea of "translocational positionality."[7] This framework facilitates the interrogation of other constructions of difference, beyond culture, based upon various identifiers and signifiers. Such a tool makes it possible to look beyond immigrant communities as homogenous groups that are bound by a collective identity in relation to others and opens up analytical insights into different narratives of belonging and otherness in the context not only of the host society but of the societies of origin, as well. As Anthias argues:

> Collective identities involve forms of social organization postulating boundaries with identity markers that denote essential elements of membership (which act to "code" people), as well as claims that are articulated for specific purposes. The identity markers (culture, origin, language, colour and physiognomy, etc.) may themselves function as resources that are deployed contextually and situationally. They function both as sets of self-attributions and attributions by others. By focusing on location/dislocation and on positionality, it is possible to pay attention to spatial and contextual dimensions, treating the issues involved in terms of processes rather than possessive properties of individuals.[8]

In the following discussion, we use the framework of "translocational positionality" to analyze the multiple ways in which Ghanaians in Canada connect with their communities and country of origin via religion, in spite of the spatial distanciation that their location in Canada imposes. The rationale behind using this framework stems from the fact that it allows us to escape the constraints of a binary division between subjectivity on the one hand and cultural determinism on the other. Rather, what we have is a dialectical approach that facilitates the appreciation of the multiple, simultaneous, fluid, and sometimes conflictual positions occupied by individuals and groups as they negotiate their sense of self and consequent attachments to cultures, religion, ethnicities, places, and nations.

We will also draw from a related schema on translocation and religion provided by Hagan and Ebaugh.[9] It is an apposite framework for analyzing how religion intersects with migration to shape the experiences of Ghanaians in Ghana and in the Diaspora. The authors point out that the role of religion in the stages of the migration process has been overlooked by both immigration and sociology of religion scholars. They contend further that the relationship between migration and religion is largely seen in historical and recent case studies that tend to emphasize the roles of the church vis-à-vis the settlement of immigrants in their host communities. Added to this focus in the literature is an interest in how religion facilitates the propagation of transnational activities. This skewed nature of scholarly work loses sight of the role that religion plays in the other phases along the trajectory of migration, prior to immigrants' settlement in their current location. Hagan and Ebaugh, therefore, suggest the need to examine how immigrants use religion at all stages of the migration process: (1) making the decision to emigrate; (2) preparing for the trip; (3) making the journey; (4) arriving; (5) joining an ethnic church; (6) developing transnational linkages.[10] During the first stage, congregants contact their priest for advice and prayer about the journey they are contemplating, spiritual guidance about its feasibility, and insights about how to proceed. The second phase involves formal religious services at which the congregation prays for the spiritual needs of the prospective migrants and their families. The church also pledges the necessary support. The religious dimension of the interregnum between departure and arrival in the country of final destination is reflected in the third stage, during which migrants rely on spiritual support from religious leaders in their home communities as they undertake arduous and dangerous journeys to their ultimate destinations. The next three stages take place in the new place of domicile. In stage four, immigrants make contact with their home pastor and church for mutual updates, and in the fifth stage, they join the "ethnic church" with an established congregation that helps its newly arrived compatriots integrate into the society and forge contacts with relevant social networks. The final stage identified by Hagan and Ebaugh relates to the establishment of transnational links between the migrant and the "ethnic church" and communities of worship in their home countries. This takes the form of spiritual and material exchanges between the two locales. This schema is very valuable in helping us not only analyze how migrants, as autonomous and interdependent agents, use religion and religious institutions creatively to structure and negotiate their journeys and experiences in the Diaspora but also understand the basis for the spiritual connections that tie the Diaspora back to its place of origin at different levels of resolution—that is, the individual and the organizational. Using this framework as a complement to the concept of "translocational positionality," this chapter focuses on Ghanaian immigrants' participation in Ghanaian churches, in both their original and their diasporic iterations, and the intersection of religion with processes of migration.

It must be acknowledged at the outset that connections to spiritual networks in travel destinations and in locales of origin, as well as perceptions of these linkages, reflect different experiences, interests, and rationales. As Shami observes, "even with the formation of collective approaches to the homeland, people who journey back and forth, their motivations, aims, representations and the kinds of landscapes they construct as they travel these circuits vary significantly."[11] Hence, it is important not to homogenize the experiences of migrants but to unpack the relationship between religion and migration for different people as we interrogate their movement across borders and integration into the Diaspora context. In view of this recognition, Shain and Barth's distinction among core, passive, and silent members of the Diaspora is useful to keep in mind as we discuss the relationships between Ghanaians in Canada and their spirituality, especially within the public sphere.[12] While core members of the Ghanaian community, such as pastors, lead their congregations to articulate their connections to the homeland and to mobilize their compatriots, passive members tend to be on the margins as church attendees but are ready to make themselves available for purposes initiated by the core. Silent members, for their part, are generally not involved in church affairs or outward displays of religiosity but may respond to initiatives by the core when necessary, whether in Canada or at home. It must be noted that a large number of Ghanaians do not attend church for a variety of reasons. These include those who did not attend church prior to coming to Canada and see no need to do so in the present context, as well as those whose absence stems from pragmatic considerations, such as work schedules. The fact that the silent members' group does not attend church should not be misconstrued to mean that the role of religion in their lives is any less important than it is for those in the first two categories. This chapter, nevertheless, focuses on narratives from, and analyses based on, the experiences of core and passive members of church congregations. In order to pursue the objectives of this research, interviews were conducted with pastors of two Ghanaian churches in Canada. Focus group discussions were also conducted with selected members of their congregations. In addition, the research drew from church documents and publications, newspaper articles, participant observations, and other secondary material relating generally to Ghanaian churches and ethnic ministries.

A point worth making here is that, while the literature tends to talk about the "ethnic church" in relation to diasporic religious congregations, it is useful to recognize that the "ethnic church" is not coterminous with the "home church" for all individuals who share an ethnic or national identity. The extent of immigrants' involvement in both a geographical and deterritorialized church is largely determined by their definition of the "home church." In this chapter, the "home church" is used to mean:

> "where one best knows oneself"—where "best" means "most" even if not always "happiest." . . . Being at "home" and being "homeless" are not matters of movement, of physical space, or of the fluidity of socio-cultural times and places, as such. One is at home when one inhabits a cognitive environment in which one can undertake the routines of daily life and through which one finds one's identity best mediated—and homeless when such a cognitive environment is eschewed.[13]

As they construct and interpellate a sense of belonging, home, location, and dislocation, Ghanaian Christians in Canada anchor their religious beliefs in a concept of the "home church" that traverses the physical boundaries of a particular state, though it incorporates it. For them, that church

> is at once a physical construct and a mental imaginary. Thus, while people may be separated from the physical construct of "home," as a result of immigration and other forms of geographical mobility, they tend to retain their attachment to that space through mental connections and outward practices that invoke that geographical location. This is the case even though signifiers of their cultures of origin are adapted to their new settings, new cultures, and by new generations.[14]

The term "home church" is thus used to refer to the broader imaginary church that one identifies with, whether physical or cerebral. The "Diaspora church" refers to the local church in the host society, while the term "mother church" is used to describe the relevant church of which a Ghana or Diaspora-based branch is a part.

Religion and Migration

The importance of religion to most Ghanaian Christian migrants does not suddenly emerge in the environment of diasporic settlement, even though the exigencies of the diasporic experience can trigger a religious epiphany for some people. By and large, it is a phenomenon that originates in their home countries and characterizes the entire migratory experience.[15] It is worth noting that a number of Ghanaian migrants interviewed for this research indicated that they committed their journeys to God prior to their departure from Ghana. The process not only involved personal, intimate appeals to God for the success of their travel plans but also manifested itself in the seeking of spiritual support from their priests and pastors. They shared their plans with the religious leaders from whom they requested prayers.

Once the decision to travel has been made, prospective migrants engage in various activities that can be categorized under Hagan and Ebaugh's second stage. Usually, in those cases where the prospective journey is legal and confirmed (e.g., for those going to school, taking up an appointment, getting permanent resident status), the priest may eventually share the plans with the rest of the congregation and ask for their spiritual support for the individual and his or her family. In those situations where the plans have not crystallized and the individual is still working through the predeparture formalities, there are a variety of spiritual interventions that are sought that do not include open solicitations for the spiritual support of fellow congregants. This practice responds to the belief among research respondents that one should not lay open for public consumption plans that have not yet materialized in order to avoid any embarrassment that might result if they do not go through. There is also the fear that one's enemies could derail the plans through witchcraft and other evil forces, if they were to become aware of them.

Spiritual interventions are invoked through fasting and prayer prior to visa appointments at the appropriate consulate or embassy, for example. It is worth noting that the visa process in African countries is generally nerve-wracking and filled with trepidation for applicants.[16] It is, therefore, not surprising that many people seek divine intervention as they proceed to the visa-application phase of their emigration plans. Cases abound in Ghana in which people have contacted pastors specifically to use their spiritual powers to ensure that visas are granted. In fact, some priests have gained popularity/notoriety in Ghana as "visa pastors" either due to testimonials from individuals who attribute their success in obtaining visas to these pastors or because the priests themselves claim to be able to ensure success in this area. Not all interventions yield the desired results. However, almost invariably, the pastors involved do not take the blame for the failures but rather point to a lack of faith on the part of the person who solicited their assistance. The practice, which sometimes requires payments from the "client"/congregant, has become so disconcerting to some members of the priesthood and the general public that it has elicited condemnation as a ploy to exploit desperate and vulnerable people looking for means to escape the vicissitudes of life in their country. A Ghanaian evangelist recently berated the "visa pastors" thus: "Some pastors have now buried repentance messages and are now preaching about how they could help people to secure overseas clearance [visas] to travel abroad without pointing out the sins of the people in our society."[17] Another warned the public about such pastors, saying that "pastors are men of God and not visa contractors, so people should not go to them for visa assistance."[18]

The third stage of the schema is particularly germane to the situation of those sojourners who have given up on legal emigration. For these people, the need for spiritual anchor is as imperative as it is for legal emigrants, if not more so, as they embark on a journey of hope that may be characterized by various trials and tribulations. They therefore turn to religious rituals that, it is hoped, will attenuate the laborious and risky ventures that they are about to undertake. This recourse to divine intervention and guidance, as well as spiritual protection, confirms findings from van Dijk's study of Ghanaian pentecostalism, which indicated that prospective migrants attend prayer camps and participate in rituals aimed at providing spiritual guidance and protection for their journeys.[19] There are stories of Ghanaians who have braved the perils of the Sahara for years in order to get to Europe, which has served, in some cases, as a staging ground for the onward journey to North America. Some contend with the marauding canines of the immigration agents who watch the harsh and unwelcoming borders of their economic or political El Dorados.[20] Those who make it to the target destinations live in constant fear of being picked up by the authorities, detained, and deported back to their home countries. Irrespective of the nature of the physical travails that these sojourners must endure, there is always the psychological turmoil that their illegal activities conjure. One of the avenues that these individuals turn to is their faith in prayer and the belief that their ultimate goal of legal residence, economic success, and/or political reprieve will be answered by a divine power. In addition to their personal prayers, they call on family members and, in some cases, pastors of their home churches to pray for them, as well. To facilitate, and express gratitude for, these interventions, the sojourner sends financial and material recompense to these networks of spiritual support.

A number of interviewees indicated that they did maintain links with the pastors in their communities of origin once they arrived in Canada. This is especially so for those who came by legal means directly from Ghana. It is not surprising that they keep in touch with their faith community in Ghana since their departures may have been formally announced to the congregations and they feel a sense of responsibility to inform their compatriots about their safe arrival and to register their gratitude for their morale and spiritual support. In some instances, individuals still have their spouses and children in Ghana, and they count on the church family to take care of them in a variety of ways, not necessarily financial. It is important, therefore, that they maintain links to the social networks provided by the church. Some respondents intimated that they still count on their pastor and church for continuing prayers and emotional support as they adjust to life in their new environments. A few mentioned that they periodically make financial contributions to the sustenance of the mother church that has supported them in various ways.

An interesting dimension of the links between the new immigrant and home churches relates to family issues in situations where the sojourner has left behind children and/or spouse(s). Some interviewees disclosed that both they and their family members have used the home pastor as a conduit for settling disputes or for addressing issues arising from geographical distance. For example, when the spouse/partner in Ghana has suspicion that the one in Canada may be engaged in a relationship with someone else, he or she may contact their pastor, who, by mail or phone, admonishes the spouse to eschew infidelity and immorality, in general, and to meet obligations to the one left behind. Interestingly, there are also instances where the complaint has come from Canada and the pastor is called upon to intervene and counsel the partner who is in Ghana. What these transnational linkages suggest is that new immigrants who had a strong attachment to their home churches still feel an affinity to them and use the institutions and agencies of those churches in ways similar to what obtained in Ghana when they were there. This seems to be the case until the individual discovers a new spiritual home in Canada, after which the ties to the mother church might be diminished, though not necessarily severed.

New immigrants have a variety of motives for joining a church once they arrive in Canada. These can be divided into what Allport refers to as intrinsic and extrinsic religious motivations.[21] The former are shaped by recourse to one's faith for meaning and guidance, while the latter are driven by utilitarian purposes. Some Ghanaian immigrants, usually those who were regular participants in congregations in their country of origin, are motivated by intrinsic considerations and seek a community of believers with whom they can develop fellowship and express their faith. In the initial stages, these individuals tend to seek any church with an acceptable doctrine that is geographically accessible. At this point they are not familiar with their locality and do not have the wherewithal to explore congregations that are not physically proximate. It is only after they establish contacts with their Christian compatriots who are members of Ghanaian churches that they begin to engage with those establishments. It appears that those Ghanaians who belonged to pentecostal and charismatic churches in Ghana are more likely to seek the diasporic versions of those churches than are their counterparts who belonged to mainline denominations at home. The main reason for this, according to the latter, is the continuity that the mainline churches in Canada provide as far as church doctrine and practice are concerned. They, therefore, feel more at home in the non-Ghanaian church environment than they would in the Ghanaian charismatic/pentecostal church. Of course, if there is a Canadian branch of a Ghanaian mainline church, they are more inclined to gravitate toward it.

In addition to the spiritual motive that underlies immigrants' connection to churches in Canada, it is important to point out that the church is also seen as a "destination of opportunity." Churches provide links to established members of the community who help the immigrant to integrate and make contacts with other social networks that help with jobs, housing, and so forth. In fact, some interviewees mentioned that they attended particular churches, even though they had no prior affiliation to the particular denomination, because someone from that congregation provided them with the necessary support and suggested that they could get more support from the congregation in question. It must be made clear, though, that the spiritual and the instrumental motives for joining particular churches are not mutually exclusive.

In the following section, we examine the specific phenomenon of Ghanaian churches in Canada. This allows us to move the discussion beyond the individual's sense of spiritual agency as they negotiate their migration trajectory to one that explores religious organization in the Diaspora at the meso-, macro-, and transnational levels.

Ghanaian Churches in Canada—Profiles and Analysis of Identity, Hybridity, and Integration

"African Churches" in the Diaspora have been identified as a growing phenomenon in the process of transnationalization.[22] In Canada, increased migration has brought with it diversity in religious beliefs, but the fundamental dominance of Christianity has remained unassailed.[23] This can be explained by the fact that a large number of immigrants are Christians, thereby shoring up the existing number of those who share the basic ethos of that religion. In tune with these developments, Ghanaian-founded and -led Christian churches are becoming a visible part of the religious landscape in Canada's big cities.[24] Some estimates put the number of "Ghanaian churches" in Toronto alone at more than 60.[25] By 2003, the members of the Ghanaian Presbyterian Church in Toronto had increased to "about 300 fully registered adults, 60 adherents and about 120 children."[26] As will be shown presently, the numbers are even higher for other churches. By and large, the Ghanaian churches fit a "niche," as opposed to a "parish," model of churches. As Ebaugh et al. note, "in the parish model, people worship in the same geographical area in which they live, while 'niche' congregations attract members from a broader geographical area who share identities, interests and/or similar tastes in worship style."[27]

The Ghanaian churches in Canada can be categorized into the three main types of African Diaspora churches identified by Adogame. They are (1) those that are branches of, or affiliated with, existing churches in Ghana and operate under the authority of the home churches; (2) those that were formed in Canada and have branches in Ghana or have the intent of establishing such branches; and (3) para-church organizations, which are informal groups of individuals who come together for prayer meetings and fellowships.[28] Prayer groups have been identified among the francophone Muslim community in Montreal, as well, an indication that these groups are represented across a variety of religious faiths.[29] For the purpose of this chapter, we focus on the first two categories. While the analysis will draw from the experiences of various churches, I will focus on two churches that respectively represent the two categories. These are the Church of Pentecost—Canada and the All Nations Full Gospel Church.

The Church of Pentecost—Canada (COP-C) is a branch of the Church of Pentecost International (COP-I), which is headquartered in Ghana. The latter was founded in 1937, in the then Gold Coast, by the Reverend James McKeown, an English missionary. It is currently run entirely by Ghanaians and has branches in more than fifty countries around the world—in Africa, Asia, Australia, Europe, the Middle East, and North America. By the end of the first half of 2003, the mother church in Ghana boasted more than a million members, 8,756 churches/assemblies, and 584 ministers, while the overseas branches had 1,904 churches, 319 ministers, and a total membership of 147,081.[30] The COP-C, which has its head office in North York, Ontario, was established in 1990 and has assemblies in the major cities of the country, including Montreal, Ottawa, Toronto, Hamilton, Calgary, and Vancouver. The Greater Toronto Metropolitan Area alone has seven assemblies. The total membership of the church in Canada, in 2004, stands at more than 2,000.

The All Nations Full Gospel Church (ANFGC) is headed by a Senior Pastor, Dr. Samuel Donkor, who founded the ministry in 1986, in Toronto, where the church currently has its headquarters. The church started as a Bible study group in the basement of his apartment, a pattern that characteristically defined the emergence of a number of Ghanaian churches in Canada. After Reverend Donkor's ordination, in 1986, he founded the ANFGC with between twenty and thirty followers. It has now grown to a membership of 1,500 people from more than fifty different countries. The church has branches in various Canadian and U.S. cities, including Hamilton, Ajax, Toronto, Ottawa, Kitchener, Calgary, Dallas, and Orlando. In addition, there are six branches in Africa and others in Europe. The ANFGC also runs the All Nations Bible College, with a student population of 100, which is aimed at training not only its own religious leaders but leaders for other bodies, as well.

Role of the Churches in the Ghanaian Community

There is a debate between those who emphasize the assimilating capacities of host cultures and those who contend that the impacts that are produced by contact between immigrants and host cultures result from complex processes of negotiation, adaptation, and reinvention.[31] As a result of these processes, immigrants retain elements of their cultures of origin, even as they adjust to the norms and practices of their new environment. Williams examines how the intersection of physical and social space affects the sense of identity among immigrants and their daily practices.[32] He argues that Diaspora life is characterized by a definitive and situated culture. Consequently, immigrants practice familiar rites in new settings and give new meanings to familiar practices and rituals, which are then exhibited during interactions among compatriots. This analysis supports the theory of "cultural remittance" as a useful tool for examining the practices, imaginings, nostalgias, and yearnings that link Ghanaians in Canada to the spiritual communities from which they have journeyed. Burman defines "cultural remittance" as

> gestures sent to an elsewhere (often conceived as home but not the only home), exceeding goods and money sent. Such gestures join points within a diasporic sphere that are not necessarily spatially contiguous, and bring to the fore imagination as social practice . . . with transformative potential. Cultural remittances play out in, and transform, diasporic locales . . . and they are often addressed to both the elsewhere evoked and the mainstream context" [of the host countries in which immigrants are located].[33]

At this juncture, it is useful to explain how "culture" is being employed here. Our use of the term derives from Anthias's three dimensions of culture: (1) culture as content or product; (2) culture as process or mechanism; and (3) culture as form or structure.[34] The first refers to cultural attributes and artifacts that are linked to particular locales or communities and provide an illustration of their symbols and practices. The second dimension pertains to the understanding of culture as an expression of a world view. It serves as the basis on which culture as content/product is built but is distinct from it. Finally, culture as form or structure refers to the patterns of knowledge and actions that characterize a society and to their institutionalization within defined structures and processes. Aberrations from these patterns lead to the application of relevant sanctions. Far from being assimilated into mainstream Canadian society, Ghanaians and Ghanaian churches in Canada are engaged in an "extraordinary process of periphery-induced creolization in the metropolis"[35] as they manifest elements of these three dimensions of culture.

Part of the reason for the growth of these churches is the fact that they offer a spiritual environment with which their mostly African members can identify. Members find the mainstream Canadian churches to be too sedate in their services. They are, therefore, attracted to the African churches, where the atmosphere replicates the exuberance, patterns, and forms of worship (e.g., dancing and drumming) found among Christian groups at home. The members of the two churches who were interviewed made it clear that they preferred a connection to the churches of their homeland to mainstream Canadian churches because the religious community assuages the nostalgia that these individuals feel for the spiritual environments of the churches they left at home by providing the best cognitive environment for their religious beliefs, routines, and rituals. As Hepner notes with regard to Eritrean churches in the United States, the growth in these organizations is largely a result of the fact that they "help maintain cultural patterns" (religious belief systems and values, language, gender roles, dress, and socialization of youth).[36] Furthermore, they respond to the spiritual vulnerabilities that are specific to the Ghanaian and African community. For example, witchcraft and the fears that it generates are still very significant concerns among Africans in Canada, even though they function in a society where these superstitions and the metaphysical trappings of this phenomenon do not hold much, if any, sway. The African churches' ability to address these concerns gives them an additional advantage over mainstream churches.

Church-based social networks provide forums where mores and values that Ghanaian members consider to be fundamental to their identities are validated and reinforced, particularly when they do not dovetail neatly with mainstream values. One such value pertains to homosexuality. Invariably, interviewees were obdurate in their opposition to same-sex relationships, which they considered to be sinful and an affront to biblical teachings. This attachment to a geographically distant yet psychologically and emotionally proximate space is a fundamental part of what defines most members' sense of their Ghanaianness, even as they operate within mainstream parameters in other aspects their lives. Similar findings came out of Yang's study of Chinese evangelicals in the United States, in which he observes that these immigrants use the ethnic church "to fend off unwelcome aspects of American ways and values while adopting others."[37]

The attraction of Ghanaian churches also derives from these Ghanaians' marginalized location within Canadian society and the perception that they are second-class citizens. The following acknowledgment by the United Church of Canada is insightful:

> In addition to not feeling valued . . . many ethnic minority members of the United Church continued to share unfortunate and similar experiences of marginalization, invisibility, and racial discrimination within the church. Cultural differences, prejudices, language isolation, as well as few accessible United Church resources and information, all presented barriers to full participation of many ethnic minorities within the household of the United Church. "The experience of many racial minority peoples is that they are frequently not seen, not heard, not taken account of. Even when they are present and participating, their contribution is often politely tolerated and received with a patronizing attitude of condescension. They feel invisible."[38]

In these circumstances, the Ghanaian churches serve as a community from within which they can articulate their sense of self and identity. Many members of the congregations are very qualified professionals who end up in low-end jobs that underutilize their skills and potential.[39] Consequently, they struggle to maintain a sense of self-worth based on the status and respect that they enjoyed in their countries of origin, and long for the benefits derived therefrom. While this process can be at once emotionally soothing and painful, as they try to resolve the dissonance produced by the differences between their Diaspora and home positionalities, the church offers a spatiotemporal cocoon where they can regain their status, even if only momentarily. The opportunity to serve as officers of the church (e.g., elders, deacons and deaconesses) confers on these individuals respect and status that may be lacking outside their church community. Furthermore, their antecedent status prior to leaving Ghana is still generally recognized and respected by their compatriots. Park and Wanpen observed similar experiences and feelings among Koreans in the United States and state:

> The majority are . . . urban middle-class professionals who migrated for personal reasons such as better economic opportunities and quality of life. The process of uprooting from one's familiar lifestyle, cultural heritage and social network creates a search for a new identity and forces one to face existential loneliness and alienation. After rerooting, the reality of finding that the "American Dream" which motivated their relocation might remain only as a dream compounds the difficulty of their adaptation and adjust-

> ment. . . . [The church] provides the immigrants with frequent and regular opportunities . . . for primary group and secondary group interactions. . . . There has been a movement to link the role of the ethnic church to ameliorating psychological distress in general and depressive symptoms in particular.[40]

The churches, then, provide a network of support for immigrants dealing with the challenges imposed by their host environment, such as problems pertaining to their immigration status. The role of the Ghanaian church community in immigration matters is very important because of the sensitive nature of immigration cases, particularly those of refugee claimants whose stories may be a mixture of truth, embellishments, and outright fabrications. Moreover, the devastation that may result from losing one's case can be far-reaching for the individual. While at the institutional level the churches do not condone false immigration claims, it is not uncommon for members to help compatriots with advice and financial support to enable them to navigate their interactions with Canadian authorities and to regularize their stay in the country. There are various means by which the churches help members to cope with and/or address social and economic concerns in the host society. As one pastor intimated, "you cannot minister unto the spiritual needs of people and ignore their physical and developmental needs because it is the latter that prepares the individual for effective spiritual development."[41]

Some of these support mechanisms are available through specific ministries in the churches, such as the women's and men's fellowships, which discuss and assist members with issues that affect them. Pastors provide counseling services and offer prayers for members who approach them with personal problems. The following testimonial illustrates the nature and perceived officacy of these services. A Ghanaian member of the All Nations Full Gospel Church, who had had a couple of accidents in very quick succession that left her in a situation where no insurance company wanted to provide her with coverage, noted:

> I know within my spirit that these were planned attacks from the devil so I made arrangements to meet with Pastor Acheampong. He provided excellent council [*sic*] and trained me for war with the enemy. . . . By God's grace the same company which will not give me insurance sent me a quote. As well, they provided me with other perks. As for the additional charges incurred by the hit and run accident, the price was negotiated and dropped

> down to something more affordable. The battle was won. . . . I thank the Senior Pastor and the church leaders for their teachings. Through Christ who strengthened me, I became a victor in the word's truest sense.

A significant number of these counseling sessions deal with marital and other family problems. The church community also serves as a network of contacts for those seeking jobs, housing, and so forth. Overall, as Manning notes with regard to West Indian carnivals in the Diaspora, the Ghanaian church communities in Canada offer

> a kind of social therapy that overcomes the separation and isolation imposed by the Diaspora and restores to . . . immigrants both a sense of community with each other and a sense of connection to the culture that they claim as a birthright. . . . They are also a means through which [immigrants] seek and symbolize integration into the metropolitan society, by coming to terms with the opportunities, as well as the constraints, that surround them.[42]

Members of congregations join or help one another to observe certain fundamental cultural practices such as the various rites of passage, and this constitutes an important dimension of the home-Diaspora connection for many Ghanaian-Canadians. They celebrate births and child-naming ceremonies, for example, and mourn deaths in the community. In Ghana, funerals are community events, and every member of the community is expected to help bereaved families organize a fitting burial for their departed relatives. This social obligation stems from a moral economy that requires reciprocal support from community members. The obligation is even more pronounced for members of the deceased's extended family, irrespective of where they may be resident. The same sense of community obligation that surrounds these activities in Ghana is replicated within the Ghanaian churches in Canada. Bereaved members of the church are supported by their fellow congregants even if they did not know the deceased. At these events, cash donations are made to help the bereaved meet their obligations to kin. The sense of communal mobilization to support the bereaved in the Canadian context is heightened by the fact that relatives who are resident abroad are usually expected to bear a significant part of the funeral expenses, particularly if they are the children or siblings of the deceased. Their compatriots, understanding the onus that this responsibility places on the bereaved, do the best they can to offer their support. The involvement of churches in funerals is even more pronounced when a member passes away. They provide emotional and financial support to those left behind and help to organize the funeral.

Events and celebrations such as those discussed in this section provide opportunities for these African-Canadians to display their material culture, which constitutes the most visible marker of their connection to the African continent. As they dress themselves in the most elaborate apparel of their cultural groups and feast on traditional cuisines, they assert their pride in their cultures of origin and their continuing attachment to them.[43]

Social Capital, the Youth, and Church Sustainability

It is particularly noteworthy that all the churches are engaged in efforts to build social capital among the youth. These efforts take different forms, including youth groups and ministries that organize peer education programs of various sorts, not only to win souls for Christ but also to address general challenges faced by the youth, offer support networks, and help them to take advantage of opportunities in the society. The COP-C, which started a youth ministry in 1994 in North York, Ontario, was motivated by the realization that "teenagers, especially those who had been passed out of Sunday school, were not growing spiritually or showing much interest in the church and its activities."[44] There are currently youth ministries in the church's branches all across the country, with a membership of more than 800, under the guidance of more than forty leaders.

The youth participate in conferences that bring together peers from across Canada and, sometimes, from the United States. The youth group of the Ghanaian Presbyterian Church in Toronto, for example, hosted the 2003 North American Youth Conference in July of that year, with participants from Toronto, Montreal, New York City, Virginia, Maryland, and Massachusetts. To generate, and sustain, the interest of young people in the churches, programs that are attractive to them, such as trips to amusement parks and other fun locations, are periodically organized. Furthermore, the churches are responding to the Internet generation by setting up Web sites for youth-related information and interactions. Chat rooms allow the youth to relate to and network with one another on religious and other matters. The Web sites also provide links to devotionals, employment, and educational resources (both secular and religious), games, movies, and so on. The COP-C Web site enables youth to post articles addressing issues that are relevant to them and their peers. The following excerpt from one such article gives a clear insight into the moralizing tone of the material that is posted:

> The young men want to wear earrings and braid their hair, so how do we distinguish between a woman and a man now? The ladies want to wear the skimpiest of clothes in the name of fashion; how do we distinguish between a prostitute and a Christian? Social status to the youth of today, is presenting oneself in as much "bling bling" as possible; be it a car, jewelry, a house or an outfit. . . . The Christian must be wary of many things in life. Today's society encourages vices such as same-sex marriage, divorce, prohibition of the Lord's prayer in school and hard drugs, all in disregard for the doctrines of God.[45]

While not all those who join the youth ministry sustain their interest in the groups, the churches are proud of the fact that they are able to keep a number of young people adhering to Christian values.

The need to encourage the youth to pursue education is a principal focus of the youth ministries. In July 2004, the Anointing Baptist Foundation of the Ghanaian Community Baptist Church in Montreal launched a scholarship scheme for high-achieving Ghanaian-Canadian youth. It is meant to help them defray the cost of their education with funding that comes from contributions by members of the church and from the Mustard Seed Foundation, in Washington, D.C. Six beneficiaries were presented with scholarships at the first awards ceremony, in November 2004. It is hoped that such gestures will encourage other youth to shoot for higher academic laurels.

The involvement of young people, particularly second-generation immigrants, in the churches' activities is very significant because the level and extent of their participation speaks to the sustainability of these Diaspora churches, which tend to be established to cater to the needs of first-generation immigrants. By building a strong foundation for the youth to participate in church activities and to take up leadership roles, these churches are hoping that the congregations will endure beyond the lifetime of the current adult membership.

Ghanaian Churches and Horizontal Integration

It has to be noted that, while these churches tend to cater principally to Ghanaian and secondarily to African congregations, they are not exclusive to those communities. Indeed, a number of them, particularly those that were founded in Canada, such as the All Nations Full Gospel Church (ANFGC), have members from a variety of national and ethnic backgrounds. This horizontal expansion of these churches is evidence of their ecumenical missions. According to the COP-I, its primary purpose is to "practice and propagate what our Lord Jesus Christ commanded in Mark 16:15–16: 'go ye into the world and preach the gospel to every creature.'" Church members believe that God had a covenant with the founders of the church to use missionaries from the Gold Coast (now Ghana) to win souls for Christ throughout the world in order to fulfill His divine purpose. In consonance with this covenant, the Pentecost International Worship Center, a branch of the COP-C, states that it is "dedicated to reaching the international community in the Greater Toronto Area for God through Christ."[46] The ANFGC, for its part, has Spanish and Tamil congregations with their own pastors. Thus, in addition to liturgies in English and in a Ghanaian language, Twi, there are Spanish and Hindi services, as well.

Beyond growing non-Ghanaian congregations, a number of the churches are engaged in community outreach programs that target not just Ghanaians but also the wider society. The ANFGC, for example, established the All Nations International Development Agency (ANIDA), in 1997, as a human development organization to help alleviate poverty and improve the lives of peoples in Canada and abroad. "Since its inception, ANIDA has been serving the local and international community in an effort to develop self-sufficient individuals and families, and build vibrant communities all over the world. ANIDA provides counseling, training, improved childcare, refugee settlement, food, medical aids and help to improve the standard of living for more than 2000 individuals and their families each year."[47] ANIDA's volunteer-facilitated Neighborhood Outreach and Help program (NOAH) assists needy families in the Greater Toronto Metropolitan Area, providing food aid throughout the year.

Another example of horizontal engagement is the churches' collaboration with Christian individuals and groups that are outside the Ghanaian community. The Ghanaian Presbyterian Church of Montreal has benefited tremendously from partnerships with extant Canadian churches. This is borne out by the following statement from the pastor of the church: "The Ghanaian Presbyterian Church joined Canada Ministries about three years ago with great hopes and expectations. The congregation is grateful to the Church of Canada for its support including the appointment of a Minister from Ghana to pastor the congregation to new heights."[48] Broader evidence of interchurch collaboration is found in the tendency for Ghanaian churches to share facilities that belong to existing Canadian denominations.

Churches as Conduits for Transnational Expression

Transnationalization of churches and the diasporization of membership provide a means whereby Ghanaian congregations in Canada participate in, influence, and are influenced by the mother church in their countries of origin. Similar reciprocal relationships exist between those churches that were founded in Canada and their branches in Ghana. Church leaders visit their branches to confer with, participate in activities organized by, and solicit support from members of their church. For example, the groundbreaking ceremony to mark commencement of work on a new church building for the Ghanaian Presbyterian Church in Toronto, in 2003, was witnessed by the Reverend Dr. Gyang-Duah, Clerk of the General Assembly of the Ghana Presbyterian Church. Leblanc and Babou have each observed similar movements among Senegalese immigrant Muslim communities.[49] The events and issues that take place in Diaspora churches intersect with those that take place within cognate institutions in their homelands and so generate mutual interest. Evidence shows that while the Diaspora branches of Ghanaian churches are generally autonomous in the day-to-day running of their affairs, they defer to the mother church in matters of church doctrine and structure. Thus, when the COP-C decided to establish a youth ministry, it sought the endorsement of the General Council of the COP-I, which gave its approval in 1996 and appointed a youth director for the ministry. A recent development among some Ghanaian churches in Toronto illustrates these home-Diaspora linkages.

In a bold move to reverse the disturbing trend of Church divisions and multiplications in the Ghanaian-Canadian communities, the leadership of the Methodist Church have taken some positive action to reunite the various factions of the Church, starting with the factions in Toronto, Canada's largest city. Throughout the weekend of December 7–8, 2003, the leadership of the Ghana Methodist Church of Toronto and the Ghana Calvary Methodist United Church of Toronto met behind closed doors in marathon negotiating sessions. These were under the spiritual guidance and supervision of the Presiding Bishop of the Ghana Methodist Conference, The Most Reverend Dr. Aboagye-Mensah, and the lay president of the Ghana Methodist Conference in Ghana, Mr Ato Essuman.[50]

The relationship between the mother church and its diasporic branches is also manifested in the posting of pastors from the former to the latter. The Ghanaian Presbyterian Church of Toronto, for example, said goodbye to the Reverend Akunor, senior pastor, in June 2003, and welcomed his successor, the Reverend Pobee, from Ghana. It is worth mentioning that the flow is not necessarily bidirectional; as the mother church expands around the world, the circulation of ministers becomes multidirectional. For instance, Apostle Anthony Miah, who took over as head of the COP-C in 2004, came from Gabon, where he had been the head of the local branch of the church for seven years. His predecessor, Apostle Ackah-Baidoo, was reassigned to Cape Coast, in Ghana. Kawakami observed similar patterns of multidimensional transnational movements within the Vietnamese Diaspora. They were characterized by "simultaneous crossing over of national borders by religious networks that were established in host countries worldwide."[51]

In addition to remitting elements of the home culture into the diasporic settings, these global movements are creating sociocultural changes within the mother churches, as well. Processes of cultural globalization, or synchronization, that are reflective of the influences of Euro-American culture have led to the emergence of new approaches, practices, and performative acts in the Ghanaian milieu that imitate the evangelistic ministries in North America.[52] These developments are not surprising because, in tandem with media images of North American religious expression, the regular flow of ministers between the home and Diaspora churches creates a circular movement not only of personalities but of ideas and liturgical genres, as well. The synchronization that defines certain aspects of religious practice in both the home and Diaspora settings helps bridge the gap between those who occupy spaces between the two worlds. It enables them, at least in the settings of these churches, to surmount the double alienation that many African-Canadians have to deal with in other realms. As Tettey and Puplampu observe, many African-Canadians do not seem to fully feel a part of their host society because they retain certain values that are different from those of mainstream society and feel discriminated against.[53] On the other hand, when they travel back to their countries of origin, they find a disjuncture, as well, because they and their home societies have changed in ways that creates dissonance for them. Consequently, they experience zones of incompatibility between themselves and their communities of origin. In terms of churches, however, the hybridization described earlier provides opportunities for a "bridgespace" that help Ghanaians escape some of that dissonance.[54]

Religious music tapes and CDs, as well as tape-recorded sermons, both from Ghana and by Diaspora-based preachers and musicians, provide a popular cultural link to the continent. Many Ghanaian homes in Canada have some form of indigenous Ghanaian Christian music or the hybrid varieties that reflect the transmutations of popular culture that have resulted from the blending of traditional African music with influences from elsewhere, particularly genres from Western popular culture. These messages and tunes provide spiritual edification for their audience, and the songs tend to be the highlight of social gatherings and church events. Videos of sermons, messages, and activities from parent churches are also shared with congregations in the Diaspora, while similar productions are made by those churches that were founded in Canada and sent to their branches in Ghana. The uses of technology echo Pendakur and Sobramanyam's findings with respect to the Indian Diaspora, where family-based video watching seems to be of critical importance in helping immigrants reproduce their home cultures abroad.[55] In the case of the Ghanaian churches, the technologies are also a means for the Diaspora to influence the home communities through the homeward flow of information, thereby creating mediascapes that are circulatory and not unidirectional.

Religious bodies also bring to the fore important questions about Diaspora mobilization via religion and its implication for socioeconomic and political developments at home. Remittances from sojourners abroad have, for more than a century, been a critical link between immigrant communities and their places of origin. Ghanaian churches serve as important sources and channels for disbursing social and financial capital to their home country. In this capacity, they epitomize the transnationalization of the moral economy that has undergirded traditional Ghanaian society. As Hall points out, the process of globalization has intensified commitments to the local.[56] In fact, the local, as far as the African Diaspora is concerned, is not only the physical here and now but also an imaginary or "distant" local. This imaginary local is defined by cultural affinity and shared origin, and, though groups or individuals may be physically removed from their communities or ethnic groups, they nevertheless maintain ethical, cultural, and pecuniary obligations and linkages. They exhibit these through mobilization of their social capital toward specific projects to benefit their compatriots.[57]

Examples of such mobilization abound in the Ghanaian-Canadian church community. For example, ANIDA has an international mission in Ghana and runs a program called Silent Cry. It is a sponsorship program for child orphans and provides the children with homes and support that allows them to pursue education from the primary to the postsecondary level. The ANFGC has also donated medical supplies to the Ministry of Health in Ghana. Furthermore, the church has established the All Nations university there to train students in various areas of expertise, including computer science, business administration, and biblical studies. It currently has 400 students. These examples support Faist's assertion that "communities without propinquity link through reciprocity and solidarity to achieve a high degree of social cohesion, and a common repertoire of symbolic and collective representations."[58]

Conflict and the Proliferation of Churches in the Marketplace of Religion

One cannot discuss Ghanaian churches in Canada without critically interrogating the basis for the mushrooming phenomenon of splinter churches. Despite the social cohesion, the construction of home away from home, and the benefits of transnational linkages that the churches provide, they have not been bastions of tranquility and harmony. Internal conflicts are, in fact, not uncommon. These clashes tend to threaten religious and socioeconomic mobilization in the context of the Diaspora church and have implications for their unity and viability. Conflicts generally do not result from disagreements over doctrine or theology but are mainly due to differences over vision and policy regarding how the church should be run and how social and financial capital should be organized for home and Diaspora purposes. There are instances where the conflicts have resulted from accusations of malfeasance against the leadership and/or the pastor for misappropriating church funds. Some cases have ended up in court or even in fistfights among the leadership, resulting in police interventions.[59]

Conflicts also flow from personality clashes between the pastor and his/her supporters on the one hand and some members and/or leaders of the church on the other. Questions regarding how power, control, and authority should be structured and exercised and who should participate in particular church-related decisions have also generated crises. A corollary to this involves conflicts that emerge when certain groups or individuals, for a variety of reasons, lay claim to ownership of the church. These claims may be based on financial and other contributions that each group thinks that it has made toward the establishment and sustenance of the church and a feeling that, in spite of those contributions, they are being marginalized. They, therefore, seek to take back the church and reestablish control. As Hepner correctly observes, actors and beneficiaries are seen "as representatives of political positions, ethno-regional communities, social classes, or kin groups . . . [e]mpowering individuals implied empowering specific collective identities over others."[60] When differences are not resolved amicably and suspicions linger, aggrieved individuals may end up breaking away and establishing a splinter church, taking with them those who support their position or believe in their cause. Some of the leaders of the breakaway faction turn into what the *Ghanaian News*, a Ghanaian newspaper in Toronto, describes as "self-ordained" and self-appointed "pastors" and "Prophets."[61]

An interesting dimension to these fissures within the churches is the commodification of religion and the attendant marketing that comes with it. Individuals who think that their stock as pastors is high within existing churches but who see no opportunity for upward mobility that will enable them to have full control over the perks of office find it expedient to branch off on their own in order to achieve the pecuniary and unquantifiable gains that come with having one's own church. The charisma of an individual pastor, and his or her perceived ability to address people's needs (both spiritual and secular), then serves as the basis for advertising the new church and attracting followers. While there is no problem with having numerous churches, the fact that many emerging churches are splinter groups, not branches, of existing ones creates competition that may be overtly or covertly negative and antagonistic. In the new religious marketplace, it is not uncommon to hear people from one church casting aspersions on other churches and raising questions about the religious credentials and personal integrity of their pastors.

Conclusion

The foregoing examination of migration, religion, and the Ghanaian Diaspora in Canada is based on the concept of "translocational positionality," which enables us to engage with issues that extend beyond the cultural. It facilitates the exploration of other dimensions of the Diaspora experience and their intersections. These include socioeconomic and political locations, spirituality, identity, the contestations they engender, the emergence of churches to respond to them, and processes of the transnationalization of church structures and activities. The framework also lends itself to an understanding of the relationship between religion and the various stages of migration, as people appropriate religion in creative ways to engage with a place beyond their immediate confines. While the focus in this chapter has been on Christians and Christian denominations, there is no doubt that prospective migrants from other faiths also make use of the institutional apparatus of their faith, such as shrines and mosques; the leaders of those institutions, for example, Imams and traditional priests; and relevant rituals to shore up the chances of a successful journey and settlement in the Diaspora.

Once they arrive in Canada, African immigrants engage with religious communities that provide them the opportunity to give expression to their intrinsic and extrinsic motivations. Increasingly, many of these immigrants are finding succor, spiritual and otherwise, within Ghanaian churches, which are assuming a significant place in Canada's urban landscape. Those who attend these churches are doing so because they fulfill a need and respond to concerns that are not adequately addressed by other religious groups. The following observation with regard to the Trinidadian Carnival in North America seems to hold true in the context of this engagement:

> [It is] not just about merriment, colourful pageantry, revelry and street theatre. [They] are born out of the struggle of marginalized peoples to shape a cultural identity through resistance, liberation and catharsis. It is these values that have facilitated [their] replication wherever the . . . Diaspora is found. [They] have acted as a bond between the diasporic community and those at home.[62]

This chapter has argued that an important development within these churches is the horizontal linkages that they are forging with groups and communities outside their core membership of compatriots from their countries of origin. The ecumenical approach to proselytizing, partnerships with existing non-Ghanaian churches, and community outreach programs all play instrumental roles in integrating the Ghanaian churches into the larger society and turning them into visible and positive models of civic and religious engagement. The churches are targeting the youth in their congregations and beyond to provide moral direction to ensure that their communities are not saddled with youth-related social problems. They are also laying the foundation for future sustainability and vertical growth by engaging the youth actively in church activities and structures.

Experience from the Ghanaian churches shows that they are highly politicized institutions, with various interests jockeying for influence, power, and control. The clash of interests has resulted in schisms within various congregations and the subsequent emergence of multiple splinter groups. These developments have eroded any potential for a unified and concerted effort on the part of various congregations of believers. Rather, they have created the basis for more extensive fissures within the larger Ghanaian communities, as these church-originated conflicts are transposed into other aspects of Diaspora life.

Notes

1. Wisdom J. Tettey, "Africa's Brain Drain: Networking Diaspora Communities for Socio-Economic Development," *Mots Pluriels* 20 (February 2002), available online at http://www.arts.uwa.edu.au/MotsPluriels/MP2002wjt.html.

2. Anthony Giddens, *The Nation State and Violence* (Cambridge: Polity Press 1985).

3. Anthony Richmond, "Globalization: Implications for Immigrants and Refugees," *Ethnic and Racial Studies* 25, no. 5 (2002): 713.

4. Wisdom J. Tettey, "Globalization, Diasporization and Cyber-Communities: Exploring African Trans-Nationalisms," in E. Osei-Prempeh, J. Mensah, and S. B. K. Adjibolosoo, eds., *Globalization and the Human Factor: Critical Insights* (London: Ashgate Publishing, 2004).

5. Floya Anthias, "New Hybridities, Old Concepts: The Limits of 'Culture,'" *Ethnic and Racial Studies* 24, no. 4 (2001): 620.

6. Homi Bhabha, "Culture's in Between," in D. Bennett, ed., *Multicultural States: Rethinking Difference and Identity* (New York: Routledge, 1998), 29–36.

7. Anthias, "New Hybridities, Old Concepts."

8. Ibid., 633; see also Arif Dirlik, "Bringing History Back In: Of Diasporas,

Hybridities, Places, and Histories," *Review of Education/Pedagogy/Cultural Studies* 21, no. 2 (1999): 95–131.

9. Jacqueline Hagan and Helen R. Ebaugh, "Calling upon the Sacred: Migrants' Use of Religion in the Migration Process," *International Migration Review* 37, no. 4 (2003): 1145–1162.

10. Ibid.

11. Seteney Shami, "Circassian Encounters: The Self as Other and the Production of the Homeland in the North Caucasus," *Development and Change* 29 (1998): 633.

12. Yossi Shain and Aharon Barth, "Diasporas and International Relations Theory," *International Organization* 57 (2003): 449–479.

13. Nigel Rapport and Andrew Dawson, eds., *Migrants of Identity: Perceptions of "Home" in a World of Movement* (Oxford: Berg, 1998), 9–10.

14. Tettey, "Globalization, Diasporization and Cyber-Communities: Exploring African Trans-Nationalisms."

15. Hagan and Ebaugh, "Calling upon the Sacred."

16. Wisdom J. Tettey and Korbla P. Puplampu, "Border Crossings and Home-Diaspora Linkages Among African-Canadians: Analysis of Translocational Positionality, Cultural Remittance, and Social Capital," in W. Tettey and K. Puplampu, eds., *Negotiating Identity and Belonging: The African Diaspora in Canada* (Calgary: University of Calgary Press, 2005); see also B. Olaniram and D. Williams, "Communication Distortion: An Intercultural Lesson from the Visa Application Process," *Communication Quarterly* 43, no. 2 (1995): 225–240.

17. "The Church Has Failed Ghana," news posting on Ghanaweb, September 24, 2004, available online at http://www.ghanaweb.com/GhanaHomePage/NewsArchive/printnews.php?ID"66596 (accessed 15 July 2005).

18. "Pastors Warned Against Visa Deals," news posting on Ghanaweb, 10 June 2003, available online at http://www.ghanaweb.com/GhanaHomePage/NewsArchive/printnews.php?ID"37596 (accessed 15 July 2005).

19. Rijk van Dijk, "From Camp to Encompassment: Discourses of Transsubjectivity in the Ghanaian Pentecostal Diaspora," *Journal of Religion in Africa* 27, no. 2 (1997): 135–160.

20. See "Mali's Dangerous Desert Gateway," BBC News, 25 June 2002, available online at http://news.bbc.co.uk/1/hi/world/africa/2063526.stm; "African Deaths in Libya's Desert," BBC News, 19 June 2003, available online at http://news.bbc.co.uk/1/hi/world/africa/3004344.stm; and "Policing Spain's Southern Coast," BBC News, 18 May 2004, available online at http://news.bbc.co.uk/2/hi/africa/3582217.stm (accessed 15 July 2005).

21. G. W. Allport, "Behavioral Science, Religion and Mental Health," *Journal of Religion and Health* 2 (1963): 187–197.

22. See Afe Adogame, "The Quest for Space in the Global Spiritual Marketplace," *International Review of Mission* 89, no. 354 (2000): 400–409, Tricia R. Hep-

ner, "Religion, Nationalism, and Transnational Civil Society in the Eritrea Diaspora," *Identities: Global Studies in Culture and Power* 10 (2003): 269–293; and Roswith Gerloff, "An African Continuum in Variation: The African Christian Diaspora in Britain," *Black Theology in Britain: A Journal of Clontextual Praxis* 3, no. 4 (2000): 84–112.

23. Reginald W. Bibby, "Canada's Mythical Religious Mosaic: Some Census Findings," *Journal for the Scientific Study of Religion* 39, no. 2 (2000): 235–239.

24. See the directory "Churches and Places of Worship in Canada" on the Afrodrive Web site, available online at http://www.afrodrive.com/AfricanChurches /default.asp?WCountryID"1. Also see "Divisions and Multiplications of Ghanaian Churches in Canada," news posting on Ghanaweb, 31 November 2003, available online at http://www.ghanaweb.com/GhanaHomePage/economy/artikel.php?ID "47078 (accessed 15 July 2005).

25. "Voodoo Rule (Part 45): Witchcraft Mentality in Toronto," news posting on Expo Times, 9 July 2002, available online at http://www.expotimes.net/backissue-sept/sept02/sept00007.htm (accessed 15 July 2005).

26. Roseline La-Kumi, "Ghanaian Presbyterian Church, Toronto," posting on The Presbyterian Church in Canada Web site, available online at http://www.presbyterian.ca/wms/resourcesA/Stories%20of%20Mission/2003/canadaministries03.h tml#gt (accessed 15 July 2005).

27. Helen R. Ebaugh, Jennifer O'Brien, and Janet S. Chafetz, "The Social Ecology of Residential Patterns and Membership in Immigrant Churches," *Journal for the Scientific Study of Religion* 39, no. 1 (2000): 107–116.

28. Adogame, "The Quest for Space in the Global Spiritual Marketplace," 400–409.

29. Marie Nathalie, "Processes of Identification Among French-Speaking West African Migrants in Montreal," *Canadian Ethnic Studies* 34, no. 3 (2002): 121–141.

30. The Church of Pentecost, "The Church of Pentecost Worldwide: Summary of Statistics for the First Half of 2003," Church of Pentecost Web site, available online at http://www/thechurchofpentecost.com/statistics.htm (accessed 15 July 2005).

31. Thomas Faist, "Transnationalization in International Migration: Implications for the Study of Citizenship and Culture," *Ethnic and Racial Studies* 23, no. 2 (2000): 215.

32. Rhys H. Williams, "Religion, Community and Place: Locating the Transcendent," *Religion and American Culture* 12, no. 2 (2002): 249–263.

33. Jenny Burman, "Masquerading Toronto Through Caribana: Transnational Carnival Meets the Sign 'Music Ends Here,'" *Identity: An International Journal of Theory and Research* 1, no. 3 (2001): 277.

34. Anthias, "New Hybridities, Old Concepts," 619–641.

35. Orlando Patterson, "Ecumenical America: Global Culture and the American Cosmos," *World Policy Journal* 11, no. 2 (1994): 104.

36. Hepner, "Religion, Nationalism, and Transnational Civil Society in the Eritrea Diaspora," 270.

37. Fenggang Yang, *Chinese Christians in America: Conversion, Assimilation, and Adhesive Identities* (University Park: Pennsylvania State University Press, 1999), 100.

38. "Ethnic Ministries," United Church of Canada Web site, available online at http://www.united-church.ca/em/background/why.shtm (accessed 15 July 2005).

39. Wisdom J. Tettey, "What Does It Mean to Be African-Canadian?: Identity, Integration and Community," in D. Taras and B. Rasporich, eds., *A Passion for Identity: An Introduction to Canadian Studies*, 4th ed. (Toronto: ITP Nelson, 2001), 161–182.

40. Hae-Seong Park and Murgatroy Wanpen, "Relationship Between Intrinsic-Extrinsic Religious Orientation and Depressive Symptoms in Korean Americans," *Counseling Psychology Quarterly* 11, no. 3 (1998): 315–324.

41. "Community Baptist Church Awards Scholarships to Montreal Ghanaian Youth," news posting on Ghanaweb, 18 November 2004, available online at http://www.ghanaweb.com/GhanaHomePage/NewsArchive/printnews.php?ID" 70073 (accessed 15 July 2005).

42. Frank Manning, "Overseas Caribbean Carnivals: The Arts and Politics of a Transnational Celebration," in J. Lent, ed., *Caribbean Popular Culture* (Bowling Green, OH: Bowling Green University Popular Press, 1990), 35.

43. Tettey and Puplampu, "Border Crossings and Home-Diaspora Linkages Among African-Canadians."

44. Church of Pentecost—Canada, *The Youth Ministry in Perspective: An Overview of the Youth Ministry in Canada, 1994–2004* (North York, Canada: Church of Pentecost, 2004), 1.

45. Abigail Ackah-Baidoo, "This Is Our Time," Church of Pentecost—Canada Web site, available online at http://www.pentecost.ca/youth/articles.html (accessed 15 July 2005).

46. Pentecost International Worship Center, "Mission Statement," Church of Pentecost—Canada Web site, available online at http://www.pentecost.ca/piwc/aboutus.html (accessed 15 July 2005).

47. All Nations International Development Agency, "ANIDA: Who We Are," ANIDA Web site, available at http://www.anida.com/wwa.html (accessed 15 July 2005).

48. Samuel K. Danquah, "Ghanaian Presbyterian Church of Montreal," The Presbyterian Church in Canada Web site, available online at http://www.presbyterian.ca/wms/resourcesA/Stories%20of%20Mission/2003/canadaministries03.html#gt (accessed 15 July 2005).

49. See Leblanc, "Processes of Identification Among French-Speaking West African Migrants in Montreal," 121–141; C. A. M. Babou, "Brotherhood Solidarity, Education and Migration: The Role of the Dahira Among the Murid Community of New York," *African Affairs* 101 (2002): 151–170.

50. "Methodist Churches in Toronto Move Toward Unity," news posting on Ghanaweb, December 17, 2003, available online at http://www.ghanaweb.com/GhanaHomePage/diaspora/artikel.php?ID"48387 (accessed 15 July 2005).

51. Ikuo Kawakumi, "Resettlement and Border Crossing: A Comparative Study on the Life and Ethnicity of Vietnamese in Australia and Japan," *International Journal of Japanese Sociology* 12 (2003): 54.

52. Paul Gifford, *African Christianity: Its Public Role* (Bloomington: Indiana University Press, 1998).

53. Tettey and Puplampu, "Border Crossings and Home-Diaspora Linkages Among African-Canadians."

54. Paul C. Adams and Rina Ghose, "India.com: The Construction of a Space Between," *Progress in Human Geography* 27, no. 4 (2003): 414–437.

55. M. Pendakur and R. Subramanyam, "Indian Cinema Beyond National Borders," in J. Sinclair, E. Jacka, and S. C. Cunningham, eds., *New Patterns in Global Television: Peripheral Vision* (Oxford: Oxford University Press, 1996), 67–82.

56. Edward T. Hall, "Monochronic and Polychronic Time," in L. A. Samovar and R. E. Porter, eds., *Intercultural Communication: A Reader* (Belmont, CA: Wadsworth, 1994), 264–271.

57. Tettey, "Globalization, Diasporization and Cyber-Communities."

58. Faist, "Transnationalization in International Migration," 96.

59. "Divisions and Multiplications of Ghanaian Churches in Canada," news posting on Ghanaweb, 31 November 2003, available online at http://www.ghanaweb.com/GhanaHomePage/economy/artikel.php?ID"47078 (accessed 15 July 2005).

60. Hepner, "Religion, Nationalism, and Transnational Civil Society in the Eritrea Diaspora," 276.

61. Ghanaian News, "Divisions and Multiplications of Ghanaian Churches in Canada," news posting on Ghanaweb, available online at http://www.ghanaweb.com/GhanaHomePage/economy/artikel.php?ID"47078 (accessed 15 July 2005.

62. Keith Nurse, "Globalization and Trinidad Carnival: Diaspora, Hybridity and Identity in Global Culture," *Cultural Studies* 13, no. 4 (1999): 662.

11

"Singing the Lord's Song in a Foreign Land"

Spirituality, Communality, and Identity in a Ghanaian Immigrant Congregation

Moses Biney

Introduction

"Africans are notoriously religious," states John S. Mbiti, the renowned theologian and scholar of African religion and philosophy. He notes that Africans carry their religion with them wherever they go—to their farms, parties, examination rooms, and parliament.[1] In essence, Africans value religion and rely on it in dealing with the vagaries of life. We can say the same about many African immigrants in the United States.

In the past decade and a half, African immigrant inflows into the United States have increased exponentially. In contrast to the modest numbers that trickled in between 1960 and 1990, a large number has entered the country, mainly as a result of the diversity visas introduced by the United States Immigration and Naturalization Service in 1990. These African immigrants, many of whom are either Christian or Muslim, have carried their religions into the United States. This is evident in the growing number of African immigrant religious congregations in the United States. Thus, in cities like New York, Atlanta, Chicago, Washington, D.C., and Miami, there are numerous churches and mosques established and patronized by Ghanaian immigrants, institutions that are undoubtedly reconfiguring the religious landscape of the America. Surprisingly, literature on immigrant religious congregations hardly reflects this reality. Scholars have paid little attention to the study of these African immigrant congregations. As a result, the nature and goals of these congregations and their influences on the lives of African immigrants in the United States and the host society have not been adequately theorized.

The central question this chapter attempts to answer is: What do Ghanaian (or African) immigrants *really* seek when they form or become members of "ethnic" congregations? This question appears simple on the surface; yet, it raises a number of issues regarding the factors that shape the formation of immigrant churches, the relationship among religion, ethnicity, and identity, and the role of spirituality and communal life in immigrant adjustment. It also questions the dominant assumption that the central aim of immigrant religious expression is the preservation of the immigrants' ethnicity.

On the basis of an ethnographic study I conducted between May 2003 and December 2004 with the Presbyterian Church of Ghana in New York, a predominantly Ghanaian church in New York City, I argue that the central concern of members of this congregation is the enhancement of spirituality and communal life, rather than the maintenance of ethnic identity. The congregation helps its members and adherents to survive in the United States by (1) reinforcing and redefining their sense of who they are and the goals they seek, and (2) providing a space and community within which their spirituality is enhanced and their welfare nurtured. After a brief discussion of the position of Ghanaian immigrants in the United States and of the church's history, we will look at four main areas of the church's life—formation, spirituality, communal life, and relationship with Ghanaian ethnic associations—that provide the basis for my argument.

Ghanaian Immigrants in New York

The state of New York is home to more Ghanaian immigrants than any other locale in the United States. According to the 2000 census, Ghanaian immigrants constitute the second largest group of West African immigrants in New York State. In the year 2000, 16,813, or 25.6 percent of the documented 65,572 foreign-born immigrants from Ghana, resided in New York State. This represented 0.4 percent of New York state's total foreign-born population of 3.9 million, 0.2 percent of United States' total foreign-born population of 31.1 million, and 0.1 percent of New York state's population of 19.0 million. Numerically, the Ghanaian immigrants pale in comparison to the large numbers of immigrants from the Dominican Republic, China, and the former Soviet Union who are also in New York.

Nonetheless, one cannot miss their presence in New York City, where they are largely concentrated.

In terms of period of arrival, Ghanaians immigrants in New York, like most other African immigrants, can be classified into two groups. The first migrated between the 1950s and the early 1990s, whereas the second came here after 1990. The first group came in very few numbers, mostly to study and, in some cases, to reunite with their families. A few others were sponsored by American friends. Many Ghanaians in the second group, which comprises most of the Ghanaians in New York City, came through the Diversity Visa Program, as a recent publication of the New York City Department of City Planning points out.[2]

The main attractions of New York City, according to some Ghanaian immigrants are its cosmopolitan ethos and the numerous job opportunities it provides. Others indicate that the presence of a large Ghanaian population and a tightly knit Ghanaian community make it easier for new immigrants to quickly adjust to conditions here in the United States.

A typical feature of the Ghanaian presence is the array of small shops owned by Ghanaians, which are becoming common in many places in New York City. These shops sell a variety of food items, clothing, prerecorded audio- and videotapes of Ghanaian music and film, and other essentials imported from Ghana. The "African market" in the Bronx, for instance, sells several raw and processed items from Ghana, including yams, plantains, "*fufu* powder," *kenkey,* goat meat, *koobi* (dry and salted tilapia), *wele* (salted cattle hind), and smoked fish.

The church is the one place where one is likely to find a cross-section of Ghanaians gathered in large numbers at a given time. Since a significant number of Ghanaians in the United States are Christians, churches of various denominations have been formed by Ghanaians over the past fifteen to twenty years. So far, no authoritative data on the number of these churches have been published. On the basis of a list of Ghanaian churches published in the July 2000 issue of *Asenta,* a newspaper devoted to news about Africa and the African Diaspora in North America, and my own counting, I conservatively estimate the number of Ghanaian immigrant churches and Christian "ministries" in New York City to be between thirty-five and forty-five. One of these churches is the Presbyterian Church of Ghana in New York, whose congregation serves as the basis for the views expressed in this chapter.

The Presbyterian Church of Ghana in New York

The Presbyterian Church of Ghana in New York (hereafter PCGNY) meets for worship services in the Sanctuary of the Mount Morris Ascension Church, a predominantly African American Church, located at 2 West 122nd Street, New York City. According to church records, the church started as a prayer fellowship in 1983 but was officially inaugurated as a branch of the Presbyterian Church of Ghana on November 24, 1985.[3] Its membership is largely Ghanaian. Nearly all of its 350 members are either Ghanaian or of Ghanaian descent. There are a few members who are European Americans (mostly spouses of Ghanaians) and a Surinamese. Among the Ghanaians, about 85 percent are of the Akan linguistic group[4]; 13 percent are Ga-speaking; and 1 percent speak Ewe. This implies that though the congregation is composed largely of persons from one country of origin, it is nonetheless multiethnic. About 60 percent of the church members are women, and 40 percent are men.[5] On the basis of the church records and personal observation during members' weekly attendance, I estimate the age distribution as follows: 10 percent are seventeen years and below, 50 percent are between eighteen and forty-nine years, and 40 percent are fifty years and older.

Diverse professionals—teachers, nurses, accountants, engineers, medical doctors, lawyers—make up the church membership. There are also a number of members who work as janitors, security personnel, hotel and bar attendants, shop and parking lot attendants, baby sitters, and aides to the aged. Aside from these, there are the self-employed, such as the cab owners and others in the transportation business, travel and tour agents, and shop and salon owners. Ghanaian immigrants generally, like other immigrants, often suffer downward social mobility when they come to the United States, particularly in terms of the jobs they perform.[6] This is also the case among members of the church, many of whom have jobs that are totally unrelated to their academic and professional qualification. A teacher with a master of science degree who had taught for many years in prestigious institutions in Ghana, for instance, is now working as a companion for an aged woman. Another person with a master's degree in history earns his living as a taxi driver.

Church Formation

The impetus to form a church, according to the founding members of PCGNY, arose from an inexplicable crisis (at least from the point of view of the Ghanaian immigrants) that hit the Ghanaian community and led to a search for God's redemption. Between 1970 and 1980, a good number of Ghanaians settled in New York State and its adjoining states, Connecticut and New Jersey. They organized themselves into community groups, which often met to celebrate the naming of newborns, birthdays, and marriages and also to mourn with bereaved families during funerals. In the early 1980s, a number of these Ghanaians died from circumstances considered mysterious by the Ghanaian community.[7] E.K., one of the founders of the PCGNY, recalls:

> The numerous and sudden deaths of Ghanaian immigrants greatly alarmed us. We wondered whether as individuals or as a group we had offended God in any way. As the deaths continued, our worries were compounded with fear; fear that we may all die in this land without fulfilling our dreams and goals, and those of our families. There was nothing we could do except to seek the face of God for an explanation, and to plead for his intervention.

The fear of death and extinction prompted some members of the Ghanaian community to start monthly prayer meetings during which they sought God's intervention. These meetings attracted more Ghanaians and eventually led to the formation of the PCGNY. From the point of view of the founding members of the church, then, what was at stake was not necessarily their ethnicity but their existence, their very survival both as individuals and as a group. Their coming together to form a prayer group and later a congregation was a natural reaction to fighting common concerns together.

Motivations of Current Members

It is a fact that people often join groups for reasons other than those of the group's original founders. In fact, institutions themselves sometimes change or deviate from their original goals. Thus, in addition to understanding the founders' reason for forming the church, we also need to know some of the reasons why *current* members joined the PCGNY. In formulating their explanations for joining, some members mentioned extrinsic factors, that is, the politicosocial and religious factors outside the church community that acted as pressures (or mostly negative forces), as their reasons for joining the PCGNY. For example, Akos, a forty-year-old member of the church, complained about the lack of congeniality and inclusiveness in the mainline American churches she had attended previously. So did Akosua, forty-five years old and a member of the Singing Band, who said she felt unwelcome and sometimes slighted in some American churches, particularly those with predominantly white members. What these and others I spoke to felt was a sense of exclusion and a lack of belongingness in their former churches. This lack of acceptance was considered by some as evidence of racism in some American churches.

For others, such as Ofori, who was a trained catechist, it was the lack of the opportunity to participate in preaching and teaching in his former church as he had done back in Ghana that made him leave. At PCGNY, he is one of the lay preachers of the church and also leads Bible studies. Mercy, a thirty-five-year-old usher of the church, says that it was the lack of a vibrant worship filled with singing and dancing that caused her to leave the American Protestant congregation she used to attend.

The belief that the theology and ethical values of most mainline churches in America have been adulterated was also an important factor causing Ghanaian immigrants to avoid those churches. Asante, for instance, left a church he was attending when he saw the pastor smoking cigarettes in the open a number of times. "I did not consider a pastor with such a dangerous habit as a good role model for my children," he said. Nana Amankwaa, a sixty-year-old member, could not help taking a swipe at Western theologians and Western Christians in general, who, he believed, have lost the spiritual importance of the Bible.

> Too much wisdom cost the crab its head.[8] These people were the ones who brought the Bibles to us in Africa but now they say they know too much. . . . Some do not read the Bible at all; others read Bibles with missing pages and yet others have inserted their own written pages into the Bible.

For many other members, it was for intrinsic rather than extrinsic factors that they cherished the PCGNY. By intrinsic factors, I mean the shared cultural and religious values of the congregation and the effervescence generated in their meetings. Such intrinsic factors include common language, common denominational tradition, familiar hymns, songs, and ritual practices, welfare services aimed at helping one another, and social gatherings at which Ghanaian foods are shared and networking takes place. It is the combination of what may aptly be referred to as "push and pull" factors that led to the founding of the PCGNY and has continued to attract members ever since. A forty-year-old woman had this to say:

> I joined the church because services remind me of home [Ghana]. Every Sunday when I come to church, I feel as if I were in Ghana. This keeps me from longing too much for home. The service, particularly the singing and dancing also helps me to deal with stress and boredom.

These factors have in many ways shaped the emphasis of the church in terms of its beliefs, rituals, and community life and have given it its particular identity. They have undoubtedly led to what both the leadership and a large percentage of the church's membership agree to be the church's two most important goals—spirituality and community.

Spirituality

"Spirituality" is an ambiguous term, one that often means different things within different religious or cultural contexts. By spirituality I refer to what Peter Paris defines as "the animating and integrative power that constitutes the principal frame of meaning for individual and collective experiences."[9] The spirituality of a people, generally, derives from and is shaped by their apprehension of, and relationship with, cosmic forces they consider to be crucial to their existence.

Among Africans, generally, spirituality involves the fostering and maintenance of a harmonious relationship between humanity on one hand and natural and supernatural forces such as God, the divinities, ancestors, and the environment on the other. African spirituality, which is often expressed through such avenues as formal worship, prayer, song, myth, art, and naming practices, has proven to be one of the most enduring aspects of African identity both on the African continent and in the Diaspora.[10] Paris rightly states:

> Metaphorically, the spirituality of a people is synonymous with the soul of a people: the integrating center of their power and meaning. In contrast with that of some peoples, however, African spirituality is never disembodied but always integrally connected with the movement of life. On one hand, the goal of the movement is the struggle for survival while, on the other hand, it is the union of those forces of life that have the power either to threaten and destroy life, on one hand, or preserve and enhance it, on the other hand.[11]

The spirituality that permeates the worship and community life of PCGNY is a hybrid of the Wurttemberg variety of pietism and Ghanaian indigenous spirituality. It is characterized by religious emotion, vibrant singing and dancing, strong belief in God as creator of all and Jesus as redeemer, belief in individual and cooperate sin, deep reverence for the Bible, holistic understanding of human life, and strong emphasis on community and fellowship. We will analyze two aspects of this spirituality—the use of the Bible and "deliverance"—in order to understand the ways in which Ghanaian and, for that matter, African understandings and expressions of spirituality may differ from those of mainline American churches.

Use of the Bible

Martha, a sixty-year-old woman, summed up the importance of the Bible to her life aptly thus: "the word of God [in the Bible] is food for my soul; it is a manual of directions for my life and a catalogue of God's promises to me." Indeed, this woman's description of the Bible reflects the general attitude of the entire church toward the Bible. To many, the Bible is an important guide not only for individual but also for community life. For most of the church members (both rank and file), the Bible contains *Onyame asem*, "the word of God," and must be the main guide and standard for Christian living. Through discussions and observation, it became evident to me that three main reasons underlie the importance of the Bible to the PCGNY. First, the Bible offers motifs and themes with which members define and make sense of their lives and sojourn in the United States. For many members, the biblical world, particularly that of the Old Testament, holds images of events, practices, and beliefs that are very similar to those that pertain in the homeland and also in their own lives as immigrants. Second, the Bible provides an authoritative guide that helps members of the church sort through the many perverse sociocultural influences that confront them and their children here in the United States. Third, it provides the church the basis for maintaining and even enforcing certain cultural and moral values.

Generally, biblical interpretation in the church is a mixture of the literal, metaphorical, and symbolic hermeneutic methods. The interpretation is always done in ways that speak to the concerns of members as immigrants and sojourners in a foreign country. This is similar to what Justin Ukpong has described regarding biblical interpretation among African Christians in general. The focus of this method of interpretation, according to him, is to "create an encounter between the Biblical text and the African context."[12] The method, therefore, involves various ways of linking the biblical text to the African context. The focus of the interpretation is always the community that is receiving the text, rather than the text or those who produced it. In this sense, the average African Christian is less concerned about the historical context and literary styles of biblical passages as about how the passages speak to his or her present situation. Such a way of interpreting scripture obviously stands in contrast to western scholarly approaches, such as the historical critical method and literary approaches. Preachers at PCGNY often present biblical stories and events as metaphorical or symbolic motifs to address issues pertinent to the members. A common example of this is the comparison of church members to the Israelites during their days in captivity and exile or during their exodus from Egypt.

A Watch Night service to usher in the year 2003 illustrates the way in which biblical teachings are used to interpret and guide immigrant lives. During this service, the preacher compared members (as they entered the New Year) to the people of Israel about to enter the Promised Land. He then used the injunctions supposedly given by God to the Israelites through Moses, recorded in Deuteronomy 11:

> We are not the people of Israel, and we are not going to occupy any geographical territory. But, like the Israelites, we are being ushered into new circumstances, new challenges, and new opportunities. And, like them, we need Moses' advice recorded in Deuteronomy 11:11–17 as we prepare to enter a new year and take advantage of all the opportunities it offers. The people of ancient Israel were told that the land they were about to occupy was made up of hills and valleys. So also we need to be cautioned that next year will be a year of hills and valleys, of ups and downs, of joys and sorrows, of successes and failures for us. Again, they were told that the land "drinks rain from heaven" and the Lord cares for the land. We should understand that

> our endeavors in the coming year will only succeed with the blessing of God. Though we may work hard at two or three jobs, though we may have the best of plans for our lives and those of our families, though we may study hard . . . an important ingredient in our lives' recipe we cannot dispense with is God's blessings. The Lord cares for our survival and prosperity and is more than willing to bless us.

Deliverance Services

On occasion, the PCGNY organizes a deliverance service. This is considered a form of spiritual healing. This type of healing, which largely employs the use of "exorcism," is believed to free the individual not only from physical illness but, more important, from all oppressive and wicked spiritual forces that disrupt his or her life. Therefore, "deliverance," as used by many Ghanaians, goes beyond physical healing to include such things as protection against witches, evil spirits, and demons that impede a person's progress in life. Such hindrances to life may take the form of addictions, barrenness, repeated miscarriages, nonachievement, financial loss, terminal and chronic diseases, or untimely death.[13] These occur notwithstanding the fact that the individual is a Christian. A person may unknowingly come under the sway of one or more of the numerous demons or fallen angels who often inhabit rivers, mountains, rocks, and trees.[14] Such a person may have inadvertently "opened a door" for the demons to enter his life in any one of a number of ways, such as involvement with occultism or secret societies, eating contaminated food, or engaging in sexual relations with an agent of demons. Other possible sources of demonic attacks are said to be curses, family/personal deities, and the like.[15] The principal idea behind deliverance is that such devilish spirits are capable of thwarting a person's progress. In the case of demon possession, there is the need for "a special man of God" who can diagnose, cast out, and bind the demon and thereby set the possessed person free.[16]

Paul Gifford is right when he suggests that the worldview behind the deliverance phenomenon is the same as that which underlies indigenous African healing practices. Both deliverance and indigenous African healing operate on the premise that there are malignant spiritual forces that seek to destroy humans or impede human progress. These forces must be overcome by the power of a superior force or being. By tapping into the power of God or gods, the priest, diviner, or deliverance official, as the case may be, can reverse the actions of these forces in people's lives. The pastor or deliverance official therefore plays a role similar to that of the priest or diviner in African Indigenous Religion. What is sought in both cases is not merely the alleviation of physical pain but total redemption from all life-threatening forces.

On November 1, 2003, I arrived at the sanctuary of the Mount Morris Ascension Church at 10 A.M. to find members and nonmembers of the PCGNY already gathered, waiting for a deliverance service to begin. I was ushered into the pastor's office, where the deliverance specialist was engaged in a "counseling" session. He sat directly opposite a middle-aged man and listened to him attentively as he spoke. He rose to welcome me and asked me to join him. I drew a chair and sat beside him. The "counselee" then resumed his story. After a lengthy narration often punctuated with sighs and sobs he exclaimed, "*Papa sre awurade ma me, na mebre*" (Sir, plead to God on my behalf for I am weary). The gist of his story was that he was an accounting officer of a financial institution and, through a mistake he had committed, the institution had lost a huge sum of money, for which reason he had been fired. As he spoke, the matter was before a law court. Since he had no job, he had failed to make some of the mortgage payments due on his house and was on the verge of losing it. The deliverance specialist held his hand and prayed for him. He then assured him that he (the counselee) would be "restored" and would not lose his home.

Soon after he was asked to leave, another person was called in. This was a twenty-four-year-old woman who had been born and raised in the United States by Ghanaian parents. The deliverance specialist asked her name and what her problem was. Emily, as we shall call her, then narrated her worries:

> For the past eighteen months, I have been having nightmares in my sleep. During the daytime, I experience depressive moods—which make me hate to do anything or associate with anybody. I often consider life not worth living. During this period, I have not been able to work well and have therefore been fired from three jobs. I have been to see different doctors and have been given antidepressants, but I see no improvement.

The deliverance specialist then asked her a number of questions, particularly regarding her sexual relationships:

> DS: Are you married?
> Emily: No, but I have a boyfriend,
> DS: Do you want to get married anytime soon?

Emily: Yeah!
DS: Are you making any plans towards the marriage?
Emily: Not really, my boyfriend is not serious about it.
DS: How many boyfriends have you had prior to this one?
Emily: [hesitantly] About eight, maybe more, I can't remember.
DS: Have you been sexually molested by anybody before?
Emily: Yeah, I never knew till three days ago when my mum told me that an uncle sexually molested me when I was young. I am so mad at him and also at my mum for not telling me earlier so I could confront him.

At this revelation, the deliverance specialist, like a researcher who had suddenly found the clue to an elusive problem, exclaimed, "Yes!" He explained to Emily that her woes were related to, and in fact stemmed from, her childhood molestation. The sexual molestation, according to him, "opened doors," that is, paved the way for demons to attack her. This initial demonic attack, he said, had led to a chain of events. It had provided the demons the opportunity to control her life, particularly her sexual life. The demons were responsible for her inability to sustain any meaningful relationship that would lead to marriage. This inability to maintain a relationship was a significant contributing factor in her depression.

As a remedy, Emily needed deliverance from these oppressive demons. She needed to be first and foremost "born again," that is, she needed to repent of her sins, ask for forgiveness, and accept Jesus as a true and personal savior. The deliverance specialist led Emily to pray for forgiveness. He then asked her to hold onto his wrist while he prayed for her and asked me to stand behind her and be ready to "catch" her, since she might fall. No sooner had he begun to pray than Emily began to spin round. I grabbed her to prevent her from falling. Together with the deliverance specialist, we laid her on the floor. Members of the church's prayer group present began to sing a Twi song that is sung in many churches in Ghana:

Yetia obonsam so o! Yetia obonsam so
[We have trampled the devil, we have trampled the devil]
Yehuru ako soro yetia obosam so.
[We have jumped high and trampled the devil]
Yetia obonsam so o! Yetia obonsam so
[We have trampled the devil, we have trampled the devil]
Yehuru ako soro, osoro, osoro yetia obonsam so
[We have jumped very high up and trampled the devil]

As we all sang, prayed, and "cast out the demons," Emily rolled, kicked, and screamed intermittently as she lay on the floor. This continued for about fifteen minutes until Emily suddenly quieted and stopped moving her body. She appeared to be sleeping peacefully. Prompted by the deliverance specialist, we said a prayer of thanksgiving that concluded the "ministration." After about five minutes, Emily woke and got up from the floor. She appeared confused for a short time and then began smiling. The deliverance specialist scheduled another appointment with her and her mother for the following day and asked her to join the main service in the sanctuary.

Communality

One important, if not the most important, concern for many Ghanaian churches at home and abroad is the promotion of a harmonious community life. The significance of communal life among Ghanaians and Africans in general is not a new subject. From the perspective of African theology, the prominent African scholar John Mbiti argues that within African belief systems there is a tendency for the concept of community to have ontological priority over that of the individual. The community largely (but not entirely) determines an individual's personhood. This happens because the community is not merely an association of individuals but rather an organic whole of which the individual is a part. This organic whole, preexisting before the individual, comprises not only living human beings but also the living dead and the unborn. Like a parent, the community provides sustenance, guidance, and protection for each of its members. Through its norms, values, and traditions, it defines the status and role of individuals and provides the context within which they are habituated or socialized. According to this perspective, human beings are viewed as intrinsically relational beings who must live cooperatively. The community therefore offers them a place wherein they can attain the fullness of their being. Mbiti's much quoted statement "I am because we are, and since we are therefore I am" describes this interrelatedness.

Identity, particularly group identity, is both an ingredient and a product of community life. A people's community life often depends largely on their identification with certain cultural symbols, beliefs and ideas, language, and practices that they consider to be historically or mythically linked to their existence and prosperity. Most of these constitute a basis for, and a vehicle for communicating, their spirituality.

This understanding of the relationship between the community and the individual is prominent among many Ghanaian immigrants and stands in opposition to the general individualistic ethos of American culture. Ghanaians who come to the United States, particularly those who have never lived in a Western country, are often rudely shocked by this individualism, which they often interpret as selfishness and lack of concern for others. Like many other immigrants, they often find that the biggest challenge they face when they first arrive is a sense of displacement, which is often coupled with alienation. Kwasi, a thirty-year-old man who had arrived in the United States about three months earlier, narrated his experience during his first few weeks in this country:

> I felt like a fish tossed out of the water unto a sandy shore. Just as the fish finds no comfort from the vast stretch of sand surrounding it, so did I find no comfort in this big country with all its big buildings and numerous people. Nothing in my past experience had prepared me for such loneliness. . . . My cousin with whom I stayed worked two jobs and was gone several hours a day. I would get out and walk round our apartment hoping to find somebody to talk to. Of course, I got nothing more than a "hi," often muttered grudgingly. All I could see were people rushing from one place to another, each minding his or her own business. I am glad I got to know this church. At least once every week I can talk with people with whom I share similar concerns.

Accounts of loneliness, boredom, sociocultural isolation, and alienation during the early part of their sojourn in the United States abound among members of the church. Narrators of these accounts often point out the help the church has provided to ease their loneliness and isolation. One person told me that she lived in a neighborhood in New Jersey that was entirely made up of European Americans and that prior to attending the church she did not know how to get in touch with any Ghanaians. Through the church she got linked up with other Ghanaians and Ghanaian associations. Now she comes to New York every weekend to attend church services and meetings of other Ghanaian associations. Another person was fortunate to find his cousins and aunt in the church. He had lost contact with them for a long time. A twenty-eight-year-old man who was desperately in need of accommodation met someone in the church who was looking for a roommate.

Aside from providing the space and the opportunity for persons to interact and link up with others, PCGNY assists members in numerous other ways, particularly in times of birth, marriage, birthday celebrations, bereavement, and other significant life events. The church has a Welfare Committee set up to cater to the social needs of members of the congregation. The pastor of the church compares this group to the seven-member committee appointed by the early disciples to "serve tables," that is, to take care of the sharing of food among the widows.[17] The job schedule of the Welfare Committee includes planning visits to the sick, collecting and collating information regarding scheduled dates for impending celebrations by members (e.g., birthdays, naming ceremonies), reviewing benefits or donations to be paid out to members, and receiving donations from members and presenting them to the appropriate persons. Members of this committee are selected from all the church groups, and they meet at least once a month. Celebrations or ceremonies planned by members each month are printed in the "events" column of the church bulletins and also are announced to the congregation on several Sundays preceding the events. The most frequent of these events are "outdoorings," or naming ceremonies, birthday parties, and funerals.

On February 21, 2003, for instance, the pastor and some of the church elders traveled to Princeton, New Jersey, a distance of about sixty-eight miles, to perform the naming ceremony for this author's child. About twenty other members of the church, in spite of the heavy rain that morning, joined the pastor and elders for the ceremony. Many of these, as well as the family of the child, were dressed in Ghanaian attire. Other persons present were friends and family of the child's parents, some coming from as far as Boston, Massachusetts.

The ceremony began with prayers, followed by the *amaneebo*, that is, an explanation of the purpose of the whole ceremony. The baby was then handed over to the pastor, who in turn asked the parents and the godparents of the child, as well as elders of the church, to join him as he performed the ritual. Holding the baby on his left arm, the pastor said a few words of welcome to the baby and then announced the name that was being conferred on him. He then addressed the baby thus:

> You came into this world on Tuesday, so we call you Kwabena.[18] Also, your parents are naming you after your grandfather, that is, your father's father, and so we call you Ohene. Your full name is Kwabena Ohene [surname].

With a spoon, the pastor then fetched a drop of plain water from a glass, put it on the baby's tongue, and said:

> Kwabena, this is water. If you [taste] water, say it is water.

Following the same procedure, the pastor put a drop of salt water on the baby's tongue and said:

> Kwabena, it is salt that you taste in this water. If you see [taste] salt, say it is salt and nothing else.

This part of the ritual, as the pastor explained during ceremony, symbolized the need for truthfulness and was aimed at instilling in the child from the very beginning the virtue of truth telling. After this, the pastor lowered the baby and gently touched the floor with him three times, saying:

> Kwabena we welcome you!
> This is the earth on which we live,
> We welcome you!
> This is the earth on which we depend,
> We welcome you!
> Live with us on this earth.

The naming ritual, which lasted about ten minutes, concluded with a prayer for the child and his family. The next session of the ceremony was for, as the pastor put it, "merry making." Before the ceremony began, assortments of prepared Ghanaian food and drinks had been brought by the family of the child and also by friends and members of the church. These were served out to all of us gathered. The rest of the ceremony was devoted to eating, drinking, and chatting. During this period, individuals and the church made donations to the child's family.

Relationship with Ghanaian Ethnic Associations

There are about eleven major Ghanaian ethnic associations in New York City, such as the Akyem, Asanteman, Brong-Ahafo, Ga-Adamgme, Okuapemman, Okwahu, United Volta, and Yankasa Associations,[19] and the PCGNY maintains close working relationships with many of these groups.

The New York associations mirror those found in Ghanaian cities, and they function as both cultural and charity groups. Many of these groups meet on the first Sunday of each month in a city building located at 127 West 127th Street, New York City. In addition to holding monthly meetings, the activities of these associations generally include organizing social and cultural programs such as dances, picnics, lectures, and health fairs, and they also raise money to support projects in Ghana. These associations operate under the larger umbrella of the National Council of Ghanaian Associations. A majority of the members of PCGNY belong to these associations. In fact, both the current and past pastors of the church are chaplains for the Okuapemman Association, which was founded two years before the PCGNY began. Each first Sunday of the month, most members leave immediately after church service to attend their ethnic association meetings.

Conclusion

I have attempted to show in this chapter that, for the PCGNY and its members, the desire for spirituality and communality takes precedence over preservation of ethnicity. Both the immediate and remote reasons for the formation of the church, as well as members' reasons for joining it, point to this fact. The need for God's redemption from death and extinction, the need for a community of faith where members respect and treat one another as equal and where members concern themselves with one another's problems, the need for vibrant worship services filled with joyful singing and dancing, and the need for good moral exemplars were given as reasons for joining the church. For most of the church members, the church offers space where they gain acceptance through worship and active participation in the church community, where their material concerns are heard and attended to, where their spiritual needs are culturally packaged and made meaningful to them, and where their cultural needs are in turn given a Christian flavor. It is a "sanctuary" where at least once a week they have their individual identities affirmed, where fellow members call them by their real names, where they can speak without being constantly reminded of their "accent," and where they can engage in their own palaver without having to look over their shoulders to see who is watching them.

Members' involvement in Ghanaian ethnic associations and the fact that the PCGNY itself emerged from an existing "ethnic" association of

Ghanaians challenge any notion that the church's chief motive is to preserve ethnic identity. Many publications on both "old" and "new" immigrants theorize that the primary sociological function of immigrant religious congregations is the preservation of ethnic or cultural identity. The central theme of Helen Ebaugh and Janet Chafetz's *Religion and the New Immigrants,* for example, is that religion maintains and reproduces ethnic identity. Immigrant religious institutions, then, "provide the physical and social spaces in which those who share the same traditions, customs and languages can reproduce many aspects of their native cultures for themselves and attempt to pass them on to their children."[20]

There is no gainsaying the fact that immigrant religious congregations play an important role in the maintenance and reshaping of ethnic identity. Indeed, religious truths are communicated through the use of ethnic languages. However, placing too much premium on this role and making it the central paradigm that guides much of the discussion on immigrant religion raises a number of problems. First, it renders immigrants' religion merely incidental to their ethnicity. Immigrant religious expression therefore becomes either a vehicle for championing ethnic interests or that which gives ethnicity its particular identity. Second, it fails to acknowledge the important theological, ethical, and psychological resources that immigrant congregations provide their members and adherents in order to address social-political and religious pressures such as racial discrimination and alienation. Third, it leaves unexplained the reasons that some immigrant religious congregations begin as ethnic "social" groups and also fails to elucidate why persons from the same ethnic group form or join different religious congregations. It is hoped that insights from this chapter, particularly its focus on spirituality and communality, will provide other ways of studying immigrant religious congregations.

Notes

1. John S. Mbiti, *African Religions and Philosophy* (New York: Praeger, 1969).

2. Department of City Planning, *The Newest New Yorkers 2000: Immigrant New York in the Millennium* (New York: Department of City Planning, 2004).

3. Presbyterian Church of Ghana in New York, *Okristoni (The Christian): A Pictorial Journal of Ghana Presbyterian Church* (New York: Presbyterian Church of Ghana in New York, 1995), 8.

4. The Akans constitute about half of the Ghanaian population. They are made up of the following peoples: Asante, Akuapem Akyem, Akwamu, Fante, Bono,

Kwahu, Sehwi, Awowin, Nzima, and Ahanta. Those represented in this church are the Akuapems, Akyems, Asantes, Kwawus, Akwamus, and Fantes.

5. Interestingly, this gender ratio is very similar to what pertains in the home church. The Clerk of General Assembly's report to the 3rd General Assembly of the Presbyterian Church of Ghana indicates that 63 percent of the church membership is made up of women, while 37 percent are men.

6. Victoria Hyonku Kwon, for instance, makes the same observation in her study of the Korean Ethnic Church in Houston. See her "Houston Korean Ethnic Church: An Ethnic Enclave," in Helen Ebaugh and Janet Chafetz, eds., *Religion and the New Immigrants: Continuities and Adaptations in Immigrant Congregations* (Walnut Creek, Calif.: Alta Mira Press, 2000), 113.

7. From all indications, this was a very troubling time in the life of the Ghanaian community. In my conversations with a number of the founding members of the Presbyterian Church of Ghana, as well as members of other Ghanaian religious and social groups, they constantly referred to these deaths. Reverend Yaw, the current pastor of the church, estimates that in one year alone about twenty-five Ghanaian immigrants died in New York City.

8. This is a translation of the Akan proverb "*Nyansa dodow nti na okoto anya ti.*" This proverb warns people who claim to know so much and often forget the very foundation of their supposed knowledge that they will end up losing their sense of what is real. I have borrowed the current translation and explanation from Kofi Asare Opoku, *Hearing and Keeping: Akan Proverbs*, African Proverbs Series (Accra, Ghana: Asempa Publishers, 1997), 342.

9. Peter J. Paris, *The Spirituality of African Peoples: The Search of a Common Moral Discourse* (Minneapolis: Fortress Press, 1995), 22.

10. Numerous scholars have pointed out the persistence, in various degrees, of African indigenous spirituality. Despite the fact that aspects of this spirituality have undergone changes as result of the influence of Christianity, Islam, and so-called Western civilization, it continues to be present in various forms among Africans and peoples of African descent. In fact, it is seen to have permeated Christianity and Islam in Africa and the Diaspora and has influenced other forms of worship, such as Voodoo, considerably. For a number of current articles on this subject, see Jacob K. Olupona, ed., *African Spirituality: Forms, Meanings and Expressions* (New York: Crossroad Publishing Company, 2000).

11. Paris, *The Spirituality of African Peoples*, 22.

12. See Justin Ukpong, "Developments in Biblical Interpretation in Africa: Historical and Hermeneutical Directions," in G. West and M. Dube. eds., *The Bible in Africa: Transactions, Trajectories and Trends* (Leiden: Brill, 2000), 11.

13. See Aaron K. Vuha, *The Package: Salvation, Healing and Deliverance* (Accra: EP Church of Ghana, 1993), 36.

14. Ibid.

15. Paul Gifford, *African Christianity: Its Public Role* (London: Hurst, 1998), 98–99.

16. Ibid.

17. Acts 6:1–6.

18. *Kwabena* is the Akan name for a male born on Tuesday.

19. Agyemang Attah-Opoku, *The Socio-Cultural Question: The Role of Ghanaian Ethnic Associations in America* (Aldershot: Ashgate Publishing, Ltd., 1996), 61.

20. Helen Ebaugh and Janet Chafetz, *Religion and the New Immigrants: Continuities and Adaptations in Immigrant Congregations* (Walnut Creek, Calif.: Alta Mira Press, 2000), 385.

12

African Immigrant Churches and the New Christian Right

Mojubaolu Olufunke Okome

Introduction

The impact of contemporary African Christian immigrants on American social and political life is not a much-studied subject. Few scholars and analysts have addressed the increasing tide of religious immigration, involving the migration of ministers, religious workers, and pastors of African churches to the United States as missionaries. This chapter addresses questions concerning the nature of contemporary African immigrant Christianity in the United States. In particular, it focuses on the issue of the political incorporation of African immigrants, and in so doing it explores the relationship between African immigrant churches and the Christian Right. Some of these connections spur the development of homogenous liturgies, doctrine, and conservative political responses to contemporary social issues and challenges, including the acceptance and normalization of conservative values. In policy terms, this devolves in the United States into support for the prolife agenda, an antigay stance, opposition to stem cell research, support for a ban on gay and lesbian marriage, advocacy of male-headed households, and support for the notion of spiritual warfare against "ancestral spirits," often interpreted simplistically as located in African indigenous religious beliefs and practices.

Given the fact that African immigrants are part of an ethnic and racial minority in most of the Western countries to which they migrate in large numbers, the history of racial exclusion and support for segregation and blatant racism within the Christian Right, and the very recent move toward racial inclusiveness, what does affinity in value systems mean for both the new African immigrant churches and the Christian Right? This is an important question because the Christian Right also advocates an end to affirmative action and multicultural curricula, as well as more restrictive immigration laws. These are measures that should benefit African immigrants, because, as blacks, they are more likely to face discrimination in employment and education and in the administration of immigration laws. Also, while the Christian Right engages in political activism and advocacy, African immigrant churches mostly claim to be apolitical and encourage their congregations to avoid overt political participation. Clear disparities in power, measured in terms of access to resources and political voice, are obvious when one compares African immigrant churches to the Christian Right. Are there any efforts to address these disparities? Politically, where do the interests of African immigrant churches lie? Which alliances are more favorable in terms of the realization of their objectives? The chapter engages in a preliminary examination, analysis, and explication of the connections between African immigrant churches and the Christian Right and their significance within the U.S. political economy.

The Christian Right: Beyond Evangelicals

Most people use the term "Christian Right" conterminously with evangelical Protestants, but, according to Grant Wacker, professor of the history of religion in America at the Duke University Divinity School, by the late 1980s, the former group could include nonevangelical Protestants from mainline denominations, secularists, Jews, and Mormons. In could also exclude some evangelical Protestants. Thus, in practical terms, the Christian Right includes "(1) evangelicals who cared enough about the political goals of the Christian Right to leave their pews and get out the vote and (2) non-evangelicals who cared enough about the political goals of the Christian Right to work with evangelicals."[1]

Historically, the origin of the Christian Right as a force to be reckoned with in American social, political, and economic life can be traced to Christian seminaries that fostered the development of biblical exegesis and hermeneutics. Movements to push the teaching of human evolution in public schools, and, after World War II, the real or perceived threat of communism, contributed to the philosophical foundations of the Christian Right. More contemporarily, the Christian Right was profoundly affected by the political and social upheavals of the 1960s. Many in the

Christian Right are also opposed to a host of Supreme Court decisions, including those banning official prayer in schools, legalizing abortion, and restricting the extent to which private Christian schools can benefit from public funding.[2]

As described by Wacker, the worldview of the Christian Right rests upon four cornerstones, including (1) the belief in moral absolutes, (2) a view of the world as a continuum from metaphysics to ethics to political affairs and everyday customs, (3) a central role for the government in providing moral guidance, especially to the youth, and (4) the need for society to commit to a set of common values, preferably the Judeo-Christian values that have guided the United States for approximately four centuries. The Christian Right objects to what it describes as the manipulative manner in which public schools treat their children, to the decline in academic standards, and especially to the manner in which liberals challenge "family values." To the Christian Right, the traditional family is besieged by the media, the schools, and government policies that encourage abortion, divorce, and fatherless families. Measures like the Equal Rights Amendment, for example, will not foster the security of ordinary women but will corrode the only tethers that keep men firmly bound to the responsibilities of home and hearth.[3] These are constructions that may very well sit well with many African immigrants who shudder at the lack of respect for authority and encouragement of children to challenge parental control in American society, favor the imposition of high standards in the educational system, support strong moral values, and look balefully upon the corruption that is purveyed in the media and its deleterious influences on their children.

In order to understand the Christian Right, one must also consider the movement's historical antecedents. If we begin from the period in the late nineteenth century that is considered the Gilded Age, we can consider the political arrangements that were salient at that time, when for ease of analysis we can categorize the Republican Party as an agent of morality and the Democratic Party as an agent of justice. As Wacker explains,

> The Republican Party perennially sought to implement in the legal and cultural institutions of the age a vision of a hardworking, churchgoing citizenry—men and women who lived by universal standards of personal uprightness. The Democratic Party, on the other hand, sought to implement a vision of equitable sharing of the nation's resources and an acceptance of social and cultural diversity as a positive good.

Of course, transformations in contemporary times have affected the Gilded Age philosophies of America's two major political parties, but thinking about that era forces us "to see the Christian Right not as an aberration but as a vigorous (or virulent, depending on one's point of view) reaffirmation of a strongly normative vision of America that has been vocalized at all levels of the culture for at least a century." It would also be unfair not to add "that the broader evangelical tradition, from which the Christian Right emerged, proved politically self-conscious and socially reformist from its beginnings in the early nineteenth century."[4] Among the positive socially conscious projects of some evangelicals in America's past are the abolitionist and the temperance movements, although other evangelicals vehemently opposed the abolition of slavery and contributed tremendously to ensuring the depth of its institutionalization and the extremes of harshness with which it was administered, and temperance was a movement that took on the nature of a top-down program of social renewal. Even if we disagree with its articulation of the issues and methods, we must not lose sight of the Christian Right's missionary zeal and its constant determination "to reach out and construct or reconstruct society in terms of a larger image of human good."[5]

African immigrant Christians consider themselves as answering the call to mission by bringing the gospel to the western hemisphere. The call to mission is taken seriously by African Initiated Churches, which have proliferated massively in the recent past.[6] Thus, the connection between African immigrant churches and the Christian Right is between two missionary efforts, one by native-born Americans and the other by new immigrants, both engaged in social construction and reconstruction for the betterment of humanity. However, this is a connection between consummate and politically savvy insiders and hopeful and sometimes politically naïve outsiders, a relationship between a sometimes xenophobic and vocally anti-immigrant movement and new immigrants who volubly express their embrace of "the American dream." This is also a connection that creates transnational linkages and communities that will profoundly affect the composition of the Christian Right in the future.

As discussed by Wacker,[7] the social science literature puts forth three main views of the new Christian Right: (1) as a right-wing radical movement, (2) as a compassionate movement engaged in the effort to preserve traditional values, and (3) as a movement engaged in working for "global economic and cultural changes, focusing especially upon the secular state as the nemesis of God-fearing people everywhere."[8] It is in this final definition that one finds a useful germ for conceptualizing the actions of African immigrant churches and the deepest connections between them and America's new Christian Right.

African Pentecostals and Social Engagement

The overwhelming majority of African pentecostal churches have their roots in African Initiated Churches. Spurred by the gaping chasm left by the lack of state responsiveness to the developmental needs of African nations that is driven by the transnationalization of the neoliberal agenda coming from the Washington consensus and purveyed with missionary zeal by the International Monetary Fund (IMF) and the World Bank throughout the developing world, the churches step in to provide comfort and, more important, to provide a roadmap to the abundant life for their members.

Some analyses view African pentecostal churches as apolitical. For example, Tim Sullivan claims that:

> few of these churches get involved in politics. While many of the more established Christian churches in Africa have taken strong political stances in support of human rights and against oppressive regimes, most of the independent churches have remained silent. Their concerns are often more basic, offering their followers a way to cope with daily issues: Will I get a job? How can I feed my family? How can I be cured of my pains?[9]

Others, however, agree with Professor Ogbu Kalu, who considers the African pentecostalist church distinctively political. In his review of Paul Gifford's book on African pentecostalism, Kalu characterizes the charismatic pentecostal movement in Ghana as political and Gifford as waffling on the issue. Gifford both subscribes to the view that this is an apolitical movement that is motivated mostly by economic forces and claims that there are some within the movement with political goals. He shows that Ghana was pervaded by political bankruptcy, economic crises, and social malaise, all of which sprang from the decay of the body politic and not from external forces. Thus, the pentecostal movement stepped in with lively music, an appeal to the youth, progressive gender ideology, and a very dynamic liturgy to build fellowship, as well as to engage successfully in primitive accumulation of capital through constantly dipping into the pockets of their parishioners in cynical manipulation of their hunger for solutions to the intractable problems that beset them.[10] In these churches, he argues, unquestioning belief, philanthropy, release from evil spirits, curses and demonic possession, and generous contributions to "the man of God" take precedence over exhortation to forsake sin and embrace hard work. These are not strategies that ensure modernization and economic development and provide valuable opportunities for mobilizing people to develop and unleash the power of their collective social capital.

While Gifford contends that the focus among pentecostals on personal achievement, materialistic accumulation and acquisition, and status prevents them from working to engender Ghana's economic development, Kalu argues that the Church must be considered in its totality, as a spiritual institution engaged in the work of God, as "a sign and witness of the reign of God in its being, saying and doing." He criticizes Gifford for unduly fixating on rhetorical pronouncements and failing to note the Ghanaian pentecostals' devotion to what he describes as the biblical "word of knowledge" and the visionary ministry as derived from the Old Testament. As an alternative, Kalu highlights the analyses provided by Birgit Meyer, Gerrie ter Haar, Stephen Ellis, David Martin, and Ruth Marshall, who find value in pentecostals' hermeneutics, doctrine, and liturgy.[11] Kalu points out that, although Gifford suggests that the pentecostals fail to see the role of human agency in fostering change, later in his book Gifford gives instances of the "spiritualization of politics" and some aspects of development. He suggests that Gifford devalues the role of spiritualism as a mode of struggle and looks askance on African cultural expressions as a wellspring from which alternative methods can be drawn by churches in their engagement with oppressive governments. Kalu suggests that the selective endorsement of a few pastors as virtuous and the rejection of the overwhelming majority as scurrilous blinds Gifford to the validity and spiritual power of the new pentecostalist churches as they "struggle to proclaim the gospel and serve society."

A close reading of Kalu's critique of Gifford provides some guidance in analyzing and evaluating the extent to which there is a relationship between African immigrant churches and the new Christian Right. Kalu cautions against critiques that are not conversant with the spiritual as well as the material basis of pentecostalist culture. Kalu's admonition generates an interest in exploring the sources of some of the fundamental principles that have become central to the doctrine of the African pentecostalist movement. Strategic-Level Spiritual Warfare (SLSW) is one such principle.

The foremost proponents of SLSW include C. Peter Wagner, retired professor at Fuller Seminary; Morris Cerrullo, an evangelist who describes himself as "a prophet to the nations"; and Frank Peretti, a prolific Christian novelist. There are raging debates among Christians on whether this is a new doctrine or whether it's biblical, and some even consider it to be a form of apostasy. [12] However, according to Gerald Ediger, SLSW has deep historical roots within the Christian practice of spiritual warfare, although it has taken new forms and is being articulated in novel ways.[13] *Engaging the Enemy,* the book edited by C. Peter Wagner, presents SLSW as a battle against territorial spirits or powerful, unseen principalities and powers that control given geographical locations. For Christianity to flourish, these powers and principalities must be identified, challenged, and conquered through prayer, with Christians waging war against them in overt demonstrations of the power of God over the realm of darkness. Thus, Christians take back these realms from evil powers and return them to God by learning and executing the methods "strategic-level spiritual intercession" and "power evangelism."[14]

There are ideological connections between the proponents of SLSW, African Instituted Churches, and African immigrant Christians, since African Instituted Churches and African immigrant churches often subscribe to what Ernest Munachi Ezeogu describes as the dialectic model, which presents gospel and culture as perpetually opposed in an irreconcilable conflict. Ezeogu points to the dichotomous "language of contrasting spatial, temporal, and circumstantial metaphors, such as these: the gospel is from 'above,' culture from 'below'; the gospel is 'divine,' culture 'human'; the gospel is 'light,' culture 'darkness'; the gospel is 'eternal,' culture 'timebound'; and so on."[15] According to the advocates of this view, the dichotomy between the gospel and culture is so absolute, and culture is so flawed, that it must defer to the gospel, which is pure and celestial. On the other hand, the dialogic model sees the possibility for culture and the gospel to be attuned and recommends their synchronization, the exchange of ideas between the two areas, for betterment.[16] Ezeogu provides ample evidence to support his claim that African Christians see perpetual conflict between the Bible and culture, causing "the popularity of a fundamentalistic viewpoint among African Christians according to which every statement in the Bible is held to be backed up by God's own authority and, therefore, not subject to re-examination on the grounds of scholarship, common sense, or experience."[17]

Ezoegu points out that a historical perspective is important in understanding the gospel/culture opposition. He argues that a great deal of residue from past missionary biases and racist ideologies persists, demonizing all things African. Talk of ancestral and territorial spirits from whom control must be wrested, the enthusiastic pursuit of demonic forces to be defeated in furtherance of the gospel, and wanton condemnation of cultural norms and practices prevail. Ezeogu argues that the African approach results in a unidimensional perspective on life in which God and what is perceived as his one true word are rigidly embraced and anything that deflects attention from them is eschewed. For Ezeogu, when unidimensionality becomes the order of the day, Christians in the embattled terrain that many African countries have become (due to deep and unrelenting economic and political crises) are encouraged to withdraw from a corrupt world, shrink from the possibility of being tainted by the unholy communities in which they dwell, and pray fervently for their own material wellbeing in a singleminded focus on survival. For Ezeogu, "The Bible has become an opiate, a tranquilizer to dull the sensitivity of African Christians to the many social, economic and political injustices that they experience on a daily basis."[18] In this sense, he is closer to Gifford than to Kalu.

Olupona's study of new religious movements in contemporary Nigeria helps to contextualize this terrain. He argues that there is a need to constantly reexamine the typologies and categories used in these studies, and he discusses the relevance of the spiritual realm to health, wholeness, and the ability to address life's challenges.[19] The African immigrant churches in the United States are the Christian part of the new religious movements in Olupona's study that

> profess a this-worldly immediate salvation and are preoccupied largely with issues germane to the existence of the human person in the daily rhythm of life . . . emphasis is laid on healing and the state of wholeness in man. Disease and illness are not necessarily seen as the result of a physical nature or cause, but of a deep spiritual and metaphysical nature. . . . A substantial part of the ritual . . . is devoted to the attainment of wholeness, good health, and to warding off misfortune and suffering. Divine healing, dreams, and visionary experiences are daily and regular occurrences in their religious life.[20]

In the following sections, we explore some of the ways in which African pentecostals in the United States are individually and collectively engaged in a creative interpretation of, and engagement with, social, political, and economic realities.

Three African Immigrant Pentecostal Churches: A Background

To further consider the questions and issues raised in the preceding section, I interviewed two pastors and one deacon who are prominent leaders of African immigrant pentecostal communities. Two belong to the Christ Apostolic Church, which is an Aladura church, and one to an evangelical church. All three interviewees are Yoruba from southwestern Nigeria. The identity of the smaller evangelical church, as well as the names of the three leaders, are concealed in this chapter for the purpose of anonymity. These interviews are a starting point in an ongoing effort to explicate the nature of political participation by African immigrant Christians in the United States. In each case, I wanted to know why and how the church came to be established in the United States. I also wanted an articulation of the church's sense of its mission, its doctrine, and its political stance.

The first interview is with Pastor Benjamin, pastor at a branch of the Christ Apostolic Church, World Soul Winning Evangelistic Ministries (CAC WOSEM). According to Pastor Benjamin, the Christ Apostolic Church was established around 1930 by the late Apostle Ayo Babalola. The CAC has its roots in Nigeria in a ministry established by an Anglican Bible study group from the 1920s. Initially, the group joined the Faith Tabernacle, an American church, and later, from 1931 to 1941, it joined the British Apostolic Church. The name Christ Apostolic Church came from the Apostolic Church controversy about whether or not medicines should be used in curing ailments and diseases. During a powerful revival led by Apostle Babalola in Ilesha, there were many miracles and healings. This strengthened the conviction that medicines were not necessary for healing to occur. Those holding these beliefs were founders of today's CAC.[21]

In this church, there is a prevalent belief in the notion that Africans have brought the gospel back to the West, thus completing a circle. CAC WOSEM, headquartered in Ilesha, is the evangelical arm of the Christ Apostolic Church. Both Pastor Benjamin and Deacon Aaron, who was also interviewed for this chapter, stated that CAC WOSEM was one of the first ministries to bring an African church to the United States.[22] The president and founder of CAC WOSEM, Apostle T. O. Obadare, established a World Soul Winning Evangelistic Ministry, which was conceived as an engine and as the preaching force that would propel the wheel of the gospel, spreading it all over the world. At a 1979 crusade in Ibadan, a prophecy was revealed to Apostle Obadare, who, having confirmed it as being from God, began his ministry in earnest.[23] The revelation was that "some of our people were going abroad and their souls needed to be saved." In response, foreign missions became a priority, and the U.S. churches were founded. Many Nigerian ministers have followed this example.[24] According to Pastor Benjamin, God saw and revealed the future trends of increased African influx to the West to his people. As a result, following the lead of Apostle Obadare, most Nigerian churches established U.S. branches led by their own people because the churches realized that their members were moving to the United States and wanted to keep them in the fold. At this particular location, the CAC WOSEM congregation is about 225 to 250 strong. The majority of the members are Nigerian. Pastor Benjamin estimates that 80 percent of the members are Yoruba, and there is a very, very small percentage of Liberians and Togolese and one Ghanaian. The church has no African American members.[25]

Pastor Isaac, senior pastor of International Ministries (a pseudonym), was my second interviewee. Pastor Isaac was trained as an electrical engineer. He became born again in 1982. In 1986, Pastor Isaac connected with the founder of International Ministries, who is his spiritual father, and until 1993 served in his ministry. He believes that God led him to become a minister while in college. He graduated from the Bible College of Ministry in 1990 and was ordained as a pastor in 1991. In 1993, he came to the United States and the next year started his ministry from "ground zero." Since he had no time for formal schooling, he registered at a Bible college for distance education that was headquartered in Indiana and earned a master's degree in theology in 2001. Pastor Isaac completed his studies for a doctoral degree in theology in 2004. When his ministry began, in 1994, there were only seven adults and two children as members. Today, he has established five churches in the United States and Trinidad and Tobago, and two are in the pipeline. The church also gives apostolic covering to about a dozen other churches in the United States.

According to Pastor Isaac, International Ministries began at the University of Ibadan in the 1970s as a nondenominational ministry for all Christian students on all campuses. It began as a literature ministry and groups of believers circulated printed materials. In 1989, the church arm of the movement was instituted to complement the ministry. Today, there are more than 100 affiliated churches worldwide. Each of these churches operates independently but is still part of a larger network. International Ministries is incorporated as a ministerial association under the Nigerian-based headquarters, but the headquarters office does not govern Pastor Isaac or his work. The relationship is believed to be necessary for mutual responsibility through institutionalized oversight to prevent egregious mistakes. Pastor Isaac is president of the church and the ministry and is responsible for overseeing the teams of ministers at the five churches that he founded. Altogether, the congregations are about 60 percent Nigerian, 38 percent Caribbean and South American (Guyanese); and 2 percent African American. According to Isaac, this is a "family church," where men lead their families to church. Approximately 60 percent of the members are men, and 40 percent women. Besides having a successful career, Pastor Isaac's wife is an ordained minister and theologian, and she contributes as an important part of the ministry team.[26]

Pastor Isaac considers himself a pioneer in founding African immigrant Christian churches in the United States. He sees the 1990s as a significant period of growth. According to him, most churches led by Africans are pentecostal, and most of them were established after his mission was already in place. The only exceptions are the Christ Apostolic Churches and the Deeper Christian Life Ministries. Pastor Isaac suggests that Africa, particularly Nigeria and Kenya, has become the international center of Christianity. African Christians are making a significant impact in the United States and throughout the world. He states that Matthew Ashimolowo, a Nigerian, leads Kingsway International Christian Center in the United Kingdom—the fastest-growing pentecostal church in Europe, with more than 8,000 current members. In Eastern Europe, Sunday Adelaja, who is also from southwestern Nigeria, is making serious strides. Isaac suggests that the same is happening in the United States, where there is much evangelizing by leaders such as the Reverend Enoch Adeboye, General Overseer of the Redeemed Christian Church of God, a church that has bought more than 250 hectares of land near Dallas, Texas, to construct a 5,000-seat auditorium and an office complex to house its North American headquarters.[27]

My third interviewee is Deacon Aaron, who is an attorney as well as a deacon and evangelist in the CAC WOSEM Church. He became an attorney in 1989 and was born into a Christian family. He has been an active Christian since his youth, and he grew up in the church, accepting Christ as his Lord and Savior when he was quite young. He has subsequently served in the vineyard of the Lord. Deacon Aaron came to the United States in the mid-1990s. He sees his ministry as one of help and encouragement. Being a lawyer gives him a beautiful opportunity to do the Lord's work both for the church and for the African immigrant community. The main goal of his ministry is to use his profession to win souls for Christ and to help Africans to adjust to their new environment. Deacon Aaron became a deacon after seven years of service in CAC WOSEM. In July 2004, he was elevated to evangelist. His branch of CAC WOSEM started in the conference room at his office and grew from five members to approximately 200 members by December 2004. The group has since moved from the office, purchasing its own building on October 28, 2004.[28]

Christianity, Culture, and Social Engagement

According to Pastor Benjamin, the CAC WOSEM mission was introduced into the United States in 1981 in response to God's call to Apostle Obadare, who was told that God's people were languishing in sin and must be rescued. Many who were Christians in Africa shed their Christianity immediately when they land at the airport. They become consumed with the struggle to survive in the erroneous belief that this will make it possible for them to advance more rapidly. The rationale for the mission to the African immigrants is that there can be no survival without commitment to Christianity.

For Pastor Benjamin, the plan to bring the gospel westward is a deliberate effort from God, based on the biblical injunction to "cast bread upon the waters and then in a few days, in due season, in time it will come back to you." Thus, Europeans planted the seed of gospel all over the world and are now in the season of harvesting. Their own culture is dying and being lost, but, because they planted the gospel, it is coming back to them. The African missionary effort, then, "is a program that will not allow any culture to die." The presumed death of European culture, which, for Pastor Benjamin, encompasses both Europe and the United States, is a spiritual death because these societies are absolutely losing all the fibers that hold Christianity together, everything that Christianity means. This is due to moral laxity and the tendency within the church to accept everything and anything. In consequence, many church buildings have become empty and are being sold, and there is a rampant proliferation of sin in the church. Because of the effort of the African missionaries, Pastor Benjamin said, "God is bringing back some sanity."[29]

Pastor Benjamin considers the United States Africans' "new land," to which they have brought Christianity. For him, from a Christian perspective, everywhere is God's land, and Christians are children of God; thus, wherever God has placed Christians is also their land, and they will most definitely survive, thrive, and succeed. He personally has given no thought to returning home for good. He feels that America belongs to him as much as to any other American. This has made him strive to do his best, contribute his best, and hope for the best. He appreciates the privilege of having a second home that he can call his own as a special blessing from God and aims to make the best of things in spite of the challenges. Pastor Benjamin emphasizes the role of the church in providing immigrants with hope for the future. He states that Christians need reassurance because the Lord said, "I did not come for the healthy, I came for the sick so I can heal them"; there is need for a healing word.

In addition to reassurance, Benjamin states that people need to be pushed. Sometimes they are stuck because they are waiting for better opportunities, but opportunities must be created with the tools in hand. People are full of excuses, such as "If I had a Ph.D., if I had a better job, or if I had a green card, then my life would be different." They must be motivated to make best of what they have. Pastor Benjamin said he pushes the adoption of proactive strategies for change among his membership. For example, the church has organized a health team to address members' health concerns and is planning to establish an entrepreneurial training program for unemployed members in order to convert them into job creators. Some have even contributed funds to help those who are seeking education, training, business grants, and loans, or whatever the need may be. The fund is still small, but there are enough skilled members to provide a core of mentors for those needing assistance.

Pastor Benjamin suggests that there is a critical mass of African immigrants developing, and, since this is a reality, there should be more use of African languages in the churches, and also support for the congregation through an emphasis on African values as a means of building and strengthening the community. Many Africans in the past privileged assimilation to ease the pains of the immigrant experience. Many believed that the best they could do is to learn how Americans do things and adjust quickly in order to get ahead and make ends meet. Many were driven by the survival instinct to conform and not rock the boat. However, he advocates a change in perspective, a reexamination of cultural values and assets to choose the useful elements and adopt them and to reject the negative elements. For this reason, Pastor Benjamin recently began a new radio program in Yoruba, in which he stresses the element of the sojourn as characteristic to the contemporary African experience. He seeks to motivate his radio, television, and physical congregations into believing that Africans can succeed in America.

Pastor Isaac similarly emphasizes a need for greater social and economic integration of the African immigrant community. International Ministries holds economic seminars where the members of the congregation and community are taught how to buy their own homes, how to finance such purchases, and how to work toward the American dream. They are encouraged not to rest on their oars but to let their equity work for them by buying other investment properties instead of keeping money in the bank. Some in the congregation have purchased several houses as a consequence.

For Pastor Isaac, it is impossible to separate a people and their culture from the practices of their faith. There is nothing like African Christianity. At the same time, he says, Christianity is international, a way of life. Race and ethnicity do not matter. Spiritual awakening is ongoing and is quite different from religious awareness. International Ministries is charismatic. People shout when they feel the spirit and sing, with lots of musical instruments and percussion. The way of worshipping in the church is African in the sense that Africans are full of life. This can be observed in the worship where dancing, feeling good, and celebration are integral parts of the service. There is a great deal of clapping, and the members of the congregation enjoy themselves during worship. The achievements of the members of the congregation are celebrated, particularly those related to seeking knowledge, going to school, and earning diplomas. When members earn doctoral degrees, they are hooded in church during Achievement Sunday. This gives children positive things to look forward to and helps to maintain values of excellence and achievement. Birthdays and wedding anniversaries are also celebrated. All celebration is accompanied by dancing and rejoicing. Music is also a way of evangelizing to bring people into the church.[30]

Deacon Aaron finds many Nigerian immigrant Christians fervent in the Lord, but he feels that the majority of them become lackadaisical. They are so comfortable that they have forgotten God, just as in the time of Prophet Jeremiah, when people forgot what God had done for them and left certainty for uncertainty. Africans do not relate to God in the proper manner. Money is worshipped and church treated as a place to visit socially on

Sunday. Many Christians have not grown in the Lord. Therefore, Satan finds loopholes to use against them. Deacon Aaron considers CAC WOSEM unique because it is faithful to the biblical charge "Be ye holy," an injunction for Christians to run away from sin and resist the devil. To engender this, CAC WOSEM Ministers are unafraid to say, "Be ye holy," and if you sin, you'll be punished. Sin has its own consequences, and a church may be compromised if it condones criminal or immoral behavior by power brokers on whom it is financially dependent. Because of the care taken to train, mentor, and guide pastors, WOSEM has successfully focused on embracing the Bible, not as literature but as the word of God, which can be properly understood only with the guidance of the Holy Spirit.

As in many African-led churches, there is a strong emphasis on family. Deacon Aaron decried the extent to which some Africans have taken negative American culture to heart and says this is hurting and destroying families. Showing respect for one's husband and elders and honoring one's wife are part of African culture, as is the responsibility to provide for one's family. This is also recommended by the Bible. He suggests that some traditions and cultures make the practice of Christianity easy. At the family level, if we follow African culture, particularly Yoruba culture, it is easy to respect and observe biblical teachings and injunctions. Deacon Aaron blames the undesirable changes in Yoruba culture on the love of money and on the adoption of cultures that do not adhere to Yoruba values. Aberrational behavior and un-Godly behavior are also damaging. Today's children are the future of Africans in America, and African immigrants will have links with their home countries only if their children are taught to love Africa and to understand African languages. Instead of being obedient to the biblical injunction to teach the children the way they should go, Africans are raising disobedient children, and parents create dangerous precedents by not giving Godly examples in their behavior.

In response to a question on the role of women within the church, Deacon Aaron claimed that there were originally more men than women in the congregation but says that the church is now following the new trend in most churches and has more women members than men. Deacon Aaron claims that there are numerous opportunities for women to play leadership roles in the church. They are deaconesses, evangelists, prophetesses, and even heads of churches. The Philadelphia and Lanham churches are led by women. The CAC, following biblical teaching, does not allow women to be ordained as pastors. However, women can perform as well as men, if not better. They teach in the Sunday School and also fill other responsible positions. The church is being opened up slowly to women for leadership, even in Nigeria. Nonhelpful CAC doctrines are also debated and changed. As a result of one change made a few years ago, people may sit wherever they please, instead of having to be segregated by sex in different sections of the church.

The Faith-Works Connection: Involvement in American Society and Politics

What about the level of social and economic and political involvement of African congregations in America, that is, their level of integration, measured by their interest, involvement and engagement in American politics, American society, and the American economy? Pastor Benjamin observes that both immigration status and their Christian background have in the past prevented African immigrants from getting involved in politics. Currently, however, more African immigrants are permanent residents, and many are U.S. citizens. Also, the reestablishment of a democratic system of government in Nigeria has inspired greater interest in politics, with some individuals even returning home to run for political office. Pastor Benjamin advocates for greater political involvement of the African Christian community. He states that while many African Christians grew up with the idea that Christians should not get involved in politics, this is wrong because the Bible says, "obey them that rule over you." Thus, the rulers had better be Christians because, even if they are ungodly, the Bible says that rulers must be obeyed. If Christians don't get involved in government now, non-Christians will dominate the government and trouble will be inevitable.

The 2004 presidential election, which the media in their postelection analysis presented as showing a radical division between the blue (Democratic) and red (Republican) states, has been described as showing the influence of "values voters." The concerns of these voters included hot-button issues such as the definition of marriage and the form it should take, prayer, abortion, and stem cell research. What position did African immigrant Christians take in the elections? What position should they have taken? Pastor Benjamin states that he was very careful not to discuss his views on whom to vote for with his congregation before the elections, but, right after the election, he was able to let them know where he stood. He says that before the election, a lot of African immigrant Christians strongly believed that they needed to vote for the Democrats because of their immigration concerns. As immigrants, it is only right that they should give much thought to immigration issues. Also, during the first Bush term, many African immigrants were unemployed. So, after the election, they were disappointed at Senator Kerry's defeat. Pastor Benjamin felt a duty to remove the sadness, and he did this by telling the people that regardless of who is in the office, God is the provider, the one who really can change their immigration status. Neither Kerry nor Bush is directly responsible for whether people "make it." It was necessary to convey this to the congregation. After that, they began to feel better. Pastor Benjamin elaborated:

> I personally voted for Bush because of those Christian values that you mentioned. He stunned me when he came into office during his first four-year term in that among the things that I have known in this day and age is that not anyone that can mention God on national television. . . . He is the only one that could invite Christians to the White House to celebrate his birthday and to sing. He is the only one that stands . . . or at least says he stands for God publicly, regardless of whether or not he was going to be voted in again. That got me. Now if you can stand for God you are going to get me. Now and some other issues about marriage: I believe that marriage should be between a man and a woman and the president said it should be. Now was the economy great during his time? I say no, but do I blame him? I say no. The reason why I say no is because I studied economics and I know that it is cyclical, I know that there is a period when there is so-called recession that is part of economics. There are times when things are great, it is part of economics, now did war have anything to do with it? Maybe yes, of course. Can war be a reality sometimes? Yes. Should we have gone to war? I don't know.[31]

Pastor Isaac was unable to speak categorically on the political affiliation of his church members. He believes that there are Republicans, Democrats, and independents. He does not believe in bringing politicians to the pulpit and does not tell church members whom to vote for. Rather, he guides them on the things that matter, which are the spiritual concerns, and expects them to use this as a guide when making temporal decisions. Pastor Isaac does not attend political meetings. Twice he got an invitation from President Bush's office and declined to participate because he does not believe in overt participation in politics. In his opinion, most Africans are more particular about the party than the person when they make decisions about how to cast their votes. This is an example of "one-way" political thinking and inflexibility. What matters for most Africans is welfare, not moral values. Pastor Isaac disagrees with this approach to life and believes that Christians should put moral values first. The church never endorses any political candidates, but individual members are free to participate in politics. They can vote for anyone, although Pastor Isaac believes that they ought to stop voting for parties and vote instead for values; he expects members to be true to their conscience. For him, the pastor must never overtly participate in politics, and neither should the church as an institution. Like Pastor Benjamin, he voted for President Bush in the 2004 election because of his moral stance.[32]

Deacon Aaron said that the church has no political affiliation, and, as an institution, it is not involved in politics. Members are not told whom to vote for but are free to join any party. It is, however, the moral duty of the church to educate the members on issues that will promote the freedom to worship God and to advise members when they need guidance. Deacon Aaron believes that most Africans tend to be Democrats rather than Republicans because the party supports immigration reform and expansive social programs. In contrast to the other two leaders, Aaron considers it a mistake for some African Christians to have voted for President Bush on grounds of morality because they based their decision on inadequate information, flawed analysis, and manipulation of the issues by the political advisers to President Bush and on the inadequate response by the Kerry team. The issues were starkly presented as a juxtaposition of prolife against prochoice politics. Both Kerry and Bush are Christians who oppose abortion, but, while Kerry believes in a woman's right to choose, Bush does not. In a hypothetical situation where abortion is prohibited by law and a member has one anyway, the member's action causes a breach with the church, but, with repentance, there is the offer of reconciliation. Kerry's position was similar to this but was not clearly articulated in a manner that would persuade Christians of his rationale. Abortion for him is a moral issue not to be subjected to government legislation. For Deacon Aaron, abortion should not be isolated as either the sole issue or the aggregation of all issues of life. The death penalty and the Iraq war are also important. Catholics are against the death penalty, but President Bush is for it. During his tenure as the governor of Texas, the state had its highest number of death penalty executions. The Iraq war also raises important questions about the value for life. The three issues—the death penalty, the war in Iraq, and abortion—should be seen as linked.

Deacon Aaron considers African immigrant Christians to be wanting in the sphere of politics, because most believe that Christians should not be politically involved. For him, this is wrong, because if Christians do not take up the challenge of leadership, unbelievers will control the political sphere. If Christians look to the Bible for guidance, they'll find examples of involvement in politics. Daniel was a governor, Joseph was second in command, and they both lived righteously and influenced other people positively. Like Pastor Benjamin, Deacon Aaron promotes greater political engagement; he made sure that the church members registered before the last elections.[33]

Challenges and Constraints to Social Engagement: Unity, Leadership, and Agenda

Pastor Benjamin observed that Africans seem to prefer taking isolated action to coming together. He suggested that a lack of trust militates against meaningful mobilization and is a longstanding problem that existed even when African immigrants were in their home countries and that is being reproduced in immigrant communities. People are afraid to form partnerships because, when it comes to making money, no one wants to trust anyone else, but without trust, nothing positive will happen. Pastor Benjamin emphasized the importance of unity and the church's role in fostering it and in offering hope and reassurance that even if things are grim today, the future will be better. He suggested that there is a strong need for ideas on how to accomplish desired goals. In his opinion, some Africans, particularly doctors, nurses, and people in the health field, have made much money, but they're still ignored, and none of their hard work is acknowledged. Many more African immigrants are in desperate straits because they lack documentation, and therefore they cannot talk, cannot shout, cannot shine.

In spite of the desire and enthusiasm for empowerment, there is little proactive action and ideological context, not in the sense of political ideology but in terms of an agenda on how to execute ideas, an audience that is willing to receive the plan, and some level of mobilization. The problems are an irrational fear of one another, a fear of being duped, and lack of legal immigration status, which has yoked African immigrants to a marginal existence mired in social and political retardation. This is why Pastor

Benjamin preaches constantly on breaking the yoke of retardation and was going to preach on the same theme later on the day of the interview.

For Pastor Benjamin, God will help African immigrants only if they begin to empower themselves economically. If they do not help themselves, no one else will. Economic self-empowerment will generate recognition for Africans, as will unity that can be demonstrated in actions such as establishing niche communities dominated by African homeowners, African businesses, African patronage of African-owned businesses, and mutual support to engender mutual progress. For Pastor Benjamin, African immigrants need to learn from other immigrants, like the Chinese, who provide employment for other Chinese immigrants in Chinese restaurants and other Chinese-owned businesses and even assist new immigrants to establish their own businesses through private, informal financing. This enables such communities to be both owners of capital and employers of labor, and they accomplish all they do through trust, and not just money. He pointed out that Haitian, Chinese, Jewish, and Italian American immigrants all have had well-established and effective institutions that serve the immigrant community. Some African immigrants are already thinking about these things, and, given the power of the imagination to inspire extraordinary change, it is only a matter of time before these things happen.[34]

Deacon Aaron agrees with Pastor Benjamin. He is very concerned with community development issues and, like Benjamin, advocates the establishment of niche communities and economies for mutual support and empowerment by African immigrants. There are many opportunities not utilized by Africans, for example, entrepreneurship based on one's expertise. Like Pastor Benjamin, Deacon Aaron observed that there is no clear leader and no clear plan to address the problems faced by African immigrants. At the church level, goals can be set to address the problems faced by immigrants.

Deacon Aaron considers the top issue for African immigrants to be the lack of legal nonimmigrant and permanent immigrant status. Deacon Aaron feels that African immigrant Christians must become further engaged in politics and in efforts to help the larger community, not just the immigrant members. There is no point in being an "African church," because being a church of Christ and God should be the goal. There is a need to plan programs that reach out to community members in order to benefit them, but most Africans do not volunteer. This needs to change because God created us to serve him and humanity, not just ourselves.[35]

For Pastor Isaac, African immigrants are becoming integrated into America socially, but they are not there yet economically, and they are not relevant at all politically. They have made no progress politically because the mindset that people brought from home has not changed. People believe that politicians cannot be good and that, particularly if one is a "God man," one cannot be a good politician. Pastor Isaac suggests that once this mindset changes, African immigrant Christians will be more effective in their political participation.

In order to ensure the success and growth of a church, Pastor Isaac believes that the mission statement of the church must be written, since having no vision implies that one is going nowhere. Leaders must also be open. Every Christian leader must have a father quality in order to progress. When asked if the privileging of the father role does not connote male dominance, Pastor Isaac explained that there are independent women pastors in the network of ministers within the church. He modified his stance by endorsing the parent as leader role for Christians. This, for him, means that the leader provides succor, must be open to changes, and must be able to change. This is crucial, because, in time, the church's style of worship may no longer appeal to the children and youth, who may want a different kind of music, praise worship, and the like. If the church does not respond in a manner that is relevant to them, the youth will leave in droves, and the church will not grow.

Pastor Isaac identified the top issues facing Nigerian and African immigrant Christians as similar to those facing most other immigrants. The top issue is health, followed by the need for education or knowledge, the decline in family values, and, for Nigerians, the redemption of Nigeria's sullied image. International Ministries emphasizes all of these areas. In terms of health, most medical findings by the American Medical Association identify African Americans as prone to most of the killer diseases. This is a cause for great concern. Christianity must be brought to the point where people can relate to it and connect it to their physical and spiritual wellbeing. In this way, the concern for health is absolutely crucial.[36]

Conclusion

African immigrant churches in the United States are growing at an extraordinary pace in an atmosphere in which the ideologies and methodologies of the religious Right are supported by the government in power.

Because of the Bush administration's policy of support for faith-based initiatives, religious institutions are likely to have privileged access to resources. They are also likely to have a great deal of influence in shaping the social agenda. Are African immigrant Christians relevant in these circles? Probably not to a great extent. Are they disinterested observers? Absolutely not. Many of the leaders and founders of the churches are well-educated and articulate; some were responsible for casting the "values" votes that swept President Bush into power, while others are critical of the reductionism in the definition of "values" and morality and of the Bush administration's social policy. Most of the churches remain conservative in their doctrine, and most have leadership structures dominated by men, although they allow for the participation of women. It is clear also that the churches have a socially conscious agenda for change.

There is clear evidence among African immigrant churches and Christians of Olupona's "theology of power," which emphasizes the importance of focusing spiritual energies on the achievement of power, wealth and success, mysticism, and a "direct mystical relationship with transcendence"; thus, "individual voluntarism and enthusiasm" are required from believers.[37] The use of organizational skill, administrative structure, and the mass media to construct a framework to challenge what is perceived as an anti-Christian social and political order is also prevalent, as are "innovations in liturgy, popular culture, music and dance" as tools for proselytization.[38] The leaders play strong paternal roles of adviser and protector, and the churches have a significant effect on the political, economic, and social spheres, even though most profess a disdain for formal or overt participation in politics.

The pastors interviewed for this study are dedicated to accomplishing great breakthroughs, spiritually and materially. As conservatives, they share an ideological affinity with some elements of the new Christian Right and would "vote their consciences." However, this group is neither homogenous nor unidimensional. There is strong evidence that African immigrant Christians would also vote to protect their material interests, and it is worth researching the extent to which this was done in the 2004 U.S. presidential elections. The increasing presence of African immigrant Christians will also cause significant changes to the religious demography of Africa[39] and the United States, not only because these Christians complicate current understandings of Christianity and religion but also because they are transnationalized actors engaged in mission reversal through transformative projects that minister to petitioners and supplicants who seek consolation, support, and mentorship in alien landscapes.[40] These churches are also socially relevant, institutionalizing philanthropic efforts by those who have "made it" to serve people who have no other way to access social welfare resources. Many of the churches are also nonprofit organizations, with 501c3 status. Thus, they are well placed to benefit from the Bush administration's support for faith-based initiatives. However, the lack of an African Christian church-specific institutional mechanism for coalitional and cooperative action necessarily limits their voice and their influence on national political, social, and economic matters. The desire for such voice and influence may cause them to give into overtures from more powerful and better organized Christian groups, as happened in the split between conservative and liberal Anglicans on the ordination of homosexual clergy, where wealthy American conservatives allied with the more numerous African and Third World conservatives to resist what they considered anathema.

As transnationalized persons and institutions in the global religious arena, African immigrant Christians and churches have formed both formal and informal linkages with transnational evangelistic networks that serve both spiritual and temporal functions of engendering ecumenical relations, as well as status elevation, in response to the challenges of immigration. The churches could become an important voice in bringing the interests of their members to the table when race relations, immigration, refugee policies, social welfare, and other issues are discussed at the local, state, and national levels. It is perhaps a function of the presence of a critical mass of African immigrant churches in Europe, or possibly the result of the longer history of African immigration there, that African immigrant churches in Europe are better at participating in larger ecumenical institutions and in public discourse[41] than are their counterparts in the United States. However, to the extent that African immigrant churches in Europe have made such strides, it is clear that the churches in the United States will do as well or better. The challenge for African immigrant Christians is to chart their own independently determined course and to plan for action in a manner that does not make them mere pawns in the power game that politics often is. This implies having the ability to set an agenda that responds to the issues identified by the churches' constituencies as important and identifying like-minded allies to work with. The Catholic Church, which is conservative on abortion and homosexuality, is very liberal on immigration, refugee policy, and issues of social welfare. Liberal Christians may also have compatible goals in these areas, although they may also express ambivalence on abortion and homosexuality. The astute African immigrant churches and Christians will make alliances based on distinct issue areas, and not on the basis of prior and blanket decision making.

It is also important to realize that overtures for alliances and coalition have and will be made to African immigrant churches and Christians by the new Christian Right, and the quest for visibility, access to resources, and influence may engender the perception that there is unity of purpose among African immigrant Christians and their Christian Right brethren. Once again, the transnationalization of Christianity shows us the possibilities for the future. There are already complex linkages that bind Christians in Africa to those in other parts of the world ideologically, spiritually, doctrinally, liturgically, and materially. African Initiated Churches and the African branches of mainline denominations have been at the forefront of the globalization and transnationalization of Christianity. African immigrant Christians and churches are bearers of these new developments to their new host countries. In the United States, they would be well advised to seek increased collaboration with the Black Church, which has previously negotiated the difficult terrain that they are traveling. The call for economic independence, unity in the body of Christ, discipline, and resistance to oppression was made in the United States by the Black Church, which predates the African immigrant church in its establishment.[42] African immigrant Christians' exhortation on these same issues would be even more effective if they could find common cause with the progressive liberal elements in the Black Church and build coalitions that devolve mutual benefits to coalitional members.

African immigrant Christians in the United States will be even more influential in the future both as part of the new Christian Right and in coalition with its opponents. Their experience is a clear indication of the manner in which the contradictions of globalization operate to simultaneously extend privileges to some and deny them to others. As social institutions with a religious mission, they must necessarily respond to the needs of their members who get the short end of the stick in the competitive global arena. Thus far, they have done so through taking a leadership role in building social institutions based on exhorting more affluent and skilled members to engage in philanthropic outreach to their less privileged sisters and brethren, to engage in information sharing, and to encourage and mentor, but their engagement with the social welfare programs provided at the local, state, and national levels remains rudimentary. Their engagement with the political process is even less developed, and they must unite, build coalitions, and deliberately consider the most successful strategies and agenda in service of humanity and the fulfillment of their mission.

Notes

1. Grant Wacker, "The Christian Right," National Humanities Center Web site, available online at http://www.nhc.rtp.nc.us:8080/tserve/twenty/tkeyinfo/chr_rght.htm (accessed December 2004).

2. Ibid.

3. Ibid.

4. Ibid.

5. Ibid.

6. Daniel J. Wakin, "Where Gospel Resounds in African Tongues," *New York Times*, 18 April 2004; Claudia Währisch-Oblau, "Together on the Way in Germany," *Reformed World* 50, no. 4 (December 2000), available online at the World Alliance of Reformed Churches Web site, http://www.warc.ch/miu/rw004/obl.html (accessed December 2004).

7. Wacker, "The Christian Right."

8. Ibid.

9. Tim Sullivan, "Christian Groups Proliferating in Africa: AIDS, Poverty, and Political Corruption Are Spawning Independent Churches That Combine Christian and Indigenous Rites," news posting on Beliefnet Web site, 3 April 2000, available online at http://www.beliefnet.com/story/18/story_1833_1.html (accessed December, 2005).

10. Ogbu U. Kalu, "Review of Paul Gifford, *Ghana's New Christianity: Pentecostalism in a Globalising African Economy*" (2004), e-mail communication, available online at http://www.utexas.edu/converences/africa/ads/94.html.

11. Ibid.

12. Richard Engstrom, Review of C. Peter Wagner, *Engaging the Enemy*, Apostasy Now! Web site, available online at http://www.apostasynow.com/reviews/engaging.html (accessed December 2004).

13. Gerald Ediger, "Strategic-Level Spiritual Warfare in Historical Retrospect," *Direction* 29, no. 2 (Fall 2000): 125–141, available online at http://www.directionjournal.org/article/?1053 (accessed December 2004).

14. Engstrom, Review of *Engaging the Enemy*.

15. Ernest Munachi Ezeogu, "Bible and Culture in African Theology, Part I," *International Review of Mission* (January 1998), available online at http://www.munachi.com/t/bibleculture1.htm (accessed December 2004).

16. Ibid.

17. Ibid.

18. Ibid.

19. Jacob K. Olupona, "New Religious Movements in Contemporary Nigeria," *The Journal of Religious Thought* 46, no. 1 (Summer/Fall 1989): 53.

20. Ibid., 58–59.

21. Interview with Pastor Benjamin, December 2004. Also See Neil Lettinga, Bethel University Web site, "Christianity in Africa South of the Sahara: AICs/Aladura," available online at http://www.bethel.edu/~letnie/AfricanChristianity/SSAAladura.html. See Matthews A. Ojo, "Babalola, Joseph Ayo: 1904 to 1959, Christ Apostolic Church, Nigeria," The Dictionary of African Christian Biography Web site, available online at http://www.dacb.org/stories/nigeria/babalola4_joseph.html (accessed December 2004).

22. Two Christ Apostolic Churches claim to be the first to establish a mission in the Americas—CAC WOSEM and Christ Apostolic Church, First in the Americas, founded in the early 1980s by the Reverend Abraham Oyedeji and located at 622 Cortelyou Road, Brooklyn (interview with Pastor Oyedeji at the Christ Apostolic Church, First in the Americas, June and July 2002). As well, there is a third Christ Apostolic Church, Agbala Itura, which was founded by Prophet Dr. Samuel Kayode Abiara, which has a church dubbed the International Miracle Center, Courtyard of Comfort, at 869 Lexington Avenue, Brooklyn. Deacon Aaron explains that the split happened in Nigeria, and each group now has different leaders and is answerable to its leaders back home. There are no formal links among the different factions, but there is no enmity, either. The bitterness from the old frictions is still remembered, but only by older members.

23. Interview with Pastor Benjamin, December 2004.

24. Ibid.

25. Ibid.

26. Interview with Pastor Isaac, December 2004.

27. Ibid. Also see Laolu Akande, "Redeemed Christian Church of God Buys Multimillion Dollar Property in Dallas, U.S.A.," Celestial Church of Christ Web site, available online at http://www.celestialchurch.com/news/newsroom/rccg_buys_land.htm (accessed December 2004).

28. Interview with Deacon Aaron, December 2004.

29. Interview with Pastor Benjamin, December 2004.

30. Interview with Pastor Isaac, December 2004.

31. Interview with Pastor Benjamin, December 2004.

32. Interview with Pastor Isaac, December 2004.

33. Interview with Deacon Aaron, December 2004.

34. Interview with Pastor Benjamin, December 2004.

35. Interview with Deacon Aaron, December 2004.

36. Interview with Pastor Isaac, December 2004.

37. Olupona, "New Religious Movements in Contemporary Nigeria," 60.

38. Ibid., 61.

39. Afe Adogame, "Engaging the Rhetoric of Spiritual Warfare: The Public Face of Aladura in Diaspora," *Journal of Religion in Africa* 34, no. 4 (2004): 493–522.

40. Ibid., 497–498.

41. Ibid., 499.

42. See for example, Amos Jones, Jr., *Paul's Message of Freedom: What Does It Mean to the Black Church?* (Valley Forge, Pa.: Judson Press, 1974).

13

African Muslims in the United States
The Nigerian Case

Yushau Sodiq

Introduction: Islam in Nigeria

Islam, the religion of submission to the Almighty God, is one of the major religions in Nigeria. There are more Muslims in Nigeria than there are Christians. Islam was introduced to Nigeria in the eleventh century by way of the Arab traders from Morocco. Of course, Islam gained no national appeal until the fourteenth century when the king of Bornu, Mai Idris Alooma, converted to Islam and through him the majority of the Bornu people and the Hausas became Muslims. Islam as a way of life was not seriously practiced until the end of the eighteenth and the beginning of the nineteenth centuries, after Uthman Dan Fodio launched Jihad against the Hausas and brought them back to pristine Islam. Dan Fodio established the Sokoto Caliphate, which reigned from 1804 until 1903, when Lord Luggard, the British administrator, conquered Sokoto and instituted indirect rule until Nigeria won its independence in 1960 from the British colonial invaders.[1]

Although Islam was known in other parts of Nigeria, particularly in southern Nigeria, before the Jihad of Dan Fodio, it was after his revivalism that Islam actually had a strong hold and influence in Yorubaland.[2] Since 1960, Islam has witnessed a rapid growth among the Yoruba people. A small percentage of Igbos from the east have also converted to Islam. At present, Islam thrives in Nigeria. The population of Muslims is about 50–55 percent of the total Nigerian population. Many educational institutions have been established at which Islamic studies are taught. Nearly all Nigerian universities offer courses in Arabic or Islamic studies, and a few others, such as University of Ilorin and Lagos State University, offer courses in Islamic law. Muslims and Christians live together peacefully in southern Nigeria, whereas there are occasionally tensions between the Muslims and Christians in the north, for reasons that are not always religious. There are twelve states that practice full-scale Islamic law in Nigeria. The Kwara State practices only Islamic family laws.[3]

The idea of migration is not foreign to Islam. Muslims immigrated to Abyssinia (Ethiopia) in 615 A.D. and sought refuge with the Christian king there. Christians received them warmly, and they stayed there for a long time before many of them returned back to Mecca and Medina. Also, when the persecution of the Muslims of Mecca reached its height, Muhammad allowed his followers to migrate to Medina, and it was there that they finally established and formed an Islamic state and put it into full practice. After the death of Muhammad, Muslims spread Islam to many parts of the world. Muslims were considered immigrants in the conquered territories. They often isolated themselves from their hosts so as to maintain their Islamic identity.[4]

Islam in the United States

The history of Islam in the United States began with the importation of African slaves into the New World. With the arrival of black slaves, Islam was brought into America. Statistics have shown that more than 10 percent of all slaves who were brought to America were Muslims. These Muslims tried to practice their religion. They offered daily prayers and fasted during Ramadan, and many of them refused completely to consume alcohol. However, because of the oppression and inhumane treatment they received from their white Christian masters, these Muslims were unable to transmit their beliefs to their offspring, who were always separated from their parents. The third generation of the slaves remembered little, if anything, about the beliefs and culture of their grandfathers. Eventually, Islam disappeared, never to be reborn in America until the end of nineteenth century and the beginning of the twentieth century. Some of the pioneers of Islam in the early 1900s were Muhammad Alexander Webb, a white convert to Islam; Noble Drew Ali, the leader of the Moorish Temple; and Wallace D. Fard, a mysterious person who claimed to have come from different countries and bore different names and titles. Wallace Fard reintroduced Islam to the African Americans in Michigan, regrouped them under the Islamic platform, and pledged to give them a new identity. He claimed that the African Americans were of Asiatic origin and descendents of Prophet Jacob (Ya'qub). Many African Americans rallied around him, listened to him carefully, and willingly accepted his philosophy and ideology of the supremacy of the black man. He thus chose Elijah Poole (later Elijah Muhammad) as his most honored and trusted minister. Wallace Fard then mysteriously disappeared, around 1933–1934. The Muslim group led by Elijah Muhammad was known then as the Lost Found Nation of Islam in the Wilderness (NOI). When Elijah became the leader, he turned the Nation of Islam into a strong, racial nationalist group. However, he helped the blacks to be proud of their color and taught them to be hardworking and respectful of their families.

Elijah Muhammad died in 1975, and his son Imam Warith Deen Mohammed took over the leadership of the Nation of Islam.[5] He immediately made drastic changes, which eventually led his followers to become part and parcel of the mainstream Muslim world community. He decentralized the Nation of Islam in 1985 and gave freedom to local Imams to reorganize and plan for themselves, a freedom that they never dreamed of. Imam W. D. Mohammed has successfully guided his people to mainstream Islam. He continuously educates them toward a proper understanding of Islam and the value of the freedom they enjoy as citizens of this great country, America. Imam W. D. Mohammed is known as an ambassador of peace. He never perceives Christians and Jews as others but sees them as inheritors of Abrahamic religion.

Nigerian Muslim Immigrants in the United States

The formation of the Nigerian Muslim Association in 1973, came in response to a felt need by the Nigerian Muslims in New York and in Washington, D.C. These Muslims wanted to maintain their Islamic identity and to prevent their families from converting to Christianity, the host religion. The NMA was not formed in protest against other Islamic organizations such as the Islamic Association of North America, the Islamic Circle of North America, the Islamic Mission, or the Nation of Islam. Rather, Nigerian Muslims feel that little attention was and is still paid to West African Islamic issues. Always, great attention is given to Middle Eastern issues or Asian or southern Asian problems; West Africa is left out and considered insignificant, primarily because it has no experts lobbying for it locally and internationally.[6]

This work is a result of my interviews with many Nigerian Muslim leaders across the United States and my own personal observations and experiences. The work on this research started in 1997, when I began to interact with Nigerian Muslims in this country. At that time, I met a number of Nigerian Muslims in Chicago at an Islamic conference conducted by the Islamic Society of North America (ISNA) and decided to pursue this research. In 2000, I attended the meeting of the National Council of the Nigerian Muslim Associations in the U.S.A. It was there that I learned that Nigerian Muslims had been running their own organizations since 1973. In order to learn more about what they had accomplished, I began to do research and to conduct interviews with many of their leaders, the Imams (prayer leaders), and Executive Committee members in New York, Washington, D.C., Chicago, St. Louis, Missouri, Philadelphia, Dallas, and Houston. My interest in this research is to identify why Nigerian Muslims established their own organizations despite the fact that they already participated in many Nigerian national and state organizations. I wanted to know how effective they were and what contributions they actually made to their Muslim communities. I also was interested in knowing how they relate to one another and interact with Muslims and non-Muslim groups, especially Nigerian Christians.

In this chapter, I argue that:

1. The NMA was formed not as a sectarian group. It was established to meet the needs of the Nigerian Muslims in the United States as they sought to maintain their Islamic identity, to teach their children in the religion of Islam, and to encourage them to marry Muslims so that their heritage and culture would be carried on. From now on, I will use "NMA" as abbreviation for the Nigerian Muslim Association in the U.S.A.
2. NMA is neither sponsored nor supported by local or international Islamic groups or movements. It is not affiliated with any group, except the Islamic Society of North America. It is free to choose its own policies and activities.
3. NMA suffers from some of the same problems that many other Muslim organizations in the U.S. face: lack of good leadership, lack of adequate planning for the future, and syncretism—the mixing of religion with cultural beliefs and values, which are, at times, repugnant to Islamic teachings.

Muslim Immigrants from Nigeria

Statistically speaking, we do not know the number of Nigerians in the United States. During President Clinton's visit to Nigeria, August 24–26, 2000, the American as well as Nigerian media put the number of Nigerians in America at 3 million; however, this number cannot be verified.[7] In the 1950s, Nigerians began to arrive in the United States to pursue higher education. Most of those who came in the 1950s and 1960s returned to Nigeria after their graduation. On their return, they assumed leadership positions and became the elite and decision makers of Nigeria. After the Biafrian war of 1967–1970, a few Nigerians from the east were granted asylum in the United States. But, as the war ended, many did return to Nigeria.

Also, between 1970 and 1985, the Nigerian government sponsored many students for study abroad. A great number of them came to the United States. The majority of those who came in 1970s returned home, whereas only a few graduates from the 1980s returned home, largely because the fall in oil prices led to economic hardship in Nigeria. However, few Muslims came as students, and few of those chose to stay in the United States; consequently, the number of Muslim Nigerians in the United States is extremely small. It is also true that some of those who were Muslims from the southern and Middle Eastern parts of Nigeria occasionally converted to Christianity in America because of peer pressure from their friends who are Christians; these Muslims by birth do not want to be perceived as different. Therefore, one finds that some of the members of the Nigerian churches in the United States were originally Muslims. Many of them do not want their parents in Nigeria to know that they have converted to Christianity.

Despite the small number of Nigerian Muslims in the United States, a handful who resided in New York and Washington areas in the 1970s decided to form an organization that would cater to their needs. While the first NMA was inaugurated in New York in 1973 with a very small number of adherents, the organization grew gradually. At about the same time, the Nigerian Muslims in Washington launched their own NMA. Later, a number of associations were launched in Chicago, Miami, Houston, Dallas, and St. Louis, and in Rhode Island, Pennsylvania, and Florida.

The goals of all these organizations are the same, although they may be expressed somewhat differently. Primarily, the aims of the NMAs as stated in their constitutions include the following:

1. To establish an organization to maintain their religious identity.
2. To reaffirm their faith in Allah and the message revealed to the Prophet Mohammed.
3. To inculcate Islamic values in adults and their children.
4. To promote good deeds and work together for the peace of all humanity.
5. To learn more about Islam and to practice it.

All NMAs are Islamic, religious, nonprofit, nonpolitical, tax-exempt organizations. They are funded by the donations of their members and receive no support whatsoever from the government or from any political organizations or foreign agents. They are not affiliated officially with any organizations in Nigeria or abroad. They are totally independent and consider themselves organizations of Sunni Muslims. Shiite Islam was hardly known in Nigeria before the Iranian revolution of 1979, led by Imam Khomeini.

It is pertinent to mention that the NMAs are often formed to resist the conversion of Muslims to Christianity. It is not uncommon among Nigerian Muslims looking for a social outing on Sundays to join their friends who attend church. They do so largely for purposes of socializing, rather than for religious reasons. Nearly all the people I interviewed commented upon what they viewed as the lack of spirituality in the Nigerian churches they attended before reverting to Islam. At the same time, many recognized the social atmosphere they enjoyed at church by meeting new friends, dating, gossiping, and dancing, particularly after long hours of hard work during the weekdays. Some members of the Nigerian mosques have gone back to their churches, complaining that there is no dancing in the mosque and that the religious services in the mosque are dull.

On a related note, one of the persistent issues in the NMAs is whether and how to separate religion from the culture. This is an issue that seems unique to the Nigerian mosques. It comes up because it was mainly members of one ethnic group, the Yoruba, who organized the NMAs. Other Muslim associations from West and East Africa exhibit greater ethnic diversity. Cultural values prevalent among the Yoruba are found to permeate daily life in the mosques; Yoruba can hardly divorce themselves from these values and practices. There are many Yoruba customs that are integrated into life at the mosque. For example, when Yoruba greet one another, they bow to each other as a sign of respect; a younger person can never initiate the shaking of hands with an older person. There are also some customs that many Yoruba do not discard, even though Islam does not endorse them, such as the intermingling of men and women at the mosque. This has at times initiated disputes within the mosque. Another sensitive issue is dancing in the mosque, which is wrongly labeled as prophetic dancing (*ijo anabi*). This practice might have been accepted initially when Islam was first introduced to win the Yoruba people, but in reality there exists no evidence to support such practice. It is purely a Yoruba cultural art that Muslims in Yorubaland accommodated and endorsed because it is a pivotal element in their social life. Any religious function, particularly a social one, that lacks dancing is perceived as dull and incomplete. Of course, men and women do not dance together in the mosque.[8]

The Structure of the Nigerian Muslim Associations

Nigerians, particularly the Yoruba, tend to be very social people and are fond of their culture. They are generally religious, too, but their religion is syncretic: a mixture of religion and culture. The NMA is formed mostly by appealing to Nigerian Muslims to come together in order to initiate *Asalatu*. The *Asalatu* refers to a weekly prayer that Nigerian Muslims perform in Nigeria on Fridays at nearly all local mosques in Yorubaland. Therein, members, mostly women, are taught and enlightened about Islam and about their responsibilities toward their God, family, and the community in general. Nigerians, even those people who know little about Islam, find the call to attend *Asalatu* very attractive and appealing. Muslims from Yorubaland would have participated in *Asalatu* or at least heard of it from their parents or relatives back in Nigeria.[9] Members invite their friends and relatives to the *Asalatu*. At times, a few others find out about the NMA themselves, particularly when a child is born and they want to give the infant an Islamic name, or they are proposing marriage and prefer Islamic marriage. On rare occasions, some Nigerians who are committed to Islam do check the telephone directories to find Muslim organizations and, if they find NMAs, they often join them.

Those who form an NMA initially gather together and have monthly meetings at members' residences on rotation. When they grow large in number, they often rent an apartment or hall, and, from the hall, they may rent a house and convert it to a mosque. Occasionally, these groups have built their own mosques from the ground, as in Houston, Texas, and in

Maryland. It is also not uncommon for Muslim groups to rent a church or YMCA, as happened in St. Paul, Minnesota, for their weekly services.

Muslims in Yorubaland and in the United States have good relationships with Christians; they consider them coreligionists and friends. They relate to one another smoothly, although there exists some tension on rare occasions due to personal interests. But, as religious communities, they get along with each other. Muslims in Dallas occasionally invite Christians to their annual functions, especially during the birthday of the Prophet Muhammad (Mawlid).[10]

In many parts of the United States, the NMA is built around the personality of the Imam, the religious leader, who often is a founding member. The NMA in Houston has a hired Imam paid by the community. This mosque was built with the support of the well-known Nigerian basketball player Hakeem Olajuwon. After the formation, the leaders deliberate on how to organize themselves as a community and how to serve the religious and the spiritual needs of their members. Since there exists no umbrella organization, each group at each local area tries out many options and adopts whatever method works and drops what does not. This results occasionally in losing some members when the leadership makes some unintentional mistakes or makes a drastic change.

Religious Programs at the NMAs

The educational programs that many Nigerian Muslim Associations follow are simple in nature and in many cases they have not been thoroughly developed or revised since the establishment of these associations. Members often meet on Sundays, rather than on Fridays, because Sunday is a weekend and everyone is free. At the meeting, they start by reciting some prayers from a pamphlet called "Prayer Book—*Asalatu,*" which is an adaptation of the prayer book in use by the Ansarudeen Society of Nigeria, in Lagos, Nigeria. The recitation is said in Arabic and lasts about forty-five minutes. Upon its completion, the Imam reads a special prayer from the Qur'an for about five to ten minutes. This is followed by a sermon in Yoruba or English language by the Imam or his deputy. The sermon addresses different topics on Islam and its practices and also addresses novel issues faced by the community of believers. Social issues are also discussed during the sermon. At the end, the members ask questions relating to the topics discussed or to any other subjects pertaining to Islam. Most sermons are in Yoruba language, except when there are people in attendance who are not Yoruba, and then English is spoken. After this, the Imam raises funds for the mosque through donations by the members. Many NMAs have no monthly fee for members, and those that require it are not strict in its collection. Thus, the association relies heavily on what it collects every Sunday as donations. Other functions that are conducted on Sundays are the performing of special prayers for members and deceased relatives.

While the prayer and sermon are in progress, the young children attend Islamic education classes, where they study the Islamic religion and Islamic values. This often involves reading and memorizing some chapters of the Qur'an. Not all NMAs offer Islamic classes for their kids. Where there are no regular classes for children, such as in Dallas/Fort Worth, parents are encouraged to enroll their kids at sister mosques and schools.[11] In general, the amount of knowledge given to students at NMAs is limited and inadequate compared to what they would receive at other Islamic schools organized by Islamic centers with greater resources. However, the leadership at the mosque is continuously attempting to improve the quality and quantity of Islamic education.

The Council of Imam and the Executive Committee

There are two leadership structures in most NMAs: the Council of Imam, which takes care of religious issues, and the Executive Committee which is in charge of managing the affairs of the association. The mosque members elect the Executive Committee, and the committee in turn elects the president. The functions of the Imam and its council, as well as the duties of the executive committee, are clearly defined in the constitution of the NMAs. Of course, there are tensions at times, but the real head of the NMA is the Imam. His advice is sought on nonreligious matters, too, and he holds the final authority in the association. While the committee members are elected, the Imam is appointed because of his knowledge of Islam, and, after his appointment, his removal may be very difficult because of the lack of an adequate procedure for appointing and removing Imams in Islam. Some community leaders attempt to set guidance on how to recruit or select the Imam, as well as how to terminate him, by offering a reasonable salary through which he will be accountable to the executive committee. As yet, such attempts have not been successful.

Both the Council of Imam and the Executive Committee arrange regular meetings of the association, but each group can also separately call for a meeting as needed. Cooperation between the two arms is expected, and, where it exists, the community develops and an atmosphere of peace and friendliness prevails. Unlike many other Muslim organizations in the United States, the NMAs often elect women to the Executive Committee to ensure that women as a group are represented and in recognition of their contribution to the progress and advancement of the community. The NMA believes that any organization that prevents women from participating has deprived itself of women's valuable contribution, especially nowadays, when women receive the same quality education as men.

Membership in the NMA

Membership in the NMA is open to all Nigerian Muslims and to other Muslims, as well. But, in reality, only Nigerians and a few Muslims from West African countries join the association. New members pay a $10 to $20 membership fee annually. As alluded to earlier, each member is also required to pay a monthly fee, but many do not pay it. Since the association does not rely on monthly fees for its operation, members are not pressed to pay regularly. Friends and relatives draw new members to the association. Many have no religious background except that they bear Muslim names and have Muslim parents. By joining the NMA, they regain their religious identity and feel proud of being Muslims again.

NMAs have little acquaintance with other Muslim groups in their locales. While their leaders often participate in social and religious functions of other Muslim groups and movements, the majority of the members rarely associate socially with members of other groups. While they pray in other mosques and attend Friday prayers, they do not regularly socialize with them. Members of the NMA complain that other Muslim groups in the United States pay little attention to sub-Saharan African issues and regard non-Arabs Muslims as less religious than Arab adherents. In addition, they directly and indirectly criticize the ways African Muslim men and women interact and dress in the mosque, which they think is too extravagant and un-Islamic at times. In other words, NMA members believe that the Arabs want them to dress like Arabs before they can be recognized as full Muslims, an idea that the NMA rejects completely.[12] Occasionally, funds are raised at Nigerian mosques for various

Islamic groups or projects. When there is a rally for the promotion of Islamic causes in the community or in other places across the United States, the NMA often participates to show its support. The NMA also seeks financial support from other groups during its annual functions and social activities. Only a small number of non-African Muslims attend NMA functions. Nevertheless, the NMA maintains a cordial and open relationship with other Muslim groups.

The NMA also keeps good relations with Nigerian Christians. Since Nigeria is a pluralistic society, there hardly exists a family in Yorubaland that has no Muslim or Christian members. In one family, one finds practitioners of every religion. Thus, in the United States, many Muslims' friends are Christians and, just as the Muslims sometimes attend church with their associates, the Christians occasionally attend a mosque whenever their friends or relatives have a special celebration. Therefore, the relationship between Nigerian Muslims and Christians is cordial. They work together and help one another as they participate in one another's social functions.[13]

It should be pointed out, too, that the NMA has, so far, no official affiliation with Muslim organizations in Nigeria. Although some members are originally from the Ansarudin Association or Ansar al-Islam in Nigeria, the associations in America are not associated with the Nigerians in Africa. Nonetheless, the NMA occasionally invites scholars and preachers from Nigeria to give lectures on Islamic issues and on Muslims in Nigeria to keep the members informed about the current issues in their homeland.

Women's Role in the Mosque

Islam preaches equality between men and women, and the Prophet granted a lot of freedom to women. However, since the death of the Prophet, women have traditionally been regarded as second-class citizens in most of the Muslim countries. In many Arab and African countries, women have no voice and place in the public; they are confined culturally and socially to the home. Nigerian women, and particularly the Yoruba, are often very social and festive, yet they rarely participate in public politics or in making decisions on social issues; men normally speak for them.[14] But, in America, Muslim women have begun to take their roles as full participants in the building of their communities. And they have started to gradually receive accommodation by men. They have been offered and granted religious titles to win their support.

In the NMAs, Muslim women play a large role in the running of the mosque and in educating the children. In many of the Islamic centers' full-time and Sunday Islamic schools, the majority of the teachers and educators are women. In some NMAs, women have been elected to become members of the Executive Committee, and they have contributed tremendously to the progress of their community. They have proven to be capable partners and assertive personalities. Some of the other Muslim groups of Arab and Asian immigrants do not allow women to be members of the Executive Committee. They argue that the Prophet did not include them. However, the Nigerian Muslim women are not excluded from decision making. In contrast, back in Nigeria, women are normally not invited to express their opinions on the affairs of the mosque, except on issues relating to women. Only then, Iya Suna (women's religious leaders) have a chance to voice their opinions, and members generally adhere to their decisions. This has changed completely in the U.S. context.

Organizational Challenges Facing the Nigerian Muslim Associations

Challenges Facing the Imams

In the 1970s and 1980s, those who founded the NMA became the leaders. The newly formed members appointed an Imam, then a president, a secretary, and a treasurer. While the other positions are easily changed as the community grows and new members increase, the Imam remains unchanged. The majority of the Nigerians mistakenly believe that the Imamship is a permanent position and that, when appointed, the Imam should not be removed unless he commits a grave sin, such as adultery or apostasy. The irony is that most Imams in the United States are not democratically elected; they are initially appointed by a handful of people to meet the urgent needs of a growing new Muslim community. Unfortunately, after their appointments, they enjoy the position and the accompanying social benefits and prestige, thus resisting all effort at removal even when they have lost the support of the members who appointed them.

In some cases, these Imams are not well advanced in Islamic knowledge; sometimes those who possess adequate Islamic knowledge lack Western education, especially administrative skills. Hence, they are ill equipped to function well and lead with wisdom. Any attempt to rectify such deficiencies is perceived as opposition or threat. Often, advice leads to division and separation, rather than to unity. Most Imams are not trained for leadership and administration of the mosque in America. Lack of training for the Imams has caused a lot of problems for the members, and yet no concrete solution has been applied to address these issues. While Christians and Jews offer rigorous training for their leaders at their seminaries and colleges, Muslim Americans have no formal training for their leaders. Many Muslim leaders in the United States therefore lack the necessary leadership qualities and administrative skills to function well in America.[15]

Challenges Facing the Executive Committee

The Executive Committee of the NMA has its own problems. The committee manages the affairs of the association and takes care of the finances. Often, the committee is made up of members who enjoy great pride in being associated with Islam and holding positions in the mosque but do not commit themselves to the teachings of Islam in their daily affairs. The committee members are those who receive Western education and have more rapport with the community because of their personalities and social activities. Most of them, for one reason or another, have inadequate knowledge of Islam and hence pay less attention to practice.

A related major challenge that is further discussed later is how to educate the NMA membership, in general, about Islam. Some members perceive any attempt toward change as threatening. They resist any genuine reform and reject any innovative idea, even when its positive result can be recognized immediately. They may resist change because of their limited knowledge about Islam, knowledge that is primarily based on Yoruba tradition rather than on true Islamic understanding.

Overcoming Organizational Challenges

Tensions between the Council of Imam and the Executive Committee cause friction and division at times and lead to deficiency in execution of the mosque programs and activities. In the constitution of the NMA, the Executive Committee and the Council of Imam are expected to meet regularly, and there is occasionally tension between the two, largely because of the aforementioned issues. Those who know more about Islam thanks to their competence in the Arabic language tend to drive people toward Arab culture and Arabic approaches to Islam, which are not always Islamic. Sometimes little respect is given to the organizational structure of the mosque and there is a preference that things be done without documentation and planning. Some members believe in oral tradition instead of writing and documentation. This lack of planning is detrimental to the communities, which lack structured activities. On the other hand, those who possess Western education and lack sound Islamic knowledge despise leaders who have Islamic knowledge and may occasionally perceive them as inferior. These groups of Western-oriented members incline to and praise modernization and secularization at the expense of Islam. Thus, there emerge conflicts of interest between the Imam and the Executive Committee. The committee is inclined to ignore the advice of the Council of Imam on the grounds that its members lack administrative skills, while the Council of Imam suspects the committee of not fully committing itself to the pristine legacy of Islam in some of its functions.

The solution to these problems lies in developing a good leadership program by educating the mosque members and the committee about the importance of marriage between Islamic knowledge and Western education. Managerial skills are also urgently needed for the leaders at the mosques if they are to deliver their message and serve the community adequately. We also suggest that Imams be trained and offered an adequate salaries based on their level of education and experience in Islamic work in the community. Their services and duties should be stipulated in their contracts. We believe that following these practices will allow the Imams to gain more credit and win the trust of their members, as it will enable members to evaluate the contributions and services of the Imams and suggest the areas that need improvement and implement them.

Other Areas for Improvement

The NMA in the United States is relatively new compared to other Christian organizations established by the Nigerians, yet it's the only Muslim organization established and run by Nigerians without any sponsorship or patronage from any Arab government or other Islamic movement. There are many areas that need drastic improvements if the NMA is to meet its goals and fulfill its responsibilities toward its members and the Muslim community in general. Some of the areas that require improvement and serious attention include (a) education, (b) planning, (c) public relations, and (d) commitment to Islamic propagation.

The level of Islamic education within the NMA is low compared to that in many other Muslim communities. Nearly 90 percent of NMA members cannot read the Arabic Qur'an, despite the fact that many of them have attended Arabic schools as youth in Nigeria. Thus, their knowledge about Islam is what they have been told and not what they have learned by reading or researching. There is a perception that learning Arabic is too difficult, and, therefore, many do not bother to attempt to learn the language. Ultimately, their knowledge about Islam remains shallow. Because of this lack of basic knowledge of Islam, they do not practice Islam and become prey to Christian propaganda, which has led some of them to convert to Christianity. In addition, much of what Yoruba Muslims know and practice about Islam has been based on Yoruba culture, which is not always Islamic.

Attempts have often been made to improve the quality of Islamic education among the members. These attempts have witnessed some success, but there are still a great number of members who perceive these changes as a threat or a selling-out of "Yoruba culture" to "Arab culture," which they equate with Islam. Adult educational programs have also been unsuccessful due to lack of access. In most cases, the nature of daily jobs in the United States does not permit many members to attend adult educational programs where they are offered.

In many NMAs, Sunday schools are established for Muslim children, who are taught the Qur'an, Arabic, and Islamic knowledge. These youth have begun to teach their parents, and at times, they are tools in encouraging their parents to attend mosques and to become more committed to practicing Islam. The Imams should pay more attention to the needs of the youth, as more than half of the Muslim population today is less than twenty years old. The leaders are concerned about the adults while they alienate the youth by not addressing their needs. The youth, who are the cream of the community and tomorrow's leaders, should be given most of the attention, and the NMA should tailor its programs to their interests.

Another significant problem faced by the NMA is lack of adequate planning. Two central areas of planning that are often neglected include planning for lectures and other social functions and planning for the future development of the mosque. As for the former, only a few members participate and know what is going on in the mosque. There are often no regular monthly meetings. The Executive Committee meets on call by the president or by the Imam, and the officers inform the mosque members of their decisions. The advice of the general body of the NMA is rarely sought. Thus, tension and ill feeling grow between the Executive Committee and the general members. If the tension is not addressed in time, it occasionally leads to division and a creation of a new association. More effort is necessary in planning activities and events and in involving as much of the congregation as possible in the decision-making process.

Further, planning for the future must be given adequate attention. The Executive Committee addresses issues as they arise, which gives the members inadequate time to resolve them properly, make genuine decisions, or provide concrete solutions. As they make improper decisions, the committee members become the subject of criticism by some members, who eventually lose trust in the ability of the committee to function and address issues diligently. Dissatisfied members express their disapproval in different ways and methods, and their criticisms are often ignored. Eventually, community progress becomes hampered, and some members have ceased to attend the mosque regularly unless there is a big function that is taking place in the community.

Some Muslims in the United States today are reluctant to publicly assert that they are Muslims because of the negative stereotypes that the U.S. media has associated with Islam and Muslims in general. Hence, some members of the Islamic movements and organizations, including the NMA, are not brave enough to propagate Islam or practice it publicly. Nigerian Muslims should not be discouraged from practicing Islam in public. The only commitment that Muslims need is the practice of Islam itself; it is the best way to propagate the religion.

Conclusion

The NMA is a growing Muslim community in the United States. It was first established in 1973 by concerned Nigerian Muslims who felt the need to educate themselves and their children about Islam in the hope of not falling prey to Christian evangelism. As they tried to organize themselves as a nonpolitical group, they encountered numerous problems; among them, leadership and syncretism are at the core. Yoruba cultural values have intruded upon religious practice. Islamic practices today among the Yoruba demonstrate the inseparability of religion and culture. The challenge of leadership is also at the center of the problem because, in Islam, there are no ordained priests, and therefore any qualified and knowledgeable person about Islam can become an Imam. The members appoint the Imams. Often, individuals impose themselves as Imams, and as time goes on, they are endorsed and recognized by the community. However, the great problem lies in effecting their removal if they are found to be incapable or aggressive or abusive in their positions. Since they are not elected and not paid any salary, the community finds it extremely difficult to remove the Imams, particularly given the social prestige attached to this position. This problem is not peculiar to Nigerians but if found in all Muslim associations and movements from different nationalities in the United States.

We have made a number of suggestions here in order to help improve the functioning of the NMAs. We believe that Imams should receive leadership and administrative training and that they should be hired on a contract basis with a paid salary. Planning activities should take place on a regular basis and should be more inclusive of congregation members. We also have suggested that actions should be taken to lessen the tension between the Imams and the Executive Committee, mainly through additional training programs and conflict resolution that attempts to bridge the divide between Western education and Islamic knowledge. There is also a need for greater effort in the area of Islamic education. While the main function of many of the NMAs is to read the prayer book, the focus should be not on reading this very particular prayer book but on a genuine attempt to improve the quality of Islamic education among the members. The teaching of the holy Qur'an and *hadith,* as well as the teaching of Islamic basic laws concerning the five pillars of Islam and Islamic values, should be given serious attention. In addition, youth education should be given priority, for they are the future of the Muslim community. Any investment of time and money on their behalf is a good investment that Muslims should proudly embark upon.

Finally, the NMAs deserve a lot of credit for their commitment to serve their fellow Muslims, for their generosity, and for their freedom from denomination, as well as from local or foreign sponsorship. The NMA Imams should also be praised for the dedication, selflessness, service, and sense of tolerance they exhibit among different groups and the accommodation of members of other religions, such as Christianity and traditional religion. Despite all of the problems we have enumerated, there is a bright future for the Nigerian Muslims in the United States. They strive to be Muslims and be more committed to their religion. They aspire to teach their children about Islam and help them receive both Western and Islamic education, and they wish to assist their children in marrying Muslim spouses. We expect that the leadership of the NMAs will improve and that the members will be exposed to universal Islam by participating and joining many other Muslim groups in their locales. They will also have increasing opportunities to work with others as Americans, rather than only on religious grounds. By taking care of one another and helping our members, we provide for our needs and find solutions to our problems, thereby reducing our reliance upon government resources. One of the most important services the NMAs provide to their members is the teaching of Islamic morality: the imperative to become a useful human being, an ethical person, who does good deeds and shuns evil and who causes no harm to himself or to any other human being, a person who submits to God and lives peacefully with others.

Notes

1. Mervyn Hiskett, *The Development of Islam in West Africa* (New York: Longman, 1984).

2. T. G. O. Ghadamosi, *The Growth of Islam among the Yoruba, 1841–1908* (Atlantic Highlands, N.J.: Humanities Press, 1978).

3. J. Akin Omoyajowo, "Interaction of Religions in Nigeria," *Caribbean Journal of Religious Studies* 5 (1983): 1–17.

4. Hiskett, *Development of Islam in West Africa.*

5. Minister Louis Farrakhan considers himself the most faithful disciple of the Honorable Elijah Muhammad and broke away from Warith Deen's group in 1978 in order to resurrect the original Nation of Islam, which he vowed to preserve. He emphasized in his speech on the Savior's Day, on February 26, 2000, that he stood for Islam and for the oppressed people all over the world. He also affirmed, in February 2000, that he is a true Muslim who recognizes one Almighty God and Prophet Muhammad bin Abdullah of Arabia. But at the same time, he noted, he would never forget the remarkable role Elijah Muhammad and his family played in his life.

6. Lisa Ann Mammel, "Nigerian Muslim Views of the U.S.: Admiration for Special U.S.–Saudi Relationship; Criticism of Anti-Islamic Bias in Foreign Policy and Media," research memorandum prepared by the U.S. Information Agency, Washington, D.C., 17 September 1990.

7. Daniel Pipes and Khalid Duran, "Muslim Immigrants in the United States," August 2002, Center for Immigration Studies Web site available online at www.cis.org/articles/2002/back802.html (accessed on 13 November 2004).

8. Yushau Sodiq, "A History of Islamic Law in Nigeria," in *Islamic Studies* 31 (Spring 1992): 85–108.

9. Ibid.

10. D. Dennis Cordel and Jane Lenz Elder, "The New Dallas Immigrants, Community Institutions, and Cultural Diversity: A Collection of Student Papers," (Dallas: S.M.U., The William P. Clements Center for Southwest Studies, 2000).

11. Ibid.

12. Mammel, "Nigerian Muslim Views of the U.S."

13. Omoyajowo, "Interaction of Religions in Nigeria," 1–17.

14. Sodiq, "History of Islamic Law in Nigeria," 85–108.

15. Yushau Sodiq, "A History of Islam Among the African-American Muslims of Richmond," in *The Muslim Journal* 67, no. 3 (July–October, 1994): 258–278.

14

Conclusion

Jacob K. Olupona and Regina Gemignani

The significance of African immigrant religious communities is evidenced by their diversity and growing numbers, as well as by their impact on American social life. As a result, they can no longer be overlooked either in academia or in public thought and policy debates. This conclusion summarizes the central points of the previous chapters and, drawing upon recent research on the role of religion among new U.S. immigrants, highlights comparisons with other emergent religious communities. This is a new field of study, and many questions remain to be answered regarding African immigrant religion. We identify some of the areas that require further attention and put forth our suggestions for future work.

The chapters in this volume portray the broad range of the African religious traditions that are currently found across America. Like that of Asian immigrants, who have established mainline, evangelical, and Buddhist (and, from South Asia, Muslim and Hindu) communities, African immigrant religion is characterized by a great deal of internal diversity. The communities discussed here include evangelical Christians who, through their fellowship and exuberant spirituality, actively address obstacles and hindrances as they adjust to dramatic changes in their social milieu; Aladura churches that holistically unite the material and the spiritual, undertaking a personal quest to discover God's presence in the midst of an often chaotic urban life; Muslim communities that negotiate divisions of religion and race, while developing a notable social and economic presence; and Orthodox Christian churches that recreate tradition as they negotiate change and continuity in their new lives. Added to these are the leaders of African Indigenous Religion who are engaging a vibrant, multiethnic community in spiritual and cultural renewal.

Within all of these varied communities there is further diversity stemming from the rich religious heritage of the African continent and the different paths that the groups take in America. A variety of Aladura churches are highly active in America, including the Celestial Church of Christ, the Holy Order of Cherubim and Seraphim, the Church of the Lord (Aladura), and Christ Apostolic Church. Mainline churches led by Africans and having large numbers of African members include Anglican, Methodist, Catholic, and Lutheran communities, among others. There are evangelical churches that primarily serve Liberian, Nigerian, Ghanaian, or Ethiopian immigrants and Catholic churches composed of members from Nigeria, Cameroon, Ghana, Sudan, Senegal, Zaire, Ethiopia, and Eritrea—each with their own styles of liturgy and worship. There are African mosques that are composed primarily of members from a single ethnic group (e.g., the Nigerian Muslim Association) and those that include a broad mix of West African immigrants. In addition to all this variety, one finds a great deal of flux; African immigrants often move freely between Christian traditions or between Islam and Christianity, and some who belong to churches and mosques also consult periodically with traditional priests. This proliferation of African religious communities is highly relevant to the ongoing development of religious pluralism in America. In regard to the U.S. context, Casanova states, "The most important characteristic [of the new U.S. immigrants] is the extraordinary religious pluralism and diversity which they bring to a country which was already the most religiously diverse and pluralistic in the world."[1]

Religion is increasingly viewed as integral to the social and cultural processes by which new immigrants to the United States collectively define a sense of belonging.[2] The chapters in this volume provide support for this idea, suggesting that for many African immigrants, religious affiliation is central to identity formation and to processes of integration and adaptation. Through deeply held beliefs and strong emotional attachments, religion provides a foundation that helps immigrants to make sense of unfamiliar surroundings, address challenges, and navigate their way in a new environment. Drawing upon their in-depth research with a broad range of communities, the authors provide evidence for the dynamic processes in which religion intersects with the African immigrant experience. They show that African immigrants do not transport a static religious and cultural tradition but rather enact their religion in creative response to their environment, and this "lived religion" becomes a key factor in their emerging transnational identities.[3] Through these processes, multiple, even conflicting narratives around identity and religion may come into play in the context of particular social and political projects.

In the context of dislocation, social marginalization and the diminishing social safety net in the U.S., religion offers immigrants an institutional framework for establishing an integrated, self-reliant, and resilient community. Like the immigrant congregations discussed by Warner, these chapters show that African immigrant religious communities increasingly encompass multiple facets of immigrant life, providing social services, recreational avenues, and opportunities for civic involvement.[4] The chapters examine, in addition to the direct forms of support offered by the communities, important intermediate outcomes of this broad engagement with members' lives. For example, much of the work provides evidence for the central role of religious affiliation in developing and expressing powerful new forms of association and alliance. Biney has suggested that religious leaders assume many of the leadership roles of family or lineage heads at home—assisting the community through rites of passage, including birth, child naming, coming of age, marriage, and death.[5] Tettey similarly describes the relations of reciprocity that are reinvented in these communities and that provide material and symbolic resources for collectively overcoming adversity. These close bonds of friendship and loyalty are critical factors in the development of trust and social capital in these newly formed communities. So far, research on this topic has mainly focused on the case of the Mouride Brotherhood, well known for its role in economic revitalization of parts of New York City.[6] More broadly conceived work is needed to understand the role of religion in the creation of social networks and the implications for immigrants' wellbeing and empowerment.

Understandings and expressions of identity within the African religious communities involve aspects of religion, gender, race, ethnicity, and nationalism. Immigrant religious groups construct unity in part through shared values and ideals. Some of the examples offered in this volume are identities based upon values such as family stability, respect for elders, education, social solidarity, and spirituality. The other side of this is the emphasis placed upon aspects of difference that are constructed through boundary formation and contrastive stereotypes. In these chapters, a prominent example of the latter is the construction of African Christian identities against images of moral laxity, extreme permissiveness, chaos, and emptiness in the West. For example, Okome describes African pastors' views of "spiritual death" in the West, evidenced in the lack of stringency within church communities and the loss of the "fibers that hold Christianity together." Tettey suggests that opposition to particular aspects of American social life (e.g., greater acceptance of homosexuality) serves as a powerful force for cohesiveness and belonging among Africans who are otherwise cut off from one another in their everyday lives. The latter point has interesting implications for the participation of Africans as "values voters" in U.S. politics—suggesting that this has much to do with dislocation and alienation and the search for a unified voice in the public arena.

Numerous theorists have pointed out that transnational identities are tied to fluidity and movement across time as well as space, "slipping from constructed past to imagined future."[7] In these essays, we have seen how dynamic constructs, such as the "home church" discussed by Tettey, express and shape the fluid nature of transnational lives. It has also been suggested that African immigrant religion provides not only linkages with the past but a collective vision for the future. A key example is the ideal of "reverse mission" in which hope, expectation, and intention infuse current experience. Such epic discourses sacralize the immigrant journey and provide a profound sense of collective purpose. The belief that African Christians are fulfilling a unique destiny, critical to world history, is central to their identity and experience as immigrants in America. Drawing on Anderson, Alonso has described the powerful, identity-affirming qualities of "epic time" as "an absolute time of Being, of first and last words, of prefiguring and fulfillment, of tradition and destiny."[8] Phrases often repeated in the African Christian communities, such as being sent out "to all the world" and "to the ends of the earth," express the possibility of collectivity in the midst of disruption and dislocation—an idea that is so fundamental to transnational identity formation.

The construction of African immigrant identities is embedded in the broader context of racial difference and hierarchy. As shown in this volume, racial identities among African immigrant communities are ambivalent and conflicting. It is not uncommon to find a critical stance against racial and cultural oppression in the African communities, and religion often plays a meaningful role here. In contexts where race becomes salient, religious and cultural practices express a racial consciousness and aim to empower the community to overcome marginalization and inequality. At the same time, there are ongoing disagreements and misunderstandings, stemming from the different and differentiated histories of African Americans and African immigrants. In some cases, these disagreements have erupted into public debate. A number of contentious issues have been raised including who qualifies as "African American," who should benefit from affirmative action policies,[9] and how best to address economic and political crises on the African continent.[10] As suggested by Beck, economic disparities that may exist in some places exacerbate the problem. At times, politicians have further stirred up debate in order to advance a particular candidate or cause.

The relationship between Africans and African Americans has emerged as a leading concern among African leaders, and religion plays a prominent role in the efforts toward positive change (although, as pointed out by Beck, religion may also serve to intensify divisions). Interestingly, although both Imams and pastors have been active in promoting unity, it is the leaders of African indigenous religion who have been particularly successful in establishing a space for positive relations. Within African indigenous shrines and temples, one finds African American perspectives, beliefs, and traditions integrated into religious practice. At the same time, Africans play a prominent role, creating programs in order to communicate aspects of African culture, tradition, and ways of life. In addition to religion and culture, there is a bridging of political issues. Discourses of equality predominate, along with pointed critiques of racism and other forms of social injustice.[11]

Beck has suggested a gradual improvement in relationships between African and African American Muslim communities. Given the U.S. legal and political context in the aftermath of September 11, 2001, this trend will likely continue. In New York City, we have observed that African Muslims often turn out in large numbers to hear African American Imams who visit the African mosque speak out against racial and religious discrimination. One African Imam explained to us that there are growing concerns in the African community about the harassment of Muslims. He stated that messages concerning discrimination are meaningful to Africans who came to the United States for greater opportunities and "may feel disappointment at such treatment by government and police." Such messages, he suggests, "touch on the reality of African immigrants who come to the U.S. thinking it's a land flowing with milk and honey." As the gap between expectation and reality widens and many immigrants become aware of the elusiveness of the American dream, it is likely that there will be greater efforts to confront and address the structures that underlie socioeconomic disparities. An important area for future research concerns the intersections among religion, African immigration, and racial identity—especially the role that religion may play as a unifying and mobilizing force.

Contributors to this work have argued that African immigrant religious communities are emerging as a key context for negotiating change in gender relations, as members reconcile more conservative values with transformations in women's income, autonomy, and status. The studies have emphasized immigrant women's agency, as evidenced in the ways in which women actively construct meanings of space, work, and gender—for example, in their debates over religious teachings about proper gender roles. This involves both the reproduction and the reinvention of "traditional" gender ideals and suggests that women are able to negotiate gender within the context of ethnoreligious identities, a point that deserves more attention in research on gender in immigrant religious communities.

Hondagneu-Sotelo argues that as gender and immigration studies become more integrated, there is increasing emphasis on viewing gender "as a key constitutive element of immigration." Gender is integral to the experiences of African immigrants—from the structuring of opportunities and responses within the global economy to relations of marriage and the family and the organization of power and control.[12] Research efforts must focus on these processes in order to better understand women's challenges and opportunities, as well as the more general ways in which gender permeates immigrant "practices, identities and institutions."[13]

African immigrant religion, and the phenomenon of African immigration itself, remains vastly understudied. As such, there are many important topics yet to be addressed. While several of these have already been discussed, a few others can be mentioned here. One major concern of many analysts and scholars is the lack of adequate statistical data on African religious communities in North America. For example, there are no consistent and accurate figures on the number and size of communities in the United States, their spatial distribution, and their rate of growth. Future work on African immigrant communities must make the collection of such data a research priority.

Another key area for future research is that of intergenerational relations. As suggested in these chapters, a prominent concern of these communities is the transmission of cultural and religious values to the youth. Studies are needed that examine the role of religion in the lives of youth—especially as related to identities, intergroup relations, and participation in civic life. This is particularly relevant for immigrant youth, who daily struggle with conflicting values and loyalties. Also, more generally, it is important at this stage to expand efforts to incorporate diverse voices into research on African immigrant religion, including perspectives that cut across generations, as well as gender, class, ethnicity, and nationality.

We suggest that this field of study will benefit by drawing comparisons with recent findings among African immigrant communities in Europe, and especially with other immigrant religious communities across America. In addition to illuminating similarities between communities as well as unique experiences, responses, and contributions, such studies will provide the opportunity to explore successful models for community development and civic engagement. Research must also be expanded to account for the spread of African immigrant communities beyond urban America. As previously discussed, the impact of increased numbers of African immigrants is currently being felt in many smaller towns across the United States, with a set of social, cultural, and economic implications very different from those that arise from migration to urban areas.

Finally, although scholars and practitioners have made significant progress in improving the visibility and promoting the civic participation of African immigrants, there is still a great deal of work to be done in this area. There is a need to develop a critical engagement between scholars and immigrant communities that will inform and focus theoretical analyses, as well as enhance the resources available to immigrant groups working toward community betterment. Recent events have shown that African religious leaders are still not seriously considered as actors in the public arena. For example, in Washington, D.C., they have been largely excluded from policymaking discussions on the role of faith-based initiatives in combating the AIDS epidemic in Africa, a topic that they are uniquely positioned to address.[14]

The remarkable diversity and vitality that characterize African immigrant religion in America are made possible by the context of religious pluralism and reflected in the ways in which African immigrant communities are actively affirming their religious identities, embracing their spiritual faith, engaging in transnational and global connections, and participating in civic life. Continued research on this important topic will further our understanding of the rich and varied experiences of the new African diasporic communities and enhance the efforts of these communities as they strive to establish a voice and presence in the American social and religious landscape.

Notes

1. Jose Casanova, "Immigration and the New Religious Pluralism: A EU/US Comparison," paper presented at the Conference on the New Religious Pluralism and Democracy, Georgetown University, April 21–22, 2005, 21.

2. See for example Elizabeth McAlister, "The Madonna of 115th Street Revisited: Vodou and Haitian Catholicism in the Age of Transnationalism," in R. Stephen Warner and Judith G. Wittner, eds., *Gatherings in Diaspora: Religious Communities and the New Immigration* (Philadelphia: Temple University Press, 1998); Jane N. Iwamura and Paul Spickard, eds., *Revealing the Sacred in Asian and Pacific America* (New York: Routledge, 2003); JoAnn D'Alisera, *An Imagined Geography: Sierra Leonean Muslims in America* (Philadelphia: University of Pennsylvania Press, 2004).

3. Iwamura and Spickard, *Revealing the Sacred,* 2.

4. R. Stephen Warner and Judith G. Wittner, eds., *Gatherings in Diaspora: Religious Communities and the New Immigration* (Philadelphia: Temple University Press, 1998).

5. Moses Biney, paper presented at the Conference on African Immigrants, Religion and Cultural Pluralism in the United States, U.C. Davis, December 2–5, 2004.

6. The Mourides illustrate the complex interactions among religion, economics, and trade and are becoming a major focus of social research as a result of their success and visibility. For example, UCLA recently hosted an exhibition on Ahmadou Bamba and Mouride spirituality.

7. Thomas A. Tweed, *Our Lady of the Exile: Diasporic Religion at a Cuban Catholic Shrine in Miami* (New York: Oxford University Press, 1997), 94

8. Ana Maria Alonso, "The Politics of Space, Time and Substance: State Formation, Nationalism, and Ethnicity," *Annual Review of Anthropology* 23 (1994): 388.

9. "African American Becomes a Term for Debate," *New York Times,* 29 August 2004.

10. Some African political economic perspectives have elicited strong criticism from African Americans. According to George Ayittey, whose views have sparked such controversies, differences in perspective stem in part from the fact that some black Americans see "their oppressors and exploiters to be white, whereas black Africans have seen both black and white oppressors and exploiters" (personal communication).

11. For example, at the April 2005 conference of religious leaders, Chief Oloye FAMA of Ile Orunmila, The Shrine, gave a presentation on unity and tolerance in Orisa worship, closing with this statement: "Orisa worship accommodates everyone and encourages peaceful coexistence." Ile Orunmila also publishes a quarterly newspaper, the *Odidere Orunmila Gazette,* which, in addition to articles pertaining to West African religious and cultural tradition, covers U.S. and international news stories involving social and racial justice.

12. The linkages between gender and the organization of power in African religious institutions is evidenced in the prevalence of "father" and "mother" roles. An example is the "Daddy General Overseer" in the Redeemed Christian Church. See Yanigisako and Delaney for an important discussion of the way in which imagery of the family signifies and legitimizes not only gender divisions but power relations more broadly; Sylvia Yanigisako and Carol Delaney, *Naturalizing Power: Essays in Feminist Cultural Analysis* (New York: Routledge, 1995).

13. Pierrette Hondagneu-Sotelo, ed., *Gender and U.S. Immigration, Contemporary Trends* (Berkeley: University of California Press, 1999), 9.

14. An important example is the invitation extended to prominent African American pastors by the U.S. secretary of state to discuss issues pertaining to Africa and the African people, especially the AIDS epidemic. A senior aide to Condoleezza Rice explained this as a need to have more African American organizations get involved in the president's Africa agenda. This event, which did not involve a similar invitation to African religious leaders, represents a significant challenge put to African immigrant religious leaders—to reverse the trend of political exclusion and to prove their vital and indispensable role in U.S. policymaking.

Contributors

AKINTUNDE E. AKINADE is an associate professor of religion at High Point University, in High Point, North Carolina. He received his Ph.D. in ecumenical studies at Union Theological Seminary in New York City. In 2000, he received a grant from the Louisville Institute to study African immigrant churches in New York City.

LINDA BECK is an assistant professor of political science at the University of Maine—Farmington. Her areas of specialization include African politics and Islamic religion and politics, and she has written numerous papers, articles, and chapters on these topics. Previously she was the acting director of the Institute of African Studies at Columbia University, and, in April 2006, she co-organized the Symposium on Africans in New York City.

MOSES O. BINEY is an ordained pastor of the Presbyterian Church of Ghana. He holds a Ph.D. in religion and society from Princeton Theological Seminary and currently serves as a postdoctoral research fellow for the Ecologies of Learning Project in New York.

ELIAS K. BONGMBA is an associate professor of religious studies at Rice University, in Texas, where he teaches African and African Diaspora religions. His forthcoming book, *On the Dialectics of Transformation in Africa,* will be published by Palgrave.

GLORIA MALAKE CLINE-SMYTHE graduated from Fourah Bay College, University of Sierra Leone, with a major in English language and literature and a minor in theology. She pursued a highly successful career in local government in the capital of Freetown and became an active member of the Church of the Lord (Aladura) (CLA), scaling its hierarchies of ministerial and administrative offices in Africa and abroad. Ms. Cline-Smythe has also represented this African Instituted Church (AIC) at various national and international conferences. She immigrated to America in 1991 and is now an executive secretary in the U.S. federal government, in Washington, D.C.

DEIDRE HELEN CRUMBLEY is an associate professor of Africana studies in Interdisciplinary Studies at North Carolina State University. Her forthcoming book, *Spirit, Structure and Flesh: Gender and Power in African Churches,* explores the interplay of gender, power, doctrine, and ritual in African Instituted Churches. Her current research project focuses on the intersection of race, gender, migration, and religious innovation in the rise of an African American, female-founded storefront church. In addition to her terminal degree in anthropology, Dr. Crumbley also holds a master of theological studies from the Harvard Divinity School.

DAVID DANIELS joined the faculty of McCormick Theological Seminary in 1987 and was inaugurated professor of church history in 2003. He has published on the history of the Black Church, especially black pentecostalism, and on writing the history of Christianity from a global perspective. He serves as a member of various research projects on religion in the United States: "Religion in Urban America," directed by Dr. Lowell Livezey, and "The Funding of Black Churches," directed by Dr. Thomas Hoyt. He has served as a member of the Lay Formation and Education project, directed by Dr. Dorothy Bass, and the Wesleyan/Holiness project, directed by William Faupel.

REGINA GEMIGNANI is a Ford Foundation postdoctoral fellow studying African immigrant religious communities at the University of California, Davis. Her interests are in public anthropology, especially in relation to the topics of social change, gender, class, and religion in Africa and the African Diaspora. Her dissertation research focused on rural development and the negotiation of gender relations in the Uluguru Mountains, Tanzania.

OGBU KALU is Luce Professor of World Christianity and Mission at McCormick Theological Seminary. He served as professor of church history at the University of Nigeria, Nsukka, for twenty-three years and as an elder in the Presbyterian Church of Nigeria. He was educated in Canada and the United States and has taught in the United States, Korea, Nigeria,

Scotland, Canada, and South Africa. Kalu has published and edited sixteen books, including *Power, Poverty, and Prayer: The Challenges of Poverty and Pluralism in African Christianity 1960–1996*, and more than 150 academic articles. Most of his research focuses on African Christianity, African church history, African traditional religions, English history, historiography, and theology.

WORKU NIDA is a doctoral candidate in sociocultural anthropology at UCLA. He is currently engaged in a Ph.D. dissertation on entrepreneurialism in Ethiopia, reconstructing entrepreneurship as social movement and an identity-making process. He has been engaged in research on ethnohistory, religion, migration, social change, and identity. He has published a book and a number of articles on Gurage society in Ethiopia. He has extensive experiences in policy formulation and cultural research-management. He crafted Ethiopia's first national cultural policy, which was passed by the parliament in 1998. He was born, raised, and formally educated in Ethiopia. He received his M.A. and B.A. degrees in social anthropology and history in 1995 and 1984, respectively, from Addis Ababa University.

MOJUBAOLU OLUFUNKE OKOME is an international political economist who specializes in African studies, gender studies, and African transnational migrations. She was educated at the University of Ibadan, Nigeria; Long Island University, New York; and Columbia University, New York. She is the author of the book *A Sapped Democracy: The Political Economy of the Structural Adjustment Program and the Political Transition in Nigeria, 1983–1993* (Lanham, Md.: University Press of America, 1998); one of three co-editors of the online journal *Jenda: Journal of African Culture and Women Studies;* and one of two co-editors of *Irinkerindo: A Journal of African Migration.*

JACOB K. OLUPONA is Professor of African American and African Studies, Faculty of Arts and Sciences, and Professor of African Religious Tradition, Harvard Divinity School, Harvard University. His major areas of specialization are religion and immigration, religions of traditional and modern Africa, and African religions in the Americas. His publications include *Religion, Kingship and Rituals in a Nigerian Community* (Stockholm, Sweden: Alqvist and Wiskell, 1991) and the edited volumes *African Spirituality: Forms, Meanings, and Expressions* (New York: Crossroads, 2000) and *Beyond Primitivism: Indigenous Religious Traditions and Modernity*

(New York: Routledge, 2004). Currently he is completing a book titled *The City of 201 Gods: Ile-Ife in Time, Space and the Imagination.* Olupona served as senior fellow, Center for the Study of Religions at Harvard University, and as fellow, African Studies Council at Yale University. He received the John Simon Guggenheim Fellowship in 1997 and an honorary doctor of divinity degree from Edinburgh University, Scotland, in 2002. With a grant from the Ford Foundation, Olupona is pioneering the project "African Immigrant Religious Communities in the United States."

YUSHAU SODIQ was educated at the University of Medina, where he received a master of arts in Islamic law, and at Temple University, where he earned his Ph.D. Author of several articles on Islam and on African Indigenous Religion, he is currently an associate professor of religious studies at Texas Christian University. He is an active member of the Nigerian Muslim Association and is passionately involved in the task of promoting interfaith dialogue and cooperation.

WISDOM J. TETTEY is an associate professor in the Faculty of Communication and Culture at the University of Calgary, Canada. His research interests include the state and public policy in Africa; new information and communications technologies; the mass media and democratic transitions; race, ethnicity, and citizenship; and the African Diaspora in Canada. He has published extensively on these issues in academic journals and books. He is co-editor of *The African Diaspora in Canada: Negotiating Identity and Belonging.*

Index